Shakespeare's Apprenticeship

Shakespeare's Apprenticeship

Robert Y. Turner

The University of Chicago Press
Chicago and London

Robert Y. Turner is associate professor of English and graduate
chairman of the Department of English at the University of
Pennsylvania. He has written articles on Shakespeare for a
number of scholarly publications.
[1974]

The University of Chicago Press, Chicago 60637
The University of Chicago Press, Ltd., London

International Standard Book Number: 0-226-81736-9
Library of Congress Catalog Card Number: 73-84195

Contents

Acknowledgments

An early version of chapter 2 appeared in *Modern Philology* 62 (1964): 1-12; I wish to thank the editors for permission to reuse that material. My indebtedness to scholars has been recorded in the Introduction and in the footnotes, but the help from friends and colleagues should be singled out here for special thanks. Professors James M. Cox of Dartmouth College, Matthias A. Shaaber, and Craig R. Thompson of the University of Pennsylvania read the manuscript and made invaluable suggestions. Professor Robert D. Bamberg of Bates College and Dr. William E. Miller of the Furness Library, University of Pennsylvania, advised and assisted me at various stages of my research. My greatest thanks are due to Professor Roland M. Frye, who read the manuscript in all its shapes and sizes and contributed through his wisdom and kindness in ways too numerous to recount.

Introduction

From the eighteenth century until about 1930 one general interpretation of Shakespeare's apprenticeship prevailed, that he learned his craft by revising the plays of others. As a factotum of his first company—probably the Earl of Pembroke's Men—he took plays already in repertory and altered scenes or rewrote speeches to improve them. In 1790 Edmond Malone gave such authority to this interpretation that readers accepted it for a hundred and fifty years.[1] He showed in detail how Shakespeare reworked two rather bad plays, *The First Part of the Contention betwixt the two famous houses of York and Lancaster* and *The true Tragedy of Richard Duke of York*, into the plays now entitled *Henry VI, Parts Two and Three*. Other "facts" were found by scholars to support this concept of the revisionist. Shakespeare's *The Taming of "The" Shrew* seemed to be a later and more artful version of *The Taming of "A" Shrew*, a contemporary play closely resembling it. His *King John* was probably a reconstruction of an earlier two-part play, *The Troublesome Reign of King John*. In the case of other early works where no specific models exist, such as *The Comedy of Errors* or *Love's Labor's Lost*, one could see how Shakespeare produced close imitations of Plautus and Lyly. *Titus Andronicus*, too grotesque with horrors to be the sole invention of Shakespeare, was taken to be either a revision or a collaboration.[2] The literary historian found in this picture of the young imitative playwright a nice contrast to the picture of Christopher Marlowe, who, although born the same year as Shakespeare, wrote five vividly original plays before his death in 1593. The legend of an untutored country boy who escaped from Stratford to London after poaching deer from Chalchote and learned his craft first by acting and then by revising fitted this contrast because Marlowe was educated at Cambridge.[3]

1

Malone rejected this legend about poaching and bolstered his interpretation of the young reviser with more convincing evidence, a contemporary quotation from Robert Greene's preface to *A Groatsworth of Wit*, published shortly after his death in 1592. Greene referred specifically to Shakespeare in a passage that makes its point with none of the airy conjecture or hearsay of an anecdote. He spoke of a "Shakes-scene" as a "Johannes factotum" who was an "upstart Crow, beautified with our feathers." Malone interpreted this allusion to be a complaint against a clever reviser who took full credit for plays that he merely polished, plays that were written by University men such as Greene himself or Marlowe.

In 1929 the publication of Peter Alexander's *Shakespeare's Henry VI and Richard III*, a study which extended upon the new bibliographic work of Pollard, McKerrow, and Greg, made clear that Shakespeare was no reviser of *The Contention* and *The True Tragedy*. Instead, these texts were corruptions of Shakespeare's original plays, *Henry VI, Parts Two and Three*. Shortly before this study appeared, Madeleine Doran arrived independently at a similar conclusion, published at the University of Iowa. Although they differed on the exact nature of the corruption, they agreed on the originality of Shakespeare's two early plays and have convinced most subsequent students of Shakespeare.[4] As a necessary correlate, Alexander reinterpreted Greene's beautified feathers as a reference to actors and not to plagiarism.[5] Their work stimulated others to reexamine the prevailing assumptions about divided authorship and revision of Shakespeare's early plays, questioning whether indeed *"The" Shrew* derives from *"A" Shrew*, whether Peele shared in the composition of *Titus Andronicus*, whether Shakespeare collaborated with Peele, Greene, or Marlowe in writing *1 Henry VI*.[6]

Research in analytic bibliography, then, changed some of the "facts" about Shakespeare's early work and has led to a reassessment of the revisionist apprentice. As Pollard noted, the assumption that a company of players would set loose an untried playwright to revise already serviceable plays is questionable.[7] Would not he need first to prove his abilities before being allowed to doctor the work of others? Contemporaneous scholarship on the kind of school training Shakespeare received at Stratford gave an additional challenge to the old interpretation. T. W. Baldwin's research into sixteenth-century school curricula established once and for all that Shakespeare, far from being untutored, was well grounded in grammar, logic, and rhetoric.[8] Consequently some spirited claims for the young Shakespeare have been put forth. E.

M. W. Tillyard saw in the early plays a carefully planned literary apprenticeship similar to Dante's and Milton's; F. P. Wilson tentatively proposed that Shakespeare initiated the fashion of the chronicle play and found him not inferior to Marlowe; Leo Kirschbaum said, "It is quite possible that we shall find that even in these early efforts he was far ahead of what Greene, Peele and Marlowe could do."[9] E. W. Talbert's *Elizabethan Drama and Shakespeare's Early Plays* gave detailed support to this supposition.[10]

If we consider the fact that in 1929 an almost new territory for Shakespearean studies opened, it is surprising how little attention has been paid to the apprenticeship in proportion to the amount of critical writing on the later plays. To address oneself to the way Shakespeare learned to master his craft is to confront a problem of literary history, and most students of his plays have been trained by a group roughly designated the New Critics and their disciples, who value primarily analyses of individual works. Such analyses are more or less self-inclosed, for the works dictate the terms of discussion. Either the critic postulates a theme and discovers how it is embodied in technical devices, or he examines technical devices for patterns that disclose a theme. A collection of these discrete analyses would not add up to literary history even if all the works discussed happened to be written in temporal proximity. As R. S. Crane has stated the problem:

The historian of the literary arts must therefore find ways of dealing with the individual works within his field of interest that will do justice at once to their multiple historical relations and to their qualities as unique artistic wholes the production of which marked the coming into being of values, great or small, such as the world had not previously known.[11]

René Wellek and Austin Warren understood this problem to be fundamental to their *Theory of Literature* (1949). At that time they found most investigations that went under the name of literary history to be either social histories, histories of ideas illustrated by literary works, or discussions of specific works arranged in chronological order. Their major distinction between intrinsic and extrinsic discussions of literature isolated social histories and histories of ideas from a true study of literary subject matter, but left them with a problem of "intrinsic" literary history. They proposed a twofold solution to the problem: how history relates to the criticism of a single literary work and how literary works relate to one another in a continuum. To show how historical considerations enter into the understanding of a specific work, they located its existence in the accumulated responses of critical readers through the ages.[12] History about literature occurs when the critic abstracts a line of change — Crane would say "causal sequence" — solely from literary works. Wellek accounted for the possibility of literary change by an analogy to evolution. Just as the scientist traces biological change by postulating the human brain as a goal toward which lower forms of life evolve, so the literary historian can postulate a goal for a group of literary works and describe all its members as steps in evolution toward it.[13] This goal acts as a standard by which all members of the group are judged, so that the claims of an individual work to be judged by its own terms are somewhat, if not largely, ignored.

The crucial decision that faces a literary historian, then, is the nature of the continuum to be postulated. Recent studies of Shakespeare's early plays indicate some of the difficulties in his choice. John P. Cutts in *The Shattered Glass* (1968) concentrates upon a single theme, self-blindness, which gets its fullest embodiment in *Richard II* when the King smashes the mirror, an act symbolizing his breakthrough to self-judgment. Cutts traces earlier manifestations of this theme through twelve preceding plays. The pattern of the shattered glass draws together references to mirrors, images, poses, shadow and substance, all embodying the theme of a character's blindness to himself. He keeps faith with the New Critics who analyze a work by two terms, theme and embodiment, and with Wellek by postulating a fully worked out theme as a goal toward which other plays are approximations. A. C. Hamilton in *The Early Shakespeare* (1967) pays closer attention to the differences in genre and discovers several patterns in the early plays that are dramaturgical rather than thematic. For instance, the pattern in the early comedies comes from the six parts of drama specified by Aristotle in the *Poetics*, chapter six. *Errors* emphasizes plot, *Two Gentlemen* emphasizes character and thought, *Love's Labor's Lost* emphasizes diction, melody, and spectacle, while *A Midsummer Night's Dream* combines all parts with equal emphasis into a satisfying whole (pp.186, 217–26). Both discussions give an impression more of personal insight than of literary history, and it is worth noting that "pattern" rather than "history" is the term favored by Cutts and Hamilton.[14]

Others, like Bernard Spivack, Anne Righter, and Ernest William Talbert, have an advantage, I think, in locating Shakespeare's plays within a continuum of sixteenth-century drama. Spivack in *The Allegory of Evil* (1958) postulates a change from abstract to literal drama and relates villains, such as Richard III and Iago, to the tradition of the

Vice figure. Anne Righter in *Shakespeare and the Idea of the Play* (1962) locates Shakespeare's dramas within a continuum of change from the mystery plays, where the spectators understand themselves to be participants in the great events of Christ's life, to drama as an independent art form, where spectators become an audience apart from events on stage. Talbert in *Elizabethan Drama and Shakespeare's Early Plays* (1963) studies the first plays in relation to contemporary dramatic conventions and extraliterary entertainment to show how Shakespeare capitalized upon the proclivities of his audience. My dependence upon their studies will be obvious in the following chapters.

As I see the continuum in Shakespeare's apprentice plays, they recapitulate phylogenetically the main historical movement in drama of the sixteenth century from the generalized didactic morality play to the relatively literal drama as a distinctive art form. Our verbal usage implicitly acknowledges this broad change, for we speak of the moralities automatically as "plays" rather than as "dramas." Even "interlude" follows this usage. "Drama" with its classical roots applies more specifically to a learned, if not professional, product and enters the language relatively late.[15] While Shakespeare's first chronicle plays can hardly be described as moralities, they exhibit many of the same assumptions and can be considered as late 1580 approximations of such works. His training in rhetoric colored his understanding of dramaturgy so that it is not far wrong to say that he composed his first chronicle plays along the lines of an oration and understood his duties to be like those of an orator, his audience to be like listeners to an oration willing to be instructed by patterns of moral behavior. The two poles of the historical continuum, as I see it, are "didactic" and "mimetic," the didactic encompassing the instructive, oratorical chronicle, the mimetic signifying drama as a particular art form with its own distinctive means of presenting a story that do not preclude moral significance.

Despite the complex history of the term "mimesis," I shall use it—not like Erich Auerbach to signify the "representation of reality"—but like Aristotle to signify the poet's process of creation which resembles the natural process of growth. A mimetic whole is not a natural whole but is similar to a natural whole. Unlike a natural individual thing whose principle of growth is intrinsic, a product's principle of growth, its form, is extrinsic, imposed by the poet-maker. Aristotle used "mimetic" in a broad sense to signify the resemblance between the formation of an artistic product and the growth of a natural thing as it becomes distinctively itself. Mimetic drama is drama which realizes the distinctive properties of its medium, drama *qua* drama rather than drama *qua* oration or drama *qua* sermon. To use "mimetic" in this way is not to deny a relationship between human activities outside a play and human activities within a play. Hamlet refers to this relationship when he speaks of acting as a "mirror" held up to nature (III.ii.20–21). Actions depicted in mimetic drama differ, as it will become clear, from actions depicted in didactic drama, but one would be hard put to it to determine this difference by measuring actions against some constant "reality" outside the play.[16]

M. C. Bradbrook has shown in *The Rise of the Common Player* (1962) how professionalism helped change the nature of drama in the 1570s. Once the actors established a permanent home and could draw upon a stable audience, they necessarily refined their craft. Drama lost its occasional flavor and in the 1580s attracted the University Wits to become professional playwrights. Peele, Marlowe, Lodge, Nashe, and Lyly — along with Kyd, not himself educated at a university, and probably Anthony Munday[17] — opened the doors to literal drama. By 1593 all these playwrights, save Munday, had for one reason or another stopped writing for the stage, leaving Shakespeare as the single major dramatist to consolidate and extend their practices until about 1599. He exploited the possibilities of his forebears and helped show the way for another great wave of playwrights that began about 1598 or 1599: Jonson, Chapman, and Dekker came into their own; Marston, Middleton, Beaumont and Fletcher soon followed. Shakespeare's apprenticeship occurred at the end of the period of the University Wits and led to the efflorescence of drama at the end of the century. His earliest plays, shaped by the strict principles of rhetoric, were gradually replaced by others which I can only describe as "mimetic." Standards of verisimilitude changed; so did his principles of characterization, dialogue, and the very nature of the dramatic experience. The continuum, then, to be found in his apprenticeship is a microcosm of the larger movement of drama through the sixteenth century.

The apprentice period, as I see it, includes that group of plays ending with *A Midsummer Night's Dream*, usually acknowledged to be Shakespeare's first masterpiece. To discuss the evolution within this group, I must postulate an order of composition, but the order I postulate depends upon the evolution which I see in the plays. So my reasoning is circular. Yet in the absence of definite dates, everyone is pushed to this kind of reasoning once the few facts and allusions to historical events have been stated. In my defense I point to the generally accepted arrangement of the early plays based on Sir Edmund Chambers's proposal that has been followed with very few modifications since 1930.[18] First I shall give the order of the plays as I conceive it, an order divided into four stages without more detailed chronological arrangement. Then I shall compare it to Chambers's order.

Stage One, from about 1588 to 1590:
    1 Henry VI and *The Comedy of Errors*
    2 Henry VI and *The Taming of the Shrew*
Stage Two, from 1590 to 1592:
    3 Henry VI, Two Gentlemen of Verona
    Richard III, Titus Andronicus
Stage Three, during the closing of the theaters because of plague:
    Venus and Adonis, The Rape of Lucrece, maybe early sonnets
Stage Four, 1594-95:
    Love's Labor's Lost, Richard II, Romeo and Juliet
    A Midsummer Night's Dream

Chambers's ordering differs mainly in the way he distributes the comedies among the chronicles and tragedies, not in the general priority of their composition within the genres:

1590-91: *2 Henry VI, 3 Henry VI*
1591-92: *1 Henry VI, Venus and Adonis*
1592-93: *Richard III, The Comedy of Errors*
1593-94: *Titus Andronicus, The Taming of the Shrew, The Rape of Lucrece*
1594-95: *Two Gentlemen of Verona, Love's Labor's Lost, Romeo and Juliet*
1595-96: *Richard II, A Midsummer Night's Dream*

I differ with Chambers's placing of *1 Henry VI* because of the persuasive arguments by Leo Kirschbaum and Andrew S. Cairncross.[19] *King John* has been omitted from my group although a strong case could be made for including it. I find tempting E. A. J. Honigmann's thesis that it was not based upon the anonymous two-part *The Troublesome Reign of King John* (ca. 1589-90) but that the order of dependence is the reverse.[20] The arguments needed to defend this thesis are so numerous that the principle of Occam's razor leads me to accept the conservative opinion without much enthusiasm, that Shakespeare wrote his play about 1596. It is difficult to see why Shakespeare, after a success like *A Midsummer Night's Dream* and at a time when he was undertaking the complex mixture of Portia's marriage with Shylock's bond, would rewrite a play

7

not in itself that much out of fashion and not part of the English history
that held his interest for ten years.

Two other floating plays are *Love's Labor's Lost* and *Titus Andronicus*. Alfred Harbage proposed that the court comedy was written originally for Paul's Boys in 1588–89 and revised in 1596–97.[21] Sylvan Barnet
follows this suggestion in his ordering of the plays for the Signet Classic
editions. Richard David, editor of the Arden Shakespeare (1951) places
it in 1593–94 (pp. xxvii–xxxi), and Louis B. Wright and Virginia LaMar,
editors of the Folger Library Shakespeare (1961) agree with Chambers.
One argument for placing it very early lies in its strong affinities with
Lyly's court comedies of the 1580s. Yet an equally convincing argument—to my mind more convincing—can be based on analogy to
Nicholas Brooke's discussion of Shakespeare's relationship to Marlowe:
Shakespeare's imitations of his vividly individual forebears were not ser-
vile; when he undertook to imitate them, he did so with confidence by
placing them in a context that reveals their limitations.[22] Just as his
echoes of *Tamburlaine* comment morally on this hero and his style, so
the echoes of Lylesque characters and style go beyond Lyly. Shakespeare's imitations argue maturity rather than uncertainty. *Richard II*,
Shakespeare's closest approximation to Marlowe, comes at the end of his
apprenticeship. So I think that *Love's Labor's Lost*, a close approximation to Lyly, comes shortly before *A Midsummer Night's Dream*, with
which it has many similarities. More troublesome is *Titus Andronicus*,
which J. C. Maxwell and R. F. Hill place at the outset of Shakespeare's
career, about 1587.[23] Hill's decision rests, as mine does, upon a conception of Shakespeare's developing technique. He sees Shakespeare's style
growing more highly patterned throughout his apprenticeship, *Richard
II* being the most severely formal. *Titus Andronicus*, according to his
tabulation of rhetorical figures, shows relatively few verbal patterns and
a high number of similarities, such as tautology and wordiness, to *1
Henry VI*. Hill concludes that *Titus Andronicus* is relatively unShake-
spearean and should be placed at the outset of his career, perhaps as a
collaboration with Peele. I shall argue that a scheme of Shakespeare's
development must take account of the kinds of experiences dramatized
as well as stylistic traits. Shakespeare wrote little introspective lyrical
verse until about the time of *Two Gentlemen, Richard III,* and *The
Rape of Lucrece*. His early characters speak about public matters in a
highly rhetorical manner; the later characters engage in increasingly
flexible dialogue that depends as much upon tropes as upon verbal patterns. *Titus Andronicus* seems to me to exhibit a wider range of emo-

tional experience than *1 Henry VI* or, for that matter, *2 and 3 Henry VI*. Further, the similarity of allusions and the proportion of suffering to action between *Titus* and *Lucrece* leads me to a date later than Hill's.[24]

The details to support my ordering will emerge in the subsequent discussion. What I want to indicate here is the problematic nature of any arrangement of the earliest plays. This calls to mind John Arthos's approach to *Pericles*, a play most probably not entirely by Shakespeare. Rather than become entangled in the question of who wrote what scene, a factual matter that can never be settled, he decided to assume that the play has an artistic integrity and then analyzed it to see what sort of coherence emerged.[25] If we let the absence of decisive facts close off investigations, our discussions of Shakespeare would be very poor indeed. We should be cautious not to postulate an evolution that rests on the exact sequence of plays, particularly the floating ones. If, for instance, someone discovers a fact that proves Shakespeare to have written *Two Gentlemen* following *Errors*, whereas I have postulated *Shrew* to have followed *Errors* because they disclose the same strict classical principles of comedy, it would not undermine my proposal about Shakespeare's development. On adjustment, it would appear that after Shakespeare composed *Errors*, he tried his hand at a new kind of comedy, that of romantic love, and, sensing his experiment to be unsuccessful,[26] returned to his earlier principles and wrote *Shrew* along the lines of *Errors*. Anyone postulating an order of Shakespeare's development must, perforce, make it schematic, whereas Shakespeare's actual growth probably took some sudden leaps and temporary retreats. It goes without saying, then, that a postulated continuum of Shakespeare's apprenticeship can claim to be no more than roughly approximate.

The Problem of Dialogue

1

A major problem for any young playwright is composing dialogue appropriate to the occasion. The way a king speaks to his messenger cannot serve to dramatize the way a lover speaks to his mistress, the rhetorical principle of decorum notwithstanding. For a mature playwright the fashioning of well-paced, actable dialogue, characteristic of the speakers and plausible in rendering an event, may come as second nature. But this facility is hardly the birthright of a dramatist. One could discuss almost any apprenticeship in drama by noting how the aptness and variety of dialogues occur. A beginner's practice might well be determined by the type of experience he feels competent to render or by the type of dialogue he has observed in other plays. What restricts him is aptness. Does the dialogue create the precise sense of the experience it dramatizes?

Our habits of critical analysis lead us to assume that dialogue follows automatically once a playwright chooses a story, for we analyze technique in terms of significance and significance in terms of technique.[1] While this approach serves us well in discerning coherence, it can blind us to issues of a playwright's development. To question the assumption that dialogue flows from the playwright's pen is one way to break the circuit of theme-and-technique. Marlowe's early play *Tamburlaine* (Part One) reveals the difficulty of adjusting dialogue to experience. He easily mastered a style appropriate to experiences of power, but when his narrative demanded more intimate experiences of love and response to beauty, he shaped and bent them to fit his style. Love turns out to be another triumph for Tamburlaine, who woos Zenocrate in the same way that he persuades Theridamas to join his army, by promises of power, possessions, and glory. When the hero senses beauty, he conceives it to

11

be in conflict with glory and therefore a temptation to be mastered. In both cases, of course, the coloring of the experiences bears out Marlowe's intention, and it is a tribute to his skill that he assimilated the intimate moment to the public mode of expression even though the final impression of the play is monochromatic.[2]

The first step in looking for evidence of Shakespeare's practice in creating dialogue is to differentiate plot from story. Given his choice of story or narrative, the dramatist faces the problem of casting it into a sequence of scenes. Even if eight Elizabethan and Jacobean "plots" did not survive or there were no references in Henslowe's Diary and in his papers to plots that were devised before scripts, we would still assume that a playwright worked from an outline of scenes before composing dialogue.[3] Collaborators would of necessity need to work from such a plot, and from Henslowe's itemized list of payments we can infer that his company sometimes discussed the dramatic possibilities of an outline before playwrights undertook full-scale dramatization. If a young playwright, working alone, formulates no such outline, he would make the same kinds of decisions, for he could not transpose a story directly to the stage. One way to become aware of his decisions is to note events of the story excluded from dramatization. For instance, the story of Romeo and Juliet entails an episode that begins the vendetta between the Capulets and the Montagues, but Shakespeare excludes it from the plot so that it does not occur on stage. The story concerns Romeo's infatuation with Rosaline, but Shakespeare chooses not to plot the story to give them a scene together. Depending upon the interpretation of the story, the playwright has at his disposal the messenger's report and can cast an event into narrative or embody it in dialogue to take place before our eyes. Another way to discover his decisions is to generalize from the dialogues he produces. Shakespeare's early chronicles, for instance, contain far more ceremonious scenes of state rendered by formalized dialogues of address and proclamation or command and assent than his later chronicles. *Errors* depends upon one experience duplicated again and again, the predicament of mistaken identities which requires one pattern of dialogue.

To see how dialogues can be discussed as patterns, I shall examine one major episode from *Errors* and compare it with a minor one from *1 Henry VI*, a comparison that may disclose some considerations a young playwright faces when he transforms a plot into his foul papers. In the third scene of *1 Henry VI* Duke Humphrey of Gloucester and his men knock at the gate of the Tower of London and are refused entrance. Their dialogue recalls Antipholus of Ephesus and his Dromio, who knock to enter their house and are locked out. The speakers vent their anger in words because the predicament keeps them from coming to blows.

>   *Antipholus E.*
>   Go fetch me something; I'll break ope the gate.
>   *Dromio S. [within]*
>   Break any breaking here, and I'll break your knave's pate.
>   *Dromio E.*
>   A man may break a word with you, sir, and words are but wind:
>   Ay, and break it in your face, so he break it not behind.
>   *Dromio S. [within]*
>   It seems thou want'st breaking. Out upon thee, hind!
>   *Dromio E.*
>   Here's too much "out upon thee!" I pray thee, let me in.
>   *Dromio S. [within]*
>   Ay, when fowls have no feathers, and fish have no fin.
>
>   (III.i.73-79)[4]

The characters need not have expressed their feelings by a play on words; they could have uttered formal denunciations or ringing proclamations. Similar episodes of knocking in *Shrew* and *Macbeth* reveal other possibilities. In *Errors* Shakespeare uses the occasion for insulting epithet and sharp retort; yet in *1 Henry VI*, where the major experience is one of power, we find the same pattern:

>   *2. Warder [within]*
>   Whoe'er he be, you may not be let in.
>   *1. Man*
>   Villains, answer you so the Lord Protector?
>   *1. Warder [within]*
>   The Lord protect him! So we answer him.
>   We do no otherwise than we are willed.
>   *Gloucester*
>   Who willèd you? or whose will stands but mine?
>   There's none Protector of the realm but I.
>
>   (I.iii.7-12)

To take a central word from an opponent's statement, twist it into a new context, and turn it against him is in itself an act of power, a control of an opponent's weapons that is both surprising and impudent. This verbal interplay works precisely to transform into a dramatic experience what would otherwise remain a flat occurrence. Shakespeare devises a dialogue particularly apt for its subject, and most likely his success plays a part in his decision to reuse it. Were Gloucester's knocking at the Tower required by the narrative, its resemblance to Antipholus's domestic confusions would be negligible. But the Duke's entrance follows from no previous plan, and it leads to no action beyond the moment. Shakespeare introduces it, so it seems, as a means of prolonging a quarrel between Duke Humphrey's faction and the Bishop of Winchester's faction. In *Errors*, although knocking at the door is a major episode, Shakespeare takes it not from the source play, the *Menaechmi*, but from Plautus's *Amphitruo* with much the same purpose in mind, to prolong and intensify the confusion of identities.[5]

A playwright faces, in writing apt dialogue, not only the problem of the right kind of interplay between speakers but a problem of sensing its natural momentum. How should he pace their talk: quickly by short speeches or slowly by long, formal speeches? How extensive should the interchange be? Obviously he needs to avoid a moment too brief to relish its distinctiveness or too long to maintain its inherent interest. Antipholus of Ephesus knocks at his own door; he cannot gain entrance; he knocks again, and he knocks again. Dialogue develops easily because the fun arises from repetition: request and denial, request and denial. Yet even repetition requires variety or intensification. Plautus used two speakers in the *Amphitruo*. Amphitryon knocks at his door and Mercury, disguised as his servant Sosia, answers him saucily. In the fragment that has survived, it is primarily Mercury's inventiveness that enlivens Amphitryon's repeated attempts to gain entrance. Shakespeare develops his episode by increasing the number of speakers. Antipholus of Ephesus is accompanied by Angelo the goldsmith and Balthazar the merchant, who discuss the dinner they anticipate before they knock. Dromio of Ephesus knocks, and Dromio of Syracuse answers. As the other outsiders gradually enter the dialogue, from within, Luce the kitchen wench (who never again speaks in the play) together with Adriana joins Dromio of Syracuse. The quarrel in the third scene of *1 Henry VI* develops by the same kind of additions. Duke Humphrey's men first knock at the Tower gate and quarrel with the Warden's men; then Duke Humphrey quarrels with Woodville, Lieutenant of the Tower; finally the Bishop of Winchester and his men enter to increase the pitch of the quarrel until their men break into a fight.

The momentum necessary to sustain any dialogue can be generated by new speakers, particularly messengers, who bring new topics to the discussion, or it can be generated dialectically by new ideas and feelings of the characters involved in the dialogue. The main pattern of dialogue in *Errors*, talk at cross purposes, depends primarily upon external nudging rather than upon characterization, for each character holds to one conception which perpetuates his confusion. Antipholus of Syracuse sees the people of Ephesus as witches and magicians. Antipholus of Ephesus sees his wife and servant as willfully recalcitrant. As new characters enter to confuse or obstruct the inevitable path toward recognition of identical twins, each speaker repeats his typical response of wonder, perplexity, or frustration. Intensity arises from repetition. The more expectations are thwarted, the more heated the responses. The more impersonal the speech patterns, the more plausible the mistaken identities. Idiosyncrasy or complexity of motivation could upset the balanced artifice.

Characters and events in *1 Henry VI* seem at first glance very different from those in *Errors*, but the patterns of dialogue reveal their kinship. Quarrels in particular depend upon simple attitudes of opposition and repetition for intensity. Just as the comic characters tend to spin out their statements on the verbal patterns of their perplexed interlocutors, so do the quarrelers in the chronicles. When Richard Plantagenet and Somerset quarrel in the Temple Garden, Act II, scene iv, one denunciation automatically sets a pattern for its response.[6]

> *Richard*
> Let him that is a true-born gentleman
> And stands upon the honor of his birth
> If he suppose that I have pleaded truth,
> From off this brier pluck a white rose with me.
> *Somerset*
> Let him that is no coward nor no flatterer,
> But dare maintain the party of the truth,
> Pluck a red rose from off this thorn with me.
>
> (II.iv.27–33)

To develop this balanced pattern of challenge and retort, Shakespeare builds the quarrel upon the symbolism of roses:

> *Warwick*
> I love no colors, and without all color
> Of base insinuating flattery
> I pluck this white rose with Plantagenet.
> *Suffolk*
> I pluck this red rose with young Somerset . . . .
> *Richard*
> Hath not thy rose a canker, Somerset?

15

Somerset
Hath not thy rose a thorn, Plantagenet? . . .
Richard
I scorn thee and thy fashion, peevish boy.
Suffolk
Turn not thy scorns this way, Plantagenet.
Richard
Proud Pole, I will, and scorn both him and thee.
Suffolk
I'll turn my part thereof into thy throat.

(II.iv.34 ff.)

Quarrels, just as the knocking on the door, do not necessarily require a play on words. Cassius's quarrel with Brutus in Act IV, scene ii, of *Julius Caesar* develops by statements of intense personal feelings, reminiscences, and judgments without dependence upon verbal wit.[7] In *1 Henry VI* characters have less to say about themselves; so they perforce repeat the same remarks with copiousness and spin out their comments by re-using their opponents' words. "Quarrel" rather than "argument" better describes the dialogue in the Temple Garden because the speakers devote themselves to insult and retort rather than to reasons for disagreeing. In fact, the immediate cause of their disagreement remains unspecified. This may well be Shakespeare's intention: to show that it has no basis in idea or value. The real significance of the quarrel, aside from the symbolism of the roses which the characters do not grasp, lies in the antagonism itself. Throughout the play the English courtiers are at odds, and their witty attention to words more than the substance of words serves well to dramatize their condition. Their pointless squabbles contrast with Talbot's fight for England's dominance in France, and it is their refusal to cooperate rather than French opposition which eventually defeats Talbot. Shakespeare's intention, then, fits the abilities of the characters to articulate their thoughts.

For purposes of argument, let us assume that a fledgling playwright selects his stories as much by the techniques he can control as by his interest in the narratives themselves. *Errors* would support this contention, for it depends upon one main experience, the predicament of mistaken identities, and requires one major pattern of dialogue. The variety of experiences demanded by the chronicle sources of *1 Henry VI*, on the other hand, belies this hypothesis. To undertake to transform the War of the Roses into four dramas, Shakespeare was not playing cautious. Yet in his embodiment of historical events, some dialogues fail to

16

capture the particular flavor of events if we take as a standard the aptness shown by the play on words accompanying the knocking on the
door. These dialogues fail in different ways: some are "flat" and others
are "thin." They can give us, if we keep in mind the possibility that
dialogues can be fashioned to be purposely flat or thin for structural
contrasts or embodiment of theme, more evidence that Shakespeare
faced problems in devising techniques proper to dramatize his plot.

Flatness can be discerned in the dialogue that dramatizes the parley
for peace in Act V, scene iv, an episode central to the action because it
brings to a close the struggle between England and France. The following perfunctory speeches conclude the treaty and end the scene:

> *Warwick*
> How say'st thou, Charles? Shall our condition stand?
> *Charles*
> It shall;
> Only reserved, you claim no interest
> In any of our towns of garrison.
> *Richard*
> Then swear allegiance to his majesty:
> As thou art knight, never to disobey
> Nor be rebellious to the crown of England,
> Thou, nor thy nobles, to the crown of England.
> *[Charles and the rest give tokens of fealty.]*
> So, now dismiss your army when ye please,
> Hang up your ensigns, let your drums be still,
> For here we entertain a solemn peace. *Exeunt.*
>
> (V.iv.165–75)

Shakespeare intends to suggest by this flat colloquy that the truce is unsatisfactory, but there is open to him the possibility for creating a sense
of anticlimax that can maintain dramatic intensity, such as the ironic
understatements which he uses later in dramatizing Richard II's submission to Bolingbroke. In *1 Henry VI* the dialogue appears to be
underwritten.

More justifiable, perhaps, are the passages of thin, quick-paced
dialogue which accompany many of the battle scenes. In Act I, scene ii,
Charles and his French forces plan to raise the siege of Orleans; they
engage in battle and are repulsed, all within the space of forty lines of
dialogue. In Act III, scene ii, Joan plans her attack on Rouen, routs the
English, taunts them from the battlements; then Talbot plans a counterattack and routs the French, all within a space of one hundred and
fifteen lines of dialogue. Speeches accompany the action much like

17

captions under a picture and do little more than lift the scene above the level of dumb show. The thinness can be justified by its relation to the structure and meaning of the play. Shakespeare chooses to sketch a number of analogous episodes to establish his theme about English bravery abroad and factions at home rather than concentrate fully upon a few crucial episodes. Joan passes not one but two tests to prove herself to Charles; Talbot champions not one but two English commanders, Salisbury and Bedford. He recaptures towns won by Joan not once but twice. Quarrels at home take place not only between Duke Humphrey and the Bishop of Winchester, but between York and Somerset and between Vernon and Basset. Of this method we may say either that thin and quick dialogue fits the multiplicity of events or that the multiplicity of events necessitates thin and quick dialogue. Even if we grant an artfulness to them, Shakespeare makes no extensive use of the technique in later chronicles except during the heat of battle scenes where circumstances perforce keep talk to a minimum.

Knocking on the door and thin and flat dialogues disclose some aspects of the problem which a young playwright faces in developing episodes by speeches. A survey of the successful dialogues in *Errors* and *1 Henry VI*, those which are sustained and apt, can give us a starting point from which to measure the early development of Shakespeare's craft. Thus far I have compared dialogues without regard to decorum of genre. It goes without saying that Shakespeare understood that domestic, everyday predicaments of ordinary people are the substance of comedy, whereas noble and ignoble deeds of far-reaching consequences for the commonwealth are the substance of the chronicles. Ceremonious dialogues have a central place in the serious plays, while witty dialogues of crossed purposes and back-chat have a central place in the comedies. Yet it has become apparent how similar they are; both kinds depend upon the sounds of words as much as upon their meanings for development, and both depend upon copious restatement rather than dialectic for momentum. These characteristics, I shall try to show, are the result of Shakespeare's training in rhetoric and of his early assumptions about the nature of drama.

∞

To generalize about the major patterns of dialogue in *Errors* and *1 Henry VI*, it is important to differentiate from the immediacy of central events which we watch taking place on stage those necessary passages, such as a messenger's report or a character's description of a plan, passages that act as the gears to help keep the story in motion and prepare for the big scenes. While this distinction is serviceable up to a point, it is not clear-cut, for a messenger's report can evoke an emotional response central to a drama. The big scene in *Errors* is that of crossed purposes; a character asserts his intention only to be surprised by his interlocutor, who asserts a counter-intention. Each assumes facts about the other which are false and, rather than question circumstances or assumptions, reiterates his intention with fervor. To take the passage between Antipholus of Ephesus, arrested for failure to pay his debt to the goldsmith, and the wrong Dromio:

> *Antipholus E.*
> How now, sir; have you that I sent you for?
> *Dromio E.*
> Here's that, I warrant you, will pay them all.
> *Antipholus E.*
> But where's the money?
> *Dromio E.*
> Why, sir, I gave the money for the rope.
> *Antipholus E.*
> Five hundred ducats, villain, for a rope?
> *Dromio E.*
> I'll serve you, sir, five hundred at the rate.
> *Antipholus E.*
> To what end did I bid thee hie thee home?
> *Dromio E.*
> To a rope's end, sir; and to that end am I returned.
> *Antipholus E.*
> And to that end, sir, I will welcome you. [*Beats him.*]
> *Officer*
> Good sir, be patient.
> *Dromio E.*
> Nay, 'tis for me to be patient; I am in adversity.

(IV.iv.9–19)

What catches our eye is the similarity between this dialogue and the one that dramatizes knocking on the door; a response oftentimes takes its shape from the words of its provocation, and it ends with a beating, not a solution. It must be admitted that I choose a passage to stress the similarity; there are other versions of this predicament that depend less upon the quick retort. Antipholus of Syracuse, for instance, stands amazed and submissive while Adriana pleads the proper duties of a husband and drags him off to dinner (II.ii.109–218); yet it too resolves into the quick-paced banter that turns on accusations of Dromio and his retorts (II.ii.186–201).

Shakespeare avoids the monochromatic impression that one gets from the printed version of *1 Tamburlaine* by the addition of set pieces, such as the description of Luce the kitchen wench by a geographical metaphor and the back-chat between master and servant who amuse themselves by passing the time. Antipholus of Syracuse and his Dromio for some forty lines spin out a pseudo-proof based on the proposition that there is a time for all things by drawing on a general fund of proverbial wisdom, colloquialisms, and commonplace observations:

Dromio S.
There's no time for a man to recover his hair that grows bald by nature.
Antipholus S.
May he not do it by fine and recovery?
Dromio S.
Yes, to pay a fine for a periwig and recover the lost hair of another man.
Antipholus S.
Why is Time such a niggard of hair, being, as it is, so plentiful an
    excrement?
Dromio S.
Because it is a blessing that he bestows on beasts; and what he hath
    scanted men in hair, he hath given them in wit.
Antipholus S.
Why, but there's many a man hath more hair than wit.
Dromio S.
Not a man of those but he hath the wit to lose his hair.
Antipholus S.
Why, thou didst conclude hairy men plain dealers without wit.
Dromio S.
The plainer dealer, the sooner lost; yet he loseth it in a kind of jollity.
                                                                    (II.ii.71–88)

And so on. Just as attention in opera centers less on what happens next than on the artfulness of song, so it pauses here to catch the ingenuity of mock logic, and, like an aria, this passage exists for itself. As for its momentum, it is self-generated. When all possible extensions of the central conceit are exhausted, it stops. It develops no situation, reveals no necessary facts of the story, and provokes no sympathy or antipathy. The speakers minimize their personal characteristics for the sake of a quick comeback that takes its relevance as much from the sound pattern as from sense. In fact, the more tenuous the relevance, the wittier the remark. The subject of the passage, Time, can be related thematically to the story of mistaken identities. Another passage of back-chat develops the proposition that time goes backwards and suggests, if grouped with this one, that Shakespeare may have intended an oblique commentary on the confusion of identities to be solved by happenstance. But our first and major impression is one of unabashed ornamentation that resembles passages of incidental, free-wheeling banter in Lyly's court comedies. In Shakespeare's canon it remains distinctive of the early style and draws on the same devices as the knocking on the door, the quarrel, and the confusion of identities.

At the center of *1 Henry VI* are moments that require ceremonious dialogues. Henry VI formally dubs Richard Plantagenet the Duke of York and later Talbot the Earl of Shrewsbury. Battle parleys abound. Talbot parleys with Joan; he challenges the Mayor of Bordeaux; Sir William Lucy parleys with Joan for the body of Talbot; Cardinal Beaufort parleys with the French for peace; Suffolk parleys with Regnier for Margaret's hand in marriage to Henry VI. One pattern shapes these moments: formal address, request, and explanation. If a command replaces explanation, it implies that the speaker has the power to enforce his request and need not bother about further words. Generalizations heighten what would otherwise be simple statements of fact. Speeches are impersonalized by syntactic patterns of exclamation and question, apostrophe and imperative.

Even though at first glance the dialogues of these ceremonies could not appear more different from the back-chat of Antipholus and Dromio, closer examination shows that they arise from the same habits of language. The funeral procession that opens the play exemplifies the style. Each speaker contributes a formalized lament for the death of Henry V that is devoid of personal characteristics. The speeches could be redistributed without any sense of distortion, or they could all be delivered by one speaker without change of content. Coincidence of phrasing with the verse unit enforces the impression of formality. The rhetorical principle of copiousness, that is, restatement of one idea in different words and images, is Shakespeare's primary means for sustaining this and other ceremonious moments. At their most intense, speeches become highly schematic. Gloucester's comment, only partially quoted here to reveal the verbal pattern, illustrates both the way intense feeling is conveyed and the way such dialogues are prolonged:

England n'er had a king until his time.
Virtue he had, deserving to command;

His brandished sword . . .
His arms spread wider . . .
His sparkling eyes . . .
What should I say? His deeds exceed all speech.
He ne'er lift up his hand but conquerèd.

(I.i.8 ff.)

Characteristic of the early style, then, is Shakespeare's eagerness to exploit the sound of words as well as their meaning. The word as word takes on a life of its own so that the pun which arises from a sound that can be detached from meaning exemplifies the special quality of this style. Today we are accustomed to look through the veil of words to the thoughts, if not things, conveyed by them. Our ideal of style might be called transparency. Shakespeare's habit of mind, quickly shifting from what is said to the means of saying it, worked within channels set by his training in rhetoric. To codify the figures so that the student can work systematically for a mastery of eloquence, rhetoricians divided them into figures of thought and figures of words. Aristotle in the third book of *The Rhetoric* recommended some figures to promote vividness and others to promote prose rhythm. Here we can see an incipient distinction that later developed into major categories. Quintilian states in the *Institutes*:

. . . there are two classes of *figure*, namely *figures of thought*, that is of the mind, feeling, or conceptions, since all these terms are used, and *figures of speech*, that is of words, diction, expression, language, or style. (9.1.17)[8]

While codification varied from writer to writer and figures varied from category to category — Sister Miriam Joseph devoted much of her effort in *Shakespeare's Use of the Arts of Language* to organizing the various categories and figures into a consistent scheme — there was always a category of figure that derived from the sounds instead of the meanings of words.

George Puttenham in his *Arte of English Poesie*, published in 1589, classified figures in a way highly pertinent to Shakespeare's practices in his early chronicles. Puttenham's three kinds are: the auricular ("apperteining to single wordes and working by their diuers soundes and audible tunes alteration to the eare onely and not the mynde"), the "sensable" ("they alter and affect the minde by alteration of sence"), and the sententious ("not only they properly apperteine to full sentences, for bewtifying them with a currant and pleasant numerositie, but also giuing them efficacie, and enlarging the whole matter besides with

copious amplifications").[9] Whether or not Shakespeare read Puttenham — Kenneth Muir argues that he did[10] — his treatise makes as clear a
statement as I can find to describe the function of the auricular figures:

And so long as this qualitie extendeth but to the outward tuning of the
speach reaching no higher then th'eare and forcing the mynde little or
nothing, it is that vertue which the Greeks call *Enargia* and is the office
of the *auricular* figures to performe.[11]

By *enargia* Puttenham meant forcefulness or vigor, the same effect I
have referred to as intensity. It is easy to see how a style that stresses
enargia would be apt to embody experiences of power. If one were to
describe in abstract terms the central experiences of the chronicle plays,
one would likely speak of them as exercises of power or struggles for
power that raise questions about the proper uses of power. Such descriptions would also apply to the serious dramas of the 1580s and early
1590s, for other chronicle plays and their immediate predecessors, the
conqueror plays that followed in the wake of *Tamburlaine*, all dramatized struggles for power. Whatever the cause, whether the playwrights'
interest in the problems of power gave them the occasion to use their
training in rhetoric or their training in rhetoric led them to dramatize
public events, the happy coincidence led to a flourishing period for
drama.

Of course, there are other aspects of rhetoric besides auricular figures
adaptable to public experiences of power. Marlowe, for instance, found
little use for auricular figures.[12] Besides forcefulness, rhetoricians generally added two other characteristics for an effective eloquent style:
clarity and aptness. While we today would have no quarrel with these
qualities, we might disagree with the Elizabethan prescriptions for
achieving them. We tend to associate clarity with simplicity. The Elizabethans saw no inconsistency between clarity and complexity. Copiousness became for them a primary means to clarity and forcefulness.
When we read Puttenham's commonplace argument for a highly fig-
ured style by analogy to rich clothes, we see in it a plea for sheer ornament, whereas he felt that natural speech would otherwise be barren
and hence ineffective without the crucial additions. Through artful
restatement an orator could make his speech irresistible. Erasmus's
treatise on copiousness was widely studied, and his praise of a luxuriant
style taken to heart. "Amplification" is the Elizabethan term for proper
emphasis, and while Rosemond Tuve cautions us that it does not signify
a lengthening but rather a bestowing of proper importance, we cannot
dismiss our contemporary understanding of the term as fortuitous.[13]

Many verbal figures depend upon repetition of sound patterns so that they benefit from copiousness. When Warwick in the Temple Garden scene of *1 Henry VI* protests that he cannot deliver a considered judgment on the quarrel between Richard Plantagenet and Somerset, he gives full weight to the fact that in other matters he would venture an opinion:

Between two hawks, which flies the higher pitch,
Between two dogs, which hath the deeper mouth,
Between two blades, which bears the better temper,
Between two horses, which doth bear him best,
Between two girls which hath the merriest eye,
I have perhaps some shallow spirit of judgment;
But in these nice sharp quillets of the law,
Good faith, I am no wiser than a daw.

(II.iv.11–18)

His position becomes inescapably clear by the detailed restatement and emphasis of his syntax, and the echoing sounds impart a certain vigor and formality which are apt for the speaker and situation. Warwick's speech, then, can be taken to exhibit the two major characteristics, auricular figures and copiousness, of the style the young Shakespeare felt satisfied the three standards of eloquence: clarity, vigor, and decorum.[14]

Whereas some events lend themselves readily to this style, others need to be adjusted and bent. Dialogues of courtship, for example, would seem to require some expression of personal sentiments, but the courtships in *Errors* and *1 Henry VI* depend for their élan upon the refashioning of single words and phrases. Once a lover declares his affection, and his lady acknowledges it, what sustains their dialogue if they do not amplify their feelings? To develop Suffolk's wooing of Margaret in Act V of *1 Henry VI*, Shakespeare prevents him from clarifying his intentions immediately. Margaret's mistrust and misunderstanding help sustain the episode. Had Suffolk clarified his purpose, her response, were it less than immediate assent, would suggest a complexity of character out of keeping with her role in the play. Not to seize the opportunity to marry the king would imply motives more complicated than ambition or greed; yet to assent immediately would truncate the dialogue. Instead, the two speakers play on the words "bondage," "freedom," and "queen."

Suffolk
Say, gentle princess, would you not suppose
Your bondage happy, to be made a queen?

24

Margaret
To be a queen in bondage is more vile
Than is a slave in base servility;
For princes should be free.
 Suffolk
      And so shall you,
If happy England's royal king be free.
 Margaret
Why, what concerns his freedom unto me?

(V.iii.110–16)

Likewise, the one courtship in *Errors* is adjusted to the major pattern of crossed purposes and uses the same parry and thrust:

 Luciana
What, are you mad, that you do reason so?
 Antipholus S.
Not mad, but mated; how, I do not know.
 Luciana
It is a fault that springeth from your eye.
 Antipholus S.
For gazing on your beams, fair sun, being by.
 Luciana
Gaze where you should, and that will clear your sight.
 Antipholus S.
As good to wink, sweet love, as look on night.
 Luciana
Why call you me love? Call my sister so.
 Antipholus S.
Thy sister's sister.
 Luciana   That's my sister.
 Antipholus S.   No . . .

(III.ii.53–60)

What is missing from these courtships—or for that matter, from any of the dialogues already discussed—are lyrical expressions of sentiment.[15] Word play is appropriate for quarrels, back-chat, and crossed purposes, but it has little potentiality for articulating tender moments.

Most revealing of the way Shakespeare dramatizes personal sentiments are the dialogues between Talbot and his son in *1 Henry VI*. The plotting indicates that Shakespeare intends these scenes to be the emotional high point of the play. As nowhere else he devotes three scenes to preparation. In Act IV, scene ii, Talbot discovers that he is trapped by an

25

overwhelming number of French troops; instead of moving directly to Talbot's defeat and death, Shakespeare inserts two short episodes, Act IV, scenes iii and iv, in which Sir William Lucy urges York and then Somerset to aid Talbot. Each refuses and blames the other for inaction. These scenes clarify the central idea of the play, that civil strife more than foreign opposition leads England to defeat in France. With a stinging sense of frustration, the audience watches two climactic episodes of the hero victimized, Act IV, scenes v and vi. To heighten the sense of helplessness and of what might have been, Shakespeare introduces Talbot's son, who has never before appeared or even been mentioned in the play and who is never again mentioned. Clearly Shakespeare uses the son to capitalize upon the audience's automatic sentiment for parent and child. From the annals we know that in fact two sons were killed in the battle, but Shakespeare suppresses reference to a second son, who was illegitimate.[16] To dramatize this climactic moment, he shapes their private conversation in the form of a debate, as if they were speakers in a public forum. Talbot urges his son to flee; his son refuses to abandon his father.

> *Talbot*
> Shall all thy mother's hopes lie in one tomb?
> *John*
> Ay, rather than I'll shame my mother's womb.
> *Talbot*
> Upon my blessing I command thee go.
> *John*
> To fight I will, but not to fly the foe.
> *Talbot*
> Part of thy father may be saved in thee.
> *John*
> No part of him but will be shame in me.
> *Talbot*
> Thou never hadst renown, nor canst not lose it.
> *John*
> Yes, your renownèd name. Shall flight abuse it?

(IV.v.34–41)

This give-and-take distills the style of the ceremony and quarrel to excite the audience rather than to express the intimate feelings of the characters. Each speaker has one point to make and, rather than reveal more and more about himself, repeats again and again his point. When Talbot finally submits to his son, it is difficult to see any new argument

26

that causes his change; the debate comes to a halt rather than to a conclusion just as Dromio's back-chat with Antipholus simply stops. The
stichomythia and copiousness differ little from the characteristics of
dialogue we have seen elsewhere in the play.

If in this episode Shakespeare achieves some success in adjusting
formal style to private scenes, we can find other moments where he does
not, particularly in the concluding scene of *Errors*. Critics have remarked upon the romantic framework of the opening and closing episodes that Shakespeare adds to his source.[17] Yet none of the characters
utters a single speech of emotional rejoicing upon discovery of his long-
lost family, not even Egeon or Emilia. With the touching moments of
reunion and reconciliation from the late romances in our minds, we
scarcely notice that the characters in *Errors* occupy themselves solely
with clearing up confusions, returning a chain, a diamond, a purse, or
rescinding the law against Egeon's death.

∞

Given this general description of dialogue in *Errors* and *1 Henry VI*, the
first difference a comparison with *Richard II* reveals is the presence of
many dialogues about intimate emotions. The simplest of these new
patterns is the response of grief to saddening news. Almost the sole
experience of Richard's queen on stage is to hear of misfortune. In Act
II, scene ii, she listens to news of Bolingbroke's return to England. Had
Shakespeare dramatized this event earlier in his career, he would most
likely have plotted it by assigning one scene to Bolingbroke's decision to
return to England and another scene to his arrival, roundly greeted by
supporters. Instead of such public events, the news of his return disturbs
an anxious, melancholy queen. By contrast, the characters in *1 Henry
VI* who hear sad news do not grieve or reflect upon misfortune. When
news arrives of Talbot's capture, Bedford resolves to return to France,
fight, and ransom him. When Henry VI receives news of Burgundy's
defection, Talbot resolves to search him out for chastisement. No scene,
for instance, depicts the English sorrowing over Talbot's death or the
French over Joan's death even though the loss of these leaders is cata-
strophic for both sides. The early Shakespeare saw in the report of bad
news the opportunity to move the action from one event to another
rather than as an occasion for emotion, such as the later Shakespeare
found stageworthy.

Much the same difference can be discovered in dialogues of comfort
or dialogues of tearful farewell. Richard II comforts Gaunt after banish-
ing his son (I.iii); Gaunt comforts Bolingbroke when they separate
(I.iii); Bushy tries to cheer Richard's queen (II.ii); the Bishop of Carlisle

and Aumerle try to bolster Richard's spirits (III.ii); and Richard speaks words of comfort to his queen as they take their last farewell (V.i). So too the Duchess of Gloucester takes sad farewell of Gaunt (I.ii); Bolingbroke bids farewell to his aged father, who assumes that they will never see one another again (I.iii); Richard bids farewell to his queen (V.i). In all these dialogues characters are responsive to one another's feelings, whereas in the earlier chronicle plays characters seldom relax the stance of challenge or defense, quarrel or intrigue. Lady Talbot, for instance, could have appeared on stage to be comforted for the deaths of her husband and son without unbalancing the emphasis upon civil quarrels at home and heroism abroad. Henry VI could have been comforted over the loss of his bravest commander in France. A brief speech of sympathy for the dying Mortimer by his nephew Richard Plantagenet occupies ten lines in a scene of about one hundred and thirty devoted to an exposition of historical facts, a proportion which suggests that Shakespeare's interest at the outset of his career may have lain more in events than in sentiments.

In order to interpret this change of interest, the question arises whether Shakespeare learned new figures or acquired different habits of writing between the years of *1 Henry VI* and *Richard II*. One obvious difference in the new dialogues is a readiness of characters to make images about their feelings. When Richard II's queen hears the news of Bolingbroke's return to England, she states how it adds to her other sorrows:

So, Green, thou art the midwife to my woe,
And Bolingbroke my sorrow's dismal heir.
Now hath my soul brought forth her prodigy;
And I, a gasping new-delivered mother,
Have woe to woe, sorrow to sorrow joined.

(II.ii.62–66)

One automatic way to talk about feelings is by a direct statement, such as "I feel sorrow," but this does very little to convey to the audience a sense of the character's feelings. The Queen tries to break through the audience's casual assent to a general term like "sorrow" by expressing her feeling rather than by stating it. To do this, she attaches her emotion to a specific and familiar act, but she could as well attach it to gestures or objects. The means of attachment are metaphor and simile. Responding to bad news becomes giving birth to sorrow; the bringer of news becomes a midwife to sorrow; the listener becomes a gasping new-delivered mother. Our sense of what it feels like to give birth coalesces with what it feels like to have premonitions confirmed, and we assent to the Queen's agony with more than a factual understanding. Our imagination has been stirred to sympathy.

This activity of translation by metaphor or simile to express feelings is instinctive, so much so that there seems to be no reason why the characters in *1 Henry VI* would not readily talk about their sentiments in this way. Yet a glance through the text reveals few passages that contain an extended metaphor. Talbot at the point when he hears news that the French surround his forces at Bordeaux develops a conceit comparable in length to the Queen's. Even after we take into account the difference between the military commander and the Queen, a comparison of Talbot's conceit with hers shows a different standard of relevance at work:

How are we parked and bounded in a pale,
A little herd of England's timorous deer,
Mazed with a yelping kennel of French curs!
If we be English deer, be then in blood:
Not rascal-like, to fall down with a pinch,
But rather, moody-mad and desperate stags,
Turn on the bloody hounds with heads of steel
And make the cowards stand aloof at bay.

(IV.ii.45–52)

Talbot's imagery differs from the Queen's because it is directed toward the audience to clarify the situation and his plan of action rather than toward another character to express the way he feels. Courage can be inferred from what he says, but it is secondary to the audience's understanding of what is happening.

The Queen's imaginative leap to create a hyperbolic metaphor requires no greater exercise of wit than the leap of associations based on the sounds of words in the dialogues of quarrel. She takes an imaginative leap from the general to the specific and from the immaterial to the concrete and selects her new context by a principle of association different from Talbot's deer park. Tentatively, then, we can say that Shakespeare's earliest characters talk little about their feelings, not because they lack a mastery of metaphor, but because Shakespeare's standard of relevance directs their choice of associations elsewhere.

These different standards, which control leaps in speech patterns, may well be determined by differing conceptions of character. It was suggested that the characters in *Errors* and *1 Henry VI* pay so much attention to words because they have little else to draw upon in developing their dialogue. The characters in *Richard II* not only talk about their feelings and sympathize with others but can remember their past, contradict themselves, intuit, and speculate on the future. A minor character, who appears briefly in *Richard II*, Act I, scene ii, to give occasion for exposition, reveals something of this new flexibility. At the end of her brief scene the Duchess of Gloucester takes a tearful farewell of John of Gaunt:

I take my leave before I have begun,
For sorrow ends not when it seemeth done.
Commend me to thy brother, Edmund York.
Lo, this is all. Nay, yet depart not so!
Though this be all, do not so quickly go.
I shall remember more. Bid him — ah, what? —
With all good speed at Plashy visit me.
Alack, and what shall good old York there see
But empty lodgings and unfurnished walls,
Unpeopled offices, untrodden stones?
And what hear there for welcome but my groans?
Therefore commend me — let him not come there
To seek out sorrow that dwells everywhere.

(I.ii.60–72)

This passage is obviously calculated to stimulate the audience's sympathy. Shakespeare renders the Duchess's loneliness first by having her try to prevent Gaunt from leaving; her attempt to detain him by thinking up things to say, her automatic request for York's visit, and then her reversal once she makes an imaginative leap to the details of such a visit, all render her sense of loneliness without dependence on explicit statement or on momentum generated by copiousness. A comparison with Mortimer's description of himself aged by long imprisonment brings out the expressive power of her remarks. Mortimer's speech is one of the few in *1 Henry VI* (II.v.3-16) that uses similes to convey a sense of personal feelings.[18] Were the Duchess to express herself like him, she would begin with a general statement, as he does about the nearness of death, and then add illustrative details, orderly and itemized, as he does with gray locks, dim eyes, weak shoulders, pithless arms, numb feet. Instead, when she begins her speech, she does not know how it will end.

We might locate the crucial difference between the dialogues of the earlier and later plays in characterization and say that the earlier characters are static speakers confined to one point of view which they elaborate only by a witty play on words or copious restatement. Of the later characters we would say that they are flexible and imaginative, complex enough to reveal themselves by degrees and talk easily about their feelings. "Process" rather than copiousness would be a term to describe the momentum of their dialogue. Such a distinction would shift the discussion from its initial focus on dramaturgy to psychological terminology and could well be an evasion of the initial investigation into Shakespeare's craftsmanship. One way to manage such a relocation of terminology would be to state that Shakespeare came to draw on psychological details as well as on rhetorical devices to develop dialogue, but this shift raises another question. Why would Shakespeare look to the way people respond rather than to the way they talk? One place to search for an answer to this question is in the standard of what is properly dramatic, and here we move into the controversial area of Shakespeare's "intentions."[19]

In *1 Henry VI* Shakespeare's uppermost intention is to dramatize historical events to show their moral significance so that the audience's understanding of event rather than a character's response to the event controls his thinking about dialogue and plot. Talbot's simile of the deer park, for instance, clarifies the situation at Bordeaux for the audience more than it expresses his feelings. The choice of roses in the Temple Garden quarrel suggests the eventual dimension of civil war inherent in the slight controversy more than it expresses what the characters themselves are thinking or feeling. In the way Shakespeare structures events, many episodes relate analogically to one another to enforce moral dicta about loyalty and selfishness in state affairs and to disclose the pattern of providential movement in history. As we have seen, the English noblemen illustrate the division of forces at home not by one quarrel but by many; Duke Humphrey quarrels with the Bishop of Winchester in the opening scene, again in I.iii, and again in III.i; Richard Plantagenet quarrels with Somerset in II.iv; later Vernon and Basset take up the quarrel in III.iv and again in IV.i. The frequency of quarreling more than any one specific quarrel is what affects the audience. In *Richard II* events occur at a much slower pace. Almost the whole of Acts III and IV dramatize Richard's submission to Bolingbroke. The significance of events depends in large part upon the way characters respond to them. How Richard responds to his loss of power is as crucial as the change in power itself. If his response to the deposition happens to be central to the plotting of that event, then we might well describe the play as tragedy, but Shakespeare does not push his dramatization that far. He devotes attention to Carlisle's prophecy of civil war, to the incipient rebellion of York against Lancaster, led by Aumerle, and to the way Henry IV governs. How Richard's deposition affects the commonwealth guides Shakespeare's choices of episodes as much as how the change of power affects Richard himself. Although the shift of significance between *1 Henry VI* and *Richard II* cannot be described as a complete change from a didactic chronicle to a mimetic tragedy, it is sharp enough to indicate a continuum of development.

The same continuum can be detected by a change of quality in the dramatic experience. In the later plays Shakespeare appears to have been relieved from the need to make events startling or bizarre. Bolingbroke need not be a chilling Machiavel, conjuring up strange tortures to destroy his enemy, or a scourge governed by evil spirits. The episodes lack any ingenious activity, such as a gunner taking aim from one part of the stage to shoot a character "on a distant tower" as we find in *1 Henry VI*, Act I, scene iv. Dramatic impact need no longer be measured against some conjectured threshold of interest in the audience. The threshold now lies within the characters of the play, and it is their interests which guide the audience's interests. Different from a group of inert listeners ready to be prompted to virtuous behavior, an audience stands ready to be engaged by the narrative, ready to extend its sympathy or laugh at what happens next.

Style, too, reflects this change of direction. Talbot, for instance, in a high-pitched reaction to Salisbury's murder, says:

Your hearts I'll stamp out with my horse's heels
And make a quagmire of your mingled brains.

(I.iv.108–9)

Sir William Lucy, when asking the French permission to bury Talbot's body, says:

O, were mine eyeballs into bullets turned,
That I in rage might shoot them at your faces!

(IV.vii.79–80)[20]

Since both speakers are sympathetic and admirable elsewhere, we cannot infer that Shakespeare intends parody by these hyperbolic comments. In his later plays villains may articulate their sentiments with such excesses, but Richard II's or Romeo's most extreme catachreses exhibit little of this particular intensity. Shakespeare must have designed Talbot's statement to raise what he took to be the audience's low threshold of interest. The early excesses of style may be explained by the enthusiasm of a young playwright and his later style by the control of a maturing taste, but enthusiasm and taste, while convincing enough, take us only part of the way in explaining Shakespeare's apprenticeship. What causes his enthusiasm for energetic style in his earliest plays? What governs his taste in the more lyrically expressive plays?

In answer, it would be possible to postulate general definitions of "rhetorical" and "mimetic" drama and then show how Shakespeare's decisions bear out these definitions. I propose instead to look at individual scenes to observe how particular decisions relate to one another, not only because this seems closer to the way Shakespeare probably speculated about the nature of drama, but also because "rhetorical" and "mimetic" are not hard and fast concepts. What is mimetic in relation to Tudor drama would need adjusting to explicate Chekhov's dramaturgy. In the next three chapters I shall examine the patterns of dialogue in Shakespeare's chronicles and tragedies to see how they reveal changes in his dramaturgy. The central line of change in the apprentice comedies reveals itself more in characterization than in the way characters talk. The discussion, therefore, falls into two parts based roughly on genre. The treatises on rhetoric insist upon the distinctions between the genres, for the poet as well as the orator must observe decorum or aptness of style to subject and effect. Just as the orator tunes rhetoric to the nature of his subject and his listeners, so the playwright tunes dramaturgy to his characters, his story, and his audience.

The problem arises, once we acknowledge the influence of rhetoric upon Shakespeare's earliest dialogues, how they shall be grouped. The most tempting categories are the three traditional types of oration: demonstrative (speeches of praise or blame), deliberative (speeches of persuasion), and judicial (debates of accusation and defense). Anyone wishing so to classify can find precedents in Donatus and Melanchthon.[21] Up to a point the scheme would work here. Scenes of persuasion have been obviously central to drama from the temptations of the Vice figure in the morality plays to Iago's manipulation of Othello. Shakespeare includes a number of such dialogues in his early chronicles, and I shall discuss them as a group. However, there is no clear-cut distinction between the demonstrative and judicial scenes. Large groups of characters engage in public confrontations, such as the quarrels already mentioned. The dialogue merges praise and blame with accusation and defense. Real controversies for debate, such as we find in Shaw's *Saint Joan* between Warwick, a spokesman for feudalism, and Cauchon, a spokesman for the church, do not appear in Shakespeare's earliest plays. Later Hector and Troilus will argue whether the standards of honor or law should govern their behavior, but judicial arguments merge into heated emotional attacks in the apprentice plays.[22] I shall therefore discuss all the public scenes of controversy, apart from the persuasions, in one group as "confrontations." As a whole these scenes dramatize experiences of power and create a vivid sense of what takes place in the forum or on the battlefield. Finally, there are the private scenes of emotion, those moments of anguish when Henry VI watches the horrors of civil war, or when in *Richard III* queens bewail their misfortunes, or when Titus Andronicus hears news of his sons' execution.

These three categories cover more or less adequately those central moments when we watch events as if they are happening immediately before us. Excluded are the mechanical scenes where news is reported or plans formulated, scenes that prepare for the central moments. Also excluded are ceremonies and pageantry, such as Henry VI's coronation, not because they are not central, but because they remain the same and reveal little about Shakespeare's developing dramaturgy.

To speak of the early dramaturgy as being "rhetorical" is to court misunderstandings, since Shakespeare never abandoned — nor could he forget — his early training in rhetorical figures, as Sister Miriam Joseph, T. W. Baldwin, Bertrand Joseph, and Brian Vickers, among others, have shown us. Madeline Doran puts the matter of the historical importance of rhetoric with clarity and succinctness:

English renaissance drama is rhetorical from first to last. If a curve is drawn from the early Elizabethan period to the late Jacobean or Caroline period, conscious rhetoric will appear as a dominant characteristic of style at both ends — at one end because verse is stiff with the devices of the schools, at the other because, supple as it is, it draws attention to its own cleverness. If we are not so highly conscious of rhetoric at the height of the period, that is only because it has become thoroughly adapted to the matter it is used to express. [23]

Likewise, with regard to Shakespeare's career, more than one critic has observed the playwright's economy: he seems never to discard even his earliest themes, dramaturgical devices, characters, and situations, but reworks them into new patterns from first to last. [24] So it can be said that Prospero's speech of farewell to his magic is as rhetorical as Talbot's farewell to his dead son. My use of the term applies to Shakespeare's general assumptions about drama at the outset of his career. He knew from Horace or the sixteenth-century humanists that art was didactic, and his theatrical experience would have confirmed this. His training in rhetoric taught him to organize language and argument to instruct and move his listeners. It is my less than novel contention that when he first shaped historical narratives for the stage, he conceived them along the lines of an oration. In this sense the earliest chronicle plays can be called distinctively "rhetorical." The later apprentice plays, while they exhibit rhetorical figures no less frequently, are shaped more to exhibit the properties of drama as a distinctive art form, guided by assumptions which I call "mimetic" to differentiate them from the features of an oration.

Confrontations

2

If one were asked what situation in itself is the most purely dramatic, one would no doubt say a clash between enemies. Likewise, we are inclined to use the word "dramatic" to describe struggles between powerful opponents. Marlowe, when he wrote *Tamburlaine* about 1587, made the confrontation of opponents a central experience in his drama and showed contemporary playwrights of the late 1580s, some who wrote conqueror plays and others, including Shakespeare, who wrote chronicle plays, how stageworthy such scenes were. In the broadest sense of conflict, of course, most dramatic scenes can be described as confrontations, but what differentiates Marlowe's is the language of the characters who oppose one another. The actors need powerful lungs and trumpetlike voices to deliver speeches fashioned by hyperbole and copiousness. We use such terms as "bombast" and "fustian"—both related to clothing, it might be noted, recalling the rhetoricians' "garment of style"—to describe this language at its worst, and terms like "heroic" or "stirring" to describe it at its best. Thomas Nashe's testimony in 1592 to the way Talbot's heroism stirred the audience comes to mind because it is just such broad simple responses as pride and tears that this vigorous style and intense experience would evoke.[1] These confrontations might be seen as the dramatic equivalents of the flyting contests between Scottish poets or the epical dispute between Beowulf and Unferth.

In developing the dialogue of a confrontation, the playwright has numerous options: what makes the characters opponents? is their struggle physical, political, or domestic? is it right against wrong, wrong against wrong, or even right against right? Only if we keep in mind how free the playwright is to cast his story into a plot can we recognize the extent of Shakespeare's dependence upon rhetoric and the conventions of his contemporaries when he was writing the Henry VI plays. Marlowe, so far as I can tell from extant sixteenth-century drama, set the fashion for the particular kind of dialogue which Shakespeare put to use in his early confrontation scenes. In Act III, scene iii, of *1 Tamburlaine* the hero's forces come face to face with Bajazeth's forces. They exchange boasts, threats, and taunts. After the warriors march off stage to battle, Zenocrate and Zabina together with their maids represent the warriors and continue the flyting until Tamburlaine reenters triumphant with Bajazeth his prisoner. Marlowe saw in this dialogue the dramatic potentiality for creating an impression of sheer power so that many speakers, not just the two leaders, engage in the confrontation. Although this fact sounds commonplace, preceding sixteenth-century drama reveals that it is not, according to my search through the extant moralities, hybrid moralities, and imitations of classical drama. David Bevington's discussion of the auspices of popular dramatic performances makes clear why traveling companies could not enact a scene of this scope because a cast seldom numbered over five.[2] Yet even in cases where more actors could be used, *Respublica* or *The Wars of Cyrus*, performed by children, there are no group dialogues of the type devised by Marlowe. Aside from circumstances of production, it seems to be a tendency of sixteenth-century playwrights to locate a conflict in two speakers with only intermittent participation by others.

No doubt one reason why Marlowe put to use the full cast of an enlarged professional company, established more or less permanently in London, was to avoid a potential ridiculousness in the quality of the dialogue. Part of the impact arises from its length. By insistent repetition of boasts the dialogue generates excitement in much the same way as a primitive dance that sustains itself through repetition of the same pattern over and over and over. The danger that characters might grow ridiculous through repetition of the same kind of talk was avoided by distribution. Marlowe withheld the entrance of Bajazeth until his representative had confronted Tamburlaine and exchanged one challenge; then the two leaders meet and clash. Bajazeth's supporters, the Kings of Fez, Morocco, and Argier, join him and are answered in turn by Tamburlaine's captains, Theridamas, Techelles, and Usumcasane; their ladies, Zenocrate and Zabina, continue the dialogue while the battle rages offstage. Thus the conversational ball, as it were, is tossed from the leaders down the line to succeeding pairs of opponents until it ends with the maids, Anippe and Ebea. What they say differs little from pair to pair; what matters is the excitement of the continuing verbal clash that creates and impression of power. Shakespeare, as we saw in chapter 1, follows the same practice in developing the dialogues that accompany knocking at the door.

More distinctive than the number of speakers in Tamburlaine's dialogue is the symmetry of the speeches, for they exhibit a stark balance.
One speech provokes its mirror opposite.

Bajazeth
Now shalt thou feel the force of Turkish arms,
Which lately made all Europe quake for fear.
I have of Turks, Arabians, Moors, and Jews,
Enough to cover all Bithynia.
Let thousands die! Their slaughtered carcasses
Shall serve for walls and bulwarks to the rest;
And as the heads of Hydra, so my power,
Subdued, shall stand as mighty as before. . . .

Tamburlaine
Our conquering swords shall marshal us the way
We use to march upon the slaughtered foe,
Trampling their bowels with our horses' hoofs,
Brave horses bred on the white Tartarian hills.
My camp is like to Julius Caesar's host,
That never fought but had the victory;
Nor in Pharsalia was there such hot war
As these, my followers, willingly would have.

(III.iii.134 ff.)[3]

The traditional structure of the stage must have exercised some
influence on the shape of Marlowe's dialogue. Leslie Hotson has shown
that the axis of the Elizabethan stage ran from left to right and not from
back to front, as it would later do with the introduction of perspective
backdrops.[4] Hotson proposed that actors oriented themselves on the
permanent London stages after 1576 in a manner close to their arrangements on the old pageant wagons and portable stages of the small
traveling companies of the earlier sixteenth century. He argued further
for a general moral symbolism of location even when literal stories were
coming to dominate repertories. The old tradition of stage right for
heaven and stage left for hell lingered as connotations to help actors
place themselves. Bernard Beckerman, from an altogether different
direction of investigation, reinforced Hotson's suggestion about symmetrical staging.[5] He took into account the large number of plays in
repertory, at least of the Lord Admiral's (or Prince Henry's) Men, the
fact that most of the actors doubled parts in each play, and the rapidity
with which new plays were introduced. From these he calculated that
rehearsal time must have been brief. Since the stage manager could
hardly devote much attention to the niceties of blocking out stage
actions, the performers must have had some handy notions about group-

ing themselves, particularly in the large, public scenes. The conditions of staging and the significance of stage locale, then, supported the playwrights' tendency to balance the group dialogue of two equally powerful factions in their confrontations.

Shakespeare's sensitivity to Marlowe's achievement becomes apparent when we consider how he adapted the dialogue of confrontation to the plotting of *1 Henry VI*. Where we would expect to find it, preceding battles between Talbot's forces and Joan's, Shakespeare avoids it. Instead, the bickering English courtiers quarrel among themselves according to the pattern set by Tamburlaine and Bajazeth. The Temple Garden scene, for instance, hardly requires the balanced accusation and counter-accusation that we find. When Somerset delivers an eight-line speech (II.iv.88-95), Richard answers it with an eight-line speech (II.iv.96-103); or when Richard speaks two and a half lines (II.iv.62-64), Somerset answers it by three and a half lines (II.iv.64-67); then they exchange one line each (II.iv.68-69). Although there are other unequal exchanges, the general pattern is one of give and take. From what the speakers say, there is little reason for the minor characters, Suffolk and Warwick, or Vernon and an unnamed lawyer, to participate at all. They pick roses, align themselves to one side or the other, and insult their opponents, thereby adding to the intensity of Somerset's accusations against Richard. Whereas on this issue the audience has no obvious reason to favor one side against the other, in the struggle with France the moral character of Talbot stimulates fierce partisanship. Tamburlaine and Bajazeth act in a foreign and pagan setting; neither one enjoys the audience's automatic approval in the way that Talbot does against Joan, who traffics with evil spirits, so that Marlowe's dialogue has about it an equality impossible for Talbot and Joan. Subsequent dramatists converted Marlowe's scene to a clash between morally unequal opponents. In Peele's *David and Bethsabe* (ca. 1587) the audience favors the king's side against Baliol when they confront one another; or in the anonymous *Thomas of Woodstock* (ca. 1592) the audience wishes for the triumph of York and Lancaster when they confront the forces of Richard II's flatterers. But Shakespeare reserved the symmetrical group dialogue for the more or less neutral clashes where we sense the power of the courtiers who rage at one another and we generally disapprove their querulousness.

When first I considered Marlowe's confrontation scenes, I thought that the full impact of the clash depended upon the audience's complete neutrality, but now I doubt whether such a stance can ever be maintained. Marlowe wrote elsewhere of man's inescapable instinct for taking sides:

When two are stripped, long ere the course begin
We wish that one should lose, the other win;
And one especially do we affect
Of two gold ingots, like in each respect.

(*Hero and Leander*, 169-72)[6]

The audience favors Tamburlaine because of his familiarity, if for no other reason. Yet Marlowe gives notice at the outset of the play that the audience's attitude will be problematic: "View but his picture in this tragic glass, / And then applaud his fortunes as you please." Events work against one's customary judgments and keep the audience somewhat off balance. With regard to this episode, for instance, the audience senses that Tamburlaine is a figure ripe for the turn of Fortune's wheel. They have watched his audacity, his overweening pride, and even his blasphemy, and consequently half anticipate his career to fit the traditional pattern of rise and fall. Bajazeth may well be the warrior to give Tamburlaine his comeuppance. Thus the audience's expectations balance their interest in Tamburlaine as the central character. Similarly in *1 Henry VI* the English courtiers reveal themselves to be so self-seeking and petulant that none can enjoy clear favor with the audience. Duke Humphrey, who becomes in *2 Henry VI* the "good duke," reveals no moral superiority until the last episode of *1 Henry VI*—long after the quarrel scenes have made their impact—when he speaks sensibly against Henry VI's marriage to Margaret of Anjou. Although we in the audience may personally favor, say, York over Somerset or Humphrey over Winchester,[7] we cannot give them our full assent because events and dialogue afford no moral sanction for this feeling. As Exeter says:

. . . no simple man that sees
This jarring discord of nobility,
This shouldering of each other in the court,
This factious bandying of their favorites,
But that it doth presage some ill event.

(IV.i.187-91)

By avoiding a simple opposition between good and evil, Marlowe created a dramatic experience appropriate to heroic conquerors and political controversy. He transmuted the style which Bottom later described as "Ercles' vein" (*Dream*, I.ii.35) or Falstaff called "King Cambyses' vein" (*1 Henry IV*, II.iv.369) into viable tender and opened a wide territory for fellow dramatists. He saw the clash of words as a displacement for the clash of swords; clearly the arrangement of Tamburlaine's meeting with Bajazeth is to give the audience the dramatic equivalent of the battle spectacle. A scene of sheer power, the confrontation exists as a quiddity, a whatness. It is fundamental for Marlowe and does not exist for the sake of something else. We know Tamburlaine is a warrior, not because we have seen him in physical struggle, but because we have seen him face Bajazeth in verbal battle. Shakespeare felt fewer scruples about putting "three rusty swords" on stage to present "York and Lancaster's long jars."[8] That he did not think these spectacles were adequate to impress the audience is apparent because he supplemented many of them with pre-battle confrontations. The presence of these dialogues before battles in 2 and 3 *Henry VI* indicates that Shakespeare sensed their dramatic quiddity. In 2 *Henry VI* the enmity between York and the Lancastrians is secretly brewing from the opening scene of the play. When the outburst finally comes in Act V, it is a moment that we have expected, and Shakespeare uses the Marlovian dialogue of confrontation to fulfill the demands of his structure for a moment of high intensity.

> *King*
> Call Buckingham and bid him arm himself.
> *York*
> Call Buckingham and all the friends thou hast,
> I am resolved for death or dignity.
> *Clifford*
> The first I warrant thee, if dreams prove true.
> *Warwick*
> Thou were best to go to bed and dream again
> To keep thee from the tempest of the field.
> *Clifford*
> I am resolved to bear a greater storm
> Than any thou canst conjure up to-day;
> And that I'll write upon thy burgonet,
> Might I but know thee by thy house's badge.
> *Warwick*
> Now, by my father's badge, old Nevil's crest,
> The rampant bear chained to the ragged staff,
> This day I'll wear aloft my burgonet, . . .
> *Clifford*
> And from thy burgonet I'll rend thy bear
> And tread it under foot with all contempt,
> Despite the berard that protects the bear.

(V.i.192-210)

Shakespeare's version exploits auricular figures far more than Marlowe's. The chronicle characters play on words and develop conceits of dream, storm, and bear in the manner of characters who pick roses in the Temple Garden scene. Their wit acts to generate the momentum of the dialogue and does not differentiate one speaker from another.[9] For equalizing the insult and retort and for sustaining the moment to create an impression of power, all characters are equally witty.

In *3 Henry VI* where there are four battles, Shakespeare wrote only two introductory confrontations. Again his choices suggest the same sense of quiddity at work to amplify the historical occasion. The first and fourth battles, the Battle of Wakefield-Sandal Castle, Act I, scenes iii and iv, and the Battle of Tewkesbury, Act V, scenes iv and v, lack the preliminary meetings, but they take their dramatic importance from what occurs after them. York is captured by the Lancastrians after the opening battle, tied on a molehill, taunted by Queen Margaret, and killed. Likewise, after the battle in Act V, the brothers York stab Prince Edward before Margaret and drive her into a rage of despair. The importance of the second and third battles depends upon the excitement of the pre-battle confrontations. Before the third battle at Coventry in Act V, scenes i and ii, Shakespeare uses the confrontation when the forces of Edward and Warwick meet; once old friends, they now express their fierce antipathy for some forty lines before Clarence enters, changes sides, and consolidates the power of York to foredoom the Lancastrians at Tewkesbury. However, it is the Battle of Towton-Saxton, Act II, scenes ii–vii, that is the turning point in the War of the Roses. Here the Lancastrian forces suffer the defeat that leads to the crowning of Edward IV. It is marked by a pre-battle clash of words and by Henry VI's meditation on the disasters of war as he sits on a molehill observing a father with his dead son and a son with his dead father. This plotting reveals something of the way that Shakespeare views the dialogue of confrontation, for he needs a second scene to moralize the civil conflict. It would have been possible for the characters to talk beforehand about the dangers of civil struggle, as Henry IV does with Vernon and Worcester before the Battle of Shrewsbury in Shakespeare's later *1 Henry IV*, V.i. Instead, Shakespeare uses the clash of words for the purpose of generating an intense excitement of power.

How the quiddity of confrontations affects the plotting of drama can best be seen in the quarrels between English courtiers in *1 Henry VI*. Shakespeare plots the narrative for frequent occurrence of quarrels, so that they are simply there as powerfully distinct moments like beads on a string. They almost never lead to events beyond themselves. They fall into two distinct groups according to the participants. One group, whose main opponents are Duke Humphrey and the Bishop of Winchester, contains three discrete meetings: I.i.33–44; I.iii.1–56; III.i.1–76. There is little reason why there should be three quarrels rather than two or four because the characters remain unchanged by their meetings even though Henry VI brings about a tentative reconciliation in Act III. The second grouping around Richard Plantagenet and Somerset fits better into the narrative; it is initiated in the Temple Garden scene, II.iv; Vernon and Basset continue it, III.iv.28–45, and again at court where Henry VI makes the gesture at reconciling them, IV.i.78–183. This enmity has a decisive causal effect in the defeat of Talbot, but even here no specific quarrel leads to the refusal of York and Somerset to cooperate in France. Each quarrel makes clear their general enmity, as does their inaction in France. In other words, all the various quarrels serve to confirm a general proposition, that quarreling between countrymen contributes more to English defeat than does the opposition by foreign power. The narrative is not plotted so that one moment prepares for another or develops a character as mimetic drama would be plotted. When dialogue creates the whatness of an episode, it has fulfilled its purpose as a concrete example. The quiddity of concrete examples, fitted together to dramatize a proposition, constitutes a didactic play fashioned in the manner of an oration.

Since the quarrels do not displace battles, the speakers ostensibly talk about matters other than physical threats and boasts although such comments usually arise in the heat of their interchange. Primarily, they demean one another, and because of this, the quarrel becomes a handy means of establishing identity. The pattern of attack and counterattack serves well to paste labels quickly on characters, adequate when they take their identities from loyalty to one side of an issue or another. For instance, when Duke Humphrey confronts the Bishop of Winchester before parliament, *1 Henry VI,* III.i, his main intention is to present a bill of particulars against the Bishop, but the dialogue conveniently takes the balanced form of accusation and retort. Once the Bishop's historical background has been narrated, his loyalty impugned, and his behavior judged improper, there is no more to say. Either the speaker amplifies by copiousness or other speakers join in to repeat with their own terms the same accusations. As the exchange continues, the pace quickens, and we can see Shakespeare using his familiar tricks to sustain the bickering and create tension:

Winchester
But he shall know I am as good —
Gloucester
As good? Thou bastard of my grandfather!
Winchester
Ay, lordly sir! For what are you, I pray

But one imperious in another's throne?
> *Gloucester*
Am I not Protector, saucy priest?
> *Winchester*
And am I not a prelate of the church?
> *Gloucester*
Yes, as an outlaw in a castle keeps
And useth it to patronage his theft.
> *Winchester*
Unreverent Gloucester.
> *Gloucester*
>> Thou are reverent
Touching thy spiritual function, not thy life.
> *Winchester*
Rome shall remedy this.
> *Gloucester*
>> Roam thither then.

(III.i.41–51)

This quarrel depends upon a discrepancy between the demands of a role and the inadequacy of an opponent's behavior to his role. Priest and Protector are only two of the many roles in the tetralogy which act as standards to measure behavior and forestall any potential questions in the audience about the characters' behavior. We learn nothing of the particular circumstances that make Winchester ambitious. Does he compensate for his illegitimate birth? Does he wish to revenge himself against his legitimate kinsman? His personal sentiments remain beyond the reach of the public dialogue. We learn instead enough to identify him as a discontented Englishman who adds fuel to the fire of controversy and prevents the commonwealth from uniting to support her valiant defenders abroad. The quarrel, then, is suited to speakers defined by their public loyalties and by clear and simple standards of behavior.

Since the patterned confrontation, exciting in itself, need not be confined to clashes among soldiers, Shakespeare found it a viable means for introducing the numerous characters quickly and grouping them with the Yorkists or the Lancastrians. The funeral of Henry V which opens *1 Henry VI* dissolves into a bitter quarrel that identifies Gloucester as protector and Winchester as a greedy, ambitious churchman. The ceremonious welcome of Margaret to England which opens *2 Henry VI* breaks out into a disagreement over Anjou and Maine, provinces in

France given to her father as a kind of inverse dowry; although in this episode Shakespeare does not preserve the symmetry of attack and insult, the various characters, as they take opposite sides on the issue and leave the stage, declare their identities and brand their opponents with such epithets as "proud prelate," "haughty cardinal," "proud" Somerset, and "ambitious" Buckingham. *3 Henry VI* opens with York's faction confronting Henry VI in parliament and demanding his crown. Here the challenge and retort explicate at a high pitch of intensity the complicated genealogy of Henry VI and York and specify by role and epithet the supporters of each claimant. *Richard III* does not open with a quarrel, but in the third scene Richard, by confronting and accusing Queen Elizabeth and her kinsmen, establishes the identities of a large group of characters and their past loyalties. *Richard II* opens with formal charges and countercharges between Bolingbroke and Mowbray that state the fact of Gloucester's murder, identify the main speakers, and establish their relations to one another. *Romeo and Juliet*, of course, begins with a version of the quarrel and develops into a fight on stage; through it the identities of Montague, Capulet, Benvolio, and Tybalt clarify their long-standing enmity.

The opening of *3 Henry VI* shows how well the balanced pattern of confrontation presents the conflicting claims for kingship because an objective interpretation of the facts is perhaps impossible. By giving both sides full display in a quarrel, Shakespeare exercises the playwright's prerogative for leaving in abeyance the decision of what is right.[10] In *1 Henry VI* the dying Mortimer narrates the genealogical details for the Yorkist claim to the throne. His account of the Lancastrians' ill treatment creates more sympathy for Richard Plantagenet than perhaps should be felt through the rest of the play. In *2 Henry VI* York himself narrates his genealogy to Warwick and Salisbury. Even though the other side presents no counterargument, the audience takes into account his partiality, a fact which mitigates against their accepting his interpretation at face value. In *3 Henry VI* the King by the sanction of the throne itself would seem to have the stronger case, but Shakespeare adds to his argument an aside:

I know not what to say; my title's weak.

(I.i.134)

He thereby neutralizes somewhat the favoritism an audience might feel toward him. The issue, then, fits with the sort of balance which the best confrontations sustain.

Yet Henry VI and Exeter make something new out of what would otherwise be a typical expository quarrel. The King offers, consistent with his meekness, a compromise: he will keep the crown during his lifetime and make York's sons his heirs. His responsiveness, unlike that of the conventional quarreler who only talks at his opponent, opens the possibility for a dialectic and brings the discussion closer to the judicial oration than before in the tetralogy. In earlier quarrels the speakers do not alter their minds; either an outsider intervenes to restore harmony, as does the Lord Mayor (*1 Henry VI*, I.iii), or they simply stop, as do the quarrelers in the Temple Garden, who utter dire predictions when they leave the stage (*1 Henry VI*, II.iv). In this later quarrel, Exeter, like Henry VI, is affected by what his opponents say, so much so that he changes his opinion and agrees with York. This responsiveness makes him a startling exception to the usual subsidiary speaker, whose role is to enforce what his leader asserts. Even so, Exeter's change of opinion remains only a matter of the moment; while he agrees with York, he does not side with him. He remains with Henry VI after the other characters depart and hopes with the King for reconciliation of the two factions. Since he appears briefly in only one other scene, his change must be explained by its immediate impact on the expository quarrel, as if Shakespeare intended to impress the audience with the force of York's claim. But the fact that Exeter remains sympathetic to Henry VI suggests that Shakespeare may have a subtler point to make that acknowledges the validity of theory and also the claims of practice. This is to say, York may present a convincing genealogical theory for prior claim to the throne, but events for three generations have established the very practical fact of the Lancastrian lineage and should be accepted to avoid chaos.[11] Just as Exeter's behavior is pursued no further, so Henry's proposal has no effect on subsequent events, for Queen Margaret rallies her supporters to attack and defeat York. The controversy, like most other quarrel scenes, leads nowhere, but in its self-contained quiddity acts like a Leibnizian monad for the entire play, reflecting in little the nature of the whole struggle.

By this time we should be forming a picture of the way our earliest impressions of Shakespeare's first chronicles—strident, even bombastic, filled with characters of little more than historical names engaged in a bewildering succession of events—merge with his rhetorical dramaturgy. While the characters may not speak in Ercles' vein, their high-pitched energy shows that they are distant cousins. The historical figures are as much orators as they are dramatic characters, for they take one side of an issue and defend it with all the devices an orator would use. And the overall plotting of events reflects the same preconceptions. Shakespeare arranges the confrontations to enforce his thesis rather than to construct a mimetic plot to dramatize the potentialities of the story itself. Episodes tend to relate vertically to a thesis which binds them together rather than horizontally to enforce a chronological narrative. The different kinds of decisions demanded by a mimetic plot can be discerned if we set comparable episodes from *Richard II* against the expository quarrel and the climactic confrontation between opponents.

∽

The quarrel that opens *Richard II* is at once close to its prototype and yet so different as to suggest a change in Shakespeare's understanding of what is dramatic. The moment is public, the issue one of power, and the dialogue symmetrical. Chivalric behavior rather than a large number of subsidiary speakers imparts a ceremonious tone to the occasion, for the quarrel is confined to only two major speakers, Bolingbroke and Mowbray. This difference, however, is incidental to the kind of exposition that sets apart the opening from its predecessors. Although it exposes, it misleads. Bolingbroke accuses Mowbray of several crimes, the crucial one being the murder of Thomas of Woodstock, his uncle and former Protector of the commonwealth. Mowbray defends himself by speeches of equal length and forcefulness. The audience listens intently to the balanced give and take for clues, but cannot determine which speaker to trust. Not until the following scene does the information come out that Richard II himself is guilty of the murder of his uncle.[12] The plotting is appropriate to a cumulative narrative where one episode prepares for the next rather than the didactic narrative where episodes, as discrete units, embody a thesis.

The mimetic plot then makes complicated demands upon the audience. The young Shakespeare as orator-playwright assumes that his audience would analogize similar episodes, but he takes care to clarify the thematic purpose behind them. When plotting *Richard II*, he either holds his audience in higher esteem or he understands them to be willing participants, eager to sympathize, curious about what comes next, rather than listeners, prepared to be stimulated to virtuous behavior. For instance, the opening scene introduces characteristics of the speakers of which the audience grows aware as their occurrence accumulates. Bolingbroke reveals a mastery of public ceremony not only in his challenge of Mowbray before the King, but later in Act III, scene iii, he takes advantage of the parley before Flint Castle to gain control of Richard, and in Act IV, scene i, he uses the ceremony of Richard's abdication before parliament to sanction his own accession; finally in Act V, scene iv, we hear of his broad hint on a public occasion that Exton kill Richard, a hint that he retracts after the deed. On the other hand, Richard fumbles during public ceremonies. Obviously he does not intend to allow the quarrel between Bolingbroke and Mowbray to develop into a trial by combat where his friend would probably sacrifice himself, but events get out of his control in scene i. Later, after he stops the combat, an act that suggests his full control, his changing the length of Bolingbroke's banishment gives us the impression of impetuosity, human though it is; certainly his refusal to follow Aumerle's advice at Flint Castle and use ceremony to parry with Bolingbroke and wait for favorable circumstances reveals this trait, for he cuts through Bolingbroke's use of ceremony.[13] No observer stands on the sidelines to describe these traits of behavior to the audience, nor is it crucial that an audience consciously formulate a statement of their observations. Certainly by Act IV when Richard II and Bolingbroke meet before parliament, their behavior comes as no surprise to us. This meeting depends in part upon Bolingbroke's not saying all he means and Richard's disrupting the public ceremony, patterns quite foreign to, say, the confrontation between Duke Humphrey and the Bishop of Winchester before parliament in *1 Henry VI*, III.i, which depends for its impact upon each character's saying what he means and his behavior being estimated solely by clear public standards.

One may object to the statement that the audience does not know about the guilt of Richard II in the murder of Woodstock, for in 1595 many members not only would have been familiar with the chronicles but might have seen *Thomas of Woodstock*, a play that has also been called *Richard II, Part One,* which dramatizes the events of Woodstock's murder.[14] Yet a similar familiarity at least by some members of the audience with the facts of the chronicles would hold for the early history plays, where Shakespeare never risks a major dramatic irony in the exposition and reveals other local ironies to the audience by asides, whispers, and soliloquy. The plotting of the earlier chronicle plays indicates that Shakespeare sees his audience in a one-way relation to stage events. Thus his function is to assault them in the manner of an orator with an enargetic and energetic style to teach them by illustrative episodes. When he comes to plot the chronicle material of Richard II's reign, he does not abdicate his role as teacher, but the moral insights emerge from the dramatized narrative in a different way. He depends upon his audience to be a willing partner and consequently turns his attention from explicit instruction to creating a self-contained world of the play where ceremonies do not always mean what is said and where anticlimactic dialogues may be more affecting than high-pitched copious ones.

By examining one anticlimactic dialogue, we can discover a second way that Shakespeare plots the career of Richard II mimetically. To attend primarily to the demands of the narrative is, among other things, to capitalize upon context. This is to say, the playwright counts on the facts of one scene to carry over to another. Although there are no battles in this play, the main opponents come face to face at the turning point of the play, Act III, scene iii. The large amount of preparation for this meeting indicates that Shakespeare intended it to be a focal point in the shift of power. Two preceding scenes depict Richard's return to England and discovery of the extent of his opposition. In the opening section of the crucial scene the dialogue moves from group to group; first, Bolingbroke speaks to Northumberland in anticipation of meeting Richard; then Northumberland speaks to Richard, who in turn sends words of defiance to Bolingbroke. With this extensive preparation, the situation fairly calls for a balanced confrontation of opponents, neither of whom at this point enjoys a clear moral superiority in the eyes of the audience. Yet when the crucial moment arrives for the central figures to speak, the dialogue takes an unusual turn toward understatement or anticlimax:

> *Bolingbroke*
> Stand all apart
> And show fair duty to his majesty. *He kneels down.*
> My gracious lord —
> *King*
> Fair cousin, you debase your princely knee
> To make the base earth proud with kissing it.
> Me rather had my heart might feel your love
> Than my unpleased eye see your courtesy.
> Up, cousin, up! Your heart is up, I know,
> Thus high at least [*touches his own head*], although your knee be low.
> *Bolingbroke*
> [*rises*] My gracious lord, I come but for mine own.
> *King*
> Your own is yours, and I am yours, and all.
> *Bolingbroke*
> So far be mine, my most redoubted lord,
> As my true service shall deserve your love.
> *King*
> Well you deserve. They well deserve to have

That know the strong'st and surest way to get.
Uncle, give my your hand. Nay, dry your eyes.
Tears show their love, but want their remedies.
Cousin, I am too young to be your father,
Though you are old enough to be my heir.
What you will have, I'll give, and willing too;
For do we must what force will have us do.
Set on towards London. Cousin, is it so?

   Bolingbroke

Yea, my good lord.

   King

         Then I must not say no. [*Flourish, Exeunt.*]
                          (III.iii.187–210)

It is as if we had been ushered up a long entrance way to an imposing portico, but when the door is opened, we find only a small, barren room. With so much to be said, we hear the flattened tones of understatement. As Richard's bitterness emerges from his excessive politeness and his clever play on Bolingbroke's words, we realize that words and meanings do not entirely coincide. Richard exhibits more wit, but Bolingbroke's quietness is an index of his superior control. The very premise upon which Marlowe devised Tamburlaine's confrontation with Bajazeth equated the power of words with the power of deeds. Yet in Richard's submission to Bolingbroke, the audience does not respond proportionately to the sound of dialogue. Shakespeare has learned to affect them powerfully with a moment of powerlessness because he has at his command the technique of dramatic irony. This means that the audience need not think or feel proportionately to the characters on stage; it also means that the audience can follow hints, sustain information from one episode to another, and react from a distinct vantage point outside the transactions of the immediate play world.

Again one might object, saying that Richard II is neither a Tamburlaine, a Richard of York, nor even a Richmond. Just as Henry VI was a weak king and seldom joined in the wrangling quarrels of his subjects, so Richard II cannot be expected to counteract Bolingbroke's forceful presence with words. In answer, one could say with regard to the King's character that he does, in fact, speak forcefully to Northumberland just before he descends from the battlement like "glistering Phaeton" to face his true opponent. He can retort sharply, as we watch him doing in the parliament scene, first with Northumberland and then with Bolingbroke. But to answer in this way is to assume that Shakespeare, had he chosen Richard II's career for his first play, would still have dramatized the meeting with Bolingbroke as anticlimactic. The peace parley between the French and English in Act V of *1 Henry VI*, as we saw in the preceding chapter, could well have used the ironic dialogue of understatement, but the discrepancy between words and meaning seems to have been less appealing to Shakespeare at this time. To convey the fact that the French do not intend to honor their treaty, he resorted to the device of whispers between Regnier and Charles. His manipulation of plot did not permit him to take the context for granted; so he did not assume that the audience would intuit through half-hearted endorsement of the English proposals that the French had no intention of honoring their treaty. It seems, then, that if an episode takes its significance from the ideas it embodies rather than from the narrative it develops, its details tend to be generalized if not commonplace in order to bear out and clarify the ideas. We might deduce that, at least on the basis of Shakespeare's apprenticeship, shades of irony become available to the playwright once an episode is relieved of its need to illustrate a thesis.

Thus the contrast between early and later confrontations, including early and later expository quarrels, provides us with a broad and rough sketch of the way Shakespeare's plotting changed between *1 Henry VI* and *Richard II*. It is now time to examine the contrast in closer detail through another version of the confrontation, which I call dialogues of triumph and defeat. Pre-battle confrontations are simple episodes that serve well to reveal methods of plotting, but they depend upon a single interaction between speakers and afford little insight into characterization. Shakespeare's flexibility appears in the way he adapts the pattern of Marlowe's dialogue to expository quarrels, and in discussing exposition, although I touched upon the characteristics of the speakers, I emphasized the relation of the quarrel to thesis and audience from its place as a segment of plot. The scenes between triumphant and defeated characters, with only slight differences from the pattern of the pre-battle confrontations, enable us to see in detail how the contrast between didactic and mimetic plotting affects characterization.

∞

The scene of triumph and defeat brings together the exultant conqueror and his defeated enemy whose relationship can only be described as one between orators, each hurling words more to hit his opponent than to express himself. These confrontations tend to be as static and discrete as the meetings before battle and, if anything, intensify even more the pitch of dialogue by concentrating upon two speakers who slow the pace by lengthy but symmetrical attacks on one another and rarely resort to the quick give and take of stichomythia customary in the pre-battle dialogues. Seldom do modulations of response or alterations of attitude result from these meetings between the victorious and the defeated, which are more verbal contests than conversations. Yet the situation of total power when one is completely victorious and the other completely his victim sets traits of character into vivid relief.

Tamburlaine's two scenes of triumph over Bajazeth set the fashion for a host of similar moments in Elizabethan plays for some ten years.[15] Marlowe shaped the dialogue to show the awesomeness of Tamburlaine's unrestrained power first when he makes Bajazeth a footstool and puts him in a cage and later during a banquet when he feeds him in his cage. In the first scene, as Tamburlaine rises on his imperial footstool, he proclaims:

Now clear the triple region of the air,
And let the majesty of heaven behold
Their scourge and terror tread on emperors.
Smile stars that reigned at my nativity,
And dim the brightness of their neighbor lamps;
Disdain to borrow light of Cynthia
For I, the chiefest lamp of all the earth,
First rising in the east with mild aspect,
But fixèd now in the meridian line,
Will send up fire to your turning spheres
And cause the sun to borrow light of you.

(IV,ii,30-40)

This quotation gives us less than half of Tamburlaine's exultation, but it is sufficient to characterize his style and sentiments. Verbs come in pairs, nouns are accompanied by adjectival phrases, and imperatives govern the syntax. Even Tamburlaine's declarative sentences convey a force of will and magnify their impact by quantitative devices such as the use of "all" and plurals: "Not all the kings and emperors of the earth, / If they would lay their crowns before my feet, / Shall ransom him" (IV.ii.92-94). The boundaries of sentences are made to stretch far beyond their customary length. Whereas Shakespeare tended to accumulate a number of short statements organized by sound patterns to create an energetic style, Marlowe multiplied the parts within a single sentence. Either way, the speeches impress us with their orotund amplitude.[16]

In addition to an expansive syntax, Marlowe depended for the impression of unrestrained power upon the excesses of disturbing hyperboles, disturbing because at this point in the play (Act IV) so many of Tamburlaine's boasts have become reality that we pause to entertain the possibility that he might well alter the brightness of his favorite stars. Counteracting this speculation is the shock of impropriety. An Elizabethan audience would have been chilled by Tamburlaine's boasts, expecting a thunderbolt to confirm their belief in man's limitations. Marlowe pushed his embodiment of unrestrained power beyond the indecorum of language into behavior. Even today without a hierarchized. society, we still sense the outrageous indignity of using the emperor as a footstool and caging him like an animal. In the banquet scene Tamburlaine's treatment moves beyond impropriety into inhumanity:

> *Tamburlaine*
> . . . Here, eat, sir; take it from my sword's point, or I'll thrust it to thy heart.
>
> *[Bajazeth] takes [the food,] and stamps upon it.*
> *Theridamas*
> He stamps it under his feet, my lord.
> *Tamburlaine*
> Take it up, villain, and eat it, or I will make thee slice the brawns of thy arms into carbonadoes and eat them.
> *Usumcasane*
> Nay, 'twere better he killed his wife, and then she shall be sure not to be starved, and he be provided for a month's victual beforehand.
> *Tamburlaine*
> Here is my dagger. Dispatch her while she is fat, for if she live but a while longer, she will fall into a consumption with fretting, and then she will not be worth the eating.
>
> (IV.iv.40–50)

This grim comedy, unlike anything on the English stage until this time, so far as one can tell from extant drama, arises from Marlowe's conception of total power, a conception that opened the gates to a new experience for drama. He showed playwrights, accustomed to the generalized group scenes in morality plays, how to exploit their training in rhetoric to dramatize with appropriate dialogue episodes of raw, brutal power.

Bajazeth puts to use the same verbal devices as Tamburlaine in counteracting his imperious assertions and outrageous treatment by defiance. He reveals no embarrassment, self-pity, or grief. Instead, he hurls curses at his opponent:

Ye holy priests of heavenly Mahomet,
That, sacrificing, slice and cut your flesh,
Staining his altars with your purple blood,
Make heaven to frown and every fixèd star
To suck up poison from the moorish fens,
And pour it in this glorious tyrant's throat!

(IV.ii.2-7)

The dialogue continues to shock through impropriety because Tamburlaine and his followers not only fail to respond to Bajazeth's fiercest words; they react to them as jokes. At the banquet Bajazeth spits out curses and evokes Theridamas's comment, "Methinks 'tis a great deal better than a consort of music" (IV.iv.59).

In *3 Henry VI* Shakespeare adapts the moment of brutal triumph to Queen Margaret's capture of the Duke of York. She places him on a molehill, mocks him with a paper crown, and taunts him with a napkin dipped in his young son's blood before she has him killed. The brutality of the scene and the way it is dramatized indicates that Shakespeare was familiar with and was even approximating Marlowe's earlier scene. When Margaret urges York to weep, "I prithee grieve, to make me merry, York" (I.iv.86), and says "Stamp, rave, and fret, that I may sing and dance" (I.iv.91), she recalls Theridamas's inhuman reference to Bajazeth's frustrated ravings as a "consort of music." The heart of Shakespeare's scene lies in two long speeches, a forty-four-line attack by Margaret, shaped like an oration, and a fifty-six-line response by York, divided into two parts; the first is an oration of dispraise against the Queen and the second a lament, which better fits chapter 4 of my discussion. For the moment, it is sufficient to say that York's lament makes a crucial difference in Shakespeare's version of Tamburlaine's brutal triumph. York, by giving vent to his feelings, creates a sympathy in the audience unlike anything that they feel for Bajazeth's curses. In both scenes there is a severity of balance between the speakers, but in Marlowe's the balance is emotional as well as verbal, for Tamburlaine's irresistible, awesome power affects us as much as any interest we have for his victim. Bajazeth's last vestige of force, his power to curse, displaces any sentiments Bajazeth might have about himself as victim and diminishes our potential sympathy. York's lament serves not to elevate Margaret's total power so much as to emphasize its brutality. Northumberland's brief interruption of York's speech,

Beshrew me but his passion moves me so
That hardly can I check my eyes from tears.

(I.iv.150-51)

reassures the audience that they too can indulge their feeling for the
rebel in this circumstance.

Margaret's speech contains little of Tamburlaine's self-congratulatory
exultation except implicitly. She shapes her attack like a demonstrative
oration and taunts York with the impropriety of his ambition. By juxtaposing her attitude to Clifford's, Shakespeare emphasizes the excess of
her cruelty. Clifford would kill the captured York immediately, but
Margaret relishes her victory and, to torment him, stretches out the
moment before death. Her remarks take the form of rhetorical questions that keep her voice from falling at the end of sentences and give it
a querulous insistence:

What, was it you that would be England's king?
Was't you that revelled in our parliament
And made a preachment of your high descent?
Where are your mess of sons to back you now?
The wanton Edward and the lusty George?

(I.iv.70-74)

The auricular figures impart an energy that enforces the sting of her
taunts. This passage is sufficient to indicate how Shakespeare's tendency
to short, repetitive units differs from the sound patterns of Tamburlaine's rolling periods, although both are apt for embodying experiences
of power.

Scorn intensifies the mockery when Margaret places a paper crown
upon York's head. Edward Hall's chronicle mentions a crown of sedges,
but Shakespeare avoids the connotations of this detail. Even though
York is brutally treated, Shakespeare never allows us to forget his rebellious behavior:

Ay, marry, sir, now looks he like a king.
Ay, this is he that took King Henry's chair
And this is he was his adopted heir.

(I.iv.96-98)

Had Shakespeare ended Margaret's speech with this mockery, York's
career would have been another mirror for magistrates, and we would
have taken an "I-told-you-so" attitude toward his death. But he di-
verged from his sources to add the napkin dipped in Rutland's blood
and turned the properly punished rebel into a grief-stricken father, and

this addition turns us against the punishers too. Hall mentions that Clifford killed Rutland in battle, but gives no evidence that York knew of this before he died.

York's answer to Margaret's taunts makes no reference to his political ambitions. He devotes the first part to characterizing her, pointing to her background as inappropriate for England's queen:

I would assay, proud queen, to make thee blush,
To tell thee whence thou cam'st, of whom derived,
Were shame enough to shame thee, wert thou not shameless.

(I.iv.118–20)

using the figure of *polyptoton* to conclude his statement with emphasis. Then he generalizes the standards by which to judge her behavior:

How ill-beseeming is it in thy sex
To triumph like an Amazonian trull.

(I.iv.113–14)

and organizes supporting details by parallel syntax:

'Tis beauty that doth oft make women proud; / But...
'Tis virtue that doth make them most admired; / The contrary doth...
'Tis government that makes them seem divine; / The want thereof...

(I.iv.128 ff.)

He uses the figure of antithesis to intensify his conclusion:

Women are soft, mild, pitiful, and flexible;
Thou stern, obdurate, flinty, rough, remorseless.

(I.iv.141–42)

Greene's parody of one line from York's speech, "O tiger's heart wrapped in a woman's hide" (I.i.137), depended for its success upon his readers' familiarity with the scene and indirectly testifies to its success. Each speaker judges the other in the same way as the participants do in the earlier quarrel scenes. She concentrates upon the discrepancy between York's behavior and his place, between his ambition and his accomplishment; he judges the discrepancy between her behavior and her nature, between her background and her role. This similarity is more than coincidental, as an investigation of some stylistic devices can show.

Both speeches contain a plethora of epithets and terms of direct address: from York's speech we find "she-wolf of France" (line 111), "proud queen" (118 and 125), "false Frenchwoman" (149), "ruthless queen" (156), "fell Clifford" (149), and "hard-hearted Clifford" (167).

Margaret addresses him twice without any title, "York" (79, 86), and adds epithets to most proper names: "wanton Edward" (73), "lusty George" (73), "your darling Rutland" (78), "valiant Clifford" (80), "poor York" (84), "great Plantagenet" (99). Of course, this repetition of the opponent's name helps preserve the oratorical situation, for one delivers a talk to, as distinct from conversing with, another, but more importantly, the epithet works to narrow the conception of character to make it appropriate to what one says. So too, the maxim, another device that occurs with enough frequency to distinguish the style of this scene, works to narrow, in this case simplifying, behavior by fitting it to a moral pattern. When York is first captured, he faces his enemies and urges them to kill him immediately. Clifford responds by saying:

So cowards fight when they can fly no further;
So doves do peck the falcon's piercing talons;
So desperate thieves, all hopeless of their lives,
Breathe out invectives 'gainst the officers.

(I.iv.40–44)

When they lay hands on York to bind and set him on the molehill, he struggles, and Clifford says again:

Ay, ay, so strives the woodcock with the gin.

(I.iv.61)

and Northumberland seconds him:

So doth the cony struggle in the net.

(I.iv.62)

These comments work to dehumanize York and help them carry out their intention to kill him. Not surprising, perhaps, is the one other place in the tetralogy where maxims occur with equal frequency: *2 Henry VI*, III.i and ii, where Duke Humphrey's enemies plan without justification first to imprison him and later to murder him. By comparing the good Duke's behavior to the wolf, the snake, and the crocodile, they simplify and falsify to make easier their acts of inhumanity. The same tendency can be applied to the speakers themselves. In the scene between York and Margaret, the Queen as orator derives force from her ability not to express her full womanhood in her speech. As victor, she abstracts herself from all the feelings she has as woman and mother in order to treat her victim so brutally. But whereas later we watch Lady Macbeth consciously going through the process of dehumanizing herself by calling on the spirits that attend on mortal thought, here the playwright has arranged her character beforehand so that the emphasis falls upon the conflict between victor and victim rather than upon the character of victor preparing for a confrontation. Margaret never reveals any trait of character that might interfere with the figure who opposes York. She gains effectiveness as a speaker much as Tamburlaine does because her character does not detract from her singleness of purpose. Her stance as opponent is fully adequate to characterize her at the moment of confrontation with York.

The later scenes of triumph and defeat provide a sharp contrast with the earlier precisely because they do not restrict a speaker's characteristics but become the occasion for releasing them. In the parliament scene of *Richard II*, IV.i, Bolingbroke with the full powers of state at his command faces Richard II, who has no choice but to abdicate in an official ceremony. The scene gets much of its dramatic power from the fact that Richard cannot constrict his behavior to his public role as opponent. His personal feelings break through to reveal pride, anger, humiliation, and bitter despair. So wide are the differences between this scene and the earlier versions that one might well raise the question whether a comparison is justified. In *Richard II* the emphasis falls on the victim, so much so that we scarcely hear from Bolingbroke at all. What he says is brief and restrained, quite unlike either Tamburlaine or Queen Margaret, who exult over their victims. Yet the situation is similar. Bolingbroke uses the helpless Richard for his purposes, and Northumberland shows no sympathy for the deposed King's anguish.

Moreover, there is evidence that Shakespeare exploits a dramatic tradition behind this scene. In order to see how aware he is of other drama, we need to consider Edward II's similar scene, when he, finding himself totally without power, must give up his crown on demand from Mortimer (*Edward II,* V.i). Marlowe's play, the chronicle of an extravagant, weak young king, has frequently been compared to Shakespeare's play on a similar career. That Shakespeare has Marlowe in mind is apparent from Richard II's echo of Faustus, if we had no further evidence:

> Was this face the face
> That every day under his household roof
> Did keep ten thousand men? Was this the face
> That like the sun did make beholders wink?
> Was this the face that faced so many follies
> And was at last outfaced by Bolingbroke?
> A brittle glory shineth in this face.

(IV.i.281–87)

I quote this passage which echoes Faustus's response to Helen of Troy as evidence not only of Shakespeare's reference to a former play but as evidence of his style. At this moment, a high point in the scene, Richard is readying himself to smash the mirror and shatter the "external image" of himself. Shakespeare intensifies the moment by verbal schemes that repeat "face" for emphasis. The devices recall the earlier scenes of triumph, but the way Shakespeare uses them changes. Here Richard's verbal play exhibits his wit. At the end of the scene, as we shall see shortly, he displays an embarrassing failure of wit, a contrast that helps dramatize his changing mood. Equally pertinent to his characterization is the fact that neither Northumberland nor Bolingbroke speaks with the intricate control of words that Richard displays, nor do they exhibit any change in their style through the scene. To recall earlier versions of meeting between conqueror and defeated, Margaret and York speak with equal facility, as do the characters in the quarrel scenes and prebattle confrontations. It is not that such variation in style is beyond Shakespeare's grasp in writing the earlier plays; rather, his intention lies elsewhere than in using wit to reveal subtle changes in the mood of his speakers.

If the general similarity between Richard II's career as dramatized by Shakespeare and Edward II's career as dramatized by Marlowe is apparent to us, the probability is strong that Elizabethan playgoers made a similar connection, particularly since Shakespeare elsewhere exploits allusions to other plays and must have assumed that at least some of his audience would enjoy them.[17] "What angel wakes me from my flow'ry bed?" in *A Midsummer Night's Dream* (III.i.116) parodies Hieronimo's cry in *The Spanish Tragedy* (II.v.1); and Pistol exhibits some recollection of Tamburlaine's heroic style (*2 Henry IV*, II.iv.148–53). Part of the pleasure of Richard II's deposition scene, at least to the more knowledgeable of the audience, lies in its resemblance to Edward II's uncrowning. I suggest that Shakespeare may well have decided to "take on" Marlowe here and "go him one better." This consciousness of the conventions of the art form is consistent with the development of professional drama *qua* drama. Concurrently in his comedies, Shakespeare uses drama to comment upon drama. Likewise, his characters grow increasingly aware of their own manner of speaking and of drama as a metaphor for their behavior. References to conventions appear to be part of the process of drama's becoming a distinctive form and part of the pleasure of theatergoers who respond to its distinctiveness.

The first stages of the way drama feeds upon itself can be seen in

Marlowe's scene, for Edward II's expression of his powerlessness depends
obliquely upon Bajazeth and Tamburlaine. Both Marlowe and Shakespeare abandon the pattern of symmetrical dialogue and pay less attention to the brutality of the conqueror than to the sentiments of the defeated. One critic has pointed out that Marlowe achieves an even greater
sense of Mortimer's power by keeping him apart from the unkinging
scene.[18] The earlier Marlowe could not have entertained such a possibility in rendering Tamburlaine's control over his victims, even if the
conqueror need do no more than look at Agydas to cause him to kill
himself (*1 Tamburlaine*, III.ii). Bajazeth's role is conceived as one half
of a confrontation, and his speeches are designed to counterpoise Tamburlaine's. To dramatize Edward II's confrontation with Mortimer's
emissaries who request that he give up the crown, Marlowe shapes the
scene almost as a monologue. Of one hundred and twenty-four lines,
the King speaks all but sixteen. Much of what he says consists of wishes,
commands, and petitions to heaven:

But if proud Mortimer do wear this crown,
Heavens turn it to a blaze of quenchless fire.

(V.i.43–44)

This appeal to the heavens echoes Bajazeth's earlier curses, but it
expresses a sense of frustration that the pagan emperor never reveals.
Bajazeth prays to the priests of Mahomet with a conviction that they will
help him, whereas Edward prays to the "heavens" rather than to a specific divine spirit or to his priests. His wish is so contrary to fact that it
becomes a half-intended mockery of his impotence. He indulges in futile wishes that, as they grow more and more impossible, become parodies of that orator who possesses the power to enforce his comments:

But stay awhile; let me be king till night,
That I may gaze upon this glittering crown;
So shall my eyes receive their last content,
My head, the latest honor due to it,
And jointly both yield up their wishèd right.
Continue ever thou celestial sun;
Let never silent night possess this clime.
Stand still you watches of the element;
All times and seasons, rest you at a stay,
That Edward may be still fair England's king.

(V.i.59–68)

Whereas Tamburlaine's hyperboles suggest the possibility that they might be actualized, Edward II's exaggerations acknowledge his power-lessness. Marlowe's reuse of his earlier style for ironic purposes resembles Shakespeare's reuse of the expository quarrel in *Richard II* for ironic purposes. A "sincere" equation between means and ends is appropriate to the orator who wishes to affect his listeners. When a playwright in fulfilling the demands of his mimetic narrative realizes that what a sympathetic character says cannot be coordinated necessarily with his own convictions or the audience's, then he becomes free to exploit the consequent discrepancies.

Richard exhibits the same ironic attitude toward his own style at least in part of his deposition scene. Near the outset when he gives up the crown, he formulates by the severely patterned language of Shakespeare's earlier characters a mock ceremony that parodies the order of the coronation: [19]

Now mark me how I will undo myself.
I give this heavy weight from off my head
And this unwieldly sceptre from my hand,
The pride of kingly sway from out my heart.
With mine own tears I wash away my balm,
With mine own hands I give away my crown,
With mine own tongue deny my sacred state,
With mine own breath release all duty's rites.
All pomp and majesty I do forswear;
My manors, rents, revenues I forgo;
My acts, decrees, and statutes I deny.
God pardon all oaths that are broke to me!
God keep all vows unbroke that swear to thee!

(IV.i.203–15)

This parody is quite clearly Richard's rather than Shakespeare's, a fact that governs the audience's attitude toward the King. Whereas Edward II's irony enforces his sense of helplessness, Richard's ironic control of his words qualifies the potential pity an audience would feel for him. Pity is a dangerous, if not dreadful, sentiment, and it is worth recalling that tragedy, according to Aristotle, stimulates pity in combination with another emotion. To feel pity, an audience must also feel in some way superior to the character in trouble, just as they feel superior when they laugh at him. In fact, pity is intimately connected with laughter, as can be seen when melodramatic episodes arranged without sufficient re-straint to tug at our heartstrings come close to evoking laughter. In this scene Richard II, who pities himself, needs some tartness or some evi-

dence of competence to counteract our indulgence of the helpless victim. Shakespeare gives him self-awareness and wit to bolster his regality
and mitigate the impression of helplessness.

In addition to the heightened awareness of both victimized kings,
Marlowe and Shakespeare devise gestures that express their inner turmoil and sustain the momentum of their speeches. It will be recalled
that Shakespeare's earliest characters develop their comments by copiousness. Placed in a situation where they take one or the other side of an
issue, they state and restate their position against their opponent's statements. By removing Edward II's opponent from the scene, Marlowe in
effect says that his king needs no continual verbal stimulation to articulate his feelings. Unlike Bajazeth, Edward struggles internally, pulled
one way and then another as he gives up the crown:

Here, take my crown; the life of Edward too;
Two kings in England cannot reign at once.
But stay awhile. . . .
See, monsters, see, I'll wear my crown again. . . .
I'll not resign, but whilst I live — . . .
Call thou them back; I have no power to speak.

(V.i.57 ff.)

Torn between his personal desire and his sense of the inevitability of
Mortimer's power, Edward II wavers in giving up the crown, extending
and withdrawing it. Marlowe's achievement in devising a process to ob-
jectify his state of mind can be gauged by placing it beside York's reaction to Queen Margaret's taunts (*3 Henry VI*, I.iv). First York announces that he is going to respond and then he illustrates his response by
images of wind and rain:

Bid'st thou me rage? Why, now thou hast thy wish.
Wouldst have me weep? Why, now thou hast thy will.
For raging wind blows up incessant showers,
And when the rage allays the rain begins.

(I.iv.143–46)

Edward II does not first vent his frustration by a furious attack against
Mortimer, as York does against Margaret, and then by a declaration of
his grief, as York does, moving systematically from emotion to emotion.
The wavering pattern of Edward's speech depicts his thoughts and feelings as if he were immediately feeling them. As a result, the interaction
of speakers differs from the give and take of their earlier counterparts.
The remarks by Leicester, the Bishop of Winchester, and Trussel, un-

adorned by rhetorical figures, are brief to the point of muteness in conveying their respect for Edward's feelings. Their restraint, guided by a wish to mitigate his suffering, fits with those dialogues of comfort and responsiveness typical of Shakespeare's later apprentice chronicles.

The moment in Richard's deposition comparable to Edward's giving and withdrawing the crown is his breaking of the mirror. Whereas Edward defines kingship solely in terms of power:

But what are kings when regiment is gone,
But perfect shadows in a sunshine day?

(V.i.26–27)

Richard acknowledges the religious dimension of kingship. For Edward the loss of the crown, as a symbol of his power, is itself the crucial event. For Richard kingship is a God-given role, and when he submits to deposition, he loses more than power; he loses identity:

I have no name, no title —
No, not that name was given me at the font —

(IV.i.255–56)

Breaking the mirror of his image, then, is the appropriate gesture to render his crisis so that giving up the crown is less crucial for him than for Edward II. It is this difference that gives Shakespeare's scene the edge, for not only do Richard's responses exhibit a greater technical and emotional range, but the whole experience of deposition is more conceptually complex. Carlisle prepares for the religious significance of the political event when he warns Bolingbroke that "this land [will] be called / The field of Golgotha and dead men's skulls" (IV.i.143–44). Several times Richard likens himself to the Son of God, and his enemies to Pilates, thereby enforcing the idea that he holds the crown by divine right.[20] While Edward II has the capacity for self-irony, he never feels the loss of himself when he gives up the crown that Richard faces because Richard takes his identity from a God-given role. Consequently, the occasion never arises for Edward II to judge himself or regret his past behavior, but Richard senses a divided nature:

Nay, if I turn mine eyes upon myself,
I find myself a traitor with the rest.

(IV.i.247–48)

What we find Richard doing here and elsewhere when he likens his position to Christ's, to priest, to clerk, and to snowman, is to measure himself against his kingship in the way that earlier characters measure their enemies. York measures Margaret against the standards of womanhood

and queenship and finds her lacking. Duke Humphrey measures Winchester against the role of bishop. But these characters do not in turn
measure themselves. In the quarrel scenes the playwright forms the
judgments and gives them to the speakers ready-made; here Richard II
undergoes a process of formulating and struggling with his judgments.
This contrast can be seen as a shift of gravity from playwright-orator to
character; whereas in the earlier plays Shakespeare stands outside
events and devises witty comments for equal opponents who deliver
them with equal dispatch, here he gives up, as it were, some of his decisions to his characters. Once characters gain the power of making
decisions about their moral nature and, as we shall see, about the way
they talk of themselves, the playwright is relieved of the need to place
them into sharply oratorical oppositions.

Northumberland acts, however, like an earlier opponent, speaking
with abrasive insistence that Richard II read a list of his "grievous
crimes." Richard at first begs "gentle Northumberland" to relieve him
of such shame, but Northumberland replies, "My lord, dispatch. Read
o'er these articles" (IV.i.243). Richard again excuses himself by saying
that his eyes are full of tears. Unaffected Northumberland repeats:

Northumberland
My lord —
Richard
No lord of thine, thou haught, insulting man.

(IV.i.253-54)

Like his predecessors, Northumberland insists upon his position and
uses like a demeaning epithet the title of address to encase his opponent
in the view that he wishes to assert, ignoring here the fact of Richard's
kingship. Richard's response echoes a moment from Edward II's scene:

Winchester
My lord —
King Edward
Call me not lord! Away   out of my sight!

(V.i.112-13)

Similarly when Bolingbroke speaks later in the scene to Richard:

Bolingbroke
Name it, fair cousin.
Richard
Fair cousin? I am greater than a king.

(IV.i.304-5)

The later victims are highly sensitized to their powerful interlocutors, responsive to their slightest phrase in contrast to their forebears who, unlike Bajazeth, appeared deaf to the most scathing epithets.

Concomitant with this sensitivity is a wider range of emotions. Edward II's responses could be described as rage, grief, despair, frustration. Perhaps the most original moment in his scene is the final gesture of hope that even he recognizes as futile:

> Bear this to the queen,
> Wet with my tears, and dried again with sighs.
> > *[He gives a handkerchief.]*
> If with the sight thereof she be not moved,
> Return it back and dip it in my blood.
>
> > (V.i.117–20)

Like his prayers and commands which he cannot resist making even though he senses their futility, his appeal to the Queen cannot possibly be effective.[21] These are the almost automatic human reactions of one who has been immobilized, like the involuntary twitchings of a trunk after the head has been severed. A comparable expressive moment comes in Richard's scene after he has smashed the mirror. Not the traditional reaction of grief, despair, or frustration, but humiliation arises from Richard's final lines of dialogue as he attempts to bolster his departure with a bit of sarcasm.

> *Richard*
> I'll beg one boon,
> And then be gone, and trouble you no more.
> Shall I obtain it?
> *Bolingbroke*
> > Name it, fair cousin.
> *Richard*
> Fair cousin? I am greater than a king;
> For when I was a king, my flatterers
> Were but subjects; being now a subject,
> I have a king here to my flatterer.
> Being so great, I have no need to beg.
> *Bolingbroke*
> Yet ask.
> *Richard*
> And shall I have?
> *Bolingbroke*
> You shall.

 Richard
Then give me leave to go.
 Bolingbroke
Whither?
 Richard
Whither you will, so I were from your sights.

(IV.i.302–15)

Richard's attempt to lead on Bolingbroke by questions and then cap them with a tart comment falls flat. The feebleness of his sarcasm expresses the spent energy of a shamed figure, and the anticlimax of this "quick comeback" embarrasses us as much as it renders his humiliation. The wit that was so apparent in Richard's earlier manipulation of auricular figures measures the extent of his disintegration as he retreats from the stage.

∞

In chapter 1 we saw how dialogues of comfort and sympathy differentiated Shakespeare's later apprentice plays from the earlier; here we see that even episodes of confrontation between opponents, designed to dramatize absolute power, can be occasions for a variety of intimate sentiments in the later plays. The contrast between earlier and later confrontations reveals primarily a difference of attitude between playwright and drama and between audience and drama. The effectiveness of the mimetic drama is no less strong than that of the didactic, but a specific impact upon the audience of a discrete scene appears to be a secondary consideration. Of primary concern is the plotting of a continuous, self-contained narrative so that one episode depends for its full effect upon another. The playwright can thereby use context to exploit dramatic irony because he assumes that the audience too holds the impressions and information from one scene to another. The form is cumulative rather than copious, so that the impact of one scene modifies a succeeding one. Likewise, the characters exhibit "process" in the sense of making up their minds as they talk rather than deliver speeches. In chapter 1 we saw the Duchess of Gloucester, a minor character from *Richard II*, change her mind in the middle of a request for York to visit her. As the plotting changes, so do the characters' patterns of dialogue.

 One possible reason why Shakespeare altered his relation toward his characters is his experience as an actor. The ghost of Hamlet, Sr., Old Adam, and Old Knowell, parts traditionally assigned to Shakespeare, indicate that he must have experienced the barrenness of enacting a one-sided prepackaged character in other plays, characters who appear to swell a scene or two. Why Vernon chooses a rose with Somerset or why Warwick sides with York never trouble us in *1 Henry VI*; they take sides to contribute their comments to the heat of controversy. If it did in fact happen that Shakespeare began to give his characters more "life" from the inside simply because he wanted to vivify his own brief roles or to satisfy fellow actors, these practical decisions led quickly to more searching decisions about plotting, for the differences between the earlier and later plays go far beyond tinkering with individual speeches. Whatever the biographical causes of change, even if we could know them, they would help us little in explicating Shakespeare's apprentice dramaturgy.

Persuasions

3

Scenes of persuasion were as useful as confrontations of opponents to playwrights of the late 1580s engaged in plotting conqueror and chronicle plays about power. As elemental an experience of power as the clash of enemies is the gradual control that one character gains over another through the artful use of words. The dialogue of persuasion would have a ready appeal to playwrights trained in rhetoric because they could transpose to the stage with very few adjustments a traditional deliberative oration. Yet such a simple version of the persuasion scene between an orator who delivers a speech and his listeners who assent hardly realizes its full dramatic potentialities. To do this, the playwright should pay as much attention to the listener submitting to the oratory as he does to the speaker exercising the artful tactics of his control. When the playwright meets the many demands of the situation, he produces one of the major experiences that drama as an art form is particularly equipped to foster. Iago's temptation of Othello comes immediately to mind or Lady Macbeth's incitement of Macbeth; it would not be inappropriate to describe Lucifer's temptation of Eve as "dramatic" in *Paradise Lost*.

For our purposes the scene of persuasion holds special importance because it acts much like a play within a play to reveal assumptions about the nature of drama. The fact that an orator controls his listener within a didactic play designed to control its audience should alert us to look for larger relationships when we examine particular scenes. Although I see no inevitable law operating, it is notable that when Shakespeare mastered mimetic drama, a play appeared within the play, first tentatively in *Love's Labor's Lost* and then decisively in *A Midsummer Night's Dream*. The playlet of *Dream*, while it may do other things, raises a question about the main function of mimetic drama which is, by definition, to create illusion. The outer audience watches the inner audience watching a play, and what the inner audience sees should alert the outer audience about what it too is watching. In didactic drama the central concern is one of values rather than illusion—I prefer to use the word "verisimilitude" here—so the values that the character-orator inculcates in his listener should heighten our awareness of values which the playwright is inculcating, especially when the character is a deceptive orator. For some reason Elizabethan drama in general tended to include microcosms that fracture momentarily the audience's perspective to increase their perception.[1] Maybe this practice resulted from an Elizabethan habit of thinking analogically, maybe it was a conventional way of realizing copious variety, or maybe it was inherent in the very nature of poetic drama to sensitize an audience by analogies as much as by cause and effect. Whatever the reason, Shakespeare's early scenes of persuasion have resonances beyond their immediate place in the narrative to the far borders of their dramas.

With regard to the topic of apprenticeship—to state roughly the contrast between earlier and later persuasions—the young Shakespeare emphasized moral clarity in the earliest chronicles and verisimilitude in the later plays. Thus far I have tended to draw examples from the very early and very late apprentice plays in establishing the contrast between rhetorical and mimetic technique of dramaturgy and have given little attention to the intermediate plays such as *Richard III* and *Titus Andronicus* where characteristics of earlier and later techniques exist side by side. The one dialogue of this transitional sort already discussed is the expository quarrel that opens *3 Henry VI*. In this chapter I shall draw more upon intermediate works like *Richard III* and *The Rape of Lucrece*, which, although it is a poem, happens to be highly important for Shakespeare's later dramaturgy. In the next chapter devoted to the change in intimate speeches of emotion, other intermediate plays like *3 Henry VI* and *Titus* will be observed to afford instances of further changes in Shakespeare's dramaturgy.

∞

In *1 Henry VI* Shakespeare confines the persuasion scene to misusers of power, Joan La Pucelle and Suffolk. Joan persuades Charles to give her control of his army (I.iii) and convinces the Duke of Burgundy to shift allegiance from the English to the French (III.iii). Suffolk courts Margaret of Anjou (V.iii) and persuades Henry VI to marry Margaret instead of the Earl of Armagnac's daughter to whom he is betrothed(V.v).

The one full-scale oration in these four episodes is Joan's persuasion of Burgundy, which should be discussed for what it discloses about the problem of an oration at once effective and wrong in a rhetorically oriented drama. Shakespeare faces a double problem of writing a persuasion that convinces Burgundy and convinces the audience that it has the power to move Burgundy without at the same time convincing the audience. He solves his problem by exploiting Joan's supernatural magnetism. Early in the play he establishes her force when Talbot first encounters Joan on the battlefield:

My thoughts are whirlèd like a potter's wheel;
I know not where I am nor what I do.

(I.v.19–20)

Before Joan speaks to Burgundy, Charles recalls to our attention this power when he says, "Speak, Pucelle, and enchant him with thy words" (III.iii.40), and Burgundy confirms it by his one comment during the oration:

Either she hath bewitched me with her words,
Or nature makes me suddenly relent.

(III.iii.58–59)

Her monologue, hedged by these testimonies, needs no dazzling verbal display to convince the audience of her persuasive power. Even so, it exhibits an artfulness that conforms to the stipulations of those such as Thomas Wilson for a good deliberative oration. Joan insinuates her primary values skillfully in the opening lines that consist of two commands, copiously expressed: first, that Burgundy look upon France as his mother country; then, that he turn his sword against his real enemy, the English. She next denounces the English as lordly and untrustworthy, citing their treatment of the Duke of Orleans as factual support (this "fact" remains a matter of conjecture, for the play never again considers it). The shape and phrasing of Joan's oration must have troubled Shakespeare less than the response of Burgundy, which, of course, his training in rhetoric could not have prepared him to create. But again Joan's magnetism gives him the means to account for Burgundy's sentiments, which he condenses into two short, bewildered speeches of assent: one, already quoted; the other, "I am vanquishèd. These haughty words of hers / Have batt'red me like roaring cannon-shot" (III.iii.78–79). Joan's magnetism — or witchery — serves even another purpose in putting the audience on its guard against her arguments. After she triumphs by persuading Burgundy to change allegiance, she concludes the episode

69

with an aside: "Done like a Frenchman — [*aside*] turn and turn again" (III.iii.85). Her comment adds a momentary complexity to her character that strains verisimilitude, for the audience must assume that she holds in contempt the man she has just worked so artfully to join her, as if Shakespeare feared the power of false rhetoric and took special care to flash a warning signal by the orator herself.[2] Certainly his caution indicates an uneasiness about his control of dramatic irony in a play where didactic considerations take precedence over verisimilitude.

When Shakespeare introduces the rebellion of Jack Cade in *2 Henry VI*, he hedges it with the same clarity of moral attitude. In Cade's first appearance, he delivers an oration to rouse the Kentish workingmen to follow him. At the outset Dick the Butcher and Smith the Weaver undercut by asides each of Cade's statements:

> *Cade*
> My mother a Plantagenet —
> *Butcher* [*aside*]
> I knew her well. She was a midwife.
> *Cade*
> My wife descended of the Lacies.
> *Butcher* [*aside*]
> She was indeed a pedlar's daughter and sold many laces. . . .
> *Cade*
> Therefore am I of an honorable house.
> *Butcher* [*aside*]
> Ay, by my faith, the field is honorable. . .
>
> (IV.ii.37 ff.)

This counterpoint was a favorite technique of the Vice figure. Sometimes he would stand aside and mock the good advice of a Virtue, and sometimes in later hybrid moralities, he would take upon himself to read a document for another character and approximate the sounds of the words to turn them to nonsense.[3] Shakespeare's adaptation, while it serves to deflate the false orator, creates another difficulty of verisimilitude: if Cade's speech is so transparent to a butcher and a weaver, how is it that he has the power to lead them to rebel? Shakespeare manages to circumvent this problem by the appearance of Sir Humphrey Stafford and his brother. Their peremptory commands:

Rebellious hinds, the filth and scum of Kent,
Marked for the gallows, lay your weapons down;
Home to your cottages, forsake this groom.

(IV.ii.110–12)

act to consolidate the workmen behind Cade and make the question of
his oratorical power finally irrelevant. They respond more against the
insults of Stafford than to Cade's transparent rhetoric. His oration,
then, serves well to introduce him as York's surrogate, whose words, like
his actions, parody his betters.

Shakespeare's need to add these moral signposts coincides with several
earlier observations about his didactic dramaturgy, first the value of
copiousness for plotting, and second the discreteness of episodes. Certainly he could not think that his audience would forget or overlook the
general intentions of Joan in her blandishments of Burgundy or York's
intentions behind the rebellion of Jack Cade. Trained in rhetoric to
value copiousness, he applies it to narrative by taking advantage of
asides even when moral attitudes are clear. Likewise, he tends to think
of his narrative as a sequence of units embodying a moral. As we have
seen, the structure of *1 Henry VI* is an accumulation of analogous episodes; the devisiveness of English courtiers appears in at least three
groups of characters; Talbot's bravery appears in three battles. In *2
Henry VI* the downfall of Duke Humphrey, occurring midway in the
play, releases the forces of selfishness which lead to civil war, so that in
the largest sense the story depicts a causal relation. Rather than concentrate upon this as Shakespeare is later to concentrate upon the causal
links between Richard II and Bolingbroke, he prefaces Duke Humphrey's downfall by dramatizing the analogous downfall of his Duchess
and prefaces the Duke of York's open warfare by Jack Cade's rebellion.

Since the false orator causes difficulties for a didactic playwright, one
may wonder why he would plot a story to present a deceptive oration.
The true orator who propounds correct values and wins the assent of his
listeners holds, of course, little interest regardless of the playwright's intentions. So there are claims of the dramatic medium that do not square
with simple didacticism which even the most moralistic playwright
needs to consider if he dramatizes a story more demanding than a par-
able. Yet the young Shakespeare manages to devise a situation that permits the good orator to deliver a forceful speech of correct values: the
contest. In this situation, which must have appealed to Shakespeare for
he uses it twice in quick succession, a good and a bad orator try to win

their listeners. In *2 Henry VI* the Cliffords speak positively for obedience to the King and turn the Kentish workingmen away from Cade, who speaks negatively against obedience to the King rather than positively for obedience to himself. In *Richard III* before the Battle of Bosworth Field Richmond's positive oration foreshadows victory while Richard's negative one points only toward defeat. These episodes provide the occasion for display of the ingenuities of rhetorical strategy and suggest not only that Shakespeare relishes the details of this art but that his audience found it equally interesting.[4] If we look behind the simple equation of good oratory with success and bad oratory with failure, we can see these contests as the forerunners of Brutus's and Antony's orations to the Romans. Like Antony, Clifford speaks verse in his appeal to the Kentish workingmen to proclaim loyalty to the King, whereas Jack Cade like Brutus speaks prose to urge them not to listen to the Cliffords. Clifford addresses them as "countrymen," and Cade calls them "base peasants." Clifford offers them a choice: relent and get mercy or follow a rebel to death. Cade offers them nothing positive and attacks Clifford's offer as false. Clifford stresses the valor of Henry V against Cade's leadership:

Were't not a shame that whilst you live at jar
The fearful French, whom you late vanquishèd,
Should make a start o'er seas and vanquish you?
Methinks already in this civil broil
I see them lording it in London streets,
Crying "Villiago!" unto all they meet.

(IV.viii.39–44)

He appeals to their patriotism and proclaims "God on our side, doubt not of victory" (IV.viii.50). Cade predicts only misfortune:

Let them break your backs with burdens, take your houses over your heads, ravish your wives and daughters before your faces. For me, I will make shift for one; and so God's curse light upon you all!

(IV.viii.27–30)

Although Cade is wrong and thus loses his followers, Clifford cannot be said to speak with complete accuracy when he appeals to the memory of the late king rather than to Henry VI. Behind this tactic is a moral judgment, for his need to refer to Henry V makes its own comment on the leadership of the present king. To this extent Shakespeare reveals a connection between the moment and the larger meaning of the drama, whereas in Joan's persuasion of Burgundy, the values of mother country raised by her speech were not well integrated, perhaps even embarrassing, to the central issues of the play.

In *Richard III* the techniques of exhortation by Richmond and Richard III to their soldiers prefigure the outcome of battle.[5] Richmond addresses his followers as "loving countrymen." Richard omits any address and for some eighteen lines never groups himself with his followers by the use of "we" or "our." In the fourth line of his oration Richmond uses "our" when he tells his soldiers why they fight:

God and our good cause fight upon our side;
The prayers of holy saints and wrongèd souls,
Like high-reared bulwarks, stand before our faces.

(V.iii.241–43)

Richard omits mention of any positive standard. Richmond characterizes his enemy as a "bloody tyrant and a homicide" who "hath ever been God's enemy." Richard devotes the main portion of his speech to denigrating his opponents with foul diction reminiscent of Cade's: "a scum of Britains, and base lackey peasants," "famished beggars," "overweening rags," "poor rats." Wolfgang Clemen praises Richard's speech as "based not on reason and principle but on feeling and imagination," exhibiting "vigorous, direct expression," and finds Richmond's to be "impersonal, clearly structured, his manner calm and undynamic" while his language is "colorless and abstract."[6] Of Richard's oration he says, "Once more the dauntless, commanding spirit, the fiery will and resourcefulness of the old Richard take over. Our disgust at his crimes gives way to reluctant admiration." Clemen's judgment is worth citing for what it reveals about dramatic priorities. He isolates aesthetic from didactic responses, and just how much at variance is his response to Richard's oration — "altogether personal, the language concrete and alive" — from Shakespeare's can be seen in his praise of Richard's tactics: "He knows that hatred of a dangerous adversary will be more effective in spurring on his men than any recourse to moral argument."[7] The events of battle prove otherwise. To bring his speech to a climax, Richmond employs a schematized syntax to list the positive rewards of victory:

Then if you fight against God's enemy,
God will in justice ward you as his soldiers;
If you do sweat. . . .
If you do fight. . . .
If you do fight. . . .
If you do free. . . .

(V.iii.254 ff.)

It should hardly surprise us that Richmond's successful oration is more highly patterned than Richard's. Like Cade, Richard lists the disasters that would follow upon defeat rather than the victories that would be gained:

If we be conquerèd, let men conquer us,
And not these bastard Britains, whom our fathers
Have in their own land beaten, bobbed, and thumped. . . .
Shall these enjoy our lands? lie with our wives?
Ravish our daughters?

(V.iii.333 ff.)

Shakespeare is remembering Cade's earlier lines, "take your houses over your heads, ravish your wives and daughters before your faces" (IV.viii. 28-29). Shakespeare's assumption, then, is that men who know what they fight for have more power than those who know only what they fight to avoid. But more to our purpose is the literal content of Richard's oration that lacks deception. Events of 2 *Henry VI* give us little evidence to question why Jack Cade's negative oration happens to be so tactically inept, but in the first half of *Richard III* we see how clever Richard can be at deception. His courtship of Lady Anne is without parallel in drama until this time in its deceptive, artful strategy. Yet to make his moral point, Shakespeare chooses not to maintain Richard's consistent use of deception in the contrasting orations. Richmond claims that both God and the English citizens wish him to win. Richard III, since he is usurper and scourge, could not make such a claim without complicating the moral contrast by irony. He does not claim the sancitity of his throne or characterize Richmond as a rebel. Richmond, however, faces the delicate issue of deposing a king, an act that certainly gets no sanction in the Homily against Willful Disobedience, by saying that Richard III is:

One raised in blood and one in blood established;
One that made means to come by what he hath,
And slaughterèd those that were the means to help him;
A base foul stone, made precious by the foil
Of England's chair, where he is falsely set.

(V.iii.248-52)

In other words, he is a *de facto* king and a tyrant, not a king by right.[8] Each speaker appeals to values literally in the sense that he conforms with the playwright's intention. As we know from Antony's funeral oration, Shakespeare later manipulates several kinds of irony at once without resorting to literal statement. Here he does not depend upon the dramatic context to preserve moral perspective, for the audience, given Richard's past behavior and character, would not have been confused by a deceptive oration. Yet Shakespeare, true to his conception of drama as a kind of oration, took no chance in confusing them about a central episode, the justified battle to overthrow a tyrant, even though verisimilitude would require Richard to deceive his followers by claiming to be a true king.

∞

Perhaps the most audacious and successful dialogue of Shakespeare's apprentice years is Richard III's persuasion of Lady Anne. Richard, not only the murderer of Anne's father-in-law whose funeral procession he halts but the murderer of her husband, woos Lady Anne, the chief mourner of the funeral and wins her. The episode is sheer invention without any basis in the chronicles and has no explicit cause, for we never learn Richard's "secret close intent" in marrying Lady Anne. Shakespeare places it immediately after the opening scene of *Richard III* to establish, much like Tamburlaine's initial persuasion scene, the irresistible power of the protagonist. With an equally audacious stroke, he introduces a parallel persuasion scene in the second half of the play between Richard and the dowager Queen Elizabeth, Act IV, scene iv, to dramatize Richard's failing power. These parallel scenes allow the audience to measure the rise and fall of Richard's career by his control of rhetoric.

Shakespeare's distinctive achievement in these dialogues lies in the interplay between speakers. Persuasions from the Henry VI plays are orations disguised as dialogues by intermittent interruptions from the listener. Richard's persuasion of Anne takes the form of a dialectical process, for her responses dictate his strategies. The fact that the experience is ostensibly a courtship may help explain why this dialogue breaks away from the rigid form of the oration. Yet a quick survey of courtship scenes in Shakespeare's preceding dramas shows that they do not take the shape of a gradual overcoming of a reluctant lady. As soon as Margaret hears from Suffolk that she would be married to England's king, she assents upon condition of her father's approval (*1 Henry VI*, V.iii). When Edward IV shifts from intimations to a proposal of marriage, Lady Gray assents (*3 Henry VI*, III.ii). In *Errors* (III.ii) Antipholus of Syracuse tries to court Luciana, but they talk at cross purposes. In *Shrew* (III.i) Lucentio and Bianca engage in one brief courtship under the guise of tutoring, but Lucentio hardly gets beyond stating his real identity. Petruchio's courtship of Katharina takes the form of a battle of wits; they parry and thrust without reaching any agreement; in fact, the comic point of the scene is that there is no agreement even though Petruchio asserts that there is (II.i). In *Two Gentlemen* the only full-scale courtship, Proteus's attempt to woo Silvia, is abortive, for she spurns him (IV.ii). It would appear, then, that Richard's courtship of Lady Anne marks a leap in Shakespeare's development of dialogue. Clemen confirms this impression by observing the new appearance of "suggestive (rather than explicit) dialogue" in this play, dialogue foreshadowed in Kyd's *The Spanish Tragedy*.[9]

The dialectic between Richard and Anne falls into three discernible stages. In the first Lady Anne dominates the dialogue, giving full vent to her anger and grief. Her automatic response, when Richard halts the funeral procession, is to express outrage at the murder of her husband and his father, but entailed in her outrage is an instinctive wish, which is her undoing, a wish to incense him to the same emotional pitch that he caused in her. This automatic response implicit in rage is one which any audience would intuit as normal, if not irresistible. Richard, however, gains immediate advantage, for he avoids reacting to her vilification as an ordinary human being would. His cool and witty remarks say, in effect, that her worst language cannot disturb him:

Anne
Villain, thou know'st nor law of God nor man:
No beast so fierce but knows some touch of pity.
Richard
But I know none, and therefore am no beast.
Anne
O wonderful, when devils tell the truth!
Richard
More wonderful, when angels are so angry.

(I.ii.70–74)

His retorts make her entire arsenal of vituperation harmless and thereby bring her to the point of exhaustion and vulnerability. Her one final gesture, a gesture of desperation, is to spit, as if to say, "I have no more words." Sir Laurence Olivier's smile in his movie version of the play is the proper response, as proportionate to his earlier witty retorts as her gesture to her earlier slander.

The second stage can be marked by the length of Richard's speeches, for he begins to dominate the discussion. Earlier in his witty responses he implicates Lady Anne in his murders by suggesting that her beauty caused him to turn against her husband and father. Now he amplifies his case. He produces tears as concrete proof of his love, saying that he never cried before, not even at his father's and Rutland's deaths. Thomas Wilson advised that "Nothing heateth sooner than fire" or "nothing moisteth sooner than water," so that an orator must be angry to engender anger and must cry if he wishes to stimulate tears.[10]

The third stage, the most artful and original, combines language and gesture. Here Richard gradually gains control of Anne through a series of commands. Having exhausted her outrage and implicated her in his behalf, he makes explicit the control over her which he has exercised from the outset. First he commands from her what is at this stage an obviously impossible act: to take his sword and kill him. The timing of this command measures how far Anne's position has changed, for had he made this proposal in the first heat of anger, her response would no doubt have been far different. After testing her passivity by this first hyperbole, he then proposes that she bid him kill himself, as if to habituate her to inactivity. Gradually feeling his way, testing how far his power extends, Richard changes the type of command from the hyperbolic to the apparently harmless and trivial offer of his ring. With the ring he gains a bridgehead to his total domination. As Shakespeare so well knew when in *Twelfth Night* character after character offers a gift in an effort to break the isolation of disguise, gifts act as an extension of oneself. Once Anne accepts Richard's ring—with all its symbolism—it only remains for him to direct her to Crosby Place and replace her in the role of mourner.

Richard's triumph suggests an almost supernatural magnetism resembling Joan's control of Burgundy. At other points in the play characters intimate that Richard is a "hellhound" possessed by the Devil and a scourge to the family York. Yet these testimonies come after his persuasion of Anne, not before or during it, as do the testimonies to Joan's supernatural power, a reversal of sequence by which the dramatic experience gives conviction to the testimonies, instead of testimonies supporting the experience. Thus *Richard III* begins to approximate mimetic drama where experiences of the narrative are primary, not illustrative, and no statement of theme is quite adequate to encompass them. In plotting the death of Talbot in *1 Henry VI*, for instance, Shakespeare knows that he can stimulate outrage in the audience if he shows the refusal of York and Somerset to come to Talbot's aid. Their mutual inhibition did not appear in the chronicles. Shakespeare invents this detail and simplifies their behavior to exhibit only enmity as their motive. Neither character speculates on how Talbot's death would affect the English forces in France, and neither is shown after the fatal battle to regret his inaction. Shakespeare appears more interested in creating a vivid response in his audience than in rendering a full and verisimilar political decision where personal hate conflicts with a sense of duty. Yet in devising Richard of Gloucester's persuasion of Lady Anne, Shakespeare complicates her responses so that their interaction takes on a richness to be found only between audience and dramatic event (rather than between character and character) in *1 Henry VI*.

Until Richard gains the crown, he is irresistible; his plans never fail. After he is crowned, he loses his gift for fun, grows tetchy and superstitious, and when he hears of Richmond's forces approaching England, for the first time contradicts himself and gives orders without plan (IV.iv.432-57). To dramatize the downward course of his career, Shakespeare composes a second persuasion scene that follows closely the form of the earlier one. Richard tries to persuade Queen Elizabeth to present him as a suitor for her daughter's hand. The fact that Shakespeare adds two such scenes to his dramatization of Richard's career when the anonymous *True Tragedy of Richard III* contains no such dialogue may be interpreted as further evidence of the way a playwright's technique helps govern the episodes he chooses to dramatize. At the conclusion of their discussion, Queen Elizabeth responds cryptically:

> *Queen Elizabeth*
> Shall I go win my daughter to thy will?
> *King Richard*
> And be a happy mother by the deed.
> *Queen Elizabeth*
> I go. Write to me very shortly,
> And you shall understand from me her mind.
> *King Richard*
> Bear her my true love's kiss; and so farewell —
>
> *Exit Q [ueen Elizabeth]*.
> Relenting fool, and shallow, changing woman!
>
> (IV.iv.426-31)

As it turns out, of course, Princess Elizabeth marries Richmond, and through this union the two houses of York and Lancaster conclude in harmony a bloody chapter of English history to establish the Tudor dynasty. Scholars have been puzzled by Queen Elizabeth's apparently contradictory behavior, assenting first to Richard's proposal and later to Richmond's. E. K. Chambers raises the problem, and E. M. W. Tillyard takes it up to point out that Richard's final judgment of her, "Relenting fool, and shallow, changing woman," came to be ironically truer than he suspected. Anne Righter in *Shakespeare and the Idea of the Play* says definitely that Richard convinces Queen Elizabeth.[11] But Shakespeare creates no intentional crux at the conclusion of the persuasion scene. The dialogue itself is strong enough to make the point about Richard's weakening power and his failure to convince the dowager queen. With the earlier persuasion scene to measure it, the audience watches Queen Elizabeth counter each of Richard III's proposals. There is no dialectical shift in her position. At every point she recalls his evil deeds:

> *King Richard*
> Then know that from my soul I love thy daughter.
> *Queen Elizabeth*
> My daughter's mother thinks it with her soul.
> *King Richard*
> What do you think?
> *Queen Elizabeth*
> That thou dost love my daughter from thy soul.
> So from thy soul's love didst thou love her brothers,
> And from my heart's love I do thank thee for it.
> *King Richard*
> Be not so hasty to confound my meaning:
> I mean that with my soul I love thy daughter
> And do intend to make her Queen of England.
> *Queen Elizabeth*
> Well then, who dost thou mean shall be her king?
>
> (IV.iv.256-65)

In the earlier dialogue Richard is never bested by Anne's comments, but here he takes the inquiring role, "What do you think?" and his statements set the conditions for the Queen's clever rephrasing. At midpoint in their dialogue Richard presents his proposal in a full-scale uninterrupted oration of forty-six lines (IV.iv.291-336) with all the artfulness at his command. After it they engage in a stichomythic exchange of about twenty-five lines that indicates his rhetoric was for naught:

King Richard
Infer fair England's peace by this alliance.
 Queen Elizabeth
Which she shall purchase with still-lasting war.
 King Richard
Tell her the king, that may command, entreats.
 Queen Elizabeth
That at her hands which the king's King forbids.
 King Richard
Say she shall be a high and mighty queen.
 Queen Elizabeth
To vail the title, as her mother doth.

(IV.iv.343–48)

And so on. Queen Elizabeth never obscures the fact that Richard has killed her sons and kinsmen. What, then, accounts for her question, "Shall I go win my daughter to thy will?" Richard utters a threat that demands a prudent temporizing response:

In her [daughter Elizabeth] consists my happiness and thine;
Without her, follows to myself and thee,
Herself, the land, and many a Christian soul,
Death, desolation, ruin, and decay.
It cannot be avoided but by this;
It will not be avoided but by this.
Therefore, dear mother (I must call you so),
Be the attorney of my love to her.

(IV.iv.406–13)

In the end he gives her no choice, but until this time the Queen's thrust and parry turn Richard's persuasive oratory into a quasi-quarrel. Shakespeare must have assumed that his audience would have been enough attuned to the strategies of rhetoric to see that Richard was unsuccessful. Her moral judgments of his behavior are as clear and accurate as Richmond's in his oration to his soldiers before the Battle of Bosworth Field. Just as Shakespeare feels no need to add any choral comment to tell the audience which oration is the better and therefore more powerful, so he feels no need to add any explanatory comment to Richard's second persuasion scene. Queen Elizabeth is not allured by his proposal; she is threatened. Twelve lines before she exits she asks, "Shall I be tempted of the devil thus?" (IV.iv.418). Lady Anne, truly misled, could never have asked such a question so near the conclusion of her dialogue. The Devil cannot tempt Queen Elizabeth because she knows who he is.

The dialogues of persuasion in *Richard III*, then, are transitional in the way that they meet both the claims of moral clarity and verisimilitude. While on the one hand Shakespeare feels no need to intrude an aside by Queen Elizabeth to clarify her temporizing strategy, he ends Richard's earlier persuasion of Lady Anne with a soliloquy that restates explicitly how wrong she is to succumb and how misleading he is:

Hath she forgot already that brave prince,
Edward, her lord, whom I, some three months since,
Stabbed in my angry mood at Tewkesbury?
A sweeter and a lovelier gentleman,
Framed in the prodigality of nature —
Young, valiant, wise, and (no doubt) right royal —
The spacious world cannot again afford;
And will she yet abase her eyes on me,
That cropped the golden prime of this sweet prince
And made her widow to a woeful bed?

(I.ii.239–48)

Both dialogues, by the interplay between speakers, show a concern for verisimilitude that is unusual by comparison with the earlier dialogues of this kind, but Shakespeare risks no moral ambiguity in these accomplishments. Plausible as Richard's persuasion of Lady Anne is, it depends upon no distinctively individual characteristics of her that one would need to learn from the story. Her anger, her exhaustion, her refusal to kill, her willingness to accept his tears at face value, all these we can sense as normal responses and need witness no prior information that she is a shallow, fickle woman or a trustworthy, decent woman. It does not grow from the narrative as Richard II's deposition scene does. Rather, it takes its credibility from standards of average behavior that playwright and audience tacitly accept in any age, part deriving from theatrical convention, part from fashion, part from general experience. There is another conception of verisimilitude that arises from coherence of the dramatic narrative where parts grow from and fulfill the données and expectations of the story. A coherent play-world of fantastic romance or science fiction has verisimilitude. One way of defining mimetic drama is to say that it imitates the coherence of the external world, not that it represents the world with naturalistic exactitude. Mimetic drama is not synonymous with either naturalistic or realistic drama. Mimetic verisimilitude need not be inconsistent with moral clarity, but in practice verisimilar behavior seldom squares exactly with moral concepts. In the next section I shall discuss a persuasion scene between the Duchess of York and Henry IV from *Richard II* that is anchored within the world of the play: it discloses additional characteristics of Henry IV, raises issues consequent upon the deposition of Richard II, and depends upon the context of events for the audience's ironic attitude. Yet if it is removed from the play and compared to Richard of Gloucester's persuasion of Lady Anne, the likelihood is that most readers would find the earlier dialogue more credible. The point of the comparison would be that Shakespeare appeals to a general standard of verisimilitude when he composes the earlier dialogue, a verisimilitude that coexists easily with the dislocations of plotting, uncharacteristic asides, and soliloquies of moral clarification. The plausibility of the Duchess of York's persuasion depends upon characters and issues which we have already come to know.

∞

Whatever the cause, unsuccessful persuasions begin to occur in Shakespeare's works, both plays and narrative poems, about 1592, while scenes of successful persuasions grow less frequent. Probably only the accidentals of his stories cause the change, but it is worth noting that full dramatization of the unsuccessful persuasion exhibits an emphasis similar to the later confrontations upon the defeated rather than the triumphant. As we might expect, the potentialities for clarifying moral values by unsuccessful persuasions happen to be almost the reverse of the successful persuasion and therefore raise different problems for integration into their dramatic contexts. It has already been stated that a deceptive orator makes for more potentially interesting successful persuasions than does the honest orator. However, an honest orator, if he is unsuccessful, can heighten our interest in a vigorous articulation of true values against an unresponsive and therefore wicked character. A deceptive and wicked orator, pleading unsuccessfully against a good but unresponsive character holds little inherent dramatic interest; given his fullest dramatization, he can stimulate little more than "you-get-what-you-deserve" response. Shakespeare quickly exhausts the meager potentialities of the unsuccessful and wicked orator. In *1 Henry VI* Joan La Pucelle, when captured, pleads to York and Warwick to spare her life (V.iv), and in *2 Henry VI* Suffolk pleads with an unnamed captain and Walter Whitmore to spare his life (IV.i). Neither captive makes any attempt to rouse humane feelings in his captors. Joan insists that she is divine and accuses York of being corrupt not to sense it. When he fails to respond, she asserts the fact of virginity without success and then pleads pregnancy. Even though Suffolk does not entangle himself in such contradictions, he maintains a similar haughtiness toward his captors. Shakespeare avoids complicating these two situations in the only way that could give them dramatic interest, by allowing the captives to cast themselves in a sympathetic but deceptive role to confuse their captors. This would demand of him a respect for the audience's awareness of dramatic irony which he does not show elsewhere in the earliest chronicles.

When a victim pleads the values of the playwright to an unresponsive captor, he sets up an occasion for choral comment, heightened villainy, and for pathos. The more effective his rhetorical techniques, the more inhumane the captor for remaining untouched and the more sympathetic the audience. Lord Say in *2 Henry VI* (IV.vii) tries to defend himself against the lawlessness of Jack Cade and his followers; in *3 Henry VI* (I.iii) young Rutland pleads with Clifford to spare his life, and after Prince Edward is stabbed by the brothers York, Queen Margaret pleads that they kill her too (*3 Henry VI,* V.v). In *The Rape of Lucrece* the heroine pleads with Tarquin to respect her chastity. In *Titus Andronicus* Tamora pleads with Titus to spare her son's life from religious sacrifice, Marcus and Titus's sons plead with Titus to allow Mutius to be buried (I.i), Lavinia pleads with Tamora to kill her to spare her honor (II.iii), Titus pleads with the senators to spare his sons (III.i) and later he kneels to heaven for pity.[12] In *Richard II* (V.v) the Duchess of York pleads with Henry IV to spare her son, accused of treachery, while the Duke of York pleads to show him no mercy. A contrast between two of these scenes, Lord Say's from *2 Henry VI* and Lucrece's plea with Tarquin, gives a clear indication of how Shakespeare begins to rethink the way values relate to episodes in mimetic drama and consequently the way they affect an audience.

Lord Say makes his first appearance in *2 Henry VI* during the episodes of the Cade rebellion and serves, as spokesman of learning, to heighten Cade's senseless destruction. (His part may have been doubled by the actor who plays Duke Humphrey and Alexander Iden, both upholders of order.) Lord Say characterizes himself in his deliberative oration as dedicated to justice and learning:

And, seeing ignorance is the curse of God,
Knowledge the wing wherewith we fly to heaven.

(IV.vii.67–68)

Like Thomas Wilson, he assumes that values need only clear and copious display to influence the listener and, agreeing with Puttenham, he uses auricular figures to impart vigor to his statements. He makes little attempt to touch his listeners directly by urging them to reflect upon their own wrongdoing. Only in his final words before he is dragged off stage to his death does he resort to this as a last desperate strategy:

Ah, countrymen! If when you make your prayers,
God should be so obdurate as yourselves,
How would it fare with your departed souls?

(IV.vii.106–8)

The reactions of Cade and his followers are those of simple, wrongheaded opponents. They judge Lord Say's learning to be dangerous and mistakenly accuse him of collaborating with the French.

In context, Lord Say's deliberative oration is skillful and effective as one side of a clear opposition between right and wrong. But it fails to move its listeners within a drama that itself is designed on the same assumptions to move its listeners. Like a play within a play, the relationship is complex: how can it both touch the outer audience and at the same time fail to move the rebels? Shakespeare solves the problem by a nice adjustment of indecorum. Lord Say's learning betrays him with Cade's followers but not with the real audience. His peroration, for instance, uses an allusion that in context sounds almost pedantic:

Here me but speak, and bear me where'er you will.
Kent, in the Commentaries Caesar writ,
Is termed the civil'st place in all this isle.
Sweet is the country, because full of riches;
The people liberal, valiant, active, wealthy,
Which makes me hope you are not void of pity.

(IV.vii.54–59)

At another point:

　Say
You men of Kent —
　Butcher
What say you of Kent?
　Say
Nothing but this — 'tis "bona terra, mala gens."

(IV.vii.49–52)

Even a sophisticated audience might well be alienated by such awkward miscalculations had not Shakespeare given Jack Cade an aside to establish without a doubt the playwright's moral perspective:

[*aside*] I feel remorse in myself with his words, but I'll bridle it. He shall die, an it be but for pleading so well for his life.

(IV.vii.98–99)

Cade's aside makes clear that it is no accident that Shakespeare chooses learning as Lord Say's major characteristic, since one of the basic premises of didactic drama is to overcome ignorance. Sheer perversity must be added to indecorum to account for the rebels' unresponsiveness to his oration.

The first evidence of a major shift in Shakespeare's thinking about the powers of oratory appears in *The Rape of Lucrece* (1593). The fact that it is a narrative poem may have some bearing on his willingness to experiment, but I doubt it. Lucrece delivers an oration which, if the stanza pattern were adjusted to blank verse, could be transferred to the stage even though it is longer than dramatic orations (lines 575–666).[13] Like Lord Say's relation to Cade and the rebels, her relation to Tarquin conforms to a simple opposition between right and wrong and a simple opposition between weakness and strength. Where she differs from Lord Say is in the complexity of her attitude toward her opponent. She argues that Tarquin should control himself, an argument that presupposes a divided self and sets her speech apart from the preceding persuasions. She does not assume, like Thomas Wilson or Lord Say, that values, once they have been clearly presented and copiously amplified, will guide behavior. Instead, she tries to awaken Tarquin's moral awareness, for she sees his ethical problem as one of putting standards to work rather than one of definition or assertion of standards:

In Tarquin's likeness I did entertain thee.
Hast thou put on his shape to do him shame?
To all the host of heaven I complain me.
Thou wrong'st his honor, wound'st his princely name.
Thou art not what thou seem'st; and if the same,
  Thou seem'st not what thou art, a god, a king;
  For kings like gods should govern everything.

(lines 596–602)

Discrepancies between a character's behavior and his social role form the main subject of earlier quarrel scenes, but they are used mainly for narrative purposes, either to identify a character or to specify improprieties that occur outside the bounds of the scene. In *1 Henry VI*, for instance, Duke Humphrey does not urge the Bishop of Winchester to realize who he is in order to control himself, but Lucrece assumes that the discrepancy between Tarquin's self and his role is a problem to overcome. Winchester pays no attention to Duke Humphrey's judgment and neither reflects on his own secret ambitions nor shows guilt about his greed or worldliness. The standards of behavior in *1 Henry VI* are talked about as proper conditions from which characters have unfortunately deviated; standards in *Lucrece* are ideals which the characters should try to put to practice.

Lucrece urges Tarquin to see himself:

Think but how vile a spectacle it were
To view thy present trespass in another.
Men's faults do seldom to themselves appear.

(lines 631–33)

Since Tarquin has already made up his mind when he confronts her, most of the complexity in her oration lies in the nature of her argument rather than in an interplay between characters, such as we find between Richard III and Lady Anne. It remains for Shakespeare to work out the possibilities suggested here in the life of Richard II, a king who purposely divides himself from his role and experiences all the self-awareness, as we have seen from the deposition scene, that Lucrece urges upon Tarquin. His deafness to her convincing oration works, of course, to blacken his character, but more significant is the fact that all her artful rhetoric cannot affect the burning resolution of the ravisher. It holds far-reaching implications for the playwright himself: how successful a cooling card could the poem be for potential Tarquins? And further, how powerful is an orator-playwright in persuading his audience or, in this case, his readers?

Not only are limitations of rhetoric implicit in Lucrece's failure to move Tarquin, but so is the direction in which Shakespeare moves in fashioning his dramas. While *1 Henry VI* reveals to an audience the proper standards of behavior so that the dramatic experiences are episodic and illustrative, the later apprentice plays dramatize a narrative process about the difficulties of trying to follow proper standards. The Henry VI plays and *Richard III* depict inadequate kings; *Richard II* and *1 Henry IV* depict the difficulties which specific kings face in trying to rule adequately. We watch, for instance, Henry VI's weakness in allowing Margaret, Suffolk, York, and Cardinal Winchester to condemn Duke Humphrey (*2 Henry VI*), but we do not watch episodes which account for his weakness. We listen to Henry VI regret the imprisonment and death of his uncle; we do not watch him facing alternatives that would lead to these deeds or questioning himself afterwards about why he did what he did. In *Richard III* we watch the evil Gloucester move relentlessly to the throne; we do not watch him questioning his conscience or learn why he must be king. He tells us at the outset of the play that he cannot prove to be a lover and therefore must be a ruler; yet within the space of several hundred lines he contradicts this assertion by wooing Lady Anne at the very funeral of the man he killed. Shakespeare purposely gives Richard a mesmeric power that suggests a character somewhat other than human. In the Olivier film version of the play that cut away Queen Margaret's comments on divine retribution to concentrate upon the wicked but human behavior of a king, the opening as Shakespeare wrote it proved inadequate for psychological revelation. It fails to provide sufficient motivation for Richard's actions, so that Olivier felt the need to add portions of a soliloquy about ambition from *3 Henry VI*. However, at the end of the play in a soliloquy before the fatal Battle of Bosworth Field Richard does face alternatives and struggle with his conscience. It is a moment of introspection not entirely consistent with the figure we have watched until this point, a Vice-like master of ceremonies whose soliloquies take the form of direct address to the audience rather than ruminations to himself. Yet this twofold char acter can be seen to fit a transitional play, composed near the time of *Lucrece*. *Richard II* depicts a king in the process of making mistakes, of struggling with the demands of kingship, and of coming to some understanding of his behavior by the end of the play. In keeping with this emphasis, *1 Henry IV* takes as its central experiences a young prince's difficulties in preparing to become a ruler. Henry VI's inadequacy remains constant, and our attitude toward him seldom varies. Richard II entangles himself in errors of judgment and differentiates a private self from his role so that he is able to give up the crown to Bolingbroke. Our attitude toward him shifts: at the outset of the play we judge him harshly, but as we watch his suffering, his judgment of himself, and ultimate recognition of his mistakes, we become more sympathetic.

Another way of stating the change of direction marked by Lucrece's failure of rhetoric is to say that Shakespeare relocates standards. Just as he relocates the standard of emotional impact from audience to character, replacing his need to create an impression of power with a need to dramatize a character's response to power, so he relocates the standard of value from outside the narrative to be illustrated by it to within the narrative as a standard which the characters try to follow. Instead of devising behavior to illustrate standards (or lack of standards) he retreats to dramatizing characters who try to behave according to standards. When the moral standard exists apart from the play to be illustrated, the playwright takes care to clarify values within the episodes to guarantee their illustrative function. When the moral standard exists within the play-world, the playwright devotes his attention to the inner consistency of his narrative. When he sees his drama as a story of a specific character struggling with particular problems of behavior, he is less likely to feel the need to break the process with uncharacteristic asides like Joan's or Jack Cade's or uncharacteristic hesitancy of deceptive characters to be deceptive, like Richard III in his oration before the Battle of Bosworth Field.

There is no persuasion scene in the later plays that consolidates the complexity of character suggested by Lucrece's oration with the verisimilitude of the interaction between Richard of Gloucester and Lady Anne. There is a version of the hapless persuader in *Richard II*, V.iii, which reveals something of the flexibility with which Shakespeare can dramatize a complex moral issue once he is relieved of the need to clarify values for the immediate enlightenment of his audience.[14] The Duchess of York pleads with Henry IV to spare her son Aumerle, accused of treachery, and the Duke of York pleads with him to punish his son as a traitor. While the Duchess has our sympathy as a mother concerned with the life of her son, the issue is not clear-cut, for the Duke, supporting loyalty to the new king at all costs, knows that the worst of evils is civil chaos. In their conflicting appeals we sense the moral dislocations that result from the rule of an illegitimate king who lacks the divine sanction to command full loyalty. The episode gives us a foretaste of the troublesome reign that Henry IV must experience, and it serves both to show by his pardon of Aumerle his intention to rule well and by Aumerle's incipient rebellion the eventual civil struggle between the houses of York and Lancaster. Both morally and dramatically the scene avoids any simple opposition between good and evil as well as any choral comment to spell out its complexities.

The way Shakespeare dramatizes the episode shows an even more startling flexibility, for the style is ironic almost to the point of comedy. When the Duchess cries to be admitted to the King's presence, Shakespeare disengages the audience by Henry IV's response:

King Henry
What shrill-voiced suppliant makes this eager cry?
Duchess [*within*]
A woman, and thy aunt, great king. 'Tis I.
Speak with me, pity me, open the door!
A beggar begs that never begged before.

King Henry
Our scene is alt'red from a serious thing,
And now changed to "The Beggar and the King."

(V.iii.75–80)

His hyper-awareness of the Duchess's style detaches the audience's serious concern and replaces it with a bemused attitude that cannot be dislodged while they listen to the subsequent arguments of father and mother for the life of their son:

King Henry
Good aunt, stand up.

Duchess
    Nay, do not say "stand up."
Say "pardon" first, and afterwards "stand up."
An if I were thy nurse, thy tongue to teach,
"Pardon" should be the first word of thy speech.
I never longed to hear a word till now.
Say "pardon" king; let pity teach thee how
The word is short, but not so short as sweet;
No word like "pardon" for kings' mouths so meet;

York
Speak it in French, king. Say "Pardonne moi."

Duchess
Dost thou teach pardon pardon to destroy?
Ah, my sour husband, my hardhearted lord,
That sets the word itself against the word!
Speak "pardon" as 'tis current in our land;
The chopping French we do not understand.

(V.iii.111–24)

The Duchess's persistence fits, of course, the requirements of copiousness and clarity, but even without the King's earlier comment about the Beggar and the King, which signals to the audience that he will be benign, her style would strike the ear as slightly comic. In context, it sounds like a parody of the sincere but strident orator, and only in context can it be discussed. If we isolate the Duchess's persuasion to consider its verisimilitude, it would suffer by comparison with the earlier persuasion of Lady Anne by Richard of Gloucester.

That Shakespeare feels free to render a serious episode by a comic style suggests a loosening of his attitude toward the rhetorical dictum of decorum. No longer microcosms of the outer drama, the serious persuasions need not be dramatized with intense seriousness to mark their importance. This suggests that Shakespeare grows surer of his audience's readiness to pick up cues and respond without moral guideposts. What they lose in moral certainty they gain in the pleasures of ironic awareness. This is not to say that all the members of the audience catch the implications of the Aumerle plot with equal perspicuity. The main point of the episode, that Henry IV forgives Aumerle — "I pardon him as God shall pardon me" (V.iii.131), is obvious and helps form their attitude toward the new king as the play ends. The problems of loyalty and moral behavior in the reign of a usurping king enrich one's understanding of the struggle for power that the play depicts, but by concentrating upon the particularities of the story itself, upon its plausibility or verissimilitude, Shakespeare leaves the interpretation open-ended. Because no choral commentator closes off judgment with an explicit interpretation, the thoughtful members of the audience are stimulated beyond the immediate response of sympathy and regret over the murder of a young, willful king, as E. W. Talbert has shown.[15] The playlets in *A Midsummer Night's Dream* and *Hamlet* indicate that Shakespeare becomes reconciled to the fact that not all the members of the audience respond to drama with the same alertness, nor, as in the case of Claudius, should they. By attending to the verisimilitude of his play-world, he does not thereby diminish its moral impact. It could be said that he increases its box-office attraction, for without a conclusive certainty about the significance of a play, thoughtful members of an audience might well be drawn to a second and third performance not only for the dramatic excitement but to ponder its meaning.

Speeches of Emotion

4

It is not difficult to see how Shakespeare used language shaped by his study of rhetoric to dramatize experiences of power, but it comes as something of a surprise to find that he composed with the same characteristics of style intimate speeches designed to express emotion. There was a strong tradition of the emotional set-speech among his contemporaries that arose from their understanding and imitation of Senecan tragedy, a tradition discussed by such scholars as Cunliffe and Clemen.[1] What Shakespeare may have learned about the set-speech from contemporary plays or Seneca would have been confirmed by his training in rhetoric, for they were of a piece. In the second book of Thomas Wilson's *Arte of Rhetorique* on the parts of a typical oration, there is a large section devoted to the topic, "Of mouing affections." Aristotle first discussed the topic as a crucial part of the problem of moving an audience to action, for an orator must know how to put them into a certain frame of mind, either to feel pleasure in wishing for something or displeasure at something to be avoided. Wilson divided his discussion into two parts, which happen to fit the concerns of the playwright: "Of mouing pitie" and "of deliting the hearers, and stirring them to laughter." His understanding of the way an orator affects his audience can be summed up by this comment: "Againe, nothing moisteth soner then water. Therefore, a weeping eye causeth much moisture, and prouoketh teares" (p. 134).[2] If the speaker is to move his audience, he must feel in the same way. Wilson amplifies his comment in this way:

Neither can any good bee done at all, when wee haue sayd all that euer we can, except we bring the same affections in our own harte, the which we would the Iudges should beare towards our owne matter. For how can he be greeued with the report of any hainous act, either in stomak-

ing the naughtinesse of the deede, or in bewayling the miserable misfortune of the thing, or fearing much, the like euill hereafter: except
the Oratour himselfe vtter such passions outwardly, and from his heart
fetch his complaints in such sorte, that the matter may appeare, both
more greeuous to the eare, and therewith so hainous, that it requires
earnestly a speedie reformation? There is no substaunce of it selfe, that
wil take fire, except ye put fire to it. Likewise, no mans nature is so apt,
straight to be heated, except the Oratour himselfe, be on fire, and bring
his heate with him. (p.133)

The playwright who adapts the assumptions of the rhetorician conceives
of a one-to-one relation between how the character feels and how the
audience responds. The character who feels passion must deliver a
speech to stimulate the audience to feel in the same way.[3]

The set-speeches of passion in the serious dramas of the sixteenth
century follow a remarkably durable formula that approximates an oration with a discernible beginning, middle, and end. Each part exhibits
its own special sentiments and stylistic devices. Wolfgang Clemen described these characteristics in *English Tragedy before Shakespeare.*
Although he devoted his main attention to the oration of grief, the
lament, any passionate speech, whether of sorrow or anger, sounds
almost like any other and adapts the same formula. Clifford's response
to the discovery of his dead father during the Battle of St. Albans in *2
Henry VI* (V.ii) fits the tradition without much deviation and can illustrate Shakespeare's early practice.[4] The set-speech usually opens with an
apostrophe to Fortune or the gods or with a question, such as "How can
I begin to find words to express my grief?" Even though the speaker
may be alone, he casts himself in the role of orator, setting himself
in the situation of petitioner or proclaimer, and in effect is aiming
his remarks at the audience. Then he moves into the main body of his
oration to exhibit his passion by the intensities of reiterated hyperbole,
cast into the syntactic forms of rhetorical question or imperative. The
form of the question suggests helplessness or perplexity; the imperative
embodies futile attempts at action or petitions for aid and relief; both
forms keep the voice at high pitch. The sentiments almost always include a petition for complete annihilation of one's enemy or of the universe and a consequent end to one's own suffering. Clifford makes no
opening apostrophe, but plunges immediately into the body of his
lament:

     O, let the vile world end
And the premisèd flames of the last day
Knit earth and heaven together.

Now let the general trumpet blow his blast,
Particularities and petty sounds
To cease. Wast thou ordained, dear father,
To lose thy youth in peace and to achieve
The silver livery of advisèd age,
And in thy reverence and thy chair-days thus
To die in ruffian battle? Even at this sight
My heart is turned to stone; and while 'tis mine,
It shall be stony.

(V.ii.40–51)

Ostensibly Clifford talks to himself, but he does not introspect or speak in a private manner; instead, he declaims as if to listeners and maintains a rhetorical stance throughout. Thus, the second and passionate part of the set-speech, succeeding an introduction, is composed of exclamations, petitions, wishes, hyperbolic descriptions of feelings that stimulate an audience to respond to the speaker's misfortunes. The third part is a resolution, a plan of some sort that fits the speech into the narrative of the play. Clifford's is to revenge his father's death. Here the syntax slackens to admit normal declarative sentences that embody factual propositions, but Clifford maintains a formality of tone by inverting normal word order:

York not our old men spares;
No more will I their babes. Tears virginal
Shall be to me even as the dew to fire;
And beauty, that the tyrant oft reclaims,
Shall to my flaming wrath be oil and flax.
Henceforth I will not have to do with pity.
Meet I an infant of the house of York,
Into as many gobbets will I cut it
As wild Medea young Absyrtus did.
In cruelty will I seek out my fame.

(V.ii.51–60)

Another frequent device is a comparison with famous sufferers from ancient times. Clemen mentions Hecuba, Priam, and Niobe as particular favorites. Clifford refers not only to Medea, but adapts the technique to conclude his speech (and get the body of Old Clifford off the stage).

As did Aeneas old Anchises bear,
So bear I thee upon my manly shoulders;
But then Aeneas bare a living load,
Nothing so heavy as these woes of mine.

(V.ii.62–65)

If we look back to *Gorboduc*, written some thirty years earlier but in the same tradition, and choose the speech of a mother rather than a soldier, we find similar structure, style, and sentiments. Videna's lament over the death of her son Ferrex (IV.i) bears out the threefold division: it begins with a question, why should she live longer? moves to hyperbolic presentations of her feelings by apostrophe, interjection, and petition; and concludes with a plan to revenge his death on Porrex, her other son.

The audience need know nothing more than the bare essentials about the characters of Videna or Clifford because their orations generate the full response toward their predicaments. Shakespeare plots *2 Henry VI* without any earlier scenes of affection between Old and Young Clifford. The play discloses none of Young Clifford's hopes, love, or attitudes toward any members of his family. His father appears for the first time in Act IV to help quiet the rebels and turns them against Jack Cade. Young Clifford appears for the first time in Act V, scene i, to join the confrontation before battle and add one more voice to the King's supporters against York and his supporters. He is much like Talbot's son, introduced just before the Battle of Bordeaux in *1 Henry VI*. In both cases we grasp immediately the general relationship between son and father, as in *Gorboduc* we grasp the nature of a mother's feeling for her dead son. These general relationships suffice as occasions for lament and resolution to act. One reason the lament enjoyed such a lengthy, vigorous life is that its very generality could be adapted to almost any character in almost any passionate upheaval, any character, that is, except one whom we have come to know in intimate detail. Juliet, for instance, delivers no lament after hearing of Tybalt's death or Romeo's exile. Idiosyncratic feelings or particular ways of speaking would interfere with a formalized lament.

The emotional set-speech, then, exhibits many of the same hallmarks of dramaturgy as the early confrontation scenes. Both tend to be discrete units that depend neither upon former details of the story or upon dramatic irony. Instead, the speaker stands in a one-to-one relation with the audience to assault them by declamation. Just as the clashes of opponents generate an impression of power in the audience, so the lamenter generates emotional turmoil in the audience. To recall Sir William Lucy's wish that his eyeballs be turned to bullets, he strains to impress upon the audience his sense of outrage at Joan and her followers over the death of Talbot. All seem designed to overcome a barrier of indifference postulated for the audience. When writing the story of Juliet, Shakespeare does not feel the same pressure to generate similar feelings in the audience as her grief over Romeo's death. He accepts the fact that the audience knows from the accumulated events that Juliet is profoundly distraught when she discovers him dead in her tomb; hence, intensity of feeling need not be proportionate to intensity of expression. We lose the sense of quiddity about scenes and speeches in Shakespeare's later mimetic plays where the narrative dictates the shape of the parts, so that it is difficult to classify dialogue into types. Conversely, the formalized or "set" quality of the lament excludes details of thinking that might individualize and integrate it into the narrative. We do not observe, for instance, Clifford's process of deciding upon revenge. First he reacts with vehemence over his father's death and then announces, "My heart is turned to stone." We observe cause and consequence, but we do not watch the stages by which he makes up his mind to be ruthless. When Romeo decides to kill himself, we do watch the stages of preparation as he sets his account straight with Tybalt, kisses Juliet, and takes his last farewell, even though when he first hears of her death he knows that he has no alternative but death. As I have stated earlier, the playwright prefashions the speeches of the earlier, oratorical characters; he relinquishes this tight control over the later characters so that they appear to decide what to say and how to say it.

For the twentieth-century reader it is easy to note the limitations of the passionate set-speech and difficult to give due recognition to its theatrical power. In our readiness to praise individuality and specificity, we would be inclined to trace Shakespeare's gradual release from the conventionality of the rhetorical set-speech, but the first four chronicle plays show that he grows more and more interested in exploiting its formal properties.[5] There are relatively few private emotional moments in *1 Henry VI*; *Richard III* contains a number of them, and *Titus Andronicus*, probably written shortly afterwards, uses the rhetorical lament as much as any other of his plays. In this same play Shakespeare begins to develop another means of emotional expression, but not at the expense of the rhetorical set-speech, which continues to appear in *Richard II* and *Romeo and Juliet*. This pattern of development, asserted by R. F. Hill in several of his essays,[6] may surprise us because we would expect a more systematic movement from the ready-made conventions in the earlier plays to more particular, lifelike speeches in the later. In fact, Shakespeare pushes further than his contemporaries the stylized properties of the lament, so that the passages by the Duchess of York, Queen Elizabeth, and Queen Margaret in *Richard III* sound more like chants than oratory. His fondness for auricular figures must have prompted him to see how well they serve the rhetorical purpose of stirring the listeners, and for a time he made no attempt to approximate the way people do in fact express their feelings.

∞

By its very nature an emotional outburst, the passionate set-speech gives immediacy to an event and serves to heighten our sense of its importance. Therefore, it is surprising to find so few such speeches plotted as reactions to events of the first two Henry VI plays. Their number increases in *3 Henry VI*, *Richard II*, and *Titus Andronicus*, and as it does, we find Shakespeare devising additional ways to express emotion. These may be grouped according to their primary means, auricular figures on the one hand, tropes on the other. The form of the emotional set-speech, outburst and then resolution to act, is easy enough to spot, but Shakespeare seldom uses the speech in its pure form, and when he abandons it in the later plays, we face a problem of isolating our subject. Emotion is, of course, always about something, so that in the widest sense dramas are composed mainly of emotional speeches.[7] Yet there is a special group of longer than average speeches that emphasize how a character feels about an event, speeches which occur apart from events, neither to interpret nor report them. For instance, when Juliet drinks the sleeping potion, Act IV, scene iii, she speaks a soliloquy that expresses her fear and her courage in overcoming that fear. Had Shakespeare omitted this speech, the story would progress with no sense of hiatus; without the speech an audience's general understanding of the drama would not be affected. Juliet could drink the potion and fall back on her bed in a sleep of mock-death without comment. Yet her hesitation heightens her action by letting us sense what it means for her to risk death. Shakespeare plots his dramatic narratives to include distinguishable speeches which articulate feelings more than facts or deeds.

1 Henry VI raises a problem as to why there are so few speeches devoted to sheer emotional response. It cannot be that Shakespeare was unfamiliar with the set-speech, for he structures the funeral procession that opens the play along the lines of a lament. It begins with exclamations, petitions, rhetorical questions, and hyperbolic judgments distributed among Bedford, Gloucester, and Exeter. The second half of the set-speech, the resolution to act, is generated by the messenger's report of bad news from France. Between the two parts Shakespeare inserts Duke Humphrey's quarrel with the Bishop of Winchester, which modifies the traditional structure. Not until Young Clifford's oration over his dead father's body in Act V of *2 Henry VI* do we find another full-scale lament. None accompanies the deaths of either Talbot or Joan, or, in *2 Henry VI*, of Duke Humphrey. In *1 Henry VI*, it will be recalled, Talbot's death is the one major public event dramatized to reveal private emotions. The one other is Suffolk's passion for Margaret, to be discussed later in this chapter. Talbot's feeling about the overwhelming force of the enemy is one of bravery, itself a quiet emotion best conveyed through understatement. Shakespeare creates intensity by adding Talbot's concern for his son, which he casts into the form of a debate with Young Talbot rather than a monologue of introspection. Yet after the battle, Talbot reenters, fatally wounded, to deliver a death speech, the one monologue of "pure sentiment" in the play. Again Shakespeare depends upon his son, for it is to Young Talbot's dead body that Talbot speaks his final lines. I shall quote part of this to demonstrate how Shakespeare avoids introspection. Talbot talks like an orator rather than — I shall say — "poet," speaking inwardly about his own feelings:

Thou antic Death, which laugh'st us here to scorn,
Anon, from thy insulting tyranny,
Coupled in bonds of perpetuity,
Two Talbots, wingèd through the lither sky,
In thy despite shall scape mortality.
O thou whose wounds become hard-favored Death,
Speak to thy father ere thou yield thy breath!
Brave Death by speaking, whether he will or no.
Imagine him a Frenchman, and thy foe.

(IV.vii.18-26)

That Shakespeare raises the pitch of expression by formalizing the sounds of words, here the use of couplets — a practice not customary in the formal lament by his contemporaries — indicates one way that he is to experiment later to express emotion.

While Talbot's death speech reveals the conversion of a public declamatory mode to the expression of private sentiment, this tells us little about Shakespeare's decision to plot events without emotional responses. On two occasions in the narrative, famous English soldiers die on stage, and it is left to Talbot to make some response to their deaths. To cite his entire response to the death of Bedford, we can detect an almost perfunctory haste in fulfilling the requirement of the situation:

But yet, before we go, let's not forget
The noble Duke of Bedford, late deceased,
But see his exequies fulfilled in Roan.

97

A braver soldier never couchèd lance,
A gentler heart did never sway in court.
But kings and mightiest potentates must die,
For that's the end of human misery.

(III.ii.131–37)

The concluding maxim serves to obviate further sentiment. It could be at this stage of Shakespeare's career—before he was writing for the Lord Chamberlain's Men—he hesitates to trust the stage to one actor speaking about private feelings. The numerous battles, staged by alarums and sallies, or the complicated staging of the gunner's son who fires at Salisbury and Talbot "on the turrets" suggest Shakespeare's estimation of what is stageworthy. Soliloquies tend to run between seven and fifteen lines, none over fifteen, and they serve practical purposes—reporting circumstances to the audience, such as Talbot's, IV.ii.42–56; stating plans, such as Suffolk's, V.iii.187–95; or making choral comments, such as Exeter's, III.i.186–200. While a distrust of private sentiment may have influenced the plotting of Shakespeare's first chronicle play, his relative estimates of public and private events certainly did. At this time public events were more important than private events, the main exception being the heroic Talbot; what he feels about the impending Battle of Bordeaux and the death of his son is stageworthy. But the impact of Talbot's death upon, say, Duke Humphrey, Cardinal Beaufort, York, or Somerset makes no demands upon the plotting because public events do not take their importance from the way they affect private lives. Later, Shakespeare plots the events of Richard II's career so that the King is a central figure, continuously involved in events. How he feels about the happenings gets as much attention as their consequences to the future of the commonwealth. The quiddity of private sentiments becomes as important for Shakespeare's dramaturgy as the quiddity of public events.

2 Henry VI omits any set-speech of response to the central disaster, Duke Humphrey's murder, because Duke Humphrey is the one character who until his death concerns us most. There is no other character of a stature whose feelings about his murder would be proportionate to the disaster. Shakespeare does include a passage for the grief-stricken King Henry before the murder that foreshadows the later mode of lyrical expression, an experimental passage that will be discussed in the next section. He reserves the declamatory style of the formal lament for Young Clifford during the Battle of St. Albans, and heated responses by the Duchess of Gloucester, Suffolk, Cardinal Beaufort, Queen Margaret. Unlike Clifford, the other characters react violently to misfortunes which they deserve. Their emotional reactions, suffering which is punishment, assume a status almost equal to that of the public events they imitate. The Duchess of Gloucester's response to her exile is mixed with chastisement of Duke Humphrey as much as it expresses her grief and shame (II.iv.19-57, 87-93); Suffolk reacts to his exile by a series of curses that in syntax and tone resemble the first half of the emotional set-speech (III.ii.309-28); the Cardinal babbles, distracted by the figure of death and the dead Duke Humphrey; his statements are cast into the same rhetorical questions and commands as those of speakers of the formal lament, his hyperboles not conjectural as theirs, but visualized (III.ii.8-18); Queen Margaret, as she dandles the bloody head of Suffolk, shapes her private sentiments in similar fashion (IV.iv.1-6, 15-18). Like these Jack Cade suffers on stage after his rebellion, but he talks in witty prose to state his impudent and audacious challenge of Alexander Iden as well as his feelings of hunger and bitter pride (IV.x). His flattened style is appropriate to reveal his misery without imparting any sense of dignity to which he aspired. His speeches deviate most radically from the formalized set-speech of emotion, but in one way or another all the speeches of suffering are modified. Shakespeare disrupts the rhythm or cuts a passage before it achieves intensity, and withholds the complete formula of the set-speech until Clifford's reaction, as if he hesitates to bestow full rhetorical power upon the wicked characters who might then bring the audience into a one-to-one relationship of sympathetic feeling.

In plotting the earliest Henry VI plays, whatever reservations Shakespeare has toward devoting time to emotional response or risking the powers of rhetoric with wicked characters, he abandons them when he plots *3 Henry VI*, the play which depicts the open struggle of civil war at its most brutal. He introduces characters into the play simply to deliver passionate set-speeches, such as the unnamed father and the unnamed son. Minor characters come regularly to the front of the stage to express their feelings about disasters. Figures such as Warwick and Clifford, hardly any more important in this play than Bedford or Joan in *1 Henry VI*, are given lengthy speeches as they die. It would appear that Shakespeare comes to accept the passionate response as a viable means for dramatizing the brutality of deeds and understands the structural possibilities for juxtaposing personal monologues with group dialogues. Yet the number of such private speeches creates problems of expression, for they cannot all sound alike. I shall postpone until the next section a discussion of the weaknesses and concentrate here upon the successes that arise from Shakespeare's willingness to experiment with auricular figures. So confident is he of their power that he risks leaving one actor alone on stage to deliver fifty-four lines, not of heated passion but of meditation. Henry VI enters the stage as a single figure isolated from the Battle of Towton-Saxton and sits on the molehill occupied several scenes earlier by York, who was taunted with a paper crown. Henry VI, who wears the real crown, is to lose it after this scene because the York forces win the battle and make Edward king. His lengthy speech thus helps signify the importance of the battle. Henry's meditation is two-fold: first he wishes for the life of a shepherd and then with the aid of *tableaux vivants* he moralizes on the civil war. After setting the scene, he begins his meditation with the conventions of the set-speech by an apostrophe and a typical wish for annihilation:

Would I were dead, if God's good will were so,
For what is in this world but grief and woe?
O God! methinks it were a happy life
To be no better than a homely swain.

(II.v.19-22)

And then he amplifies his wish:

To sit upon a hill as I do now,
To carve out dials quaintly, point by point,
Thereby to see the minutes how they run —
How many makes the hour full complete,
How many hours brings about the day,
How many days will finish up the year,
How many years a mortal man may live;
When this is known, then to divide the times —
So many hours must I tend my flock,
So many hours must I take my rest,
So many hours must I contemplate,
So many hours must I sport myself;
So many days my ewes have been with young,
So many weeks ere the poor fools will ean,
So many months ere I shall shear the fleece.
So minutes, hours, days, weeks, months, and years,
Passed over to the end they were created,
Would bring white hairs unto a quiet grave.

(II.v.23-40)

This virtuosity creates an impact of a primitive chant — to enchant the audience. Shakespeare, it appears, is willing to leave one actor alone because he feels confidence in the power of repetitive verbal sounds to fix their attention and stir them.[8] Henry's wish to be a shepherd both helps account for the triumph of York, occurring simultaneously off-stage, and mitigates the harshness of judgment which we cannot avoid placing on the ineffectual king. Stirred by Henry's yearning to live a life other than a king's but aware of the battle which he cannot lead against rebels, the audience hovers between pity for his helplessness and blame for his inadequacy. The severe stylization manages to create a delicate balance, affecting us while keeping us at a distance from Henry's sentiments.

When an unnamed son enters with the dead body of his father and an unnamed father enters with his dead son, the symmetry of these generalized pairs fits with the style of the meditation. Not unexpectedly, when these unnamed soldiers speak, they sound like Videna from *Gorboduc* or Clifford from *2 Henry VI*, about whom we know as much as we do of these orator-characters:

> *Father*
> But let me see. Is this our foeman's face?
> Ah, no, no, no! It is mine only son!
> Ah, boy, if any life be left in thee,
> Throw up thine eye. See, see what show'rs arise,
> Blown with the windy tempest of my heart
> Upon thy wounds, that kills mine eye and heart.
> O, pity, God, this miserable age.
>
> (*3 Henry VI*, II.v.82–88)

Henry's sympathetic response is expressed in a similar manner:

> Woe above woe, grief more than common grief;
> O that my death would stay these ruthful deeds!
> O, pity, pity, gentle heaven, pity!
>
> (II.v.94–96)

Not only the style, but the structure of Henry's meditation recall the formula of the set-speech. His chant about the life of a shepherd depends upon the same sort of expressive syntax as does the conventional opening section of the lament, and his choral commentary upon the suffering fathers and sons resembles the second part of the lament, not so much in coming to a plan of action as in relating itself to the specific facts of the narrative.

In *Richard III* Shakespeare reuses the stylized characteristics of Henry's monologue to express grief and embody gnomic wisdom. The large number of women in the cast of characters differentiates the play from its predecessors, and it is they who deliver the changing figurations. The details of Richard III's career may well have demanded the appearance of Lady Anne and Queen Elizabeth: Shakespeare's interpretation of his career demanded the oracular voice of Queen Margaret, brought back from France without historical sanction; but the old Duchess of York, who did not appear in the earlier chronicles, where she would have been as much a part of events as she is here, if not more, can be justified mainly by her additional voice to the repetitious expressions of grief. One passage approximates so closely Henry VI's monologue as to establish without question Shakespeare's dependence upon his earlier experiment:

Son
Was ever son so rued a father's death?
Father
Was ever father so bemoaned his son?
King Henry
Was ever king so grieved for subject's woe?

(*3 Henry VI*, II.v.109–11)

In its later reworking:

Queen Elizabeth
Was never widow had so dear a loss.
Children
Were never orphans had so dear a loss.
Duchess of York
Was never mother had so dear a loss.

(*Richard III*, II.ii.77–79)

In Act IV three wailing women sit upon the ground to lament and comment upon the pattern of justice in events:

Queen Margaret
I had an Edward, till a Richard killed him;
I had a Harry, till a Richard killed him:
Thou hadst an Edward, till a Richard killed him;
Thou hadst a Richard, till a Richard killed him.
Duchess of York
I had a Richard too, and thou didst kill him;
I had a Rutland too, thou holp'st to kill him.
Queen Margaret
Thou hadst a Clarence too, and Richard killed him.

(IV.iv.40–46)

The musical repetition of sound underlines the simplicity of justice to produce a mysterious sense of inevitability that indicates together with the dreams, curses, and oaths the supernatural force of providence working its way through the events of *Richard III* to unite the warring houses in the Tudor line.

Shakespeare gives another turn to his experimentation with patterns of sound in *Richard II* and *Romeo and Juliet*. Rejecting his rhetorical principle that sound patterns should stimulate feelings in the audience similar to feelings in the speaker, he redirects the relation of sound to meaning in accordance with the audience's relation to mimetic drama. He devises contortions of feelings in the character without regard for producing comparable responses in the audience.[9] An early instance of the redirected emotional speech occurs when Gaunt on his deathbed puns on his name for eleven lines (II.i.73–83). As if to defend this unusual sound pattern, Shakespeare writes for Richard II: "Can sick men play so nicely with their names?" (II.i.84). Gaunt takes the occasion to chastise Richard rather than account for his style, implying that his anguish and sense of urgency are explanation enough. In a second passage of similar intensity, Richard contorts sounds after he gives up the crown to Bolingbroke before parliament:

> *Richard*
> Your cares set up do not pluck my cares down.
> My care is loss of care, by old care done;
> Your care is gain of care, by new care won.
> The cares I give I have, though given away;
> They tend the crown, yet still with me they stay.
> *Bolingbroke*
> Are you contented to resign the crown?
> *Richard*
> Ay, no; no, ay; for I must nothing be;
> Therefore no no, for I resign to thee.

$$(IV.i.195-202)$$

His final pun on "I" recurs in a similar passage, perhaps the most contorted of all, spoken by Juliet in reaction to the Nurse's fumbling account of Tybalt's death and Romeo's banishment:

> What devil art thou that dost torment me thus?
> This torture should be roared in dismal hell.
> Hath Romeo slain himself? Say thou but "I,"
> And that bare vowel "I" shall poison more
> Than the death-darting eye of cockatrice.
> I am not I, if there by such an "I"

103

Or those eyes' shot that makes the answer "I."
If he be slain, say "I"; or if not, "no."
Brief sounds determine of my weal or woe.

(III.ii.43–51)

The audience need not in response to this complex word-play feel in the
same way as Juliet, but it should infer the pressure of feeling that makes
her speak this way. Her speech marks the limit to which Shakespeare
carried his experiments in the expressive use of sounds that take precedence over the sense of what is being said. While he never abandoned
the auricular patterns, he gradually replaced in passages of emotional
response sensible figures by "sensable" figures, to use Puttenham's term.

∞

Lyrical passages of emotional response are more appropriate to mimetic
drama and therefore grow in frequency during Shakespeare's apprenticeship. By "lyrical" I mean roughly the style of a speaker who finds
equivalents of his feelings in images. To convey how he feels, he usually
describes a hypothetical scene without clearly marked stages of beginning, middle, end, unadorned by the heightened syntax of question and
imperative or auricular figures. This is a customary way for anyone to
express his feelings, a way refined by lyrical poets whether they write in
1590 or 1950, but not for the orator or character in rhetorical drama of
the late 1580s and early 1590s. Sir William Lucy's catachresis, wishing
that his eyeballs become bullets, is an image designed to inoculate the
audience with a sense of outrage similar to the one the speaker feels
against the French enemies of dead Talbot (*1 Henry VI*, IV.vii.79–80).
To choose a less familiar example from *3 Henry VI*, when Edward hears
of his father York's death, he utters a sentiment customary to the rhetorical lament:

Now my soul's palace is become a prison.
Ah, would she break from hence, that this my body
Might in the ground by closèd up in rest.
For never henceforth shall I joy again;
Never, O never, shall I see more joy.

(II.i.74–78)

Both speakers use images, but implicit in their choice lies the assumption that the listeners are inert and would remain unmoved by something less extreme. Furthermore, Edward's fragment exemplifies the
form into which the declamatory speaker casts his images: a wish
("Would she break from hence"), a proclamation ("For never henceforth shall I joy again") intensified by repetition and auricular figures.

3 Henry VI can be discussed as a transitional play because the dialogue contains a number of emotional responses, both declamatory and lyrical. Shakespeare's willingness to include less insistent and more lyrical passages of descriptive imagery, usually comparisons of tears to rain and sighs to wind, arises at least in part, I think, from his attitude toward the War of the Roses. He takes no clear-cut position for one side or the other, but dramatizes the horrors of civil struggle for both sides. To recall the one powerfully declamatory sequence, Henry VI's meditation on the molehill, the speeches of the unnamed father and the unnamed son draw us close to their grief, but we never learn which side each fights for. Events lead us to feel that the Yorkists do wrong to attack the King, and yet we watch the King's own doubt about his claim to the throne in the opening scene and his subsequent weakness that not only emboldens the Yorkists but fosters Margaret's brutality, which in turn intensifies the antagonism. To dramatize the horrors of the conflict, Shakespeare needs to include passages of emotional response. Yet it is the nature of the declamatory set-speech to draw in the audience to feel as the speaker feels. This power does not square with Shakespeare's general attitude. So too, his prodigality in covering a multitude of events works against any tendency to equip every suffering character with a formalized set-speech. Senecan drama, where the emotional declamation fits precisely, is restricted both in events and characters, so that while Medea or Hercules may utter lengthy speeches to express their tortured souls, the playwright does not load the text with a large number of such intense moments for a number of characters. *3 Henry VI*, structured to show forth the story from beginning to end rather than to concentrate in Senecan fashion upon the climax with retrospective reports, dramatizes the emotional responses of Henry VI, York, Edward, Richard, Queen Margaret, Queen Elizabeth, Warwick, Clifford, the unnamed father, and the unnamed son.

Granting the fact that all these speakers should not declaim, the very number sets a problem for lyrical descriptions too, for all characters cannot liken their tears to torrential streams and their sighs to tempests. Shakespeare and his contemporaries, however, found a ready source for emotional expression in comparing physical gestures to extreme states of nature.[10] The unnamed father, for instance, describes his grief for his dead son:

Throw up thine eye. See, see what show'rs arise,
Blown with the windy tempest of my heart
Upon thy wounds.

(II.v.85–87)

Richard of York, after Margaret hands him the napkin dipped in Rutland's blood, adapts the images to the syntax of the declamatory lament:

Bid'st thou me rage? Why, now thou hast thy wish.
Wouldst have me weep? Why, now thou hast thy will.
For raging wind blows up incessant showers,
And when the rage allays the rain begins.

(I.iv.143–46)

Another variation upon the motif can be rung by refusal to weep or sigh. Queen Elizabeth, when she hears of Edward IV's capture, considers her pregnancy and says:

Ay, ay, for this I draw in many a tear
And stop the rising of bloodsucking sighs,
Lest with my sighs or tears I blast or drown
King Edward's fruit, true heir to th'English crown.

(IV.iv.21–24)

In a more famous passage Richard of Gloucester takes the same position when he hears about the brutal death of his father York:

I cannot weep, for all my body's moisture
Scarce serves to quench my furnace-burning heart;
Nor can my tongue unload my heart's great burden,
For selfsame wind that I should speak withal
Is kindling coals that fires all my breast
And burns me up with flames that tears would quench.
To weep is to make less the depth of grief.
Tears, then, for babes; blows and revenge for me!

(II.i.79–86)

Richard's brother Edward responds to the same news with a traditional wish, already quoted, for universal annihilation, a contrast to the idiosyncratic and fierce response of Richard that indicates one way to particularize emotional responses.

Warwick's death speech suggests the direction that Shakespeare eventually takes in particularizing sentiments. Warwick develops his feelings within a description of his past life. If we recall the quarrel scene, characterization of rhetorical personae requires little familiarity with the details of their lives other than loyalty to one side of a conflict or a discrepancy between social role and behavior. As Warwick begins to speak, we see that he is akin to these characters. He opens with the orator's stance:

Ah, who is nigh? Come to me, friend or foe,
And tell me who is victor, York or Warwick.
Why ask I that? My mangled body shows,
My blood, my want of strength, my sick heart shows,
That I must yield my body to the earth.

(V.ii.5-9)

Here the conventional question expresses his dazed condition as he regains momentary consciousness, first calling to anyone, then addressing
himself. Once he describes his wounded condition, he turns to sentiments about Fortune's wheel, more appropriate to *A Mirror for Magistrates* than to a narrative of civil war.

Lo now my glory smeared in dust and blood;
My parks, my walks, my manors that I had,
Even now forsake me; and of all my lands
Is nothing left me but my body's length.
Why, what is pomp, rule, reign, but earth and dust?
And, live we how we can, yet die we must.

(V.ii.23-28)

The concluding couplet recalls Talbot's pious commonplace spoken over
the body of Bedford, *1 Henry VI*, III.ii, and would fit him or any other
character equally well. Warwick's sentiments about his parks and manors, although apparently more particular, are typical symbols of the
exalted fortune of one who falls. Had we been acquainted at some
earlier point with Warwick's pride in his estates, the symbols would have
been modified by the story to become characteristic particularities.
Likewise, Montague, Warwick's brother, mentioned for the first time at
the end of his death speech, serves the moment for a general, not a particular feeling. Warwick's grief for his dead brother supplies a ready-
made situation that carries with it typical sentiments reminiscent of
Talbot's son, who was suddenly introduced into *1 Henry VI* to capitalize
upon typical feelings at the moment of Talbot's death. To particularize
these feelings, Shakespeare need only introduce Talbot's son earlier or
plot an episode of cooperation and affection between Warwick and
Montague. To do this would be to place narrative before oratory,
whereas Shakespeare sees drama as analogous to an oration. Consequently, a character appears at any point that didactic purposes require
him and need have no dramatic past in order to deliver an emotional
set-speech. While Young Talbot is given more preparation than Montague, his father makes no reference to his past private life as Warwick

107

does. Shakespeare appears to introduce these details into Warwick's death speech to give it distinctiveness, but this is disproportionate to Warwick's role in the play. Particularization of feelings, it would seem, depends upon details of narrative, so that declamatory set-speeches fit better into rhetorically conceived drama than into mimetic drama.

The way Shakespeare constructs Lucrece's responses to her rape provides a model for the way he works himself free of the emotional set-speech, free not in the sense of abandoning it, but free to use means other than variations upon the orator's devices and conventional metaphors. Over half of the poem is devoted to Lucrece's response to her rape, a proportion that suggests Shakespeare's increasing dependence upon the feelings and thoughts of participants to give an event its meaning. It is fascinating to watch Shakespeare try out the typical devices of the lament in meeting the demands of his story, using and reusing them until, as if out of a sense of exhaustion, he devises another means of expression.

In brief outline, Lucrece after the rape assumes an orator's stance with an apostrophe to Night, beginning line 764, petitions help for her predicament, describes her tears and moans, and imagines hyperbolic conditions which could hide her shame. Then, beginning line 876 she addresses Opportunity and intensifies her comments by severely patterned verbal schemes. Next, she turns to Time (line 925), characterizing it, petitioning for aid, questioning why it permitted Opportunity to work against her, and concluding with a series of curses against Tarquin. This segment could serve as a compendium of the traditional techniques of the passionate set-speech. As she begins to reflect on herself and see that she rails in vain (1016–29), she moves to the next phase by resolving on a plan of action. Before calling her maid and writing a note to Collatinus, she extends her oratory by addressing the sun, the birds, herself, even her hand. The voice of the poet then intrudes after she sends the groom with her message:

The weary time she cannot entertain,
For now 'tis stale to sigh, to weep and groan.
So woe hath wearied woe, moan tirèd moan,
    That she her plaints a little while doth stay,
    Pausing for means to mourn some newer way.

(lines 1361–65)

This is as much as to say that Shakespeare, having exhausted the conventions of the set-speech, is casting about for some new way to render her feelings.

How he does it is to introduce a painting of the fall of Troy (lines 1366–1568). Lucrece examines the "piece of skillful painting" in detail to nourish her passions and responds with sympathy to Hecuba's anguish and with revulsion at Sinon's duplicity. The inset tableau serves locally as an allegory for Lucrece's predicament, but it also serves to relieve Shakespeare of the need to generate feelings by rhetorical stimulation. The implications are far-reaching, for the tableau indicates his trust in the facts of a story to move an audience (or reader). Lucrece drops her role as orator and becomes an observer, turning away from her reader-listener, whom she addresses obliquely when she invokes Night, Opportunity, and Time, to face the picture. Her new direction relieves Shakespeare of the need for systematic organization of her response. Either the chronology of the narrative or the process of her observation, instead of introductory address, wishes, questions, petitions, and finally resolution, can shape the response. Just as we appeal to the familiar when we try to define something new, so Shakespeare juxtaposes a famous story to Lucrece's. Even though we understand from her story just how Lucrece feels, our understanding is consolidated and confirmed by another situation which we already know.[11] By using one narrative to develop another, Shakespeare commits himself to strengthening his outer narrative, as he is to do in subsequent plays by specifying how one character interacts with another, by adding details to create a sense of the play "world" with its own setting and atmosphere, and by tightening the relations of cause to effect.

The narrator's comments make explicit the mechanics of expressiveness that remain implicit in dramatic dialogue. First Shakespeare describes what an ordinary viewer might see — "that one might see" (1386), "that one would swear he saw" (1393), "there pleading might you see" (1401), all phrases implying that the reader need not necessarily see these details. Then he describes what Lucrece sees. The two parts of his description would be unnecessary if he were not suggesting the selectivity of vision. When Lucrece sees Hecuba, she "shapes her sorrow to the beldame's woes" (1458), and when she spots Sinon "But Tarquin's shape came in her mind the while" (1536). Not only her interpretation of the details but the selection of details indicates her state of mind.

Our sense of Lucrece's feelings arises from an inference about her mental activity only intimated by the poet here but given explicit formulation by Bushy in *Richard II* when he explains to the Queen why she is troubled by premonitions:

Each substance of a grief hath twenty shadows,
Which shows like grief itself, but is not so;

For sorrow's eye, glazèd with blinding tears,
Divides one thing entire to many objects,
Like perspectives, which rightly gazed upon,
Show nothing but confusion — eyed awry,
Distinguish form.

(II.ii.14–20)

Whereas Lucrece expresses grief by selecting Hecuba to compare with herself, Richard's Queen expresses grief by projecting omens into things around her. The audience, intuiting the cause from its effects, senses the feelings in much the same manner that they do when listening to Juliet's or Richard II's contortions of words, such as their play upon the sound and meaning of "I," "eye," and "aye."

Titus Andronicus must be discussed in connection with *The Rape of Lucrece*. Aside from the fact that both stories take place in ancient Rome, their structures resemble one another too closely to have been composed at widely different periods. All of Act III and much of Act IV dramatize Titus's reactions to the outrages perpetrated by Aaron, Tamora, and her sons, a proportion similar to the attention given to Lucrece's reactions to Tarquin's outrages, and both exhibit the same movement through traditional rhetorical set-speeches to the expressive tableau. When Titus has lamented his sons' imprisonment and Bassianus's exile, then the mutilation of Lavinia's hands, he reaches the point where he exhausts the emotional set-speech. After he hears that Lavinia's tongue has been cut out, he imagines a picture rather than looks at a narrative painting:

For now I stand as one upon a rock,
Environed with a wilderness of sea,
Who marks the waxing tide grow wave by wave,
Expecting ever when some envious surge
Will in his brinish bowels swallow him.

(III.i.93–97)

His tableau is shorter than Lucrece's and is imagined, obvious differences that are due to the conditions of theatrical performance, but like hers, the details of his picture express his feelings which have isolated them for description. Both pictures can be classified as *translatio*, that is, one thing replacing another. Puttenham gave three reasons why one needs to translate: for want of a better word, for pleasure of ornament, and for enforcement to make a thing more significant. All three can apply to Titus's imagined picture and suggest an impact upon the audience different from that of the passionate set-speech.

Anyone can testify that he feels satisfaction when he is able to restate a proposition in his own words. A pleasure arises from the activity of incorporating it into one's thinking and from testifying to the understanding of a new proposition. Likewise, when one discovers a synonym for a new word, he feels more comfortable with it; so too when one discovers a religious or philosophical explanation to account for perplexing events. Metaphor and allegory provide us with a less rigorous and more hypothetical or playful translation that produces a satisfaction which may be called "poetic." This hypothetical *translatio* that makes a sudden link can delight us with its spontaneous rightness. Some pleasure akin to this satisfaction was probably what Puttenham had in mind when he spoke of the pleasures of ornament that *translatio* gives us. Titus first translates his feelings about so many disasters into being engulfed by the sea and then adds another translation of the sea as a wilderness. Our satisfaction at the rightness of his translation can be described as assent, for it confirms, like Lucrece's picture, our sense of his feelings which we have intuited from the dramatic context. Significantly Shakespeare introduces expressive tableaux only after Lucrece and Titus have established their feelings by rhetorical set-speeches, as if he were unwilling to trust them with a full expressive burden or unsure that the audience would sense the full expressive import. Later, of course, the pleasure at the rightness of *translatio* replaces the approximate emotion that the rhetorical set-speech generates.

To take another of Titus's pictures of grief which adds gestures and incorporates a variation on the motif of tears:

Shall thy good uncle and thy brother Lucius
And thou and I sit round about some fountain,
Looking all downwards to behold our cheeks
How they are stained, like meadows yet not dry
With miry slime left on them by a flood?
And in the fountain shall we gaze so long
Till the fresh taste be taken from that clearness,
And made a brine-pit with our bitter tears?

(III.i.122–29)

The entire situation relieves much of the expressive burden from the image of tears, but a more crucial difference from the earlier references to sighs and tears is Titus's inclusion of himself in his picture. Lucrece must compare herself to Hecuba because her picture is a physical presence. Titus's picture, being hypothetical, permits him to take his place within it and throw the main task of *translatio* on the surroundings and on his behavior. His reference to himself in a new context implies an inner life beyond what Lucrece's straightforward allegory is capable of suggesting.[12]

∞

The innovation implicit in these descriptive tableaux and their aptness for mimetic drama become clear when we look back to the few tableaux in the early Henry VI plays that anticipate them. As might be expected, almost all such descriptive passages occur in soliloquy where the speaker need not use his rhetorical style to attack or influence other characters, but to inform the audience. In *2 Henry VI* York's first soliloquy gives his private interpretation of the loss of Anjou and Maine that reveals his ambition for the throne. He compares himself to a "silly owner" who must stand aside while pirates plunder and squander his goods; so Suffolk and Henry VI give away Anjou and Maine for the hand of Margaret, daughter of a minor king (I.i.220–229). York's son Richard almost duplicates this use of picture when he reveals his aspirations for the throne in *3 Henry VI*, again in soliloquy: "I do but dream of sovereignty, / Like one that stands upon a promontory" and then develops this picture (III.iii.134–143); he repeats his point by likening his search for the throne to "one lost in a thorny wood" (III.iii.173–181). These speakers use the tableau to clarify their emotions for the audience in a way that recalls the one extended *translatio* from *1 Henry VI*: Talbot's comparison of his soldiers' predicament before Bordeaux to a herd of deer "parked and bounded in a pale" (IV.ii.45–52). Talbot's passage differs from York's and Richard's because he is sympathetic. The tableau is especially appropriate for an unsympathetic character's responses in the rhetorical chronicle plays because it does not draw the audience into a sympathetic bond as a declamatory set-speech would. The one tableau that reveals best the dynamics of clarification while distancing the audience, most revealing because most awkward, is Henry VI's picture of his feelings when Duke Humphrey is arrested by Suffolk and Cardinal Beaufort with the support of Queen Margaret, York, Somerset, and Buckingham (*2 Henry VI*, III.i). The King's little allegory, spoken just after the Duke's arrest and before Henry leaves the stage to the plotters, separates him from them:

Thou [Duke Humphrey] never didst them wrong nor no man wrong.
And as the butcher takes away the calf
And binds the wretch and beats it when it strains,
Bearing it to the bloody slaughterhouse,

Even so remorseless have they borne him hence;
And as the dam runs lowing up and down,
Looking the way her harmless young one went,
And can do naught but wail her darling's loss,
Even so myself bewails good Gloucester's case
With sad unhelpful tears, and with dimmed eyes
Look after him and cannot do him good.

(III.i.209-19)

Even though the tableau serves well enough as a comparable predicament, we cannot ignore the connotations which make the comparison of
the Duke to a calf and the King to a cow unfortunate. No doubt Shakespeare intended to reveal Henry's sympathy toward his uncle while at
the same time disapproving of his passivity, but the comparison pays too
high a price. Max Black, in discussing metaphor, observed that we hold
in balance both items of comparison and do not omit the one when the
other is substituted: "interaction" rather than "substitution" better describes the relation of tenor and vehicle.[13] If this holds true for metaphor, it holds more so for a comparison where both terms are explicit.

Henry VI, York and Richard of Gloucester devise pictures to clarify
their feelings for the audience and for that reason find one-to-one relations between themselves and figures within their descriptions, so that
their pictures work explicitly as similes. But a character like Titus
Andronicus, by placing himself in an imaginary environment, does not
restrict his conception of himself to one lost in a thorny wood, a victim
of pirates, or a cow, but suggests numerous possibilities for other hypothetical surroundings or other expressive gestures. His open-ended picture implies a faculty of imagination like the playwright's, capable of
inventing other tableaux, whereas the more definite, closed picture of
York or Henry VI suggests a pedagogical facility to clarify feelings in the
character more limited than the playwright's. We in the audience who
sense the feelings that are translated by an imaginary picture intuit an
extra dimension of awareness in a character who can separate himself
from the self he places within his tableau.

There is only one short step from the imaginary picture to a first-
hand description as a means of expressing emotion. Romeo, when he
first sees Juliet, need not declare his feelings as Suffolk does when he first
sees Margaret of Anjou, nor does Romeo need to devise a little tableau,
as does Titus to express his feeling; all he need do is to describe her by
specifically selected images which evoke the feelings that produce them:

O, she doth teach the torches to burn bright!

It seems she hangs upon the cheek of night
As a rich jewel in an Ethiop's ear —
Beauty too rich for use, for earth too dear!
So shows a snowy dove trooping with crows
As yonder lady o'er her fellows shows.

                                        (I.v.44–49)

To measure the expressiveness of his description, we need only set it
beside Suffolk's response to Margaret's beauty, taken from *1 Henry VI*:

O, stay! [*Aside*] I have no power to let her pass.
My hand would free her, but my heart says no.
As plays the sun upon the glassy streams,
Twinkling another counterfeited beam,
So seems this gorgeous beauty to mine eyes.
Fain would I woo her, yet I dare not speak.
I'll call for pen and ink and write my mind.
Fie, de la Pole, disable not thyself.
Hast not a tongue? Is she not here?[14]
Wilt thou be daunted at a woman's sight?
Ay, beauty's princely majesty is such
Confounds the tongue and makes the senses rough.

                                        (V.iii.60–71)

Both speakers respond to beauty, both fashion generalized comments
upon beauty, both shape a simile by placing the comparison before the
term to be compared. The difference in Romeo's passage could be located in his far richer figures. Suffolk lacks the inventiveness to turn a
verb to metaphorical use ("teach the torches"), nor can he combine the
figures entailed in Romeo's simile of "rich jewel in an Ethiop's ear" with
the metaphorical verb "hanging" and the personification, "cheek of
night." While it is possible to measure Shakespeare's development by his
manipulation of simile and metaphor, it is subsidiary to his attitude
toward the kind of poetry proper in dramatic situations. Suffolk casts
his feelings into a conflict between hand and heart, then between hand
and tongue, which he articulates by antithesis, self-address, question
and answer. He engages in a little dialogue with himself. When Shakespeare composes Romeo's speech, he apparently feels that the intensities
of rhetorical conflict are unnecessary to hold the attention of the audience capable of intuiting the richness of his emotion from the richness of
his description. The simplicities of the earlier passage arise not from any
inherent difficulties of metaphor and simile but from a standard of
dramatic relevance.

The lyrical tableau, whether imaginary or immediately descriptive, is more appropriate to the character in mimetic than in rhetorically conceived drama. Sensitized to immediate experience, able to evoke hypothetical pictures, he not only gives the impression of a richer inner life but in fact talks more about himself than his earlier counterpart. The rhetorical character takes an outward stance, facing his interlocutor, who is either a friendly listener able to be persuaded or an opponent to be accused. As we have seen, his dialogue gets its momentum from copiousness. He asserts his loyalty to one side of an issue, states his identity, and attacks the inadequate behavior of his enemy, but for him to be modified by a confrontation, to add an unexpected sentiment, change his attitude, or draw on intimate resources of character is rare indeed. The Duchess of Gloucester in *Richard II*, a minor character in a mimetically conceived narrative, is able to modify in mid-speech her request for York to visit her. The mimetic character creates the impression of a richer inner life, not only because he is more flexible, but because the narrative leaves something unspoken. The playwright can count upon context as much as upon words to help express feelings because mimetic narrative is cumulative, and he assumes that an audience carries over the impressions of one scene to another. Thus an audience can sense from a situation how a character is going to respond so that when it hears his tableau, the details of the *translatio* coalesce with its expectation to evoke a special pleasure of assent. At times, of course, a character's emotional response may surprise the audience so that its pleasure is one of inference from details to the feelings that cause them rather than assent to the hypothetical *translatio*. In either case, the fact that the character need not state explicitly how he feels contributes to our impression that the present moment does not encompass or reveal him fully.

Another means available to the playwright for expressing emotion has yet to be discussed, a psychological momentum possible in developing the lyrical tableau. Without being systematized like the declamatory set-speech, the lyrical speeches discussed thus far have been straightforward presentations, moving in deliberate fashion from sentence to sentence. Yet the movement of a lyrical speech may also be expressive of the emotion that generates it. In chapter 1, I observed that Juliet does not simply recall a fact; she tries to remember it. The movement of her speech approximates a psychological process, a structure that helps realize the fullest potentialities of emotional response in the apprentice plays. It goes without saying that such an expressive movement fits well with the cumulative structure of the dramatic narrative that adapts to the claims of story as story rather than to the claims of a general thesis.

∞

The painting of Troy puts Lucrece in the position of an observer instead of an orator so that her speech follows the direction of her eyes rather than the structure of an oration. As she looks from Sinon to Hecuba, her spontaneous movement guides what she says. Shakespeare, of course, arranges what she sees, but he designs the sequence to express "spontaneous" experience rather than to follow the tested order of an oration. Two speeches from a later play, the final soliloquies of Romeo and Juliet, can show us how far Shakespeare moves from his reliance on the structure of the rhetorical set-speech in approximating the process of a mind under the pressure of great feeling. Juliet's speech occurs just before she drinks the sleeping potion, and Romeo's just before he kills himself in Juliet's tomb. Both speeches express reactions to misfortune, and both conclude with resolutions to act so that they resemble the earlier set-speeches in enough ways to allow significant comparison. [15]

The narrative could move ahead without Juliet's soliloquy, but we would feel little sense of the risk she takes in drinking the potion. Her speech heightens her action by dramatizing fear, an emotion in itself significant because it is expressed so infrequently by the conventions of the rhetorical set-speech that work so well in rendering the intensities of wrath and grief. One earlier moment of fear comes to mind, Richard III's soliloquy as he awakes from his dream about ghosts before the Battle of Bosworth Field, which takes the form of an internal debate with his conscience. Juliet at the outset of her soliloquy recalls Richard III, who describes his feelings objectively:

Richard
Cold fearful drops stand on my trembling flesh.

(V.iii.182)

Juliet
I have a faint cold fear thrills through my veins.

(IV.iii.15)

And just as he divides himself into two voices to debate, she talks to the Nurse, the vial, the dagger, and herself:

Nurse!—What should she do here?
My dismal scene I needs must act alone.
Come, vial.
What if this mixture do not work at all?

116

Shall I be married then to-morrow morning?
No, no! This shall forbid it. Lie thou there.

(IV.iii.18-23)

The short phrases create an impression of breathlessness and suggest her
tension. At this point the resemblance to Richard's soliloquy breaks off,
for unlike his struggle with his conscience, Juliet's speech develops speculation on what might happen. By its very nature, fear is anticipatory,
and Shakespeare approximates its dynamics by a sequence of increasingly violent hypotheses:

What if it be a poison which the friar
Subtly hath minist'red to have me dead . . . ?
How if, when I am laid into the tomb,
I wake before the time that Romeo
Come to redeem me? . . .
Shall I not then be stifled in the vault . . . ?

(IV.iii.24 ff.)

She does not now talk about fear, but becomes fearful. As her speech
reaches a crescendo, her picture of what might happen grows more
vividly detailed:

Where bloody Tybalt, yet but green in earth,
Lies fest'ring in his shroud . . .
. . . what with loathsome smells,
And shrieks like mandrakes torn out of the earth.

(IV.iii.42 ff.)

As her picture grows more fearsome, the syntax loosens; the phrases
follow hard on one another without control, as if her reason has given
over syntax to emotion. We might say that Shakespeare almost paints
himself into a corner because, if Juliet becomes so intensely afraid, what
can bring her to drink the potion? With the stroke of a sure dramatist,
he exploits the liveliness of her imagination to conjure up a picture of
Romeo too.

O, look! methinks I see my cousin's ghost
Seeking out Romeo, that did spit his body
Upon a rapier's point. Stay, Tybalt, stay!
Romeo, I come! this do I drink to thee.

(IV.iii.54-58)

With this gesture, we watch the resolution of her speech, composed as if
she were living it phase by phase without regard for the audience's feel-

ing the same fear. Her love overcomes her fear, a movement attuned to Juliet's actions throughout the play.[16]

Unlike hers, Romeo's final soliloquy is retrospective and interpretative, but like hers, it makes significant the moment, for with only a brief comment he could have killed himself and satisfied the demands of the narrative. Through the speech we learn what Romeo's suicide means to him. To develop his comments, Shakespeare adapts the old techniques of address, rhetorical question, and exclamation, having Romeo talk first to Juliet, then Tybalt, again to Juliet, and finally to his eyes, arms, lips, and the vial of poison. One fact which separates him from an orator is that he knows less than the audience and therefore cannot inform them or stimulate similar feelings in them. More important, the movement of his comments follows the unsystematic movement that he makes, walking back and forth from bier to bier.

His opening lines set him apart from an orator, who would in his desire to influence his listeners hardly allow an unnecessary ambiguity in what he says:

How oft when men are at the point of death
Have they been merry! which their keepers call
A lightning before death. O, how may I
Call this a lightning?

(V.iii.88-91)

Is he saying that, soon to be released from his life without Juliet, he is merry and asks for words to express it (*how* may I call this a lightning?), or is he saying that he does not feel merry like most men before death (how may I call *this* a lightning?)?[17] An actor may settle the ambiguity by the way he reads the line. If he does not, he preserves an indecisiveness which we feel appropriate to the moment: since Romeo "knows" Juliet to be dead, he is glad to die; yet since his feelings about dying are not happy — as they should be if she were dead — we would like him to trust those feelings as cautionary. Then he turns to Juliet:

O my love! my wife!
Death, that hath sucked the honey of thy breath,
Hath had no power yet upon thy beauty.

(V.iii.91-93)

The unsuspected truth in his observation reveals how the devices of an oration can be turned to expressive purposes. We in the audience who know how close Juliet is to reawakening are torn between hope that he will discover the truth and the apprehension that he will kill himself before the moment of her return to life.

Next, he walks to Tybalt's bier to even the acccount of his past misdeeds and set straight his life's record:

Tybalt, liest thou there in thy bloody sheet?
O, what more favor can I do to thee
Than with that hand that cut thy youth in twain
To sunder his that was thine enemy?
Forgive me cousin!

(V.iii.97–101)

This moral concern helps prevent Romeo's attitude from affecting us as negative, either cynical or despairing, even though his final comments may intimate these feelings by their detachment, as we shall see. He turns again to Juliet's lifelike beauty:

Why art thou yet so fair? Shall I believe
That unsubstantial Death is amorous,
And that the lean abhorrèd monster keeps
Thee here in dark to be his paramour?

(V.iii.102–5)

The repetition of his observation about Juliet's vital beauty heightens our poignant awareness of what might have been and keeps our responses distinct from his. The unusual image of death has been isolated by critics who relate it to the general theme of *Liebestod* in the play; as such it serves to strengthen the unintentional irony of Romeo's remarks.[18] What is intentional is his shift to a quasi-humorous attitude that creates a shade of feeling hardly to be found in the earlier rhetorical laments:

For fear of that I still will stay with thee
And never from this pallet of dim night
Depart again. Here, here will I remain
With worms that are thy chambermaids.

(V.iii.106–9)

The fanciful, almost sardonic explanation of why he will kill himself deflates the elevated tone that would be essential for the traditional lament. Jocularity about the seriousness of death would by the standard of rhetorical decorum be improper, but by the claims of mimetic drama—that is, by the claims of immediate circumstances—it is justified in particularizing Romeo's attitude:

119

> O, here
> Will I set up my everlasting rest
> And shake the yoke of inauspicious stars
> From this world-wearied flesh.
>
> (V.iii.109–12)

By this proclamation he faces directly the act of suicide, but it too states more than it intends. His apparently self-willed resolution, echoing his earlier one-line response to the news of Juliet's death, "Is it e'en so? Then I defy you, stars!" (V.i.24), is not so clear-cut, for his choice fulfills the exact plan of the stars. The irony separates our feeling of pity from his feeling of determination. G. B. Harrison, among others, has discerned a pun in his comment: "setting" up his "rest" is a metaphor from primero, a card game, whose connotations enforce the attitude of jocularity implicit in the earlier image about Death as amorous.[19] In the same vein, Romeo puns with his final words:

> O true apothecary!
> Thy drugs are quick. Thus with a kiss I die.
>
> (V.iii.119–20)

Shakespeare's use of puns is not new, but their use is new in such a moment of utmost seriousness. Talbot's or Warwick's death speech contains no such breaches of decorum. Like Gaunt's pun on his name as he is dying or Juliet's pun on "I" when she fears Romeo's death, Romeo's puns seem to require a detachment of mind more appropriate to quarrels than to moments of ultimate seriousness.

Romeo's freedom to link primero with suicide coincides with the freedom of expression which Shakespeare enjoys when he develops a mimetic narrative without primary regard for instructing an audience. His treatment of the Duchess of York's plea to Henry IV in *Richard II*, V.iii, is another instance of this freedom. In both cases the freedom is somehow attached to the manipulation of dramatic irony. Romeo is one of the first major characters, if not the first, who dies not knowing what the audience knows (Talbot may be considered ignorant of York's and Somerset's mutual inhibition); even Clarence finally discovers the role of his solicitous brother in his murder. The discrepancy between what Romeo sees and the audience sees coincides with Romeo's ability to devise statements which do not, even from his own point of view, say all they mean.[20] Perhaps it is a rule of dramatic composition that characters speak like their playwrights. Just as in rhetorically oriented drama characters tend to speak like orators, so in mimetic drama that exploits the ironies natural to the stage the characters speak ironically. Irony possesses no inherent value, but here it helps particularize Romeo's feelings by suggesting complexities of attitude that cannot be encompassed in such terms as "fear," "despair," or "resignation." So while Lucrece's scrutiny of the picture of Troy opened the way for a looser structure of the emotional response, it tightened the range of expressiveness to specific shades of feeling unavailable to the rhetorical set-speech.

It is obvious that any drama, in so far as the playwright takes advantage of the distinctive resources of the stage, must exhibit discrepant awareness among the characters. If the playwright takes seriously a character's viewpoint, if Richard II's queen responds to facts colored by her grief, or if Romeo describes objects under the influence of his feelings, it follows that lines of perspective are kept distinct so that the characters become differentiated by how they see as well as by what they know. Such niceties of awareness do not always fit, however, with the priorities of rhetorically conceived drama. For instance, the unnamed captain in *2 Henry VI* knows fully all the facts of Suffolk's evil behavior, including his presumably secret love of Queen Margaret. How the captain comes to learn his secret is less important to Shakespeare than his full denunciation of Suffolk at the moment of his execution. When Shakespeare gives priority to a character's viewpoint, it follows that the mechanics of intrigue become as important as their moral significance. Concomitantly, the interplay among characters becomes more complex so that it is not adequate to group them as friend and opponent, active speaker and passive listener, strong and weak, or triumphant and defeated. Again we see that the claims of narrative as specific story take precedence over the claims of a general thesis. It is to this topic, the claims of dramatic narrative upon discrepant awareness in Shakespeare's early didactic and later mimetic plays, that we turn to draw together observations on his uses of dramatic irony.

Moral Equations

5

Minor matters of dramaturgy oftentimes reveal a playwright's assumptions as clearly as do his essential choices. Until now I have examined Shakespeare's dialogues, which I take to be the results of essential choices in plotting his stories. Now I want to supplement this approach by examining two minor matters of technique which will give further clarification to Shakespeare's assumptions about mimetic and didactic drama. The two topics, the extent of a character's awareness and the use of comic attitudes toward serious events, are unrelated to one another; yet they happen to fall into similar patterns that disclose something of the way Shakespeare's principles work. His earliest characters, for instance, appear to be governed by tacit moral equations. That is, how much they know depends upon their moral character. Likewise, the audience's attitude toward characters is governed by a similar equation: they are sympathetic to the good and antipathetic toward the wicked. These equations obviously do not hold for the later mimetic plays. The immediate explanation for this break would be that the narrative itself rather than its moral significance makes first claim upon Shakespeare. To get beyond this proposition, I have more than once stated figuratively that Shakespeare turns over decisions to his characters in the later apprentice plays. It is this figurative statement that needs further examination. It means, in effect, that Shakespeare takes into serious account how the characters view events.

To take the characters' viewpoints into serious account is to abandon any authoritative interpreter of events and to dramatize events that defy authoritative interpretation. What the characters say and feel gives events their significance, not what the playwright imposes from above upon events. Mimetic drama, which fosters the particularities of narrative, operates on the assumption that human experience cannot be cut to a pattern of moral concepts. Something is always left over. The audience participates by weaving its way through a number of partial judgments to reach its own final, if not conclusive, judgment. Inevitably mimetic drama generates a multiplicity of judgments. That Shakespeare accepts this fact can be seen from the few times he depicts an audience on stage. In *Love's Labor's Lost, A Midsummer Night's Dream,* and *Hamlet*, he shows all to clearly how reactions vary. By contrast the public orators like Marc Antony, Menenius, or Sicinius and Junius Brutus produce unanimous responses from their listeners, as does the orator playwright who tailors his narratives to establish a clear didactic reaction. Yet we cannot infer that Shakespeare throws up his hands when he undertakes mimetic drama and assumes that anything goes. Obviously there are more and less adequate responses in the audience just as there are on stage. The loss of uniformity in response is balanced by heightened moral awareness. Whereas the earlier rhetorically structured chronicles confirm the audience's moral sentiments, the later mimetic chronicles show that categories are not clear-cut, that moral rules cannot be applied to human experience in absolute measure. In the earlier chronicles, judgments come easily because even the most apparently neutral decisions of dramaturgy have moral significance.[1] In the later, Shakespeare retreats and allows the characters to struggle with partial judgments not unlike the way an audience does in its everyday life.

∽

That the wicked are secretive and the good speak their minds are the first facts to notice about the characters' awareness in the early chronicles. In *1 Henry VI* Bedford, Talbot, Exeter, Henry VI, and Sir William Lucy are plain speakers with nothing to hide, whereas the Bishop of Winchester informs the audience at the end of the opening scene about his secret plan to gain control of the young King and rule the commonwealth. Again in Act V, scene i, he tells the audience that he will either triumph over Duke Humphrey or "sack this country with mutiny." Since nothing comes of either soliloquy, we can only infer that Shakespeare intends the sheer activity of plotting to characterize him as wicked. In the anecdotal intrigues, one inserted into *1 Henry VI* to characterize Talbot, another inserted into *2 Henry VI* to characterize Duke Humphrey, the plotters fail to get their way. The Countess of Auvergne plans to trap Talbot, but he manages to outsmart her (*1 Henry VI,* II.iii.); Simpcox tries to deceive Henry VI by claiming a miraculous gift of sight, but

Duke Humphrey exposes his pretense by a few shrewd questions (2 *Henry VI*, II.i). An equation of goodness with awareness is not out of keeping with didactic drama which assumes that enlightenment fosters virtuous behavior.

Yet a difficulty arises because if an intrigue is to be plausible, the victims must not know what the intriguers (and maybe the audience) know. Shakespeare, however, cannot bring himself to dramatize his good characters as being unaware, a fact that reveals something of his early assumptions about the way an audience sympathizes, since dramatic irony tends to pull them toward the characters who know and away from the ignorant. Major plotters, such as York in 2 *Henry VI*, achieve success over virtuous characters, but when the occasion arises for denunciation, others know the plotters' secrets without benefit of discovery scenes. In 2 *Henry VI* in addition to York's plot, Margaret and Suffolk plot the murder of Duke Humphrey; Jack Cade plots a rebellion. Warwick and Henry VI know immediately that Suffolk is guilty of Duke Humphrey's murder; when the unnamed captain denounces Suffolk, he knows not only about the murder, but also about his love for Queen Margaret, a matter which we in the audience assume to be of the utmost secrecy even to the court and certainly not familiar to humbler citizens. Likewise, at Bury St. Edmunds when Suffolk, Cardinal Beaufort, and York accuse Duke Humphrey, he answers by exposing with such accuracy their personal ambitions and secret intentions that it startles us how he knows his enemies so well. His denunciations raise a problem of verisimilitude not so much about the means of his enlightenment, for we can assume an offstage discovery as well as shrewd guesses, as about Henry VI's passivity before his truth. We wonder why the King permits the good Duke's arrest and can answer only tautologically that Henry VI is weak. Shakespeare is more concerned to preserve the good Duke's superiority in the accusation scene than he is to motivate the King.

The rebellious Jack Cade is transparent to all, good and wicked alike. Shakespeare's interest in making Cade's deceptions clear to his followers leaves open the problem, mentioned earlier, of Cade's success. Why would they follow such an obvious charlatan? We assume that their greed for spoils overcomes any scruples about their leader, but this is our assumption rather than a decision embodied in dialogue. Shakespeare could have written discovery scenes in which Henry VI finds out about the guilt of Suffolk or Duke Humphrey learns the plans of his enemies, but his interest lies more in composing public scenes of accusation and defense than in scenes of discovery, the facts of which the audience already knows. To plot discovery scenes would be to place the need for the characters to know before the audience's. In that case, Shakespeare would be taking the characters' viewpoints seriously. By assuming knowledge on the part of the good characters, Shakespeare puts his audience first, composing dialogues of didactic clarity between accuser and accused to stimulate their indignation or approval.

He plots events "from above," as it were, rather than from the characters' points of view. It is easy, for instance, to see how events in *2 Henry VI* could be slightly modified to take account of the intriguer York's point of view. Since at the end of the first scene he reveals himself to the audience as ambitious for the throne and in Act V defeats the King's forces at St. Albans, it would be possible to keep him in the forefront of the audience's attention and to organize many of the events around his gradual rise in power. The plotting would acquaint us with his intimate feelings about events, his anticipations, his plans, his reactions. Duke Humphrey's fall in Act III, for example, is crucial to York's rise. Yet the accusations before the parliament at Bury St. Edmunds, Act III, scene i, take place through a centralized dialogue. Our attention moves from Margaret to Suffolk to Henry VI so that York remains only one among the accusers. We do not hear how he personally feels during the episode. Afterwards he announces his further plans in soliloquy, but these arise more as a consequence of the messenger from Ireland than from Duke Humphrey's emprisonment. One can say that a centralized dialogue of accusation fits Shakespeare's intention to dramatize collective responsibility for the murder of Duke Humphrey and the collective anguish that results. Yet this is to acknowledge the playwright's position above his characters'. Had Shakespeare been interested in building the plot around York's rise, he probably would have kept him before our eyes in Act IV rather than turn over the stage completely to Jack Cade. As it stands, while we know from York's soliloquy that Cade acts as his surrogate and while we grant that the chaotic scenes of rebellion are superbly created, suitable to their own mode, we could have witnessed a scene between York and Cade, planning their tactics. Even a momentary dialogue between them would consolidate York's central position by vivifying what we hear only in soliloquy. But enough speculation on what might have been.

Richard III is the first of the noncomic plays to take advantage of characters' points of view. The comedies from the outset of Shakespeare's career exhibit control of discrepant awareness. As Harry Levin has noted, *Errors* is plotted mainly from the position of the stranger twin in a new city rather than from that of the local twin irritated by events which do not go according to customary pattern.[2] *Shrew* is plotted from Petruchio's vantage point so that we learn of his plans and are not privy to Katharina's intimate responses. The reasons why comic stories encourage plotting by strict lines of awareness will emerge later; here it need only be said that Shakespeare never conceives them as having the same high rhetorical purpose that the Henry VI plays have. In taking seriously the various characters' points of view when he comes to *Richard III,* he does not abandon high moral purpose, maybe because of the experience he has gained from writing comedies, maybe because he takes as a model for Richard the Vice figure whose success demands secrecy. We are drawn by the magnetism of Richard's comic exuberance and cannot avoid seeing the initial episodes of the play from his angle of vision. He tells us his plans to murder Clarence and woo Lady Anne, and he comments to us intermittently about his successes. It is here that Shakespeare's early equation of awareness and goodness breaks down, although not entirely because Richard's victims—except the two young princes whom we do not watch being killed—one way or another get what they deserve. Our feelings not only toward Richard but to his victims become complicated by an involvement that does not agree with our moral judgments.

Plotting to take account of a character's point of view can be restated as plotting to capitalize upon a natural property of drama, that is, irony. This means, among other things, to create a complex emotional experience, for the audience is drawn to the character, regardless of his moral sentiments, who knows more. The relationship may not be one of approval, but the bond of shared information overrides feelings of approval or disapproval to establish a kinship. This kinship can be intensified by arranging the order of introductions and the distribution of soliloquies. Inevitably the first character on stage claims our interest—as Richard or Iago does—and it is with some effort that the playwright breaks this claim. When a character confides in us about his secret plans, he usually makes us conspirators. The plotting of *1 Henry VI,* on the other hand, never breaks the equation of sympathy with approval for Talbot or antipathy with disapproval for Joan. Our attitude toward them remains constant and uncomplicated. Even though Joan plots to take Rouen, Act III, scene ii, and informs us beforehand, Shakespeare arranges events without exploiting the irony of her superior information. She executes her plan immediately so that she enjoys only a brief moment of superiority over her enemies. However, Richard of Gloucester enjoys his superior position for many scenes. Like the villain-hero Barabas, the Jew of Malta, Richard draws us into his ken and allows us to experience vicariously his irresponsible release from moral strictures while he triumphs. The plotting permits us to indulge some of our anarchic impulses within a narrative of poetic justice that exorcises them at the end when the ghosts reassert Richard's moral responsibility and when Richmond triumphs. Of course, we never forget Richard's villainy when we share his point of view. The plotting encourages us to take a hypothetical stance to entertain a fictional narrative as if it were happening. The partial point of view draws us in temporarily, permitting us to experience a range of emotions and viewpoints that we would scarcely allow ourselves in everyday life. In this way mimetic drama operates upon us in its distinctive capacity, turning us into an audience rather than into a congregation or a class of pupils.

While our interest in Richard does not coincide with our approval, our reaction to Lady Anne, his victim, is equally difficult to square with moral equations. No doubt most of us regret and even sympathize while we watch over Richard's shoulder as he seduces her by his artful rhetoric. Yet when Richard reminds us after the event in soliloquy how quickly she has forgotten her good husband and her father-in-law, we shift again, modifying our attitude in a way that Joan or Talbot never demand of us. But it is in the episodes dramatizing Hastings's entrapment and death that Shakespeare creates the most complex effects with irony, effects of morbid humor unlike anything in the Henry VI plays. His two scenes, Act III, scene ii and iv, are prefaced by Richard's plan to test his friendship by a visit from Catesby. If Hastings will not agree to the Protector's coronation, then "Chop off his head!" (III.i.193). When Catesby sounds him out, Hastings fails the test by saying,

I'll have this crown of mine cut from my shoulders
Before I'll see the crown so foul misplaced.

(III.ii.43–44)

Shakespeare phrases his remark, of course, to echo Richard's earlier hypothetical command and to underline its irony. Even so, it would be less ironic if the scene did not open with a messenger from Lord Stanley warning Hastings of danger. Shakespeare appears to miss no opportunity to exploit the irony of Hastings's blindness so that we cannot avoid being amused at a very unamusing matter of life and death. In the same scene, for instance,

Catesby
'Tis a vile thing to die, my gracious lord,
When men are unprepared and look not for it.

Hastings
O monstrous, monstrous! and so falls it out
With Rivers, Vaughan, Grey; and so 'twill do
With some men else, that think themselves as safe
As thou and I, who (as thou know'st) are dear
To princely Richard and to Buckingham.

(III.ii.62–68)

The following council scene depends equally upon broad innuendo and unintentional irony. The fact that the dialogue of this public group scene lacks the high rhetorical style weighted with auricular figures, ceremonious address, and balanced response indicates what Shakespeare feels about the inherent dramatic interest in the double meanings. The ironic force of the dialogue relieves the need for the typical formality of style to be found in the usual public scene.

Buckingham
We know each other's faces; for our hearts,
He knows no more of mine than I of yours;
Or I of his, my lord, than you of mine.
Lord Hastings, you and he are near in love.

Hastings
I thank his grace, I know he [Richard] loves me well.

(III.iv.10–14)

Shakespeare continues to mine this vein:

Hastings
His grace looks cheerfully and smooth this morning;
There's some conceit or other likes him well
When that he bids good morrow with such spirit.
I think there's never a man in Christendom
Can lesser hide his love or hate than he,
For by his face straight shall you know his heart.

Derby
What of his heart perceive you in his face
By any livelihood he showed to-day?

Hastings
Marry, that with no man here he is offended.

(III.iv.48–56)

Through all of this discussion the audience knows that Richard plans to condemn Hastings to death. Such pointed discrepancies between intended meaning and real meaning are both easy and conventional. Pedringano's banter with the hangman (*The Spanish Tragedy*, III.vi) or Barabas's dialogue with Ithamore and Bellamira as he urges them to sniff the poisoned flowers (*The Jew of Malta*, V.i) come immediately to mind. But Shakespeare does not avail himself of this severe irony until he relaxes the orator's control over plotting that is guided by moral equations.

While the audience might from its vantage point of extra awareness pity Hastings's helplessness, it cannot avoid some alignment with his amused opponents who mislead him with their pious mockery. Yet an amused attitude is not quite adequate for Hastings's experience. After he is condemned, he undergoes a discovery, recalling the warnings, recognizing the pattern of punishment for his sins, and becomes morally aware of himself. Such discoveries become possible when Shakespeare plots his narratives to take account of the characters' points of view and preserve the boundaries of awareness. What characters know differentiates them; but so does their capacity to learn. The fact that so many characters in *Richard III* — Clarence, Rivers, Grey, Vaughan, Hastings, Lady Anne, Queen Elizabeth, and Buckingham — experience moments of moral awareness about their past deeds suggests the impact of technique upon subject matter. In the earlier Henry VI plays characters go to their deaths on stage, moments when it is natural to survey the past and comment upon one's life, with no regrets for their past deeds. To take the immediately preceding play, *3 Henry VI*, the three main participants in the civil war who die on stage, York, Clifford, and Warwick, never judge their past behavior.

Richard III exhibits more than local ironies, for discrepant awareness lies at the very heart of Richard's career. It becomes clear, as events unfold, that while Richard is hewing his way to the throne of England, he is unintentionally doing the work of Providence by punishing those treacherous participants in the War of the Roses, scourging England in preparation for renewed health under the Tudor monarch. Queen Margaret senses a pattern in events, and others discern parts of it. The audience sees more of the pattern than Margaret, for it witnesses the dreams before Bosworth Field and Richmond's final speech of victory when he announces the union of the two houses with his marriage to Elizabeth of York.[3] Shakespeare plots Richard III's career to take account of varying degrees of awareness so that even Richard, crafty-smart though he is, does not see all. On the other hand, when no one can sum up "the" meaning of events, as we find to be the case in the later mimetic plays, it follows that Shakespeare feels no urgency to protect the good characters against ignorance. Romeo and Juliet, to take the obvious example, never learn what the chorus tells the audience in the opening lines of the play, that their love is "star-crossed" and will end their parents' strife.

∞

An awareness beyond the awareness of facts, difficult to describe because it encompasses moral principles, practical judgment, and sensitivity to the feelings of others, becomes crucial to the plotting of Shakespeare's later mimetic plays. By taking seriously into account this awareness—I shall for the sake of brevity call it "moral awareness"—Shakespeare particularizes his narrative and discourages ready didactic judgments in his audience. *Richard II*, for instance, is plotted to take into serious account different degrees of moral awareness in characters engaged in deposing a king. The attitudes of Bolingbroke and Richard himself, the judgments of Carlisle, York, and Gaunt, all combine to give us a complicated view of the central events, none of which is entirely adequate, but none of which can be disregarded in our response to the deposition. It would be possible to describe similar attitudes at work in the contemporaneous *Romeo and Juliet*. While the two young lovers' attitudes toward love attract our greatest interest and affection, we sentimentalize the play if their awareness becomes the one we ourselves assume. Friar Laurence's judgments cannot be entirely discounted, nor should the attitude of the Capulets toward socially arranged marriages. Each viewpoint has its shortcomings, and while the lovers' attitude—perhaps I should say "attitudes," since Juliet views things somewhat differently from Romeo—is the most appealing, it contains an element of recklessness that De Rougement and Mahood have explicated for us. For purposes of comparison, it is better to confine this discussion to *Richard II*, which can be measured against earlier chronicle plays.

One may immediately object that any drama takes into account the characters' moral awareness so that the plotting of *Richard II* is no more or less mimetic or didactic than *2 Henry VI*, where Shakespeare includes the judgments of York, Suffolk, and Margaret about the death of Duke Humphrey, or *1 Henry VI* where characters pluck roses in the Temple Garden. Yet the differences in moral awareness of the characters who pluck roses count for less than the fact that they choose to be either for or against Richard Plantagenet. As we watch the responses to the murder of Duke Humphrey in *2 Henry VI*, we generalize from them to the issue of right against wrong. Even though York's reason for the

good Duke's death differs from Suffolk's or the Cardinal's, these differences matter less than the collective selfishness in ridding the commonwealth of the one figure who prevents them from falling into civil strife.
The difference between the characters' opinions about the death of
Duke Humphrey and the characters' attitudes about the deposition of
Richard II is a difference between a multiplicity of voices and a multiplicity of judgments.

While it is easy to make a case for the relative unimportance of differing attitudes in the Temple Garden scene, it is harder, for instance,
in *3 Henry VI*, where the experience of shifting loyalties and treachery is
a primary dramatic issue. Yet even in this later play Shakespeare encourages us to generalize immediately from the particular opinion to
the moral pattern. In Act III, scene iii, to take a central episode in
which Warwick shifts allegiance from Edward IV to Queen Margaret,
Shakespeare arranges dialogue so that Warwick's interpretation of his
change is shown finally to be negligible. The scene takes place in the
court of Lewis of France. Margaret and Prince Edward request aid from
Lewis to support their opposition to Edward IV; then Warwick enters,
an emissary from Edward, to arrange his marriage to the Lady Bona.
Lewis entertains Warwick's proposal until interrupted by a messenger
with news that Edward IV has married Lady Grey. In anger, Warwick
vows allegiance to Queen Margaret, and the scene concludes with their
planning, together with Oxford and Lewis, to attack the York forces.
The episode depends upon a variety of viewpoints, the central one being
Warwick's. Until the arrival of the messenger, the issue discussed is the
legitimacy of the English king. Oxford accuses Warwick of treason to a
king he obeyed for thirty-six years. Warwick retorts and urges Oxford to
"leave Henry and call Edward king." Oxford explains the basis of his
loyalty:

Call him my king by whose injurious doom
My elder brother, the Lord Aubrey Vere,
Was done to death? and more than so, my father,
Even in the downfall of his mellowed years,
When nature brought him to the door of death?
No, Warwick, no! While life upholds this arm,
This arm upholds the house of Lancaster.

(III.iii.101–7)

He bases his loyalty upon personal history rather than upon any theoretical conviction about the true king. With this speech in mind, we are
primed to compare Warwick's motive for change after he reads the

letter announcing the marriage of Edward IV to Lady Grey:

King Lewis, I here protest in sight of heaven
And by the hope I have in heavenly bliss
That I am clear from this misdeed of Edward's—
No more my king, for he dishonors me.

(III.iii.181-84)

Had the plotting of events included some earlier scene that dramatizes Warwick's dedication to honor, the audience would generalize less easily about his reason for change of allegiance. While we have no reason to doubt his sincerity—honor is as plausible a value to explain his behavior as any—Warwick's explanation fits with Oxford's reason for loyalty to Henry VI, or for that matter, Edward's sudden attraction to Lady Grey or Clarence's anger at his brother and defection to Warwick, dramatized in the immediately preceding scene. All act from personal motives rather than from objective standards that would stabilize their political behavior. After experiencing this multiplicity of opinions, the audience arrives at a general position, something like this: personal motives should not interfere with loyalty to one's king, or civil strife arises when subjects replace loyalty to their king by private desires.

If the audience of *Richard II* fails to take into account the different attitudes and judgments of Bolingbroke, York, Northumberland, and Aumerle, but lumps them together as inadequate, they will see the deposition simplistically as a sin against God's anointed. Shakespeare, however, balances gains against losses so that events do not confirm Carlisle's interpretation as absolute. The Bishop of Carlisle is spokesman for the orthodox interpretation of divine right and opposes the deposition of Richard II in vivid terms: "The blood of English shall manure the ground / And future ages groan for this foul act" (IV.i. 137-38). Earlier, upon Richard's return from Ireland, the Bishop bolsters his flagging spirits by similar forceful speeches about his rightful position as king. His prophecy to Bolingbroke, ". . . this land [shall] be called / The field of Golgotha and dead men's skulls" (IV.i.143-44), does indeed come true with the War of the Roses, foreshadowed in the play by Aumerle's attempt at rebellion. Should he not, then, be taken as the choral commentator of the play?

Had Shakespeare plotted Richard II's career to affirm this interpretation, he could have supported it by characterizing Bolingbroke as a clear ambitious villain. At no point does Bolingbroke confide to the audience his aspirations for kingship even though it would have been a simple matter of a short soliloquy or a brief aside, additions which Shakespeare does not hesitate to supply elsewhere. One might retort that Bolingbroke's actions speak for themselves. Yet it is Richard who submits to his cousin. A hundred lines before the King comes "down, down. . . like glist'ring Phaeton," (III.iv.178) Bolingbroke sends a request for his inheritance:

Henry Bolingbroke
On both his knees doth kiss King Richard's hand
And sends allegiance and true faith of heart
To his most royal person; hither come
Even at his feet to lay my arms and power,
Provided that my banishment repealed
And lands restored again be freely granted.

(III.iii.35–41)

That his inheritance is rightful Shakespeare establishes by York, who earlier warns Richard of the danger in taking from his cousin what belongs to him by ancestry:

Take Hereford's rights away, and take from Time
His charters and his customary rights;
Let not to-morrow then ensue to-day;
Be not thyself—for how art thou a king
But by fair sequence and succession?

(II.i.195–99)

If Bolingbroke speaks of his intention more for effect than from conviction, Shakespeare could have made it clear by a brief aside. One can object again that Bolingbroke's public words do not necessarily coincide with his private thoughts so that while we hear no explicit aside, we do well not to take his remarks at face value. If one is cautious—and I am willing to grant that the circumstances as well as Bolingbroke's other behavior in the play encourage us to be cautious—this highly sensitized attitude gives additional evidence of the way Shakespeare's plotting here works on the audience. It puts us on the qui vive for the possibility of suppressed meaning, and at the same time warns us against any final judgment of Bolingbroke based on his intentions.[1]

While we may be uncertain about his intentions, Bolingbroke's actions show him to be a more efficient ruler than Richard. Shakespeare arranges parallel situations in order to measure the two rulers against each other (rather than against some abstract standard of good management). At the beginning of Act IV, a strategic place just before the deposition scene, Bolingbroke faces a problem of allowing his first cousin Aumerle to go into trial by combat for the death of their uncle Woodstock, the same predicament which opens the play. Before the dilemma where both alternatives are disagreeable, it is a mark of prudence to avoid choice and hope that in time the dilemma vanishes. Certainly Elizabethans had acquaintance with such temporizing—some would say indecisiveness—by their Queen. Bolingbroke first attempts to postpone any trial by combat until the Duke of Norfolk returns from exile. Carlisle says that he is dead, a fact that makes explicit Bolingbroke's strategy, for in spite of this information he continues to postpone combat, and we hear nothing more of it. Earlier Richard II wants to take the same course and avoid exposing his first cousin and friend to trial by combat, but he lacks authority or prudence to back up his statement, "We were not born to sue, but to command" (I.i.195). At the end of the play our impression of the usurper king is one of qualified wrongdoing, borne out by his forgiveness of Aumerle and a plan for a crusade to the Holy Land in repentance of his implication in Richard's murder. It seems unlikely that Essex's followers would have asked for a performance of this play the night before they marched on London had Bolingbroke impressed them as a clear villain.

The Bishop of Carlisle is not the only character who talks about the role of Providence in human affairs. When the Duchess of Gloucester, for instance, urges John of Gaunt to revenge the death of her husband and his brother, he twice says that he leaves the solution up to heaven, statements that occur at the outset of the play:

But since correction lieth in those hands
Which made the fault that we cannot correct,
Put we our quarrel to the will of heaven,
Who, when they see the hours ripe on earth,
Will rain hot vengeance on offenders' heads.

(I.ii.4–8)

He predicts, in other words, that Richard, guilty of murder, will be punished by Heaven. As if to enforce the point, Shakespeare adds another, more specific statement:

God's is the quarrel; for God's substitute,
His deputy anointed in his sight,
Hath caused his death; the which if wrongfully,
Let heaven revenge.

(I.ii.37–40)

These comments do not contradict Carlisle's interpretation so much as they supplement it. The fact that God's anointed representative is deposed by mortals does not mean that God remains helpless before man's behavior, nor does it mean that Providence is denied by man's willful actions. We see instead that God's mysterious pattern is affirmed even through mortal opposition to the human embodiment of His authority. Consequently, a startling juxtaposition in Act III makes sense. On his return from Ireland, Richard, confident that his sancity will protect him, says:

God for his Richard hath in heavenly pay
A glorious angel. Then, if angels fight,
Weak men must fall; for heaven still guards the right.

(III.ii.60–62)

At this very moment Salisbury enters to announce that all Richard's Welsh supporters, twelve thousand men, have abandoned him. Without any need of the supplementary comments by a Gaunt or a York, the audience could see this news a mockery of Richard's claim to divine sanction. Still later when York reports the populace's cruel treatment of Richard on his entry into London, he says:

That, had not God for some strong purpose steeled
The hearts of men, they must perforce have melted
And barbarism itself have pitied him.
But heaven hath a hand in these events,
To whose high will we bound our calm contents.

(V.ii.34–38)

M. M. Reese finds such passages so convincing that he makes the murder of Woodstock, an event that occurs before the beginning of the play, the cause of Richard's downfall.[5]

For a playwright to take seriously the characters' moral awareness is not only to plot events to include several plausible interpretations of events; it is to acknowledge that interpretations themselves have the status of events. A character's change of awareness can become a viable dramatic experience. At the center of the play Richard comes to an awareness that adversely affects his behavior. In Act III, scene ii, once he has learned, detail by detail, the loss of his troops and supporters, he sinks to the ground in despair to "tell sad stories of the death of kings." In this condition, facing death, he sees no difference between himself and other men:

Throw away respect,
Tradition, form, and ceremonious duty;
For you have but mistook me all this while.
I live with bread like you, feel want, taste grief,
Need friends. Subjected thus,
How can you say to me I am a king?

(III.ii.172–77)

135

In short, he makes a distinction between kingship and his private self, a distinction that enables him to give away his crown. Without this separation, of course, it would be impossible for him to resign his state to Bolingbroke. Later he learns the error of his distinction between his role and his manhood. During the deposition scene he wonders what name he now has, and later in his soliloquy, the only one he is given in the play, he surveys his life, judges his behavior, and comes to a realization:

> But whate'er I be,
> Nor I, nor any man that but man is,
> With nothing shall be pleased till he be eased
> With being nothing.
>
> (V.v.38–41)

This is to say that manhood alone is inadequate in this world; without a role, no man can be content until he be eased with being nothing.[6] To state the proposition another way, fulfilling one's role is the one possible source of contentment that man can enjoy in this world. Richard, having given up his role, is consequently free to assume any number of roles in his imagination but his role is God-given, not a matter of free choice, a fact that applies not only to him but to Bolingbroke.

Such moments of discovery differ from discoveries of fact as Henry VI experiences when he learns of Duke Humphrey's death. Henry VI's discovery has no effect upon his moral outlook. Change of moral awareness becomes important to the plotting of *Richard III* when Richard's numerous victims become aware of their past sins. Yet these moments occur, as it were, on the periphery rather than at the center of the drama, which concerns the rise and fall of Richard. Richard II's interpretation has such an effect upon events that his moral awareness itself becomes a dramatic event, another way of saying that Shakespeare takes into serious account a character's viewpoint.[7]

As we weave our way through the complexities of events and opinions, fitting one comment against another, we sense the costs as well as the advantages of a divine-right monarch. What does it mean to be ruled by a king who combines God's sanction with all too human inadequacies? Shakespeare complicates his answer by having the King participate in his own unkinging and by showing the usurper to be a competent ruler. Our sympathies with the unkinged King combine with our disapproval, and our disapproval of Bolingbroke combines with respect for him. The difficulties of a clear-cut judgment about events are reflected in the episode of Aumerle's treachery, already mentioned. Juxtaposed to the scene of Richard's death, it foreshadows the struggle between the houses of York and Lancaster, but at the same time it characterizes Henry IV as a restrained and forgiving king.

Although no character in the play can be said to interpret the full complexity of events, York comes closest to the level-headed participant who gives each side its due. Like John of Gaunt, he is Richard's uncle and at the outset of the play establishes himself as adviser to the young, foolish King, who does not heed his warning about the dangers of appropriating Bolingbroke's inheritance. When Richard leaves for Ireland, he appoints York his deputy, whose consequent behavior casts his role as choral figure into question. He tries to raise a force to oppose the return of Bolingbroke, but it is unsuccessful. When he confronts his rebellious nephew, he denounces him as a traitor to the King and sums up his position in these words:

> . . . my power is weak and all ill left;
> But if I could, by him that gave me life,
> I would attach you all and make you stoop
> Unto the sovereign mercy of the king;
> But since I cannot, be it known unto you
> I do remain as neuter. So fare you well —
> Unless you please to enter in the castle
> And there repose you for this night.

(II.iii.154-61)

This passage could be construed as the posturing of a hypocrite, but it can better be seen as a dramatic counterpart of the attitude which the audience must take toward events. York acknowledges the claims of divine right and the consequent proper behavior of the King's subjects, and at the same time recognizes that practical circumstances prevent him from doing anything about it. Lacking the power to apprehend his nephew as a traitor, he accepts the fact that the offender is still his nephew, who has also been wronged, and offers him shelter for the night. He never denies Richard's right to kingship, but after the King has submitted to Bolingbroke and given up the crown, York tenders his undivided loyalty to the new King, illegitimate though he is, for he recognizes that Henry IV is the alternative to chaos. In Act V York, strenuous to the point of cruelty, insists that the new King show no mercy to his son who is a traitor. Here he can affect circumstances where before, in Act II, he is helpless before them. We cannot therefore generalize about his behavior by saying that he sacrifices principle to circumstance and chooses always the easier course. That critics have disagreed over York's behavior indicates something of the complexity of this drama and the demands which it makes upon our attention.[8]

In short, York's behavior and judgment show that the principle of divine right should indeed guide public behavior, but that it is an ideal standard which circumstances make difficult to uphold. We see how men ought to behave and how in practice they do behave, failing to live up to the ideal through human weaknesses and uncontrollable circumstances. Richard should have maintained his God-given role, and Bolingbroke should have remained his loyal subject. But Richard rules imprudently, even sinfully in killing his uncle, and Bolingbroke, a popular member of the royal family and a practical ruler, seizes the opportunity to be king which Richard helps bring about. By refusing to simplify events, Shakespeare realizes the peculiarly dramatic potentialities of his medium which lacks an authoritative narrator and which can present at least two plausible sides to an issue.[9]

In Shakespeare's earliest chronicles, moral equations hold between good characters and the audience's sympathy because he shapes events to embody moral laws. Given the power of dramatic irony to draw an audience to take sides with the knowing against the ignorant, he hesitates to allow his good characters to be ignorant, since it is desirable to encourage an audience to rejoice in their successes and regret their failures. Moral equations break down in mimetic dramas not because Shakespeare becomes perverse and encourages his audience to favor the wicked but because he accepts the fact that moral law does not relate to human behavior according to clear patterns. The good may or may not know facts; our sympathies may lie with the mistaken and ignorant when the play renders the difficulties that characters face in living up to proper standards. To dramatize these difficulties, Shakespeare takes seriously the point of view of his characters; they struggle to make the sorts of decisions which he makes when he fashions didactic drama. Like Lucrece, who sees Tarquin's ethical problem as one of putting into practice ethical standards rather than one of discovering what the standards are, so York, who acknowledges the proper behavior of subjects to their king, struggles with a situation where the King himself fails to behave according to standards. It is no accident, I think, that the topic of mercy becomes a central issue in Shakespeare's dramas that follow the rhetorically didactic plays. Justice lends itself to straightforward application, and in *Richard III* we watch Richard's victims being punished for their sins. Later Portia pleads with Shylock to take into account the particularities of Antonio's case and forgive him. To be merciful is to acknowledge the importance of individual circumstances. So too Shakespeare takes into account mitigating circumstances when he plots the moral behavior of characters in his later mimetic plays.

∞

In the early chronicles Shakespeare's use of comic episodes and comic attitudes follows the same moral dictates as his use of discrepant awareness. Our laughter coincides with our disapproval; it is not mixed with concern or sympathy. Sidney in the *Apology for Poetry* talked of two possible responses to comedy, a laughter of scorn and a feeling of delight. The comic moments in Shakespeare's earliest chronicles produce only the laughter of scorn. Two patterns of dialogue evoke this response at its least complex. During the quarrel scenes, for instance, we may laugh when characters degrade one another with witty epithets. In another type of dialogue, observers stand aside and ridicule characters to stimulate our laughter, an arrangement that Shakespeare uses especially to dramatize wrong-headed courtships. In *1 Henry VI* when Joan is engaged in persuading the Dauphin to appoint her leader of his troops, Alencon and Regnier stand aside and speculate on their behavior (I.ii.118–23), attributing sexual motives to the Dauphin and causing us to laugh. A fuller version occurs in *3 Henry VI* when Clarence and Richard stand aside to observe Edward IV's courtship of Lady Grey (III.ii). The same pattern serves to deflate Jack Cade's oration to his followers, a dialogue already discussed. If we look afield to *Two Gentlemen of Verona*, Julia stands aside in her disguise as a page and deflates Sir Thurio whom Proteus is reassuring about his courtship of Silvia (V.ii). When Suffolk courts Margaret in *1 Henry VI*, Shakespeare varies the arrangement, allowing Margaret herself to stand aside and deliver witty comments upon Suffolk while he meditates in asides upon his plan to woo her for himself in the name of the King (V.iii). In all these dialogues of double viewpoints, the laughter created by the detached observer is scornful, and in all cases Shakespeare generates our disapproval for the characters engaged in courtship. In none do we feel any uneasiness about our laughter, for the characters' behavior is indeed wrong, and we agree with the observers who ridicule them.

Any full discussion of the way Shakespeare puts comedy to use in his early serious plays would raise an issue about genre and recall Sidney's almost contemporaneous dictum against mixing hornpipes and funerals, but I confine myself here to what the comic episodes disclose about Shakespeare's early apprenticeship. A full discussion would be complicated by the influence of the popular native tradition of the morality play that does not fall into classical patterns of comedy and tragedy and by the chronicle plays which the editors of the first folio classified as a third genre. One way to deal quickly with the issue is to say that Shakespeare has less interest in the prescriptions of genre than in entertaining his audience. This would assume that Shakespeare takes entertainment to be something apart from generic considerations, an assumption that his dramaturgy scarcely supports. Heming and Condell grouped his plays according to genre, and even though we find them fumbling with *Troilus and Cressida* or *Cymbeline,* their classifications are generally serviceable. As the next chapter will argue, Shakespeare takes very seriously at the outset of his career the prescriptions of sixteenth-century humanists' program of education that places the utmost stress upon the discipline of rhetoric. Fundamental to their prescriptions is the principle of decorum which the orator breaks at his peril. The playwright can break the principle while still taking it quite seriously, as we see Shakespeare doing in the case of Lord Say's oration to the Kentishmen. Sidney declares a mixture of hornpipes and funerals to be improper. Had he been a playwright, he might well have considered that improprieties can be dramatically effective.

Hastings's ironic dialogues in *Richard III*, while not precisely what Sidney had in mind, stimulate a sense of impropriety in the audience. The discrepancy between what Hastings knows and what we know produces an attitude which, if we do not laugh, keeps us at a distance from him so that we do not take his experience, a matter of life and death, with the kind of seriousness it would otherwise demand. Normally we define as serious whatever threatens man's well-being or his capacity for happiness. Yet the arrangement of Hastings's dialogue militates against this normal response. Many of the comic episodes in Shakespeare's earliest chronicles and tragic plays create this same unsettling effect. We laugh or almost laugh while at the same time feel that perhaps we should not. Our sense of impropriety indicates that something is morally askew.[10]

In another matter of life and death, the trial by combat between Horner and his servant Peter in *2 Henry VI*, we are similarly discomforted by the comic depiction. Shakespeare creates a quasi-amused attitude toward the event, not by using unintentional irony in the manner of Hastings, but by a purposeful flattening of style.[11] So too neither the cowardice of Peter nor the drunkenness of Horner leads us to suspect the sudden disaster. Later in the play Jack Cade's behavior stimulates our laughter even though it has, to say the least, serious consequences. He not only kills Sir Humphrey Stafford and defeats his forces; he delivers ruthless sentences against the unnamed follower who calls him "Cade" rather than "Lord Mortimer," the Clerk of Chatham for being able to write, Lord Say for his learning, and Say's son-in-law. Even at his most threatening, Cade never escapes ridicule from his followers.[12] It could be argued that although Cade's and Peter's behavior raises issues of life and death, Shakespeare assures us by making them comic that they are not to be taken seriously, that they are parodies of their betters,

140

examples of what happens in a commonwealth where the nobility is selfish and the King weak. It then follows that the lower class is presumptuous, no more than an irritant, a symptom of the real trouble, so that indecorum is the note to hit in rendering their behavior.

Such an explanation would conform to the sixteenth-century humanists' prescriptions about the proper dignity for characters of tragic stature, but it cannot take account of those episodes involving Richard of Gloucester, Aaron, or Saturninus which create a similar uneasiness in the audience. Theirs is an intentional impropriety arising from their refusal to take seriously what ought to be serious. Richard, for instance, says:

Simple plain Clarence, I do love thee so
That I will shortly send thy soul to heaven.

(*Richard III*, I.i.118-19)

Like the Vice figure he refuses to reckon with moral responsibility; unlike the Vice he eventually answers for his refusal. We in the audience cannot avoid participating in his attitude and, if we do not laugh, we cannot preserve the proper seriousness toward the funeral of Henry VI when Richard says:

But first I'll turn yon fellow in his grave.

(I.ii.260)

His typical style, a peculiar mixture of grandiloquence and colloquialisms, as Wolfgang Clemen has observed,[13] exhibits the kind of verbal humor that arises when serious rhetoric is placed in an inappropriate context. When Buckingham suggests that they ride to greet the young prince who journeys to London for his coronation, Richard phrases his response with copious overstatement that is as amusingly inappropriate as his understatement about sending Clarence to heaven:

My other self, my counsel's consistory,
My oracle, my prophet, my dear cousin,
I, as a child, will go by thy direction.
Toward Ludlow then, for we'll not stay behind.

(II.ii.151-54)

Buckingham, too, can generate a smokescreen of words with the same exuberance, as, for example, when he urges the crown upon a coy Richard, meditating between two divines. Although this "persuasion" and Richard's equally overstated protest concern the throne of England and the health of the nation, the verbosity of these two con men, displaying their excesses before a simple Lord Mayor, make us succumb to laughter, a laughter that measures our susceptibility to the power of

141

Richard. Yet our laughter is not the laughter of pleasure which comedy affords. Somewhere in the background is our awareness that we are laughing at events whose consequences are crucial. Gradually the tone changes when Richard becomes king. He takes on a tetchy, superstitious attitude and is troubled about Richmond, who reestablishes dramatic proprieties by a style which has been described by some as dull and conventional, too much seduced, no doubt, by Richard's vivacity to recognize the moral equation implicit in decorum.

Other comic episodes exhibit variations on the same equation between impropriety and immorality. In *1 Henry VI*, Joan, for instance, laughs at Sir William Lucy's style when he requests the body of Talbot by identifying it by some twelve titles:

Here is a silly stately style indeed!
The Turk, that two and fifty kingdoms hath,
Writes not so tedious a style as this.
Him that thou magnifi'st with all these titles,
Stinking and flyblown lies here at our feet.

(IV.vii.72-76)

Sir William Lucy's excesses generate Joan's sneer, but whereas he errs on the side of propriety, she ignores propriety. Even Coriolanus's enemies, who kill him, recognize his worth and give appropriate tribute to his corpse, but Joan's contempt argues a mean spirit. In *Titus Andronicus* Aaron exhibits one of his stylistic tricks of inappropriate understatement:

They cut thy sister's tongue, and ravished her,
And cut her hands, and trimmed her as thou sawest.
   Lucius
O detestable villain! call'st thou that trimming?

(V.i.92-94)

When Aaron kills the nurse, he says:

   Weeke, Weeke!
So cries a pig preparèd to the spit.

(IV.ii.146-47)

Shakespeare reverses this impropriety when he dramatizes Saturninus's sentence of death upon the old clown. The bumbling low comic figure who confuses "Jupiter" with "gibbet maker" becomes an inadvertent messenger for Titus Andronicus and delivers his arrows that carry pleas for justice. Appearing on the scene in Act IV after the slaughters and mutiliations, the clown strikes a homey note of everyday reality. When Saturninus, irritated by Andronicus's petition, sentences the clown to death, we are as shocked by his lack of proportion as we are by Aaron's. In both cases the disjunction between response and event strikes us as immoral.

In *Romeo and Juliet* and *Richard II* similar discrepancies occur between what is serious and the attitude taken toward it, but the audience's reaction cannot be described as either the laughter of scorn or an uneasy awareness that something is morally askew. Mercutio and Romeo crack jokes at the moment of death; Bolingbroke senses a ridiculousness in the very serious plea by the Duchess of York for the life of her son. We in the audience sense these dislocations as enriching the experience without evoking moral condemnation. Mercutio says:

Ask for me to-morrow, and you shall find me a grave man. I am peppered, I warrant, for this world.

(III.i.95-97)

and his attempt at a comic pun serves to strengthen the high seriousness. Likewise, Romeo shares something of Mercutio's lightness of heart when explaining why he will kill himself:

       Shall I believe
That unsubstantial Death is amorous,
And that the lean abhorrèd monster keeps
Thee here in dark to be his paramour?
For fear of that I still will stay with thee
And never from this pallet of dim night
Depart again.

(V.iii.102-8)

Near the end of *Richard II*, the Duchess of York pleads with Henry IV to spare Aumerle whom York has just revealed as a traitor. Her speeches, shaped by copious use of antithesis, recall Sir William Lucy's style in the way they exaggerate on the side of propriety. Like Joan, Henry IV reacts to the intense moment after York has urged no mercy for his son by saying:

Our scene is alt'red from a serious thing,
And now changed to "The Beggar and the King."

(V.iii.79-80)

We share his perspective and sense no indecorum in his comment that suddenly releases the tension created by the Duchess's plea.

These later characters do not attack someone else but treat lightly

143

their own serious predicaments and exhibit a detachment that in the earlier plays was the property only of opponents in confrontations or observers in ironic courtship scenes. The context or the plotting of the narrative prevents us from feeling any moral dislocations. From the general movement of the narrative we know the moral nature of the speakers and the seriousness of circumstances. Details of the story affect the way we interpret the manner of speech, not the manner of speech the way we judge the episode.[14] Perhaps the boldest example of sympathetic impropriety occurs in *Titus Andronicus* alongside the dislocations of moral uneasiness. Titus laughs after he has suffered the knowledge of his daughter's mutilation and the sacrifice of his own hand and is sent the heads of his two sons and his hand:

Marcus
Why dost thou laugh? it fits not with this hour.
Titus
Why, I have not another tear to shed.

(III.i.265–66)

Quite obviously we take our cue from the situation rather than Titus's style and sympathize rather than feel uneasy about the impropriety of his reaction.

One can generalize from the episodes by saying that as orator-playwright, Shakespeare assumes that the audience should be drawn to feel as the good characters feel and disapprove of the bad. As mimetic playwright he leads us to sympathize with the wrong-headed, such as Richard II, or be amused at the morally decent, such as the Duchess of York or Juliet's nurse. It might be taken as a rule of thumb that the persuasive tactics of didactic drama become offensive in a mimetic context. The more a character makes a direct appeal for our sympathy, displaying innocence, goodness, and suffering, the more we resent bestowing our favor. When the innocent, good, and suffering character, if there happens to be one so categorically perfect in a mimetic drama, makes light of his situation and turns his face from the immediacy of his anguish, we are unreserved in our sympathy. Decorum is governed by moral equations in the didactic chronicles, equations that are too restrictrive for mimetically conceived narratives. Even the earliest contemporaneous comedies of Shakespeare exhibit a sense of decorum more complicated than what we find in the Henry VI plays. It would seem that Shakespeare's practices in generating laughter by events of *The Comedy of Errors, The Taming of the Shrew,* and *Two Gentlemen of Verona* probably contribute to his practices in *Romeo and Juliet*, if not the earlier *Richard III*. To investigate this possible influence, we must turn to the principles that govern the plotting of these early comedies.

Neo-classical Stipulations

6

Critics have often remarked upon the wide variety among Shakespeare's earliest comedies and have interpreted it as evidence of his willingness to experiment. Bertrand Evans, for instance, finds the young playwright trying his hand at four kinds of comedy: the Roman (*Errors*), the farcical (*Shrew*), the romantic (*Two Gentlemen*), and the satiric (*Love's Labor's Lost*).[1] In view of my postulate that there is a steady line of development in the chronicles and tragedies, henceforth grouped as the "serious" plays, this diversity in the early comedies poses a problem. Is there any discernible line of development in the first five comedies? If there is, does it correspond to the changes occurring at the same time in the serious plays?

To postulate a line of development in the early comedies and the major terms for discussing it, I must first consider a prior question of genre. Why group Shakespeare's early plays into two categories, serious and comic? The first folio groups them into comedies, tragedies, and histories. Had Shakespeare written more tragedies during his early years, I would no doubt have grouped them together as another category and discussed its distinctive problems of dramaturgy. As it is, my discussion makes the two earliest tragedies subsidiary to the trend of development in the chronicles, many of which are in themselves "tragic." Given the first twelve plays, my grouping does approximate Heming and Condell's, who, as editors of the first folio, arranged Shakespeare's plays according to the subjects and principles that guided Shakespeare's dramaturgy. These principles, at least for tragedy and comedy, were enunciated by the sixteenth-century humanists who combined their admiration for the ancient dramatists with a conviction that drama should encourage good behavior. Didacticism alone would not necessitate a division of drama into the genres of tragedy and comedy, for the popular native tradition of the moralities, designed to instruct, fitted no such categories. The humanists based their conception of genre upon the practice of the Greek and Roman playwrights and interpreted the parts of each genre, such as character, plot, diction, as functions of didactic purpose.

These humanists were the same men who preserved the status of rhetoric as a central discipline in the school curriculum because they understood it to be a chief instrument for fostering virtuous action. Poetics was subsumed by the discipline of rhetoric, for the chief end of drama and poetry was to instruct and delight (or instruct through delight). The concept of decorum indicates how closely the two were linked: decorum guides the orator to adjust style to his audience and subject and it guides the playwright to adjust style, character, and subject to genre. As tragedy depicts the fortunes of great men, so comedy depicts the fortunes of ordinary men. The rhetorical high style, appropriate to affairs of state and the sufferings of great men, hardly fits the domestic problems of everyday people. This is not to say that elevated diction and heavily patterned syntax do not occur in Shakespeare's comedies, but usually they are inappropriate and therefore laughable, as when Petruchio declares his chivalric intention to "protect" Katharina from her own wedding feast. As the tragic narrative begins in calm and ends in turmoil, so the comic narrative begins in turmoil and ends in calm; as tragic events are historical, so comic events are fictitious; as the tragic plot stimulates pity and fear, so the comic plot generates laughter. In effect, Shakespeare's school training in rhetoric, which exerted such an influence over his earliest chronicle plays, exerted a similar influence over the very different practices in his earliest comedies. It is the pronouncements of the sixteenth-century humanists on comic characterization, plotting, style, and laughter that give us the terms for understanding the line of his development through the first five comedies, pronouncements that Shakespeare would have absorbed in his school training and in school plays, either Latin productions or English adaptations such as *Jack Juggler* or *Gammer Gurton's Needle*.

From *The Comedy of Errors* to *A Midsummer Night's Dream*, Shakespeare's development appears to cover less extreme changes than it does from *1 Henry VI* to *Richard II*. F. P. Wilson has suggested that Shakespeare almost single-handedly developed the form of the chronicle play; he faced no such task in writing comedies. One reason for this lies in the very nature of Roman comic plots which are sequential, unlike Senecan

147

tragic plots which are climactic. Sequential plotting that approximates chronological time fits with the instinctive native plotting of the moral-ities, which trace Mankind's life from beginning to end. Consequently Terence and Plautus exerted a continuous appeal as models for imita-tion to Elizabethans and Jacobeans, whereas Seneca, equally admired, required extensive modification, as the differences between Kyd's popu-lar *The Spanish Tragedy* and his translation of the Senecan closet drama, *Cornelie*, reveal. Not only did Plautus or a Renaissance coun-terpart, Ariosto, supply ready models of humanist comedy, but Lyly's court comedies and the clown portions of the hybrid moralities, such as Simplicity's episodes in Robert Wilson's *The Three Lords and the Three Ladies of London,* provided rich material for Shakespeare. It may be well to add here that such a rich store of dramatic conventions would affect Shakespeare's training as much as the theoretical comments of the humanists. Practice did not contradict theory. What he learned in school about the principles of comedy would have been confirmed, if not in every detail, by contemporary plays.

A second reason why Shakespeare's comic dramaturgy does not duplicate the pattern of the serious plays has already been suggested in the fifth chapter, on discrepant awareness. The very conditions of laughter require an audience to respond differently from the characters on stage, a condition that lies closer to the potentialities of drama *qua* drama than the orator's techinque of causing tears by tears and anger by anger. Rather than change his comic principles between *Errors* and *Dream*, Shakespeare appears to develop greater flexibility in applying them.

A third reason lies in the kind of instruction that the humanists prescribed for comedy. Basing their observations upon the practices of Terence and Plautus, they could hardly prescribe an insistent didacti-cism. Instead, they formulated a concept of comedy as a mirror of manners which reveals to the audience patterns of behavior to imitate or avoid, usually, since comedy stimulates laughter, patterns to avoid. The nature of comic instruction will be discussed later in the chapter; suffice it to say here that Shakespeare was encouraged at the outset of his career to be obliquely instructive. *Errors* and *Shrew*, while organized for moral purposes, reveal greater attention to story as story than does the con-temporaneous *1 Henry VI*, where details tend to illustrate a thesis.

Sixteenth-century humanists, whether Sir Thomas Elyot or Sir Philip Sidney or their Italian counterparts, generally agreed on a large number of principles that can be fairly described as a tradition.[2] Their pronouncements take as their starting point the writings of Cicero, Horace, Quintilian, and Donatus, the fourth-century commentator on the plays of Terence. The tradition has been thoroughly discussed elsewhere, but the way the principles affect the details of Shakespeare's dramaturgy needs to be examined. Considering the specificity and force of this tradition, one finds it surprising to turn to a survey of the criticism of Shakespeare's comedies in the twentieth century (excluding the late romances) and to read John Russell Brown's summary of it:

A retrospective view of the study of Shakespeare's history plays or imagery reveals sustained critical and scholarly argument with progress marked by a few outstanding books. But, in the period under review [about 1900 to 1953], there is no clear line of development in the study of the early comedies. . . . there is much detailed work to report but little concerted effort.[3]

While this is defensible with regard to detailed criticism of specific comedies, we can find a broad similarity of approach in many of the central books of the period: writers establish two different categories of Elizabethan comedy which they may describe in varying ways but which are "realistic" or "classic" on the one hand and "romantic" or "native" on the other.

Many critics place Shakespeare in the category of "romantic" and Jonson in the "classical." If one takes the broad view of Shakespeare's comedies, including *The Merchant of Venice, Twelfth Night, All's Well,* and *The Tempest,* it becomes obvious that his comedies differ from Jonson's, a difference that is most easily confirmed by the kinds of story that depict love even though the comedies of the first decade hardly dramatize love in the same way as do the late romances. If matters of dramaturgy receive the major emphasis in a definition of the two categories, then the classification is far from clear-cut. E. C. Pettet, who finds Shakespeare's comedies to be primarily romantic in *Shakespeare and the Romance Tradition* (London, 1949) excludes *Errors* and *Shrew* from his discussion and discerns a bemused detachment toward love, a detachment that one can also relate to the sixteenth-century neo-classical principles of comedy. Nevill Coghill, in an essay that faces squarely the issue of neo-classical comedy, states that the essential qualities of Shakespeare's comedies reside in the romance tradition, not classic but gothic in origin. The way he defines the two types can be seen in this passage:

I have tried so far to show Shakespeare's dependence on, or agreement with, a medieval conception of Comedy as a story starting in trouble, ending in joy, and centred in love; and I have suggested some of the philosophical implications of this picture of life and their conformity with a medieval and Christian understanding of reality. I have exampled the opposed "corrective" view of Comedy favoured by Renaissance critics, a view which owes nothing in form to the Middle Ages but goes back to Donatus and his fellows directly.[4]

Some questions immediately arise about the way he separates his types: does the form of the romance, as he states it, not fit the comedies of Terence? Northrop Frye, for instance, finds the form of New Comedy to be essentially the same as that of the late romances of Shakespeare.[5] Does Coghill's picture of the two traditions do justice to the facts? Madeleine Doran observed that the distinction between "medieval" and "classical" varies from age to age, so that what the Elizabethans took as classical does not necessarily coincide with what we view as classical today. Not only is it difficult to separate the two, since "most medieval ideas about literature are themselves classical in ultimate origin," but "the fresh study of classical literature and literary theory only helped to interpret and justify something already familiar in living literary tradition."[6] While Doran's comments call into question Coghill's categories, she establishes two somewhat similar categories for comedy, one emphasizing realistic, social criticism and the other dramatizing romantic fortuitous stories of love: "there is far more mingling of the two kinds than there is separation. Jonson's comedy is the "purest" on the social side; Peele's, perhaps, on the romantic side. Nearly everybody else's, even Shakespeare's, is more or less mixed, with emphasis on one side or the other depending on temperament and interests" (*Endeavors*, p. 182). And taking another, more recent discussion of comedy, M. C. Bradbrook's *The Growth and Structure of Elizabethan Comedy* (1955), she finds Shakespeare's comedy to be a synthesis of two traditions, the "learned" and the "popular." Although John Russell Brown may be accurate about the absence of progress in the analysis of Shakespeare's comedies, it strikes one that the general approaches tend to be remarkably similar. Critics establish two categories, one of which is "romantic" and the other in some way different from romantic. A few critics like Coghill put Shakespeare's comedies decisively into one category, but most find them to be a mixture.

Since two such terms appear to be serviceable, my problem is to specify them and see how they are mixed in the apprentice comedies. H. B. Charlton, whose major terms are "realistic" and "romantic," formulates a broad statement about the mixture better than most:

They [Elizabethan playwrights] were required to beat out a play which should be comic and romantic at once. . . . the whole history of Elizabethan comedy is a tale of the reluctance of comedy to compromise itself with romance.[7]

Charlton develops his conception of the comic by an examination of Latin comedy and the way it related to Roman society rather than by what sixteenth-century humanists said about Latin comedy. My procedure will be to show how difficult it was for the neo-classical stipulations for comedy to encompass romantic sentiments and romantic behavior. To formulate a tentative and rough statement of Shakespeare's early development, it would not be wide of the mark to say that he sought to introduce romantic sentiments and behavior into neo-classical "mirror" comedy. His first efforts, *Errors* and *Shrew*, follow closely the stipulations of the humanists so that romantic sentiments play little part. *The Two Gentlemen of Verona* makes the first break in his practice by introducing romantic love as a central experience for comic purposes of mirroring; whether it was written before or after *Shrew* matters little—it could be that he experimented soon after writing *Errors*, and not pleased with the results of *Two Gentlemen*, returned to the tried and true principles in writing *Shrew*. *Love's Labor's Lost* and *A Midsummer Night's Dream* constitute Shakespeare's first successes in incorporating romantic sentiments and behavior into mirror comedy, and they bring to a close the first phase of Shakespeare's solution to the problem. *The Merchant of Venice* and *Much Ado about Nothing* represent another approach to the same problem of mixing. While on the face of it Shakespeare's first five comedies appear to be a miscellaneous group of experiments, as Bertrand Evans has stated, underlying their differences is a set of principles that make them variations on one kind of comedy. The first step in examining the apprentice playwright's dramaturgy is to state these principles, familiar as they are.

∞

For a discussion of Shakespeare's early comedies, the stipulations of what can be described as a neo-classical tradition of comic theory in the sixteenth century can be systematized into four topics: meaning, plot, character, and emotion; the topic of emotion, central for my purpose, can be subdivided into emotion of character and response of the audience. The fundamental statement of the tradition comes from Cicero who in *Pro Sexto Roscio Amerino* (16.47) said, "I think, in fact, that these fictions of the [comic] poets are intended to give us a representation of our manners in the characters of others and a vivid picture of our own daily life."[8] Donatus attributed to Cicero a similar state-

151

ment which rephrases this idea more vividly and was consequently cited more often: "the imitation of life, the mirror of custom, the image of truth."[9] "Manners" and "custom" are the words in these quotations that come closest to specifying the kind of behavior appropriate for comic display. But the main intention behind both is to assure us that comedy is morally relevant to our lives. However, the conception of the mirror is broad enough to cover almost any play, as Hamlet's application of it to "The Murder of Gonzago" shows, and the exact way in which comedy is morally relevant to our lives is equally open to interpretation, as two different sixteenth-century writers can show. Sir Thomas Elyot, writing in *The Governor* (1531) tells us how one sixteenth-century humanist regarded the plays of Terence and Plautus:

. . . they be undoutedly a picture or as it were a mirrour of man's life, wherein iuell is nat taught but discouered; to the intent that men be-holdynge the promptnes of youth unto vice, the snares of harlotts and baudes laide for yonge myndes, the disceipte of seruantes, the chaunces of fortune contrary to mennes expectation, they beinge therof warned may prepare them selfe to resist or preuente occasion.[10]

Nicholas Udall, writing just a few years later, justified *Ralph Roister Doister* (1541) on the ground that sheer mirth can be profitable:

. . . nothing more comendable for a mans recreation
Than Mirth which is used in an honest fashion:
For Myrth prolongeth lyfe, and causeth health.
Mirth recreates our spirites and voydeth pensiuenesse,
Mirth increaseth amitie, not hindring our wealth,
Mirth is to be used both of more and lesse,
Being mixed with vertue in decent comlynesse.[11]

In short, Donatus's statement was broad enough to relieve the play-wright of obvious didacticism. It has already been stated that a comparison of *Errors* with *1 Henry VI* would bear this out. In fact, the Abbess's advice to Adriana sounds much like Udall:

Sweet recreation barred, what doth ensue
But moody and dull melancholy,
Kinsman to grim and comfortless despair,
And at her heels a huge infectious troop
Of pale distemperatures and foes to life?

(*Errors*, V.i.78–82)

While the concept of comedy as a mirror of everyday life is broad, it placed certain decisive restrictions upon the humanist Elizabethan playwright who knew the power of romance. *Mucedorus*, derived from Sidney's *Arcadia*, was one of the most popular Elizabethan plays, if we can judge from the number of times it was reprinted.[12] A romantic narrative usually takes the form of adventure in which two admirable lovers are separated by circumstances, frequently wondrous, forced to undergo a series of tribulations that bring out their virtues and the constancy of their love until they are happily reunited at the conclusion. It is a form not far removed from that of plays based on sacred history and legend, such as *The Life and Repentance of Mary Magdalene* (ca. 1550-66) by Lewis Wager that exhibits the didactic techniques of the morality. *Sir Clyomon and Sir Clamydes* (ca. 1570) and *Common Conditions* (1576) show how a playwright could adapt the dramatic devices of the morality to romance. Both the native popular dramatic tradition and the Elizabethan taste must have made the romantic narrative tempting to a young playwright; yet Shakespeare did not succumb until he was a mature dramatist. Ben Jonson, more typically a humanist playwright, railed at the romance throughout most of his career, particularly through his gulls who relish its wild improbabilities. Puntarvolo fancies himself a wandering knight and forces his wife to engage in pretenses of chivalric romance (*Every Man Out of His Humour*, II.ii); Asotus would bestow on his mistress the name Lindabrides, "Emperor Alicandroes daughter and the Prince Meridian's sister" from "The first Part of the Mirror of Princely Deeds and Knighthood" (*Cynthias's Revels*, III.v. 27-36). Jonson's attitude is consistent with a remark made by Donatus some thirteen hundred years before: "To utter a counterfeit is a fault, a fiction an ingenuity, a lie a folly. We are deceived by counterfeits, we are delighted by fictions, we despise lies."[13] Keeping foremost the purpose of comedy as a mirror of custom and an image of truth, he praised Terence for avoiding the improbable and the fantastic.

Observations about plot were equally general—so general, in fact, that they can hardly be described as stipulations. "Plot" is a term that may designate story, the action of a story, the form of a story to be dramatized, or the structure of a drama, and like our critics today, sixteenth-century commentators applied the term without technical precision. Closely related to plot is "argument," a term revealing the intimate link of rhetorical theory to dramatic theory.[14] Argument means the gist of the story, the whole action reduced to a brief statement (see Herrick's *Comic Theory in the Sixteenth Century*, pp.91-94) and is the stuff from which the plot is constructed. The one value which commentators demanded consistently of plot was variety. Terence spoke of simple and double plots in the prologue to the *Self-Tormentor* when he explained how he built his play from two simple Greek plots; in fact, all his plays except the *Mother-in-law* are duplex and can easily be said to satisfy a taste for variety. Shakespeare created variety by multiple plots in *Shrew, Labors,* and *Dream,* where several groups of characters are engaged in similar stories; in *Errors* and *Two Gentlemen* several groups of characters are engaged in the same story. No doubt Renaissance commentators were drawn to approve variety as much from contemporary taste as from admiration for Roman comedy. Even so, variety can be seen as a value consistent with the principle of comedy as a mirror because if comedy is to expose our manners and customs, it would show them most sharply by contrasts. Bradbrook sees this variety through contrasts as a principle governing the organization of *Dream.* [15] Variety led the theorists to commend the duplex over the single plot as well as the complex over the simple plot. Aristotle made the observation with regard to tragedy that a simple plot contains nothing unexpected, no reversal of fortune or discovery. Offhand, it is difficult to conceive of a comedy which would have a simple plot, for the unexpected, either to characters or to audience, would seem to be crucial to the laughter and merriment. Certainly Shakespeare devised no simple plot. In *Errors* and *Two Gentlemen* the discovery and reversal of fortune occur together; in *Shrew* and *Labors* they are distinct; in *Dream* a reversal of fortune occurs in the forest, but there is no discovery scene as such. An unusual discovery occurs for the audience at the very end of the play, but the characters themselves remain in the dark about the crucial facts. This difference suggests some independence in Shakespeare's plotting as he matures, particularly with regard to the position of the audience towards events on stage.

In addition to variety, the commentators agreed upon a general outline by which playwrights should construct their plots, so general and practical that it would be difficult not to follow. The opening section, the protasis, necessarily encompasses the exposition and may start the bustle of affairs. The next section, the epitasis, develops the complication: the knot is tightened, the bustle increases. The final section, or catastrophe, is marked by a reversal of affairs that brings about the cheerful outcome. T. W. Baldwin has traced the elaboration of this formula during the sixteenth century into the five-act structure. [16] Yet the typical elaboration preserves the general threefold division, identifying acts one and two with the protasis, but adding a distinction to the epitasis, the catastasis or counterturn, in acts three and four, thereby equating act five with the catastrophe. Commentators approved the bringing together of all the characters in a final cheerful union, the way Terence closes his *Eunuch*. This practice would not be open to writers of the morality play, as David Bevington has shown us, where doubling for the sake of variety increases the number of characters far out of proportion to the number of actors, but it was possible for school plays and within the limits of professional companies. Shakespeare brought all the major characters together for the conclusions of *Errors, Shrew, Labors,* and *Dream*, but not once in the contemporaneous Henry VI plays. In *Labors* even after Holofernes and Sir Nathaniel have retreated in humiliation from the Show of the Nine Worthies, they return to join in the closing songs of spring and winter; since they add nothing in character, their final appearance can be attributed only to Shakespeare's desire to assemble the whole community. At the end of *Two Gentlemen*, the low comic servants do not go into the forest, but this exception is not important enough to deny Shakespeare's general practice. It can be said, then, that Shakespeare followed the stipulations of the sixteenth-century commentators in plotting his first five comedies, but not much can be made of this because the stipulations are broad enough to cover almost any decisions that a playwright might make.

The humanists located their most restrictive stipulations for mirror comedy in matters of character and characterization, and being restrictive, these stipulations became especially important to Shakespeare's apprenticeship, for they set the boundaries against which he reacted. Marvin T. Herrick in his helpful study of comic theory in the sixteenth century, explains why the theorists made character the center of their attention:

Emphasis upon characterization was the natural result of the traditional emphasis upon the didactic function of comedy; for comedy was supposed to present a mirror of everyday life which showed the spectator what he might follow and what he should avoid. In other words, the lesson of comedy came largely from the characterization, from the *ethos* and the decorum exhibited.[17]

If we keep in mind that these theorists were confronted on the one hand with the plays of Plautus and Terence, their raw material, and on the other with the principles of rhetoric, we can see why character bore more burden of meaning than plot. Faced with a multiplicity of intrigues and predicaments, the commentators were forced to abstract to a high degree before being able to make significant moral propositions that would cover them. One way to limit the process of abstraction was to talk in terms of a group's behavior rather than mankind's, or in terms of a character's representative behavior rather than a group's. When a comic predicament displayed idiosyncratic or bizarre behavior, it could be placed in perspective by generalizing to "typical" behavior, typical, that is, of a character.

The critics' first step in discussing character was to construct classifications, thereby restricting the possibilities of what is appropriately comic. Just as Thomas Wilson laid out the places by which an orator may develop a demonstrative oration, so Erasmus, Melanchthon, Minturno, Badius, and other commentators on comedy listed the attributes for developing a character: he should be differentiated by age, sex, country, as well as habits, disposition, inclinations, and emotions.[18] In itself, this sort of categorization seems inconsequential, but entailed in the attributes of character are judgments about decorum which do have consequences. Badius, for instance, insisted upon decorum of sex, social status, and moral character: the male sex is more constant and serious than the female; manly deeds and speech should never be confused with womanly behavior; a slave should not speak like a hero; an honest woman should speak differently from a wanton hussy, and a wise man from an ignoramus. Robortellus pointed out that weaving and spinning are commendable accomplishments in people of low birth, but not praiseworthy in gentle folk. The highest virtue in a servant may be a vice in his master; refraining from theft, for instance, may be praised in a servant, but hardly in a man of honor.[19] These pronouncements on decorum appear to us simple enough, but they had far-reaching effects on the practices of playwrights. Cicero's and Donatus's subject matter of comedy, manners and custom or the lively image of everyday life, suddenly takes specific shape in patterns of decorous and indecorous behavior that lend themselves readily to specific prescription for creating laughter.

First let us consider how classification determines the portrayal of a comic character's inner life. His social class becomes in effect his motivation. Why is a young man improvident? Because it is the nature of a young man. Why is an old man miserly? Because it is the nature of an old man. Type characters are tautological; their dialogue exhibits their loyalty, and their loyalty determines their dialogue. Neither reveals inner motives which would personalize and particularize their behavior. To hear specific reasons why Adriana is shrewish would be to deemphasize her typicality and would thereby lessen the mirrorlike function of her behavior.[20] The sixteenth-century commentators did not counsel against personal motivations; instead, they stated that comic characters should be consistent. Erasmus, for instance, in *De Rerum Copia* advises the writer, whether he constructs serious or comic characters:

Either follow tradition or invent what is self-consistent. If haply, when you write, you bring back to the stage the honoring of Achilles, let him be impatient, passionate, ruthless, fierce; let him claim that laws are not made for him, let him ever make appeal to the sword. . . . If it be an untried theme you entrust to the stage, and if you boldly fashion a fresh character, . . . have it self-consistent.[21]

Robortellus makes the principle of self-consistency stronger by insisting that it exclude change. If a poet introduces a person as cowardly, greedy, proud, he should keep him the same throughout the play. Some characters in Terence's comedies change, such as Micio and Demea in *The Brothers*, a fact that raises a difficulty which the commentators solved as best they could:

I say that change of character ought not to be admitted unless some very good reason is expressed, which is strong enough to bring it about; just as Demea expressed the reason for his change at some length.
(Riccobonus, *Poetica Aristotelis*, 1587)[22]

Given the fact that a character's behavior is understood by his classification, it readily follows that change is difficult to account for, so that whatever change occurs, the playwright locates the cause more in external circumstances than in change of heart. The change of Katharina dominates the dramatic experience of *Shrew*, for example, but we watch Petruchio's methods of taming rather than the stages of her psychic adjustment. In line with this, one critic has observed that Shakespeare could have extended the episodes of taming indefinitely.[23]

It follows that inner conflicts are inappropriate to comic characters. Aeschinus in Terence's *The Brothers* expresses a conflict between desire and duty when he faces a choice between betraying his brother Ctesipho and bearing the blame for kidnapping the music girl. As Herrick tells us, sixteenth-century commentators reconciled this exception with their principles by labeling his scene a "tragic complaint."[24] While this solution appears to beg the question, it follows consistently from the restrictions on a comic character's emotions laid down in Quintilian's *Institutes*. His long pronouncement is central to this discussion and needs to be quoted in full:

Emotions, however, as we learn from ancient authorities, fall into two classes; the one is called *pathos* by the Greeks and is rightly and correctly expressed in Latin by *adfectus* (emotion): the other is called *ethos*, a word for which in my opinion Latin has no equivalent: it is however rendered by *mores* (morals) and consequently the branch of philosophy known as *ethics* is styled *moral* philosophy by us. But close consideration of the nature of the subject leads me to think that in this connexion it is not so much *morals* in general that is meant as certain peculiar aspects; for the term *morals* includes every attitude of the mind. The more cautious writers have preferred to give the sense of the term rather than to translate it into Latin. They therefore explain *pathos* as describing the more violent emotions and *ethos* as designating those which are calm and gentle: in the one case the passions are violent, in the other subdued, the former command and disturb, the latter persuade and induce a feeling of goodwill. Some add that *ethos* is continuous, while *pathos* is momentary. . . . The emotion of love and longing for our friends and connexions is perhaps of an intermediate character, being stronger than *ethos* and weaker than *pathos*. There is also good reason for giving the name of *ethos* to those scholastic exercises in which we portray rustics, misers, cowards, and superstitious persons according as our theme may require. For if *ethos* denotes moral character, our speech must necessarily be based on *ethos* when it is engaged in portraying such character. . . . The *pathos* of the Greeks, which we correctly translate by *emotion*, is of a different character, and I cannot better indicate the nature of the difference than by saying that *ethos* rather resembles comedy and *pathos* tragedy. For *pathos* is almost entirely concerned with anger, dislike, fear, hatred, and pity.

(Book 6, ii.8–20)[25]

Of particular significance for us is Quintilian's separation of the emotions of love and longing for friends from the violent feelings of tragedy and from the mild, characteristic emotions of comedy. Placed in an intermediate range, these feelings became in the sixteenth century the province of a third type of drama, tragicomedy, by definition an intermediary between the two major dramatic genres.[26] Quintilian's restriction of comic sentiments to those which are constant and typical fits well with the principle of comedy as a mirror of custom and with the classification of characters according to social types. It also fits with the humanists' definition of laughter which is, in effect, the audience's primary emotional response to mirror comedy about social types.

The laughter proper to mirror comedy is essentially the laughter of scorn and depends upon the principle of decorum. Cicero, again, set the direction of thought on the subject by a remark in *De Oratore* which can be traced to Aristotle:

The seat or province, so to speak, of the laughable lies in a certain ugliness and deformity; for those sayings are laughed at solely and chiefly which point out and designate something ugly in manner that is not ugly.

(2.38.236)[27]

There is only one short step from his comment to the notion of decorum. What constitutes ugliness of manner? Trissino in his *Poetics* (1529) even though he does not mention the term, takes that step when he enumerates the details that are laughable:

But if the object that is presented to the senses has some mixture of ugliness, it moves laughter, as an ugly and distorted face, an inept movement, a silly word, a mispronunication, a rough hand, a wine of unpleasant taste, or a rose of unpleasant odor moves laughter at once, and those things especially cause laughter from which better qualities were hoped, because then not merely our senses but also our hopes are slightly offended, and such pleasure as this comes to us because man is by nature envious and malicious, as is clearly seen in little children, for almost all of them are envious, and always delight to do evil, if they are able.[28]

The audience applies its general standard of decorum, and when behavior or attributes are found wanting, it laughs. Trissino gives indecorum a moral dimension by grounding the inclination to take pleasure from the imperfect in man's sinful nature. Yet an audience also applies a standard of kingly decorum to Richard II and finds his behavior wanting, but does not laugh. The definition of comedy delineates the boundaries or behavior to manners and customs of everyday life which exclude the actions of great men with ultimate consequences, that is, matters of life and death. Implicit in Trissino's discussion of indecorum is the element of surprise, and Madius (1550) stresses the importance of the unexpected in laughter.[29] While this concept calls attention to the element of time in the dynamics of laughter, it does not add anything substantive to the understanding of the laughable as a species of the improper.

Sir Philip Sidney made a significant addition to the discussion of laughter in his *Apology for Poetry*. Whether or not Shakespeare read his essay is not so important as the fact that Sidney tried to expand the thinking about laughter in much the same way that Shakespeare generated another kind of laughter in comedy. Sidney did not abandon the traditional notion of the ridiculous, but contrasted the response to it, which he called the laughter of scorn, with the feeling of delight in a complex passage that deserves full quotation:

But our comedians think there is no delight without laughter; which is very wrong, for though laughter may come with delight, yet cometh it

159

not of delight, as though delight should be the cause of laughter; but well may one thing breed both together: nay, rather in themselves they have, as it were, a kind of contrariety; for delight we scarcely do, but in things that have a conveniency to ourselves, or to the general nature; laughter almost ever cometh of things most disproportioned to ourselves and nature. Delight hath a joy in it, either permanent or present. Laughter hath only a scornful tickling. For example, we are ravished with delight to see a fair woman, and yet are far from being moved to laughter. We laugh at deformed creatures, wherein certainly we cannot delight. We delight in good chances, we laugh at mischances; we delight to hear the happiness of our friends or country, at which he were worthy to be laughed at that would laugh; we shall contrarily laugh sometimes to find a matter quite mistaken and go down the hill against the bias, in the mouth of some such men, as for the respect of them one shall be heartily sorry, yet he cannot choose but laugh; and so is rather pained than delighted with laughter. Yet deny I not but that they may go well together; for as in Alexander's picture well set out, we delight without laughter, and in twenty mad antics we laugh without delight, so in Hercules, painted with his great beard and furious countenance, in a woman's attire, spinning at Omphale's commandment, it breedeth both delight and laughter. For the representing of so strange a power in love procureth delight, and the scornfulness of the action stirreth laughter. But I speak to this purpose, that all the end of the comical part be not upon such scornful matters as stirreth laughter only, but, mixed with it, that delightful teaching which is the end of poesy.[30]

When Sidney differentiates laughter from delight by their objects, the two responses are clear. Difficulty arises when he relates them to the purposes of comedy, scorn for foolish behavior and delight at its instructiveness. "Delight" covers, so it seems, two different reactions: delight in a pleasant object and delight in being taught to scorn a ridiculous object. Apparently he would find that all comedy which acts as a mirror of custom and an image of truth generates a mixed response of laughter and delight, and would reject silly behavior—the kind that Hamlet disapproves in the undisciplined antics of a clown—which produces only the laughter of scorn.

Delight in relation to sympathy happens to describe the response appropriate to the kind of comedy which dramatizes the tribulations of lovers, that is, the romance or tragicomedy. Sidney attached delight to Hercules spinning at the wheel, "for the representing of so strange a power in love procureth delight; and the scornfulness of the action stirreth laughter." But if the characters face heroic challenges and demonstrate virtues of constancy, patience, and fortitude, we would not only admire but be delighted at the rewards of happiness they receive. This kind of story depicts the very range of feelings which Quintilian excludes from comedy and reveals patterns of behavior to imitate rather than to avoid.

Yet there is still another kind of delightful laughter suggested by Sidney's quotation but not explicated either by him or by other sixteenth-century humanists, a laughter of kinship or goodwill. It arises from sheer animal spirits, the kind of laughter typical of small children at play. It is the kind of laughter that uneasy adults affect at parties to generate a sense of camaraderie. It is the kind of laughter that old-fashioned manuals of public speaking understood when they advised a speaker to begin with a joke. It is the laughter of fun that Max Eastman recognized and made central to his book *The Enjoyment of Laughter*. [31] And it is the sort of laughter that Shakespeare's later apprentice comedies seem designed to stimulate. The audience's response cannot be described as sympathetic delight, which is appropriate to the romance, nor can it be described as the laughter of scorn, which implies disapproval; instead, it is best described as a laughter of "kinship" that entails both recognition of shortcomings and acceptance of them as part of the human condition.

In summary, the story which best embodies the neo-classical stipulations of the humanists about behavior, plot, character, and laughter is the intrigue. Usually a lustful youth and his cunning servant plot against a crabbed and miserly father to bring about marriage to an apparently unsuitable young girl. Variations on this situation appear in Shakespeare's *Shrew, Two Gentlemen,* and *Dream,* to mention only his apprentice plays. While love happens to generate the ingenuities of plotting, it does not appear as a rendered experience on stage, at least in the typical examples of Roman and neo-classical comedies. Whatever amorous sentiments need to be expressed are spoken by the young man not to his love but either to himself or in confession to his servant. These are brief and quickly dissolve into practical considerations of plotting. Just at the plotting suppresses personal sentiments, so it emphasizes the need for judgment. By its very nature intrigue divides the characters into two groups, one blind to the facts. It is a short step for the playwright to intensify the blindness by another sort, the blindness of hypocrisy. We laugh at the characters' follies as well as at their failures to be aware of the intriguers' plans. The father not merely opposes his son's marriage; he insists on his own "wisdom" and exhibits an exaggerated sense of self-importance, usually enforced by an entourage of friends like himself, a pedant, a doctor, a lawyer, with a parasite to flatter them all. A variation on this intrigue plot is the story of mistaken identities where both sides exhibit a blindness to the central facts, a blindness that also provides occasion for indulging characteristic blindnesses of vanity and hypocrisy. *Errors*, of course, fits this pattern. We laugh the laughter of scorn not only at the mistakes about identities but also at the hot temper of Antipholus of Ephesus, the pomposities of the pedant, and the strident behavior of the shrew.

Central to this story, whether intrigue or mistaken identities, is the discovery scene. The crabbed father regains perspective and recognizes the rightness of his son's desire. The pedant is brought up short, the shrew adjusts to her proper place, and it turns out that the young girl, thought to be improper, is respectable and rich after all. Northrop Frye would see in this conclusion the establishment of a new society which signifies the triumph of man's vitality.[32] The sixteenth-century commentator and critic would describe the event in terms of judgment and decorum. The father learns a lesson and adjusts his sights to what is appropriate for his son. A reordering of judgment occurs within the play that approximates the principle of judgment evoked for the audience watching the play. Their laughter at improprieties is a type of recognition similar to the discovery scene, both carrying out the principle of comedy enunciated by Cicero and Donatus.

Against this background we can set Shakespeare's earliest comedies to see that he explored problems of judgment and tried to extend the principles of neo-classical comedy to encompass the sentiments and behavior of young lovers. The question to be asked is not whether Shakespeare read the humanists, English and Italian, mentioned here, but how well their discussions relate to his dramatic practices. Certainly he shared their general principles about education, and at the barest minimum we know that he was familiar with some of the plays they discussed: Plautus and Ariosto. As a practicing dramatist, he may have gained his understanding of the potentialities of comedy through specific plays, such as *The Menaechmi* or *The Supposes* or Lyly's court comedies, plays which confirm the principles of the humanists. Yet their theoretical statements can give us terms to understand what he was doing. Lyly too exemplifies the same twofold effort in trying to hold to the principles of mirror comedy while extending them to the experiences and sentiments of lovers.[33] These playwrights could have abandoned themselves to the unrestrained delights of romance and produced such works as *Sir Clyomon and Sir Clamydes* or *Mucedorus*. Instead, they accepted the stipulations of the humanists and gradually tested their elasticity.

∞

The diversity in Shakespeare's first five comedies, so apparent at first glance, loses some of its sharpness after we survey them in the light of the neo-classical principles of the sixteenth-century critics, for the comedies fall roughly into two groups. *Errors* and *Shrew*, because of their close conformity to the rules, make a class by themselves. *Two Gentlemen*, because it attempts to dramatize the predicaments of romantic love as the central experience, can be seen as a transition to *Labors* and *Dream*, two plays that solve the problem of encompassing the sentiments of love within the principles of neo-classical comedy. These five plays, then, follow a line of development similar to the one in Shakespeare's serious plays, where personal responses become increasingly important to the dramatic narrative.

Errors and *Shrew* form a group because, among other reasons, the characters exhibit their typicality as if they were cut according to the specifications of the poetic treatises. The major figures take their identities from their domestic roles, the minor from their professions. Wife interacts with husband, old suitor with young girl, servant with master, father with children, all of them exhibiting attributes customary to these categories. With impropriety as the main source of laughter, these characters deviate from the standard of domestic harmony so that the wife is shrewish, the husband "unfaithful," the master intolerant, the servant "inefficient." Antipholus of Ephesus is irritated by his servant; so is Petruchio; Adriana is shrewish; so is Katharina; Luciana is an attractive sister; so is Bianca; Dromio seems willfully to confuse his master's orders; so does Grumio. When the minor characters need to be identified by no more than profession—an episode in *Shrew*, for instance, demands of the tailor and haberdasher no further attributes— it is a simple matter of showing them with an exaggerated sense of importance. A tailor sees himself competent in matters of fashion; a pedant thinks himself remarkably learned; or a constable sees himself as the bulwark of law and order.

If characters were to be fashioned according to type, what standards did the commentators apply to differentiate the more successful creations from the less successful? Donatus praised Terence for variety, achieved by contrast. Of the *Eunuch* he said:

Here is shown a multiplex, dissimilar concourse of persons who are yet kept separate by the force and design of the poet so that no confusion of speech occurs.[34]

Modern critics echo his observation when they praise Shakespeare's early comedies; M. C. Bradbrook, for instance, in *The Growth and*

Structure of Elizabethan Comedy devotes two chapters to "character as plot" and comments upon "the interplay of contrasted groups of characters" in *Dream*.[35] Yet Shakespeare's chronicles and tragedies cannot be said to be sparsely populated. We find a duplex plot in *Shrew*; we find another in *Lear*. By count, *Hamlet* contains more characters with specific names than does *Dream*, and this count includes Peaseblossom, Cobweb, Moth, and Mustardseed, who appear only momentarily to indulge Bottom's whims. The difference lies in the kind of attention given to the characters rather than in the number. In comedy the group seems larger because our attention shifts focus so rapidly from one character to another, a fact which helps preserve the audience's distance from predicaments and encourages laughter. It would be harder, for instance, to become involved with Romeo and Juliet if we were also concerned about the problems of a second pair of lovers; say Benvolio falls in love with Rosaline at the Capulet ball and woos her intermittently throughout the play. In Shakespeare's first five comedies it is difficult to isolate the major characters in the same way that we can point to Richard III, Titus Andronicus, or Richard II from the early serious plays. Only two titles of his comedies refer to single characters: *The Taming of the Shrew* and *The Merchant of Venice* (*Pericles* and *Cymbeline* obviously belong to a different group), both of which indicate the principle of characterization as a social type. On the other hand, most of the tragedies and histories bear single proper names as titles.

The title of *Shrew* leads us to ask whether or not Katharina constitutes an exception to the mode of characterization we find elsewhere in the first two comedies, for she changes through the course of the play. Furthermore, her aberration differs from the improprieties of behavior in *Errors*, where all difficulties vanish once the characters discover the true nature of circumstances, everyone except Adriana. It is significant that she too, is a shrew, and her aberration arises not entirely from external causes, as the two lectures given to her during the course of the play suggest, but from a blindness to the principle of wifehood. Once she has been jarred into recognition by Emilia's ostensibly sympathetic questions, we assume that she will change her attitude. One of the comic aspects of Katharina's instruction is that Petruchio does not lecture to her; laughter arises because what he says does not coincide with what he does. He speaks of concern for his wife's diet and rest while she goes hungry and sleepless. Hers is a school of will, will in the sense of both desire and power. As teacher, Petruchio exerts man's superiority through sheer force, guided, of course, by a shrewd plan. The instruction—or taming—follows a pattern from the physical to "spiritual" matters. He thwarts her will by physical discomforts, first by means of travel (narrated by Grumio), then by deprivation of food and sleep. Next, he makes clear that her clothing depends on his will, then her pleasure on his whim, and finally he gives her a capricious command, to praise the fresh young maidenly beauty of wrinkled Vincentio, that makes clear her dignity depends on him—even her reputation for sanity. The plotting includes no discovery scene or lecture. In their absence lies the very substance of the comedy, for we laugh because it is necessary to tame Katharina like a falcon. In effect, her behavior evokes the same standard of decorum, the same kind of laughter, and the same expectation for fulfillment that we apply to the other type characters.[36] Had Shakespeare given us some inner glimpse of her, a conflict, let us say, between an affection for Petruchio and her stubborn pride, then she would have been akin to the complex heroines of his later comedies. As it is, we judge her behavior to be temporarily out of kilter.[37] With proper cause she assumes her proper role in the order of things so that her story need evoke from us no more than a ready generalization or proverb to cover the matter.

Paucity of intimate sentiments, particularly sentiments of romantic love, also sets *Errors* and *Shrew* apart from the later apprentice comedies. There is, however, one occasion for the expression of love in *Errors*. Antipholus of Syracuse declares his affection for Luciana, but he delivers his remarks when she reminds him of his marriage to Adriana. Their dialogue falls into the dominant pattern of the play, the dialogue of crossed purposes, so that their misunderstandings generate one more occasion for laughter. Antipholus's one uninterrupted speech of love states his willingness to risk all for Luciana. This declaration gains its expressive power from a series of hyperbolic commands and a fanciful description of the idolized lady rather than from a description of his feelings, which are stated flatly and briefly:

Are you a god? Would you create me new?
Transform me then, and to your power I'll yield.
But if that I am I, then well I know
Your weeping sister is no wife of mine,
Nor to her bed no homage do I owe.
Far more, far more, to you do I decline.
O train me not, sweet mermaid, with thy note,
To drown me in thy sister's flood of tears!
Sing, siren, for thyself, and I will dote.

Spread o'er the silver waves thy golden hairs,
And as a bed I'll take them, and there lie;
And in that glorious supposition think
He gains by death that hath such means to die.
Let Love, being light, be drownèd if she sink?

(III.ii.39–52)

We must not lose sight of the fact that Antipholus speaks this within a frame of comic misapprehension. Far from evoking similar feelings in Luciana, the speech leads her to lecture him on the duties of a husband. In Act V, when the two could express their sentiments unfettered by misconceptions, they remain silent.

Recent critics of *Errors* make much of Antipholus's declaration of love and connect it with Egeon's sentence of death, the addition of Emilia, Antipholus of Syracuse's soliloquies on identity, and the family reunion to show how Shakespeare "deepened" his source play. Implicit in their argument is an understanding of farce as some lesser form in a hierarchy of genres, inappropriate to Shakespeare's genius; so they set out to show how even his first comedy goes beyond the limitations of farce by adding such topics as "death," "love," or "identity" that have special value in themselves.[38] As Peter G. Phialas puts it in *Shakespeare's Romantic Comedies,* which discusses *Errors* as a forerunner of Shakespeare's treatment of romantic love:

But the fact remains that *The Comedy of Errors*, though in the main concerned with the farcical mistakings of identity, touches briefly a theme of far greater significance, the ideal relationship of man and woman.[39]

If indeed themes can have value apart from the way they are dramatized, one might respond that in this play the experiences of love and marriage serve to develop the theme of what constitutes identity. Had Shakespeare intended to develop such an ideal relationship between man and woman, he missed his chance in Act V, where Luciana and Antipholus of Syracuse could have expressed their sentiments. Yet they remain completely silent. Some of the best essays on the play, such as those by Harold Brooks and R. A. Foakes, identify various themes within the comedy, but they too assume that the real values are serious and somehow distinct from the farce. Brooks, who finds the themes to be "relationship between human beings, depending on their right relationship to truth and universal law: to the cosmic reality behind appearance, and the cosmic order," states that the themes are intimately related to the action and yet is somehow impelled to write the following:

[*Errors*] resembles the *Ion* and *The Confidential Clerk* in matching a mystification about identity, at the level of intrigue, with an exploration of serious issues appropriate to such a plot. Less than half the total number of lines (some 750, I estimate, out of some 1750) are mainly devoted to the essentials of the intrigue comedy. About 300 are elaborations of comic rhetoric; the remainder develop the romance interests, and, with the comic rhetoric, point the themes. Even so rough a criterion confirms that the play is not to be regarded as a farcical intrigue-comedy and little more.[40]

While I do not wish to dispute Brooks's statement of theme, I question whether the farce is to be praised because of its "serious" issues. Surely the problem for analysis is to show how Shakespeare puts such topics to comic uses. About Egeon's sentence of death, for instance, Harry Levin states,

The framing figure of Egeon contributes an emotional tension, at the very outset, to what would otherwise have remained a two-dimensional drama.[41]

Yet this tension is short-lived because we infer as soon as we learn about his two sons in the same town where he is sentenced that all will turn out happily. Isn't it the very power of farce to transmute potential threats and "serious" themes to matters for laughter and joy? Shakespeare appears to be testing the power of his story by the very lengths to which he adds what would otherwise be "serious." Rather than separate the "comic intrigue" and "comic rhetoric" from the themes, we should ask how it is that themes, quite serious in other contexts, become the stuff of farce.

The neo-classical principles of sixteenth-century humanists cannot satisfy all our questions about the dynamics of comic attitudes, but they can prevent us from overemphasis on sentiments of love or sympathy for a condemned father, a misunderstood wife, or a beaten servant. If these principles encouraged playwrights to devise comedies closer to farce or satire than works like *Twelfth Night*, we need treat them with no less respect for that. Farce affords its distinctive pleasures that arise from its very limitations. It has the power to make us laugh at cuckolds, shrews, beaten servants, unpaid goldsmiths, unjust laws, even potential incest. Shakespeare did indeed change and add to his source play, but to make it more the kind of drama that it is, not to romanticize or soften it. The critics who best observe the particular comic power of the play for me are Paul Jorgensen and G. R. Elliott, even though others may be more thoroughgoing in their account of the themes.[42]

In *Shrew* the *duplex argumentum* allows several scenes to dramatizing the love and courtship of lovers. Petruchio's courtship of Katharina raises no problems about lyrical sentiments, for it takes the form of a battle of wits, built from stichomythia, epithet, and pun, which create a dialogue like the quarrels of the chronicle plays. Lucentio's courtship of Bianca is a different matter. When he first sees her, he falls immediately in love and expresses his sentiment with no more than a gesture toward lyricism. His speech, in fact, is unique in the play. I quote its entirety:

But see, while idly I stood looking on,
I found the effect of love-in-idleness
And now in plainness do confess to thee,
That art to me as secret and as dear
As Anna to the Queen of Carthage was,
Tranio, I burn, I pine, I perish, Tranio,
If I achieve not this young modest girl.
Counsel me, Tranio, for I know thou canst.
Assist me, Tranio, for I know thou wilt.

(I.i.147-55)

Like Antipholus, he places the emphasis elsewhere than on the direct articulation of his sentiments. The only passage which directly expresses his feelings is: "I burn, I pine, I perish," and he delivers this not to Bianca but to his servant. Since it builds upon a no doubt intentionally inadvertent comparison of himself to Dido, it was designed to strike the audience as funny. His one moment of courtship with Bianca on stage, Act III, scene i, occurs when he is disguised as her Latin tutor, restrained from any full expression of his feelings by the presence of Hortensio, also disguised and also trying to woo Bianca. This arrangement of suitors in contest directs our response toward laughter rather than to sympathy with the young lovers. Lucentio states his love intermittently with Latin phrases to disguise his intention from Hortensio, but this trickery allows him to communicate no more than his identity and his desire. Hortensio, impatient and suspicious, quickly diverts our attention to his courtship, which he carries on through phrases of musical instruction. Neither tutor gets farther than statement of rudimentary facts. When next we see the suitors and Bianca, Act IV, scene ii, the major business is Hortensio's withdrawal from the contest. The lovers devote their private conversation to plans for marriage so that the audience must infer that their courtship has progressed offstage. The romance of the "normal" young lovers, which contrasts to the taming of Katharina by Petruchio, serves as occasion for comic disguise, double talk, and intrigue rather than expression of intimate feelings.[43]

R. B. Heilman has written a sane account of *Shrew* as a farce that measures the inadequacy of such critics as H. C. Goddard and Nevill Coghill, who would sentimentalize Katharina. Heilman says, "The essential procedure of farce is to deal with people as if they lack, largely or totally, the physical, emotional, intellectual, and moral sensitivity that we think of as 'normal.' "[44] He supports his classification by observing how quick-paced and automatic, even mechanical, the action is. Lucentio falls in love as soon as he sees Bianca; when the two Vincentios confront one another in Act V, neither pauses to reason about the mistaken identity, but takes recourse to insults and blows. Yet no one gets hurt even though Katharina breaks a lute over Hortensio's head, Petruchio beats Grumio, and he trains Katharina like a falcon. Heilman's classification agrees with Quintilian's stipulation about the range of emotion proper to comedy even though he speaks of a subgenre of comedy.

Farce would be decidedly an inadequate category for *Two Gentlemen,* the comedy in which Shakespeare adjusts the neo-classical stipulations to cover the experience of love. Expressions of affection abound: Julia tears up Proteus's letter and then cherishes every little piece of paper (I.ii.101–30); Valentine describes to Proteus at length his devotion to Silvia (II.iv.165–74); Proteus woos Silvia while Julia watches in anguish (IV.ii); and Proteus delivers two introspective soliloquies that disclose his struggle between the feelings of friendship for Valentine and desire for Silvia (II.iv.189–211; II.vi.).[45] This story of romantic tribulations is plotted to dramatize how the characters feel as well as how they behave, but the audience responds with none of the sympathy or pity that later Romeo and Juliet evoke. The experience of love remains within the province of comedy because Shakespeare makes romantic love a distinguishing attribute of the courtier class. As the title directs us, the comedy is about not two ordinary men, but two gentlemen who feel love.[46] It follows that the plotting must set against this class another of those who do not feel romantic love. This class, represented by the servants Lucetta, Speed, and Launce—remains distinct not only by social position and sentiment but by their criticism of those they serve. If romantic love with all its attendant follies becomes a natural attribute for young lords and ladies, can we describe as scornful our laughter at their behavior? Events show their love to be inevitable and irresistible as well as irrational, so that the laughter of scorn is hardly an adequate response. As we shall see in the next chapter, an attitude which both recognizes the limitations of the young lovers and at the same time accepts them as inevitable can be described as the laughter of kinship or the laughter of acceptance.

The story of *Two Gentlemen* raises a problem about classifying natural romantic sentiment which the stories of *Labors* and *Dream* solve. If romantic love is a natural attribute, then all the courtiers and ladies should feel in much the same way. Julia, Valentine, and Silvia do feel alike in being constant to their first love. That Proteus's emotions differ is demanded by the story, for they set the difficulties to be resolved. What causes his difference in feeling is never clearly revealed although his proper name indicates that something other than love must be the cause. The abstraction "Proteus" like the abstraction implied in "Valentine" fits uneasily with the specific "Julia," but it discloses something of Shakespeare's thinking about motivations when writing this play. Type characters act from tautological motives. Proteus's love changes because, as his name indicates, it is his nature to change. We in the audience could describe his feeling as "passion" or "lust" rather than true love, but this distinction would only shift the ground of our difficulty. When faced with the question why Proteus feels passion while Valentine feels true love, we return to the observation that it is in their natures (and names) to feel this way. A comedy, of course, might well be based on such a distinction of feeling, but the dialogue, as it stands, provides no such terms for understanding the sentiments; we must import them from outside the play, a procedure which a critic takes at his peril. Nor can we say that Proteus's change is similar to Katharina's, embodied in the person of Silvia as hers is embodied in the person of Petruchio, because the plotting stresses his inner conflict. Two soliloquies reveal his struggle between the value of friendship and his feeling for Silvia. When Proteus repents, it is Valentine's characteristic unselfishness and friendship which cause him to change his affection for Silvia, and it is Julia's characteristic devotion, revealed by her disguise and adventures, that regenerates his former love. In spite of their virtues, the external causes that account for his repentance, we feel unconvinced by his conversion, for the dramatization of the story has raised questions about his inner feelings, and we await a full expression of his regret, which is not forthcoming.[47]

Shakespeare's assumptions about comic characterization fit with neoclassical stipulations of the sixteenth-century commentators, and while they cause a difficulty with the story of *Two Gentlemen*, they square with the stories of *Labors* and *Dream*. In *Labors* the central predicament raises no distinction between the young courtly lovers. Navarre and his attendant lords set absurdly idealistic standards for themselves only to discover how human they are when they fall equally and in-evitably in love. The comedy traces the courtiers' adjustment to their own human nature.[48] In *Dream* the four young lovers face a predica-ment similar to the one in *Two Gentlemen,* but here the cause is ex-ternalized in the juice of love-in-idleness, a delightful invention to show how lovers can alter their emotions without reason. Lysander and Demetrius are to the audience's eyes equally appropriate for marriage to Hermia; throughout the play we can hardly distinguish them. Yet to her eyes, a lover's eyes, there is no comparison between the one she loves and the one her father approves. There is no demonstrable "reason" why she prefers Lysander. The escapades in the forest bear out in almost allegorical fashion the fact that the lovers behave foolishly, that is, un-reasonably. The juice of a simple flower serves to make objective the irrationality of affection. Theseus interprets the lovers' behavior for us, articulating the standard of decorum by which we judge. We see that lovers act under the influence, like poets and lunatics, of imagination or fancy, embodied in "fantastics," and we laugh at their irrationality.[49]

Symmetry would demand that *Venus and Adonis* exercise an in-fluence as important for the early comedies as *The Rape of Lucrece* exercises for the early histories and tragedies. Since the later three of the early five comedies take romantic love as their central experience, it could be that the writing of *Venus and Adonis,* either shortly before or after *Two Gentlemen*, influenced Shakespeare's thinking about the ways to render love in dialogue. One can discern a similarity of at-titude—bemused tenderness—between the exhilarating anguish of Venus in love and Julia in love. But it is difficult to specify closer links between the poem and the comedy. Elizabethans made no sharp dis-tinctions between narrative and dramatic tragedy; Willard Farnham, Howard Baker, Lily B. Campbell, and Virgil Whitaker, among others, have shown how closely verse narratives, especially those in *The Mirror for Magistrates*, influenced stage tragedies. The erotic epyllion, by its very subject, would necessarily be less influential.

The best account of the way the poem relates to the plays, an essay by Norman Rabkin, stresses a pattern of thought common to the two forms. On more local matters of technique, J. W. Lever has said, "But the poem is, in fact, not a comedy or a tragedy. It is not a drama. It is occupied with narrating a myth.[50] In so far as Venus is a tautological character, the goddess of love who loves, she is comparable to characters in the early plays, comic or serious; in so far as she is an immortal god and female who undertakes to woo a mortal and male, she exhibits indecorus and laughable behavior. Yet more to the point, Elizabethan comedy exhibits a variety of characters in their social guises to accompany and indeed affect their sentiments. While Venus and Adonis exhibit characteristics incidentally similar to dramatic characters, they show no distinctive qualities about lovers that, so far as I can tell, were influential on the later comedies. What is distinctive about *Venus and Adonis* is nondramatic; what it shares with the comedies, it shares in general.

∞

Roughly speaking, Shakespeare's development through the first five comedies can be described by his effort to combine the experiences of romantic love with the general principles of neo-classical comedy, a movement which broadly approximates the change from the rhetorically oriented to the mimetic serious plays. A comparison between the two should lead us to understand more about the meaning of "rhetorical" and "mimetic" as they apply to Shakespeare's early plays even though the terms do not fit the early comedies in the same way that they do the serious plays. For instance, *Errors* and *Shrew* are conceived like mirrors, artifacts that reveal foolish patterns of behavior to be laughed at and avoided, whereas the early chronicles are conceived like dramatized orations, also artifacts within the real world that are designed to instruct. The later plays, comic and serious, present themselves not so much as special items within the real world as little self-contained worlds. The way the playwright changes his methods of plotting to affect the audience's reactions clarifies this difference.

As instructive artifacts, the early plays reflect the audience's already formed general opinions. In *1 Henry VI,* for instance, the characterizations of Talbot and the French enemies exploit the audience's sense of patriotism. *Errors* and *Shrew* likewise depend upon general standards of behavior, such standards as we apply automatically to shrews, young men in love, gullible pedants, inefficient servants. Consequently, the audience feels no hesitation about their approval or disapproval of characters in *1 Henry VI* or *Errors*. Clearly designed, the narratives conform to explicit themes, such as Katharina's concluding speech on the duties of a wife, that never raise perplexities of the kind evoked by *Richard II*. The audience's values are confirmed, and they are encouraged to put them to practice. But just as in the real world of everyday affairs, we have difficulty in classifying behavior by categories of what is to be avoided and what is to be imitated, so too in the later apprentice comedies, judgments seldom remain unqualified; laughter is hardly ever entirely scornful, and the foolish usually have enough insight to measure the wise. Likewise, the interplay of Bolingbroke and Richard II cannot be dramatized by the patterns of rhetoric that serve to render the interactions of Cardinal Winchester and Duke Humphrey. The later characters behave in ways that fit neither the earlier conventions nor clear-cut categories of judgment. Verisimilitude replaces instruction as the primary consideration of the playwright. In *Labors* we laugh most readily at Armado and Holofernes, but they have the ability to measure Navarre and his courtiers; and Navarre's academy, whom we laugh at almost as easily, is mocked by the Princess of France and her ladies; yet we come to learn that even their mockery has its limitations. The later apprentice plays hold up hypothetical worlds to the real world to affect our sympathies and judgment in complex ways like events in the real world, not like dramatized orations or mirrors that reflect general patterns of behavior.

The audience faces head-on the artifacts of the rhetorical chronicle and the mirror comedy, which confirm the values they already hold, but the audience must participate in the mimetic comedy and chronicle, sympathizing in spite of disapproval, laughing without rejecting, waiting for crucial information, adjusting first impressions and snap judgments. The comic worlds of *Labors* and *Dream* even contain their own dramas. In my view, it is inevitable that Shakespeare's development toward "mimetic" drama would incorporate playlets into his plays, playlets that raise the plays to a status comparable to the real world which contains plays. In his realizing the potentialities of drama as drama, he would inevitably incorporate self-criticism, for like a human being who individuates himself by awareness of his particularity so drama becomes most itself when it can dramatize a little drama.

Comic Characterization

7

What practical help in characterization did playwrights get from the sixteenth-century commentators and rhetoricans who discussed comedy? Two dramatists, writing shortly before Shakespeare, have left us some evidence of the way their general propositions were interpreted. Richard Edwards says in the prologue to *Damon and Pithias* (1571):

In comedies the greatest skill is this: rightly to touch
All things to the quick, and eke to frame each person so
That by his common talk you may his nature rightly know.
A roister ought not preach—that were too strange to hear,—
But, as from virtue he doth swerve, so ought his words appear.
The old man is sober; the young man rash; the lover triumphing in joys;
The matron grave; the harlot wild, and full of wanton toys:
Which all in one course they no wise do agree,
So correspondent to their kind their speeches ought to be. [1]

His statement on the decorum of speech could be supported by almost any handbook of rhetoric that describes the school exercise of *ethopoeia*, sometimes called a figure and sometimes a kind of oration or theme, that delineates the character of a hypothetical type or historical person from within, as it were, by self-description and manner of speech. [2]

When Edwards speaks of the proper function of comedy, to touch things to the quick, he restates the traditional idea that comedy presents a "lively image of our everyday life" or a "mirror of custom." George Whetstone in his "Epistle Dedicatorie" to *Promos and Cassandra* (1578) talks much like Edwards:

For to worke a Commedie kindly, grave olde men should instruct: yonge men should showe the imperfections of youth: Strumpets should be lascivious: Boyes unhappy: and Clownes, should be disorderlye. [3]

Where do they learn that old men ought to be sober, young men rash, and matrons grave? Cannot old men be rash, such as Hortensio in *Shrew*? Cannot young men be cautious like Antipholus of Syracuse? Whetstone and Edwards appear to have understood the classifications proposed by the humanist critics and rhetoricians as dictating the way specific characters are to be created. Yet when we look at a specific character like Bottom, we question whether his desire to play all the major parts of the playlet can be said to be typical of his class of Athenian workmen. To begin with a class and deduce the appropriate attributes in creating characters is to produce generalized figures whose patterns of behavior mirror the audience's behavior in a direct and deductive fashion. The playwrights who did apply theory to practice in this way no doubt caused Dryden to observe that the characters in New Comedy seem to be all alike.

These playwrights have confused the understanding of character with the formation of characters. It is unlikely that Shakespeare shaped Bottom's character by first considering the class of Athenian workmen or workmen in general. Snug the Joiner and Peter Quince differ from Bottom, yet all three belong to the same class. What Shakespeare does is to give each member his outstanding characteristics and, following Quintilian's dictum, keeps them constant so that Bottom's behavior is typical, but it is typical of himself. His exuberant self-confidence is no momentary aberration. Had the story of Bottom revealed that his mother, let us call her Volumnia, urged him throughout his childhood to take leading parts, had she instilled in him a distaste for playing second fiddle, we would sense some motive other than his status as workman, and his typical trait would evoke a response other than laughter of scorn. Since neo-classical comedy restricts itself from revealing the inner workings of a character, the audience looks automatically to social place for satisfying its curiosity about the causes of human behavior. Shakespeare does not neglect emphasis on Bottom's membership in the group of workmen; the range of his responses coordinates with theirs; his style of speech is prose like theirs. Characters within the comedies interpret behavior by the same categories as the audience does. All Ephesians engage in witchcraft; all pedants are credulous; shrews need to be put in their place. Inadvertently we may have happened onto one of the powers of comedy. We are easily satisfied with explanations by kind, the sort of explanation that fosters provincialism and bigotry. It lies within the power of comedy to take our instinctive readiness to understand human behavior in simplistic terms and convert it to harmlessness by a story that allows our indulgence. This attitude is always partial and inadequate in the real noncomic world. The sixteenth-century theorists did not, of course, talk this way, but the hardiness of their prescriptions may well owe something to the fact that they support this basic pleasure that comedy does afford us.

Comic characterization, then, entails not only the attributes that differentiate one character from another, but the class, role, or place to which the character belongs, and we must add the standard of decorum which we implicitly associate with that class. By the way that comedy evokes or shapes this standard, the playwright asserts much of his individuality. Shakespeare learns to work on our sense of decorum through contrasting the critical attitudes of various characters. At the same time that he extends the principles of neo-classical comedy to encompass the experience of romantic love, he draws our attention to the limitations of groups of characters, their feelings, their manners, and their speech. To do this, he turns the characters into critics of one another and themselves. Since the sixteenth-century humanists linked the standards of decorum intimately to laughter, Shakespeare may have seen his efforts to sensitize us to standards of behavior as a way of affecting our laughter.

We in the twentieth century, who know how complex are the springs of laughter, can smile if not laugh at the explanation which locates the response in decorum. Techniques of comedy cannot be taught any more than the dynamics of laughter can be explicated, we say and settle back, content with the felicities of Shakespeare's genius. Yet from everyday experience we know that laughter admits of many different shades. A young child, an adolescent, and an adult do not always laugh at the same behavior; when they do laugh together, the timbre differs. This difference in timbre indicates difference in attitude, and attitude is shaped by experience and judgment. Likewise, Elizabethan laughter must not have been like Roman laughter, for historical circumstances give shadings to the audiences' attitudes. So too, Lyly's audience laughed differently from Jonson's, and Jonson's from Shakespeare's. But to press discriminations within laughter this far is to be pushed into saying finally that comedies themselves are different. The sixteenth-century commentators were not off base—though no doubt incomplete—when they maintained the generality of their observation that standards of judgment were involved in laughter. We can at least make a beginning toward understanding shades of laughter as well as something of characterization when we ask what Shakespeare's early comedies suggest as proper or normal social behavior. Comic characterization does not confine itself to contrivance of vivid attributes. The richness of Shakespeare's later comic characters lies as much in the way he manipulates our understanding of their social role or place as it does in our recognition of their ethos. Just as we cannot grasp the way that Verrocchio creates the effect of a smile if we look only at the lips and ignore the eyes and bone structure of his portrait busts, so too with Shakespeare's comic characterizations. Where he discloses most vividly his convictions on matters of decorum, at least to twentieth-century audiences, is in his low comic characters, so that I shall begin discussing characterization with the Dromios, Launce, Speed, Costard, and Bottom. Then it becomes easier to locate the techniques for presenting Julia, Proteus, Berowne, Hermia, or Lysander.

∞

If the low comic characters are servants, and almost all are in *Errors* and *Shrew* with the exception of the tinker, Christopher Sly, some obvious potentialities for indecorum and laughter follow automatically. The servant can be inadequate to his role as slow as Launce, as hungry as Speed, as confused in carrying out his master's orders as Costard or Puck—or he can be too adequate, clever enough to reverse roles and control his master, as Tranio momentarily does with Vincentio. Such interplay of master and servant exerts a constant comic appeal. Plautus used it and Shaw used it. No doubt Shakespeare would have created incompetent or clever servants or irascible or stupid masters whether or not he had read Terence or was influenced by the humanist tradition of the sixteenth century. Yet our laughter at John Tanner's chauffeur (*Man and Superman*) differs from our laughter at Pamphilus's servant Davus (*The Andria*) or at Antipholus's Dromio. Shakespeare from the outset of his career sees in low comedy a reflection of the social hierarchy, part of what Lovejoy calls the Great Chain of Being, what Tillyard calls the Elizabethan World Picture, and C. S. Lewis calls the Discarded Image. It has to do with what Ulysses calls "degree" and Cordelia calls her "bond." Luciana articulates the doctrine when she instructs Adriana that her role as wife is to obey and please her husband. Shakespeare gives it a more conspicuous place at the conclusion of *Shrew* when Katharina explains her obedience to Petruchio.

Shakespeare's understanding of the doctrine converts Plautus's story of mistaken identities into a story of isolation and fulfillment. Father separated from children, wife from husband, brother from brother, the family is isolated by the confusion of identities which is a temporary condition before fulfillment in domestic harmony. The consequent identities are domestic; we think of Egeon as a father and Antipholus as a brother, not as traveling merchants; we think of Luciana more as a sister than as a romantic lover. Yet their roles as members of the family hardly seen conducive to laughter, for lack of fulfillment is not itself comic. Accepting "degree," we see no discrepancy between how a proper father ought to act and how Egeon acts, or how Antipholus of Syracuse as a brother acts, or Emilia as a mother. When Egeon and Antipholus of Syracuse speak of their longing for their family, their comments are sober and touching. Where Shakespeare does find matter for laughter is in the discrepancy between how a master should treat his servant and how the Antipholi beat their Dromios. There are four beatings in *Errors*, but, interestingly enough for those who speak of the way Shakespeare softens Plautus, there are only threats of beating in the *Menaechmi* and only one beating in the *Amphitruo*.[4] Another source for laughter in both *Errors* and *Shrew*, the improprieties of the shrew, has in common with the mistreatment of the servant a relationship of power. It is worth returning to the way Luciana — and later Katharina — describes the degrees of nature and society: she interprets them as degrees of power, of dominance and submission or command and obedience rather than in terms of fulfillment. Our laughter of scorn, then, comes in large part from the improprieties of command and obedience.

Much of the low comic behavior arising from the improprieties of master and servant is slapstick. The brothers Antipholi are harsh masters, irritable to the point of beating their servants; in moments of exasperation both Petruchio and Katharina beat Grumio. The Dromios and Grumio, as best they can, carry out the offices of servant, and strangely it is because they are unjustly punished that we laugh.[6] The particular timbre of our laughter arises from a forced recognition of the harsh realities of command and subservience. The dynamics of our response can be clarified by comparison with laughter at episodes of cozening which present unsentimental pictures of the susceptible gull, dramatizing the proverb, "A fool and his money are soon parted." If we sympathize at all, we side with the victim, but dramatization seldom tips the scales toward the victim, for sympathy inhibits laughter. It cannot be said that the cozener is praised, since the cards are stacked so that deception is inevitable. We laugh not because we experience a surprise but because we are forced to acknowledge an unpleasant fact that we would rather ignore, that some human beings are victimized regardless of their good nature. Entailed in our response is the feeling that the gull is not seriously harmed; his capacity for happiness remains unchanged, but so do his susceptibilities. Cuckold or minority jokes work in much the same way. They expose harsh realities and force audiences to acknowledge what they would rather avoid. Since divorce today provides a release from unhappy marriages which were once conditions to be endured, these jokes have a faded appeal for us. Similarly, comic routines of servant and master cannot affect us as forcefully as they did an Elizabethan audience whose lives were intimately acquainted with the harsh realities of servants. In their society the servant had little recourse from unjust masters. Our laughter is a forced acknowledgment of this unpleasant fact of reality that we would prefer to avoid.[7]

To exploit the harsh facts of service, Shakespeare could have dramatized a number of situations: disagreements between master and servant over serious or trivial matters, punishment by a mistaken or cruel master, provocation by a mistaken or real disobedience. Some playwrights of the 1580s and early 1590s pushed their interplay to the breaking point: the good servant leaves a harsh or unproviding master, as in *Gallathea* (ca.1584–88), or a bad servant leaves a good master without understanding his virtues, as in *The Rare Triumphs of Love and Fortune* (1582). In Shakespeare's comedies of the 1590s only Launcelot Gobbo leaves his master, Shylock, to join Bassanio, but only with the permission of both. Shakespeare never depicts the lazy, inefficient, greedy servant and therefore never capitalizes upon justifiable chastisements and beatings, at least in the early comedies; Caliban comes to mind immediately from a later period. During the years of his apprenticeship it is mainly in the comedies of Robert Greene that truly inadequate servants appear: Miles in *Friar Bacon and Friar Bungay* (ca. 1589–92) or Adam in *A Looking Glass for London and England* (ca. 1587–91). If we generalize to say that Shakespeare finds undeserved punishment of greater comic appeal, we must face an objection that the predicament of mistaken identities in *Errors* demands this sort of interplay between master and servant. In answer, one could say that Shakespeare might have chosen to depict a mischievous Dromio, seizing opportunities to use Antipholus's purse when it accidentally comes his way. Or the visiting Dromio could engage in merchandizing exploits of his own to compound the confusion of his master's relations with the native Ephesians. Shakespeare chooses instead to exploit the comic possibilities of unjust punishment and continues to mine this vein in *Shrew*.

One comic episode in *Shrew* generates the laughter of acknowledgment by reversing the relationship of master and servant so that we laugh not at unjust beatings but at the master as victim. Grumio's scene in Act IV, scene i, gives a foretaste of Shakespeare's mastery of low life that appears in the Henry IV plays. Before the entrance of Petruchio and Katharina, the main business of the dialogue is a narration of their wedding journey from Padua. It is conducted with byplay between Grumio and Curtis — in prose — to suggest that their customary relationship is one of quarreling which they have refined by long practice to high art. Later the tavern group in *2 Henry IV* and the crowd at Ursula's tent in *Bartholomew Fair* are to give full scope to the art of affectionate insult. Our laughter at Grumio and Curtis takes some of its force from the resemblance to the behavior of their betters, the newly married couple.

When Petruchio enters with his new bride, both disheveled from the journey, the dialogue modulates to another kind of laughter. He demands to know why his orders have not been carried out. Without undue emphasis, Grumio delivers a hilarious explanation, spinning out elaborate details to excuse the seven servants who fail to greet their master in the park. The audience listens, knowing that Grumio has devoted his time to gossip rather than to preparations for his master's arrival. Implicit in his speech, contrived on the spur of the moment with an unsuspected ingenuity, is a long training period in which he developed the expertise of inventing excuses rather than performing his duties. His speech, extraneous to the central matter of Petruchio's swaggering and intimidation of Katharina, gives us another glimpse of the way forces balance themselves in a society of "degree." We respond with the laughter of acknowledgment at the "inadequate" servant while Petruchio responds simply with "Go, rascals, go, and fetch my supper in" (IV.i.123).

Like the Dromios, Grumio suffers the hot tempers of Petruchio and Katharina, but the Dromios have no separate scenes of low life. Shakespeare confines their experiences to one relationship, the misunderstanding and unjust treatment by their masters. This relationship generates a laughter of forced recognition at the way things are in a hierarchy that depends upon command and obedience, the same hierarchy that also affords the standards of decorum for laughing at the shrew, the pedant, and the courtesan. On the whole, our laughter evoked by *Errors* and *Shrew* can be understood by Sidney's term, the laughter of scorn, the laughter that arises from our judgment that behavior deviates from the standard of decorum.

Yet one episode of mistaken punishment in *Errors* raises the possibility for discriminating attitudes contained within this "laughter of scorn." Implicit in scorn is the audience's detachment from what it laughs at : scorn implies superiority. Is this an accurate response to Dromio of Ephesus who delivers this speech after several unjust beatings?

I am an ass indeed; you may prove it by my long ears. I have served him from the hour of my nativity to this instant, and have nothing at his hands for my service but blows. When I am cold, he heats me with beating; when I am warm, he cools me with beating. I am waked with it when I sleep, raised with it when I sit, driven out of doors with it when I go from home, welcomed home with it when I return; nay, I bear it on my shoulders, as a beggar wont her brat; and, I think, when he hath lamed me, I shall beg with it from door to door.

(IV.iv.27–36)

The insistent rhythms of this speech create an intensity that appears to claim from us a response more intimate than detachment and sounds much like another troublesome speech, Shylock's "Hath not a Jew eyes?" (*Merchant*, III.i.46–64). Twentieth-century audiences respond with a sentimentality that would no doubt have surprised an Elizabethan. Shylock's speech is designed to justify revenge, and it could be said that Dromio's speech exaggerates the plight of the servant with a conscious exuberance to generate by its very energy laughter in the audience. Still, it is hard not to accept the possibility that the playwright aims at affecting more than our sense of impropriety. In short, Dromio's speech brings out the strong sense of injustice from the point of view of the victim to implicate and slightly discomfort us. The harsh realities which force upon us the laughter of acknowledgment stimulate our sense of complicity in recognizing them. Surely no man or woman who laughed at cuckold jokes laughed with complete innocence any more than one today laughs at minority jokes with innocence. Merriment about fondness for liquor has about it a complicit acknowledgment that the enjoyment is tinged with risk, however slight it is. We hardly make jokes, for instance, about the pleasures of iced tea. Without any wish to complicate the matter, let me say that the laughter of forced acknowledgment cannot be identified with a laughter of superiority. Much of the laughter at shrews, at knocking on the door, at Dr. Pinch and the gullible pedant, at the December wooer, can be described as the detached laughter from a superior viewpoint. The laughter at the harsh realities of servants entails our forced acceptance of the way things are, a laughter that prefigures the responses evoked by the later comedies. In them Shakespeare seems inclined to develop episodes that stimulate the laughter of kinship, forcing us to acknowledge the realities of our human shortcomings especially in matters of courtship and romance.

∞

Quintilian excludes the sentiments of friendship and love from the constant emotions which comprise *ethos* or character that he takes to be the proper subject for the comic mirror. Shakespeare, however, understands the sentiments of romantic love to be a distinguishing characteristic of courtiers. As such, love is integral to his conception of the social hierarchy and, to dramatize it as distinctive of gentlemen, he sets in contrast the low comic characters as a group untouched by romantic sentiments. The interplay of servant and master changes into a relationship far more complex than command and obedience which we find in *Errors* and *Shrew*. The low comic character acts to measure the limits of his betters, and the plotting reflects this different conception, for Launce and Speed appear in four episodes apart from their masters, whereas the Dromios have none, and Grumio only one. The episode of Grumio and Curtis shows us that, once the servants are set apart, we automatically sense an analogy with other characters in other episodes. So too with Launce. Immediately after Proteus takes farewell of Julia (II.ii) Launce narrates his poignant farewell to his family, using one shoe to represent his mother, another to represent his father (II.iii). His praises of a milkmaid, assessing her capacity to work, her physical defects and advantages (III.i.264–360), follow Valentine's and Proteus's idealizations of Silvia and precede Proteus's advice to Sir Thurio on the proper manner of courtship (III.ii). In Act V at the height of emotional turmoil when Proteus has been spurned by Silvia and when Julia, in a page's disguise, suffers with the knowledge of her lover's infidelity, Launce appears on stage to soliloquize on his sufferings brought about by the indiscretions of his dog Crab.[8] Speed, Valentine's servant, acts as a clear-eyed critic of his master's behavior rather than as a low comic parallel. With a greater verbal facility than Launce, he can judge his master because he enjoys a freedom from the befogging sentiments of romantic love. And blinding they are, for just after Speed first describes to Valentine his transparent and foolish behavior, Silvia appears; having asked Valentine to write a love letter for her, she refuses it and lets him keep it for his pains. Too much in love to see her conceit, Valentine becomes dejected, and it takes Speed, the detached observer, to interpret her action.[9] Unquestionably Shakespeare means the courtiers, by the range and quality of their sentiments, to be set above their servants, but the relationship is hardly a simple one of possession and deprivation.

Romantic love in Shakespeare's early comedies is no such ennobling sentiment as Britomart's or Prince Arthur's in *The Faerie Queene* but is closer to the one John Lyly dramatized in his first two comedies, *Campaspe* and *Sapho and Phao*. Alexander the Great in the earlier and Sapho in the later are rulers subjected to the temptations of love for people of lesser rank. Events make apparent that for a conqueror or queen to succumb to such feelings would be a severe breach of decorum. Love appears as a temptation to be resisted by reason or counteracted by the value of honor so that happiness at the ending is defined by overcoming the temptation. We cannot conclude from these two stories that Lyly disapproved of love for rulers but only that something more important, like honor, must help discriminate among romantic sentiments. His later comedies, *Gallathea* and *Love's Metamorphoses*, make no such discriminations but stress the irresistible power of love in overcoming apparently insuperable opposition. Shakespeare emphasizes both the irresistible and the irrational qualities of love in *Two Gentlemen*, irrational in the logical sense of causing contradictory behavior and irrational in the ethical sense of causing deviation from reasonable rules of moral behavior. Julia's famous letter scene — she wants to read and cherish it, yet refuses to disclose her feelings before Lucetta and tears it up — dramatizes early in the play the way love provokes contradictory behavior.[10] Proteus's inability to control his sudden love for Silvia and Valentine's inevitable succumbing to love after his initial sneers dramatize its irresistible force. Given such a description without noting the way Shakespeare plots events, one would assume that he intends his audience to take a censorious attitude. To be shown as comic, romantic behavior would, it seems, stimulate the laughter of scorn. Yet the presence of low comic characters helps guide the audience to accept rather than censure the lovers' behavior, or to put the matter more precisely, they prevent the audience from either extreme of approval or scorn.[11]

Proteus's betrayal of Valentine threatens the happiness of two innocent and well-intentioned characters so that the audience is tempted to become intimately involved in their plight, but Shakespeare plots events to deflect these feelings by sheer comic foolishness. In the opening acts, once Launce, Speed, and Lucetta make clear that the entanglements of romance are the attributes of the gentle class, we in the audience are not encouraged to make the kinds of discriminations among romantic sentiments as we do in the first acts of *Romeo and Juliet*. There Romeo's attitude toward Rosaline, the Capulets' attitude toward Paris as a husband, the Nurse's expectations for Juliet, and Mercutio's interpretations of Romeo's feelings are all set in contrast to the sentiments of the two young lovers. When Proteus's threat develops in Acts III and IV of *Two Gentlemen*, Shakespeare bolsters our critical detachment by interspersing scenes of analogous emotional experiences, such as Launce's catalog of the milkmaid's virtues. It is difficult to remain deeply involved in predicaments when they occur in tandem with obviously ridiculous events. At one of the most threatening moments, when Valentine is banished, Launce comes on stage quite obviously to make us laugh. He announces the sentence of banishment but confuses the word with "vanish." When Valentine despondently says that he is "nothing," Launce is willing to put his remark to a practical test with a blow. His behavior serves in the simplest way to counteract our involvement. This is Shakespeare's first comic narrative that gives the audience scant assurance that all will turn out happily.[12] In plotting it, he is not entirely successful, particularly in Act V where the troublesome question of Proteus's conversion arises. When Shakespeare next undertakes a similar comedy, not until *The Merchant of Venice*, he still lacks complete mastery of adjusting comic tone to serious threat. In *Two Gentlemen* he depends in large part on the low-comic behavior and the critical stance of the servants to maintain the audience's distance; significantly they make no appearance in the final scene of discovery, conversion, and forgiveness.

More important than this ridiculous behavior for deflecting the audience's involvement is the way the servants measure the limitations of their betters and foster the audience's critical attitude. Launce, cut off from the mysteries of romance, fastens onto the practical concerns of everyday life when praising his milkmaid; what he misses in the heights and depths of sentiment is replaced by commonsense and hardihood. Valentine is too enraptured to think of dinner, but Speed cannot feed on the chameleon's dish. Julia, after watching in anguish Proteus's courtship of Silvia, turns to find the host, who has accompanied her, asleep. The natural hierarchy of social place, described by Luciana and Katharina in terms of command and obedience, has thus become a more complex arrangement of advantages and limitations. What one gains by virtue of his position is balanced by what he loses.

As an audience watches the play unfold, it modifies its judgment, adjusting its laughter at comic limitations by awareness of compensating gains. In the first scene of the play we watch Speed banter with Proteus for a tip and laugh at his wit, for his behavior conforms with our conventional conception of a servant. Yet in his next scene, when he judges Valentine's behavior and interprets Silvia's conceit of the letter, we modify our conception of "servant," for he makes claims on us as a critic. Launce's first appearance, like Speed's, leads us to categorize him in a way that must be modified by his later behavior: the sudden sharp awareness when he says, "I am but a fool, look you, and yet I have the wit to think my master is a kind of a knave" (III.i.261–62), his little triumphs of wit over Speed, and his attitude toward the milkmaid. So too for the major characters. As the play unfolds, we adjust our estimations. Julia's pluckiness, for instance, in her adventure as a page and her resilience in the face of Proteus's change of feelings add much to our first impression of a young girl with a love letter. These changes of impression about character need mean nothing more than the simple fact that, as stories unravel, characters inevitably grow more complex because they engage in more activities. Aside from the fact that in *Errors* we make no significant adjustments of our first impressions of the Dromios, Antipholus of Ephesus, or Luciana, the changing impressions would count for very little if they were not coordinated with a change in the audience's fundamental judgment. The very nature of social place as it emerges through changing impressions, critical views, and analogies is one which has limitations. Consequently we laugh at the same time that we acknowledge this is the way things are. Valentine is foolish by Launce's standards, and Launce's love would be inadequate by Valentine's standards. Neither needs to be explicitly critical of the other, but juxtaposed each acts in his own way to measure the other. We need not judge Valentine's romantic behavior by some ideal of rationality and control, for we see that he lacks the practicality Launce shows in abundance. Judged by some ideal, Valentine would be found wanting and the object of the laughter of scorn. We respond to each one, with the virtues and deficiencies of his place, by the laughter of acceptance, acknowledging that this is the way things are. Midway between scorn and approval, this response recognizes by laughter the limitations of behavior and yet does not contain the assumption that the limitations could be avoided. It is the comic response appropriate to a hierarchy of social place.

The play within the play scenes in *Love's Labor's Lost* and *Dream* realize the complexities of the social hierarchy more explicitly than any other moments in the early comedies. The central action of *Labors* is, roughly speaking, the adjustment by Navarre's academy to the claims of their flesh and blood. The King of Navarre and his attendant lords discover that they set themselves standards which, by ignoring the limitations of their human nature, are not only unrealistic but presumptuous.

The main story is supplemented by several low-comic characters who exaggerate the discrepancy between what they think they are and what they are. Don Armado affects the manners of a Renaissance courtier, Holofernes thinks himself the epitome of wit and learning, and Sir Nathaniel admiringly agrees.

The narrative dramatizes the very process of adjusting standards by the characters that the audience itself undergoes toward events of *Two Gentlemen*. The first part of *Labors* sets forth the improprieties, and the second the exposures, realizations, and adjustments. Although this summary may lead one to think that the play resembles Ben Jonson's comical satires, it fits with Shakespeare's customary attitude toward decorum because the governing subject is love which Jonson, true to the humanist principles of comedy, did not dramatize until late in his career in *The New Inn*. Jonson's humour characters affect roles that denature them and are thus harmful. Navarre, his courtiers, and Armado attempt to be more than themselves, but fail. Their exposure leads not to a change in themselves as do Jonson's satires so much as an adjustment to be themselves. Holofernes, on the other hand, would fit into a Jonsonian comedy, for his exposure is not a recognition but a shaming, the results of which are never pursued within the play. It is difficult to dramatize convincingly the conversion of ingrained folly; at best shaming can be traumatic and a change intimated. Most of the exposures in *Every Man Out of His Humour* follow this pattern, and so does Malvolio's in *Twelfth Night*. Shakespeare, then, prudently arranges for Holofernes and Sir Nathaniel to retire after the Show of the Nine Worthies so that they are forgotten in the final sentences, forgiveness, and adjustments.[13]

Moth and Costard exercise the function of servant-critics. Moth, the witty page, banters with his master Armado, who remains unaware of the way he is mocked and deflated. Moth is not only akin to Lyly's pages, but his dialogue with Armado (I.ii) bears a strong resemblance to Epiton's dialogue with Sir Tophas in *Endimion* (III.iii).[14] As critic, Moth resembles Speed, while Costard resembles Launce. Costard makes no direct criticism of Navarre's impossibly strict dedication to his studies, but his very presence serves to comment on Navarre's folly. After being caught with Jaquenetta, in disobedience of the King's stricture that none shall keep company with a woman for three years, Costard says, "Such is the simplicity of man to hearken after the flesh" (I.i.212). His remarks to Navarre, like this one:

> *King*
> This maid will not serve your turn, sir.
> *Costard*
> This maid will serve my turn, sir.

(I.i.281-82)

formulate no shortcomings in the King's policies, as Berowne's remarks do; he is merely himself and, like Launce, sufficient to measure the limitations of his betters. Don Armado and Holofernes, too, act as critics in an oblique way by serving as exempla for Navarre and his academy, but Navarre sees them as objects of amusement. At the outset were he and his lords perceptive enough, they might have discerned in Armado's pretensions, including his ornately learned letter condemning Costard, a cooling card for academic courtiers. Holofernes first appears in Act IV as the kind of figure Navarre and his lords might well have become had they pursued blindly the ideal of learning divorced from what Costard calls the simplicity of the flesh. While the pedant does not in his first scene appear before the academy, the audience senses clearly enough the relevance of his affectation.

The Show of the Nine Worthies brings face to face the social groups to measure one another and lead the participants as well as the real audience to a flexible sense of decorum. The servants turned actors are led by Holofernes, who chooses the subject of the Nine Worthies even though they are but five. Holofernes, himself, intends to play three roles. The outrageous discrepancy between role and actor entertains the audience by its unintentional impropriety, and like a mirror comedy the show exhibits a pattern of truth. Berowne recognizes the analogy, if not the precise relevance: "A right description of our sport, my lord" (V.ii.519). The courtiers laugh, as they should, at their image, but theirs is the laughter of scorn. Shakespeare devotes much of the remainder of the play to modifying this kind of laughter, for mockery lacks awareness of one's own limitations and happens to be the contrary of the attitude that first encourages Navarre and his men to set for themselves a rigid program of study. Both assume that men should conform to ideal standards of human behavior.

As a result of the audience's mockery, Sir Nathaniel and Holofernes leave the stage in shame. Costard corrects the audience's opinion with no malice by reminding them that Sir Nathaniel has other qualities:

There, an't shall please you, a foolish mild man; an honest man, look you, and soon dashed. He is a marvellous good neighbor, faith, and a very good bowler; but for Alisander—alas, you see how 'tis—a little o'erparted.

(V.ii.575-78)

If the parson is inadequate to his role as Alexander, his role is also inadequate to represent him. Holofernes's one direct remark to the audience when he is laughed off stage makes the same criticism, but less effectively:

This is not generous, not gentle, not humble.

(V.ii.621)

His comment goes unnoticed in the courtiers' merriment, but we in the outer audience would do well to heed it. Mockery is corrective for others, but it fails to account for the fallibility of the mockers and should not therefore be the final attitude which a mirror comedy evokes.

While the confrontation of the low-comic characters with the courtly audience calls our attention to the limitation of mockery, the appearance of Mercade makes it forcefully. The dominant mockers of the playlet are the lords, whose vulnerability as mockers is obvious to us in the outer audience, but the ladies are mockers too, not so much of the playlet but of the lords, and their vulnerability is less obvious to us. Mercade may be a later addition by Shakespeare; certainly the presence of several duplicated passages in Act V indicates revision in this part of the play.[15] If the announcement of the King of France's death represents Shakespeare's maturer consideration, it pushes further the directions already within the playlet: to humanize by revealing limitations. Preceding events depict the Princess of France as particularly sharp-tongued. Her banter with the forester in Act IV, scene i, appears to pad the scene with extraneous wit if we overlook her opening remark. At the outset she makes an admiring comment on Navarre spurring his horse uphill, a comment that intimates a love for him at a point in the play when she has little assurance that he would respond in kind. Later in the scene she rejects with an acerb wittiness the praise of the forester and bewilders the simple man. This moment, while it gives us a glimpse behind her courtly façade, reveals an indifference to the feelings of the forester. Mercade's announcement of death, itself a reminder of the final human limitation, has the immediate dramatic effect of humanizing the Princess so that her grief stimulates our awareness of her vulnerability and our sympathy. This movement fits into the direction indicated by Costard's and Holofernes's remarks during the playlet. So too the last laughable episode in the play, the literal exposure of Armado;

his embarrassment over having no undershirt is, I think, intended to be funny, but it exposes Armado's humanity in a way we would never have suspected had we seen only his opening dialogue with Moth. Both the inner and outer play stimulate the laughter of scorn and then modulate it into the laughter of acceptance as we watch the characters hearken to the simplicities of their flesh.

In *A Midsummer Night's Dream* Shakespeare makes the laughter of scorn itself the object of laughter, and it too becomes one of man's limitations. The playlet in the final act of this comedy dramatizes the laughter of scorn as a symptom of human blindness to reality. We laugh at it and must sense how restrictive it is if we are to differentiate ourselves from the audience on stage. The low-comic characters choose to perform "Pyramus and Thisbe," as improper to their abilities as the Show of the Nine Worthies to the performers in *Labors*. Yet the Athenian workmen remain happily insulated in their own view of themselves, untouched by the audience's laughter at their expense. In the same way the stage audience, as blind to their own limitations, fail to see how the playlet mirrors their shortcomings. Their failure should warn us in the outer audience by analogy, a relationship that remains comically implicit in the structure of the play. The story of Pyramus and Thisbe turns on a misinterpretation of fact because the lover Pyramus allows his fancy to control his behavior. So too, the four courtly lovers behave in the forest like Pyramus, the fairies being "fantastics" or creatures of fancy who, in allegorical fashion, work upon their fancies.[16] Theseus in his central interpretative speech (V.i.2–27) clarifies for us the significance of the forest episode by stating the similarity of lunatics, lovers, and poets, all of whom allow their fancy rather than reason to govern their behavior.[17] Given these terms for understanding events, we in the outer audience are prepared to analogize the workmen's behavior who are playwrights or lunatics—it hardly matters which—with the lovers' behavior.

The standard by which we judge how foolish or unrealistic are their actions is the standard of cool reason. Theseus and Hippolyta, who appear to be controlled and reasonable, have been in their youth susceptible to the powers of Titania and Oberon, and as we watch the fairies bless the house and the wedding bed at the end of the play we recognize the continuing power of the fantastics and fancy over their marriage. Irrationality, of course, is more explicit in the other characters. Like Pyramus, who kills himself over a bloody scarf that he takes to signify Thisbe's death, Demetrius alters his love on the basis of no real fact. Neither can differentiate reality from his imaginary version of reality. The same confusion appears in the production of the playlet. The workmen trouble over the impact of an imaginary lion upon the ladies and cannot decide what properties could be left to the imagination, such as moonshine, and what properties should be present on stage to assist the enactment of the story. Nor can they differentiate between what items should be represented, such as walls, and what should be enacted, such as characters. To determine the difference, they would need to be rational, for reason, as Theseus tells us, is the faculty of grasping what is real and what is not. The audience on stage laughs at the actors' confusion, scornful but unaware that they too have been unable to differentiate the fantastic from the real, and suddenly at the end of the play when Puck steps out of his role to address us, we in the outer audience see too that we have failed to differentiate, for we have watched a play, a product of imagination, a mere fancy or dream as the title warns us, and we have taken it as reality. In an ever widening circle, our comic attitude encompasses ourselves so that the final laughter modulates from scorn to recognition and adjustment, accepting as one inevitable part of the human condition a blindness not only to the difference between reality and fancy but a blindness that produces the laughter of mockery.[18] Unlike the Show of the Nine Worthies, the playlet of Pyramus and Thisbe generates no shame; all remain insulated in their satisfied sense of themselves.

The low comic characters as actors exhibit an analogical relationship which Shakespeare begins to explore in Launce's absurd behavior. There in *Two Gentlemen* the emphasis falls on the difference between the low comic and his betters, each measuring the other. Here in the playlet Shakespeare brings all ranks together not only to measure one another but to reveal their kinship. To see how everyone shares in the limitation of irrationality is not to collapse the distinctions of social place. Shakespeare observes the variety in manners and customs to keep vividly distinct the social differences. Adhering strictly to Richard Edwards's practice, Shakespeare gives the workmen prose to speak when they do not attempt the doggerel of their playlet, the lovers rhymed verse, and the rulers blank verse. When Puck is most himself, he chants a rhymed, four-accent line. As in *Two Gentlemen*, the low comics feel none of the anguish the lovers feel; instead they enjoy a compensatory enthusiasm that balances their place in the order of things. We might say that what Theseus and Hippolyta gain in dignity by virtue of their status, they lose in sheer vitality, although to say this may be to equate dramatic necessities too rigidly with social attributes.

The question now facing us is what development, if any, Shakespeare's characterization of low comics reveals. If we confine ourselves to characterization in the strict sense of inventing attributes, then Bottom differs little from Launce. If we look beyond to the kind of laughter stimulated by low comic characters, differences appear. Certainly the difference in behavior and the difference in the kinds of separate scenes between *Errors-Shrew* and *Two Gentlemen* confirm the proposition that Shakespeare takes a major leap when he introduces romantic love as a subject for comedy. This new experience changes the underlying sense of social place and the timbre of our laughter. If we can discriminate further degrees of change, we must locate them in the kind of awareness evoked in the audience as it laughs at the comic improprieties on stage. Events in *Errors* and *Shrew* capitalize on the ready standards an audience brings to the theater, expectations about the proper harmony of husband and wife, master and servant, goldsmith and customer, young maiden and suitor. When characters fail to measure up to standards, we laugh. The slapstick beating of servants, I suggested, stimulates laughter of forced recognition somewhat different from the laughter of scorn, evoked elsewhere in these plays. In *Two Gentlemen*, while the follies of lovers generate the laughter of scorn at the outset of the play, later events show this attitude to be inadequate, so that, although still aware of their shortcomings, we recognize that the standards of rationality and control are ideals which human nature cannot quite fulfill. *Labors* makes this adjustment of ideals to human nature the main thread of the story and encompasses the laughter of scorn (or mockery) as an attitude itself inadequate. In *Dream* the laughter of scorn becomes an object of laughter. When we laugh, we laugh at the laughers. *Dream* makes the clinching revelation as a mirror comedy about the laughter of acceptance, showing us how we personally have been trapped by the same confusions as the characters on stage. We cannot avoid acknowledging our standard of rational discrimination as an ideal, since it makes us objects of laughter. In brief, Shakespeare's development can be measured by the expanding degrees of critical awareness that his comedies stimulate in the audience. Maybe Sidney was right in attaching the feeling of delight to our experiences of learning. Yet the pleasure I refer to entails some sense of relief as well as an enlarged awareness. By acknowledging that shortcomings are part of the human condition, we are in effect relieving ourselves from the strict demands of our standards. This is not to say that we abandon standards, for that would be as extreme a position as mockery. Instead, Shakespeare's later apprentice comedies encourage us to take a balanced attitude; we recognize that man cannot always go in full-dress, but we would take less pleasure in this recognition if we concluded that full-dress should never be worn.

∞

One difference between "high" and "low" comic characters is the sheer quantity of time they are on stage. The low comic characters can, because they appear intermittently in short episodes, exhibit one or two readily identifiable traits which they repeat on each reappearance. Repetition of a familiar trait in new circumstances gives pleasure by confirming the audience's initial understanding and thus reassuring them of the simplicities of explanation by class or profession, a social attitude which comedy allows them to indulge. Yet one or two readily identifiable traits are seldom sufficient to sustain our interest in major comic characters. One way for the playwright to follow Quintilian's stricture on ethos, a stricture that is practical if the character is to be the object of our scornful laughter and hold our interest, is to multiply the number of high comic characters so that no one need dominate our attention for long. *Errors, Labors,* and *Dream* scatter attention over a large group of "major" characters, thereby modifying the quantitative distinction between high and low comic characters. Another way is to devise a composite character, a simple collection of attributes. To take Antipholus of Syracuse, he responds with wonder at the strange ways of the Ephesians at some points and with irritation at others; he loves Luciana, beats his apparently inefficient servant, and searches for his long-lost brother. The audience never troubles about the nature of the self or substance which underlies his various activities and responses, a substance to which we give the word "character." We raise no question about an underlying character that would hold together all his attributes because he gives no indication of a distinct inner life. His plans and motives coincide with his behavior so that he suffers no inner conflicts, faces no moral choices, and reveals no short circuit between an inner self and outward actions. We in the audience feel no difficulty in coordinating his various responses; he loves Luciana, we understand, because he is a young man, and it is natural for young men to fall in love; his irritation with Dromio we know to be characteristic of masters;

his desire to hunt for his lost brother we attribute to his membership in the family. Yet the story leads us to make one tacit distinction among his attributes, separating the conditional from the unconditional. Antipholus's irritation at Dromio is conditional upon their misunderstandings; his love for Luciana is an unconditional trait of being a young man; so too his desire for fulfillment within his family. His comic improprieties are conditions of temporary circumstances. We assume that Adriana will become a patient, obedient wife once she has been instructed properly, that Luciana will love Antipholus once she learns that he is not her brother-in-law, and that Antipholus will not beat his servant once he learns the source of confusion. We assume that our standards of proper behavior are "normal," so that some of Antipholus's traits are temporary aberrations from the real and "constant" attributes of his class.

The distinction between a normal and a temporary trait is one more way to account for the seeming contradiction between Quintilian's statement that comedy reveals ethos or constancy of character and the fact that characters oftentimes change traits of character, even in purer examples of neo-classical comedy such as Ben Jonson's. This applies to the example of change discussed earlier, Katharina's, whose basic character we tacitly assume is to be an obedient wife. In short, our general sense of the social hierarchy rather than any underlying, particular substance serves to hold together the attributes implicit in manners, responses, and actions. So too the movement of the comic narrative gives us pleasure because our expectations are fulfilled at the conclusion when the major characters conform to our sense of normal social place.

Disguise is a device to help the playwright compound attributes without necessarily relating them to an inner self. Shakespeare may have happened onto disguise by choice of story; the sources for the subplot of *Shrew* and the Julia-Proteus plot of *Two Gentlemen* contain disguises. But he returns to it again and again in his major comedies. The complexity of character achieved by the tension between Julia's disguise as Fidele and her feelings as a young maiden in love can be gauged by her "natural" or normal character.[19] She is a young girl of constant devotion, bold enough to follow her love, spunky enough to become Proteus's page when she learns of his infidelity. In sum, she is made up of those qualities sufficient to account for her actions with no suggestion of further "character" not expressed in behavior. Even when she experiences the complex desire to read and cherish Proteus's letter but refuses to acknowledge to Lucetta that she cares about it, she explains her behavior in the same fashion that mirror comedy encourages the audience to understand, by relating it to its type:

What fool is she, that knows I am a maid,
And would not force the letter to my view!
Since maids, in modesty, say "no" to that
Which they would have the profferer construe "ay."

(I.ii.53–56)

In disguise she is prevented from either stating or explaining her sentiments. The double meanings in her dialogue with the host as she watches Proteus woo Silvia, and in her dialogue with Silvia when she describes Julia, impart a sense of depth to her character. Something remains unspoken — as rare in a rhetorical mirror comedy where verse is intended to articulate as a mute in opera. The unspoken sentiments give an impression of an inner self without the attendant memories, inner conflicts, and hypothetical tableaux that build the complexities of a tragic or chronicle character.

The success of disguise in compounding character helps us appraise the difficulties Shakespeare faces in constructing Proteus's character, for he must struggle with himself, choosing between his passion and his friendship for Valentine, not to mention abandoning Julia. This inner conflict, unique in the early comedies, raises the problem of a self which is distinct from the changing passions. As we have already noticed, Proteus's behavior differs from that of the other three romantic lovers and cannot therefore be explained by the class he belongs to. So too, the name "Proteus" gives little help to Shakespeare, for a protean character would feel no need to question his behavior, since it is automatically changing. Proteus is no personification, but is cut from the same cloth as the other characters of the play.[20] Shakespeare's difficulty can be seen in the way Proteus talks to himself. Naturally the young apprentice takes the readiest way to render Proteus's inner conflict, the soliloquy. That he needs two of them which almost follow one another (II.iv.191–214; II.vi.1–43) suggests the difficulty facing him.[21]

When Julia talks about herself, she speaks from the viewpoint of Fidele, but Proteus has no such clear external locus for his comments about himself. The opening statements of his first soliloquy reveal an uncertainty about where he stands, inside or outside of his feelings:

Even as one heat another heat expels,
Or as one nail by strength drives out another,
So the remembrance of my former love
Is by a newer object quite forgotten.

(II.iv.189–92)

The artificial order of his comparison evokes the image of a speaker who knows what he wishes to say beforehand. Yet his next sentence indicates that he has no certainty about what he intends:

It is mine eye, or Valentine's praise,
Her true perfection, or my false transgression,
That makes me reasonless to reason thus.

(II.iv.193–95)

This could be read as a rhetorical question, delivered with the same control as the opening sentence, but I think that we should take Proteus's words at face value: he ponders the motive for his change of heart and questions why he feels the way he does.[22] If not, his soliloquy becomes a bemused, even cynical meditation on his change of feeling. His question would become just a pose of perplexity, and this would make him more at home in *The Importance of Being Earnest* than in *Two Gentlemen*. Not that Shakespeare is incapable of self-irony. In his next comedy Berowne exhibits amusement at his own behavior, and his mode of expression leaves no doubt about how he regards himself. Proteus neither stands entirely apart from himself, aware of his own behavior, nor expresses his sentiments entirely from within to render the experience of a confused, dazzled young man. Generally speaking, in his first soliloquy he stands outside his feelings and describes them accurately to the audience:

. . . for now my love is thawed,
Which, like a waxen image 'gainst a fire,
Bears no impression of the thing it was.
Methinks my zeal to Valentine is cold,
And that I love him not as I was wont.

(II.iv.197–201)

and he diagnoses his behavior, the key word being "reason":

'Tis but her picture I have yet beheld,
And that hath dazzled my reason's light,
But when I look on her perfections,
There is no reason but I shall be blind.

(II.iv.206–9)

Proteus's wavering style becomes apparent when we place it against

Berowne's clearly focused style in *Labors,* where Shakespeare succeeds in rendering the inner conflict of a comic character. Berowne is both a smitten lover and a cynical critic of love.[23] In one soliloquy he speaks from a firm base outside his feelings, points to their foolishness, and accepts them helplessly. In another he speaks from the inside, trying to be critical, but remains confused and captivated by Rosaline. For instance, in the first soliloquy he mocks the figure of Love, the object of his love, and himself with copious use of diminishing figures in the controlled fashion of the cynical orator:

And I, forsooth, in love!
I, that have been love's whip,
A very beadle to a humorous sigh,
A critic, nay, a night-watch constable,
A domineering pedant o'er the boy,
Than whom no mortal so magnificent.
This wimpled, whining, purblind, wayward boy,
This signor-junior, giant-dwarf, Dan Cupid,
Regent of love-rimes, lord of folded arms,
The anointed sovereign of sighs and groans.

(III.i.162–71)

It is in this soliloquy that he makes the famous comparison of a woman to a German clock and describes Rosaline as

A whitely wanton with a velvet brow,
With two pitch balls stuck in her face for eyes.

(III.i.185–86)

By contrast, his second soliloquy comes from within and lacks the control of the earlier. We watch the process of thought as it is occurring rather than thought organized in set form, like an oration:

The king he is hunting the deer; I am coursing myself. They have pitched a toil; I am toiling in a pitch — pitch that defiles. Defile — a foul word! Well, set thee down, sorrow, for so they say the fool said, and so say I, and I the fool. Well proved, wit! By the Lord, this love is as mad as Ajax: it kills sheep; it kills me — I a sheep. Well proved again o' my side! I will not love; if I do, hang me. I' faith, I will not. O but her eye!

(IV.iii.1–8)

Later Rosalind in *As You Like It* exhibits the same flexibility in moving from deeply involved lover to witty critic of love, but she, like Julia, has a disguise to help keep distinct her attitudes. Berowne shifts from one to the other without puzzling us about where he stands with regard to his feelings.

What enables Shakespeare to succeed with Berowne can be described as self-awareness, a description that is easy to make but hard to explain in terms of dramatic technique.[24] An awareness of self creates a sense of self which is apart from a collection of attributes, an inner substance that cannot be equated with the sum of its parts. If Berowne is aware of his love, that part of him which generates the awareness must be in addition to the feelings of love. He is not, in other words, a tautological character, a lover who simply exhibits the behavior of a lover. Proteus has a similar complexity; his behavior does not illustrate himself. There is a short circuit between his desires and his behavior so that he struggles between the feelings of friendship for Valentine, loyalty to Julia, and his desire for Silvia. When he describes his feelings, the problem arises as to the basis from which he speaks, his "ethos," to use Quintilian's term. Is his basic character identifiable with the true feelings of friendship for Valentine and love for Julia while his desire for Silvia is a passing fancy? This could be a possible interpretation, but the name "Proteus" suggests otherwise, and the soliloquy, expressed from within and from without, gives no certainty as to which is the "real" or inner Proteus.

Another way of stating the difference between the successful characterization of Berowne and the puzzling characterization of Proteus is to consider their relation to the playwright rather than to an inner self. As we have seen elsewhere, the playwright stands behind rhetorical characters and makes their decisions for them, shaping their set-speeches on the model of an oration. Valentine, for instance, gives us a better example of the playwright's locus than Proteus, for he exhibits none of the wavering that we find in Proteus's soliloquy. When Valentine is exiled from Verona, he reacts in a soliloquy to state his loss, and he expresses it copiously through the help of rhetorical question and balanced syntax:

And why not death rather than living torment?
To die is to be banished from myself.
And Silvia is myself; banished from her
Is self from self, a deadly banishment.
What light is light, if Silvia be not seen?
What joy is joy, if Silvia be not by?

(III.i.170–75)

To conclude his soliloquy he sums up his thoughts in a neat antithesis:

Tarry I here, I but attend on death,
But, fly I hence, I fly away from life.

(III.i.186–87)

In short, his soliloquy exhibits the consciousness of loss without self-consciousness, and as such it fits the demands of a rhetorical character. His location toward his feelings remains stable like an orator's because he is clearly a good character, and his soliloquy acts like an oration to convince us of his intense feelings.

When Shakespeare abandons his position as orator-playwright, he figuratively turns over decisions of motive and expression to the characters so that they lose the assurance of the rhetorical characters and gain the ability to express their thoughts in the very process of thinking them, as Berowne shows in his second soliloquy of love.[25] He also shares Titus Andronicus's ability to stand outside and be aware of himself, an extra awareness that Proteus needs as a basis for his soliloquy. Proteus stands outside, but his locus appears to reside in the playwright rather than in himself. It is no coincidence, I think, that a play within the play occurs in the same comedy that characters become self-aware. When Berowne takes over from the playwright the ability to express his feelings in the process of thinking them and the ability to stand outside of his feelings and criticize them while still committed to them, so other characters become playwrights in the literal sense of producing a play within the play.

This is not to deny Shakespeare the ability to dramatize a self-divided character within rhetorically oriented drama. Characters like Suffolk in *1 Henry VI* struggle with their feelings. Shakespeare writes internalized debates between two voices, adapting the same pattern that works well between characters in the public forum. It is the solution that he uses for Richard III's soliloquy before the Battle of Bosworth Field when Richard debates with his conscience. And, as might be expected, Shakespeare resorts to the same device in Proteus's second soliloquy to dramatize his inner division. In fact, the rhythms of Proteus's debate either echo or anticipate Richard III's soliloquy.[26] As Proteus says,

Fie, fie, unreverend tongue, to call her bad,
Whose sovereignty so oft thou hast preferred
With twenty thousand soul-confirming oaths!
I cannot leave to love, and yet I do;
But there I leave to love where I should love.
Julia I lose and Valentine I lose.
If I keep them, I needs must lose myself;
If I lose them, thus find I by their loss:
For Valentine, myself; for Julia, Silvia.

(II.vi.14–22)

so Richard III says:

Richard loves Richard: that is, I am I.
Is there a murderer here? No. Yes, I am:
Then fly. What, from myself? Great reason why—
Lest I revenge. What, myself upon myself? . . .
O no! Alas, I rather hate myself
For hateful deeds committed by myself.
I am a villain. Yet I lie, I am not.
Fool, of thyself speak well. Fool, do not flatter.
My conscience hath a thousand several tongues,
And every tongue brings in a several tale,
And every tale condemns me for a villain.

(V.iii.183–96)

The staccato phrasing, the abrupt shifts, and the compact logic of both speeches create a sense of the divided character that satisfies us without need of the extra dimension of self-awareness that would raise the problem as to which of the two voices is the "real" substantive self.

Berowne, not only self-divided but aware that he is self-divided, takes his place as the comic counterpart of those characters in Shakespeare's later mimetic dramas who recall their past, project themselves into the future, and imagine hypothetical tableaux. Yet Berowne differs from them because, in line with Quintilian's comments on ethos and pathos, Shakespeare directs our attention to the traits which as a comic character he shares with his group, not his idiosyncrasies. We find in the comic characters no conflict like Richard II's between his private feelings and his public role, nor distinctions like the one between the intense refined sentiments of Romeo and Juliet and the coarser, more conventional sentiments of their parents and friends. Berowne's awareness sets him apart from the other members of Navarre's academy at least temporarily, but his awareness serves the primary purpose of stressing the limitations of a typical romantic lover, irresistibly drawn against his better judgment to the simplicities of the flesh. Critical awareness, whether it be Speed's or Berowne's, leads to recognition of limits and to the laughter of acceptance. In *Dream*, the comedy written after *Labors*, Shakespeare gives more attention to setting one group of characters against another than to one character's awareness of himself. While each group's point of view gets full claim on our attention to draw laughter from the consequent dramatic ironies, Shakespeare makes no further innovations here in comic characterization.[27]

199

The chapters on Shakespeare's serious plays began with the rhetorical uses of language and then moved to the characterization of the speakers. Thus far in the discussion of the early comedies, I have stated that the speech of comic characters should be fashioned according to the decorum of type, but I have emphasized the type over the manner of speech. Earlier we saw how an episode of knocking at the door in *Errors* uses the same pattern of dialogue as a quarrel scene in *1 Henry VI*. The question naturally arises as to the way Shakespeare expands language for comic purposes at the same time that he is widening the scope of rhetorically shaped language in the serious plays to include lyrical expressions of emotion, and it is to this question that we now turn.

Comic Uses of Language

8

The sixteenth-century humanists related the comic uses of language to types of character by the principle of decorum because speech is a kind of behavior, and its misuses can evoke the laughter of scorn as much as improper manners. In its broadest formulation this principle works well to disclose the comedy in Armado's ornate style or Costard's confusion of meanings, but it is more adequate to account for Shakespeare's use of comic language in the serious plays, such as the Jack Cade scenes, than in even his earliest comedies. Here the comic uses of language depend upon operations more complex than recognition of improprieties. I shall concentrate upon two kinds of comic language, verbal wit and verbal humor, both of which may be classified broadly as types of indecorum. No doubt a greater variety of categories is needed to make a full account of Shakespeare's verbal comedy, and much of his comic language, including the quibble, will slip by my discussion. Even so, verbal wit and verbal humor serve to extend my line of inquiry into Shakespeare's apprenticeship. Given the preceding discussion of rhetoric in the chronicle plays, the question arises as to the way language contributes to the purposes of mirror comedy. The way Shakespeare uses verbal wit helps to answer this question, while his use of verbal humor helps to discriminate something of the particular power of comedy and to show the limitations in my discussion of the laughter of scorn and the laughter of acceptance.

Verbal wit rather than verbal humor is the category we more readily associate with Shakespeare's comic characters, who exercise unusual control over words, reusing a word to bring out an unexpected meaning or taking a customary usage and throwing it into an unexpected context. The quick comeback, the smart saying, the pun, all the uses of words which call attention to themselves and startle us into laughter can be classified as verbal wit. To say this is to go against the customary classification of clever and stupid speakers,[1] but even the misusers of language, such as Bottom, Dogberry, and Mrs. Malaprop, depend for their comic effect upon the playwright's cleverness so that the distinction based upon degrees of consciousness within the characters is not a primary one. Passages such as Antipholus of Syracuse's banter with his Dromio on the nature of time or Peter Quince's prologue to "Pyramus and Thisbe" use words that call attention to themselves and startle us into laughter. Most of us would probably agree that these could be classified as examples of verbal wit. Yet there are other passages, equally laughable and equally dependent on words for their effect, that exhibit no clever manipulation. Adriana, for instance, delivers an earnest academically shaped oration on the duties of a husband to a stranger whom she mistakes for her husband (*Errors*, II.ii.109–45). We laugh at the irony of her situation, but "irony" is insufficient to account for the length of her speech or the attention to details of argument and ornate phrasing. The comic predicament releases the audience from its normal concern for rhetoric and enables it to laugh at precisely the care and correctness of discourse that it would otherwise take seriously. It is doubtful that Elizabethans, without their intense respect for eloquence and the powers of rhetoric, would have relished the fun in Adriana's oration. Some twentieth-century critics find her oration to be quite touching.[2] This otherwise serious and appropriate use of language in comic contexts, which occupies a central place in the early comedies (except *Two Gentlemen*), can be described as verbal humor. Shakespeare's uses of verbal wit coordinate with the general line of his development in the first five comedies, but his use of verbal humor does not. It raises a question about the distinctive power of comedy as a mirror of manners and shall be postponed until I have traced the changes in Shakespeare's early uses of verbal wit, uses which do fit the purposes of mirror comedy.

∞

Verbal wit expresses the high spirits of the speaker and heightens the awareness of the audience. One may question whether it can be classified as "indecorum" because a witty character exercises unusual control over language, bringing out unexpected but nevertheless apt uses of words. Madius in his *De Ridiculis* (1550) added "admiratio" (astonishment, wonder, or surprise) to ugliness (or indecorum) as a cause of laughter.[3] "Admiratio" serves well to account for our response to witticisms, for it encompasses not only a startled response to the unexpected, but also a delighted approval at the rightness of the unexpected. Madius's discussion covers both the unexpected in things (*res*) and words (*dicta*). In his desire for support from ancient authorities, he found confirmation more in what they said about the uses of language than in things, support sufficient for our purpose here. Aristotle says, for instance, in *The Rhetoric,* when he talks about the uses of metaphor:

> Liveliness is specially conveyed by metaphor, and by the further power of surprising the hearer; because the hearer expected something different, his acquisition of the new idea impresses him all the more. His mind seems to say, "Yes, to be sure; I never thought of that."[4]

Marvin T. Herrick says that, although Madius found no support in Cicero, he could have used a comment from the *Partitiones Oratoriae,* "A statement is pleasing which has surprises (*admirationes*), suspense, and unexpected issues" (9.32).[5]

Fortunately for us, C. S. Lewis has traced the gradual constriction in the meanings attached to "wit" from Cicero to Addison and Pope in a graceful and learned essay that moves parallel to the list of meanings in the OED. Of special interest is his analysis of Falstaff's comment, "I am not only witty in myself, but the cause that wit is in other men" (*Henry IV, Part II,* I.ii.10–11), which he finds to encompass both the older meaning of wit as good sense and the newer meaning of "mental agility or gymnastic which uses language as the principal equipment of its gymnasium."[6] William G. Crane has shown how the study of rhetoric in the sixteenth century helped to push the general meaning of wit as mental proficiency toward the specific meaning of proficiency in word-play.[7] The most helpful account of word-play which today we would describe as witty is C. L. Barber's. He isolates that feature of usage which separates witty from ordinary talk: "the *physical* attributes of words are used by wit: a witticism capitalizes on 'external associations,' that is to say, it develops a meaning by connecting words through relations or likenesses not noted or used in the situation until found."[8]

In Shakespeare's comedies, the passages of repartee, by their unexpected meanings, heighten our awareness and tune up our judgment. Since improper conduct directs our thought to proper standards and witty dialogue sharpens our attention, the laughter of scorn coordinates nicely with the attitude evoked by repartee, both alerting what can be described as our mental faculties. If our attitude toward the witty character can be specified, it must be something close to admiration. When he uses his wit as a means of attack and mockery, he directs our laughter toward his victim; our response is a mixture of admiration, surprise, and scorn, a response that can be seen to fit with the laughter of impropriety at shrews or pedants, discussed in the last chapter. More complicated is the situation where two witty characters talk together. For the moment, suffice it to say that verbal wit by heightening awareness serves the same general purpose of instruction that the laughter of scorn does, so that both fit Shakespeare's two early mirror comedies.

By the impression of sheer energy created by the dialogue and by the attention devoted to verbal byplay, we can sense the comic impact it must have made upon Elizabethan audiences, but twentieth-century audiences do not respond with much intensity, a difference that cannot be explained entirely by changes in the common uses of words. Like cuckold jokes, verbal wit derives part of its power from conditions of the times, not only education in rhetorical figures but taste which arises from a variety of causes including assumptions about art, artifice, and nature. Though not synonymous with fashion, taste is allied to fashion, and it may be well to begin the discussion of Shakespeare's uses of verbal wit by describing the fashion of witty dialogue when he started writing for the stage. For the extensive passages of closely written wit combats in the earliest comedies draw some of their force from dramatic fashion established by Lyly's court comedies.

John Lyly laid down the challenge to any playwright of the late 1580s and early 1590s who would display versatility with words. He set the pace by mock logic, riddles, and elaboration of fanciful metaphors which Shakespeare and some contemporaries took as models. Although it lies outside my purpose here to support the observation, a comparison would show us that none of the University Wits came close to Shakespeare in adapting Lyly's devices. For every verbal trick of Lyly's we can find a counterpart in Shakespeare's apprentice comedies. Robert Wilson, who wrote *The Three Ladies of London* for an adult company about 1581 before Lyly's comedies for child actors set the fashion, attempted no dialogues of sustained verbal wit; when he composed a sequel about 1588, *The Three Lords and Three Ladies of London,* the clown Simplicity engages in verbal banter with three small and sharp-tongued pages.[9] Wilson stressed the comic disproportion between physical size and verbal facility more than he did ingenious connections between sounds and meanings. Robert Greene mainly in *James IV* (1590-91) attempted to incorporate Lylesque banter: Slipper, a servant, shows his quick wit through riddles and pseudo-proofs, proving that ale and toast are the compass of the whole world (II.i.173-82) and enumerating the ten properties which women and horses have in common (I.ii. 95-107); Eustace engages Ida in a witty dialogue about her embroidery as an oblique means of courtship (II.i.48-71).[10] The clumsiness of all these approximations to Lyly's dialogues serves to impress us with Shakespeare's agility, for he not only duplicated Lyly, device for device, but moved further to show how verbal ingenuities exhibit the limitations of their speakers. A detailed comparison of these devices is set forth in the following section; the reader may wish to skip to the next section, a discussion of the ways Shakespeare adapts verbal wit to his comic purposes.

∞

The ways in which Lyly exhibits verbal wit through the quick, unexpected but relevant response can be classified as pun, syntactic pattern, metaphor, proverb, and pseudo-logic, a classification that covers most of the devices which comic drama presented in "witty" dialogue.[11] The simplest response displays the pun:

Dicke
What calst thou the thing wee were bounde to?
Mar.
A raughter.
Raffe
I will rather hang myself on a raughter in a house, then be so haled in the Sea, — there one may haue a leape for his life.

(Gallathea, I.iv.5-8)[12]

Many of Shakespeare's servants in the early comedies shape their responses to their master's comments according to this pattern.

Adriana
Back, slave, or I will break thy pate across.
Dromio E.
And he will bless that cross with other beating:
Between you, I shall have a holy head.

(Errors, II.i.78-80)

Sometimes a response takes its sharpness from the verbal form of the preceding statement either by repeating it or by reversing it:

Alchemist
. . . he hath stolen my apparell, all my money, and forgot nothing but to bid mee farewell.

Raffe
That will I not forget; farewell, Maister.
   Alchemist
Why thou hast not yet seene the ende of my Arte.
   Raffe
I would I had not knowne the beginning.

(Gallathea, III.iii.6–10)

So too in Shakespeare:

Armado
I love not to be crossed.
   Moth (*aside*)
He speaks the mere contrary — crosses love not him.

(Labors, I.ii.32–33)

A literal statement may be turned into a metaphorical one, or a metaphorical meaning may be reinterpreted literally, revealing a secondary meaning not intended by the speaker. To take an example from *Midas:*
   Pip.
Tush! euerie thing that *Mydas* toucheth is gold.
   Pet.
The deuil it is!
   Pip.
Indeed gold is the deuil.
   Licio.
Thou art deceiued wench, angels are gold.

(I.ii.124–27)

Likewise, in *Errors:*

Luciana
Spake he so doubtfully, thou couldst not feel his meaning?
   Dromio E.
Nay, he struck so plainly, I could too well feel his blows; and withal so doubtfully, that I could scarce understand them.

(II.i.51–54)

The riddle and the pseudo-proof permit extended answers which turn on the double meaning of words, similar sounds of words, customary sayings, and clichés. To take a relatively simple example from perhaps Lyly's earliest comedy, *Campaspe:*
   Manes.
I will proue that my bodie was immortall: beecause it was in prison.

206

Gran.

As how?

Manes.

Didde your maisters neuer teach you that the soule is immortall?

Gran.

Yes.

Manes.

And the body is the prison of the soule.

Gran.

True.

Manes.

Why then, thus to make my body immortal, I put it to prison.

(I.ii.30–39)

In a similar manner Launce, for instance, proves that his milkmaid is desirable because she has more hair than wit:

More hair than wit—It may be. I'll prove it: the cover of the salt hides the salt, and therefore it is more than the salt; the hair that covers the wit is more than the wit, for the greater hides the less. What's next?

(*Two Gentlemen*, III.i.347–50)

The riddle takes much the same form. One speaker states an apparently impossible proposition or poses it as a question. It puzzles the listener, who asks how it is possible. The answer usually takes the form of a pseudo-proof.

Tophas.

But alas, *Epi,* to tell thee the troth, I am a Nowne Adiectiue.

Epi.

Why?

Tophas.

Because I cannot stand without another.

(*Endimion*, III.iii.17–19)

It is possible to cite more far-fetched propositions that provoke longer answers. Proteus proves, for instance, that Speed is a sheep, and Speed proves that he is not (*Two Gentlemen*, I.i.84–97); Dromio proves that Time goes backward (*Errors*, IV.ii.55–62); Moth proves that he can move "swift as lead" (*Labors*, III.i.49–55). Closely resembling the pseudo-proofs are dialogues which extend the points of comparison of a far-fetched metaphor beyond the bounds of plausible ingenuity. In *Midas* the pages take an unpromising comparison of teeth to keys of a virginal and expand it at length (III.ii.84–93); in *Endimion* Epiton and

207

Dares consider the foul witch Dipsas to be like a meal (III.ii.92-105), and Sir Tophas elaborates upon the metaphor that Love as the Lord of Misrule keeps Christmas in his body (*Endimion,* V.ii.5-16). In *Labors,* Rosaline, Maria, Boyet, and Costard similarly extend the metaphor of courtship as archery (IV.i.107-38).

∞

Verbal wit, to recall an earlier statement, expresses the high spirits and energy of the speaker. His exuberance fits comedy as easily as the power inherent in confrontation scenes fits the chronicles. In comedy the wit combats work best when they are disproportionate to their primary dramatic function. By being excessive, they create a sense of sheer vitality. Lyly achieves an impression of excess by plotting his narratives to emphasize discontinuity. Interposed between episodes of his major story are scenes of apparently irrelevant byplay, usually between servants or pages. In his earliest comedies he makes little attempt to integrate the secondary group of characters into the main story. In *Campaspe* the episodes centering on Diogenes or his servant Manes remain detached from the episodes about Alexander's love for Campaspe. Though they are causally disconnected, Lyly gave them subtle thematic connections. In his later plays, such as *Endimion,* the scenes of counterpoint hold together as a kind of subplot; Sir Tophas's love for the foul witch Dipsas parallels the main story of Endimion's love for Cynthia. Either way, the secondary characters intervene with brief scenes often just long enough for the embellishment of an absurd metaphor sustained beyond the limits of what anyone would think possible. No doubt the fact that all of Lyly's plays except *The Woman in the Moon* were written for child actors bears on his manner of plotting, for the length of ingenious dialogues are developed sufficiently to exhibit artful delivery but do not demand the modulations of performance which a trained actor sustains.[13]

The particular nature of Lyly's achievement in creating vitality through purposeful discontinuity suggests difficulties facing a playwright who adapts verbal wit to a narrative drama that stimulates interest in what happens next. Verbal wit — I shall confine the discussion to sustained passages and exclude incidental remarks — depends upon quickly shifting contexts determined not by the story but by the words themselves and the associations they evoke. While the audience's attention is sharpened by spontaneous improvisations, it tends to suspend its concern for what happens next so that passages of verbal wit work like songs in a musical comedy. That Lyly was aware of this can be seen from the prologues and epilogues he appended to his plays, disclaiming any intention to engage "serious" attention:

Wee present neither Comedie, nor Tragedie, nor storie,
nor anie thing, but that whosoeuer heareth may say this,
Why heere is a tale of the Man in the Moone.[14]

Shakespeare is less willing to sacrifice the sustained interest in a character's fortunes and inserts lengthy passages devoted to pure displays of wit
infrequently even in the earliest comedies.

Given the fact that a quick interchange sharpens our attention, it
would seem that such dialogue would work best to introduce a theme or
implant a concept in the minds of the audience. In Lyly's *Midas,* for
instance, Pipenetta lists the properties which an egg shares with gold
(II.ii.15–54), bringing into playful juxtaposition a natural object, char-
acterized by its potentiality for life, with a rare substance which, for all
its value, cannot balance the value of even the simplest organic substance, as Midas learns in the central story of the play. In a similar set
piece, detached from the main course of events, Antipholus of Syracuse
banters with his Dromio on the nature of Time (*Errors,* II.ii.63–108).
Antipholus says, "There is a time for all things," and Dromio disputes
this for some forty lines. What seems incidental is central, for the action
of the play shows that there is a time for all things, including a reunion
of long-lost brothers, husband and wife, parents and children. Shakespeare puts the static set piece to frequent use in *Labors* where passages
of banter fit easily into the narrative for no apparent reason other than
the fact that the courtly characters simply wish to amuse themselves.
Rosaline, Maria, Boyet, and Costard talk about courtship in terms of
archery (IV.i.107–38); Rosaline and Katharina talk about love and
death (V.ii.11–29); and Armado talks with Moth about great men who
have succumbed to love (I.ii.62–85); all these passages appear incidental and yet introduce concepts that gradually illuminate behavior in
the central story.

In one way Shakespeare uses the wit combat that does not follow
Lyly's practices, to dramatize the relation between master and servant.
Quick retorts become the servant's surrogate blows in these slapstick
worlds of the early comedies where giving as much as one gets is a primary satisfaction:

Adriana
Back, slave, or I will break thy pate across.
Dromio E.
And he will bless that cross with another beating:
Between you, I shall have a holy head.

Adriana
Hence, prating peasant! Fetch thy master home.
  Dromio E.
Am I so round with you as you with me
That like a football you do spurn me thus?
You spurn me hence, and he will spurn me hither!
If I last in this service, you must case me in leather.

(II.i.78–85)

Lyly tends to keep his witty pages apart from their masters during interchanges of wit except when the masters are to be discredited, such as Sir Tophas in *Endimion,* the alchemist and astrologer in *Gallathea,* or the greedy fathers in *Mother Bombie.* The main exception occurs in his first play, *Campaspe,* where Diogenes quips with everyone from Alexander the Great to his servant Manes, always with the intention of teaching them and demonstrating his independence from them. Elsewhere masters quip among themselves, and their servants or pages exchange quips among themselves.[15] This restraint points to an unspoken assumption that quickness of wit is for Lyly a significant characteristic of the human hierarchy, and it is tempting to see Lyly's personal predicament at court reflected in this nicety. Among the educated and talented young men drawn to court by their humanist conviction — as G. K. Hunter has shown[16] — that their learning should serve society, Lyly must have grown acutely aware that natural ability seldom coincides with patronage or social rank. Dialogues between master and witty servant in *Errors* and *Shrew* suggest that Shakespeare takes that fact for granted without sensing that it calls into question the hierarchy of social place. Indeed, he sees verbal wit as one more way to bolster the social order, for it acts as the servant's safety valve in maintaining his position at the command of an unsympathetic or unjust master. The exchanges of wit, where the servant gets his chance at a comeback, symbolic though it is, act to complement the moments of slapstick where the servant must suffer unjustly at the hands of a mistaken master.

Earlier we saw that a master's unjust punishment stimulates the laughter of recognition at harsh realities we would rather avoid facing. Laughter at the servant's witty retorts is more akin to Sidney's laughter of delight; we take sides with the servant and are delighted that he has scored a point or two in a little game where the loser is indifferent to the outcome. "Game" is a useful classification for the servant's retorts because he acts to deflect his energy into harmless channels. All of us at one time or another have played such behind-the-stairs games when we are frustrated or thwarted by powers that brook no other recourse, and consequently we intuit Dromio's game and feel a kinship with him when he scores a point. Our laughter, hardly of scorn, signifies our fellow-feeling.

Games of wit that displace strong feelings and release energy in what seems to be disproportionate to the occasion occur elsewhere in Shakespeare's early comedies, particularly in moments of courtship. Badinage sustains those first encounters of lovers without at the same time shattering propriety by untimely declarations of feeling. In the love game, as D. L. Stevenson aptly describes it,[17] interest is first exhibited and tested, like a mating dance, before feelings can be disclosed. The initial dialogue between Navarre's academy and the Princess's retinue dramatizes this interplay, but Shakespeare takes care to assure the audience at its conclusion about the meaning of what occurred by writing an explication of the ironies for Boyet to deliver (*Labors,* II.i.226–47). Later, in *Much Ado about Nothing* Shakespeare intimates the fascination which Beatrice and Benedick hold for one another through similar wit combats. Earlier, in *Shrew* Petruchio's courtship of Katharina is more combat than love game and conveys little sense of an unspoken romantic attraction behind his conventional praise and her retorts. Edward IV's wooing of Lady Grey in *3 Henry VI* exemplifies the thorough uses of verbal wit, the King suggesting discreetly, the lady parrying his thrusts without being impolite, each making a tentative point until the King realizes that he must propose marriage to satisfy his desire (III.ii). For the most part in the chronicles, plain speech is held up as the standard of propriety, set by such characters as Duke Humphrey and John of Gaunt. In the comedies, where manners and customs are mirrored, the ironies of wit-play oftentimes satisfy the claims of manners; yet here too wit implies shortcomings of some sort, either in the speaker or in conditions.

It is the shortcomings of wit that Shakespeare explores in his later apprentice comedies, all the while preserving the exuberance and delight that we sense in Lyly's plays. Because he forces us to see around the edges of wit and recognize it as an adjustment rather than as a model for discourse, we assert his superiority to Lyly with regard to this kind of comic dialogue. I can conceive of someone wishing, after one of Lyly's court comedies, that he could speak so cleverly; I cannot conceive of one feeling this way after watching Shakespeare's *Labors,* where wit shapes the dominant pattern of dialogue. To generalize about Shakespeare's most witty characters, Feste, Lear's fool, Hamlet, perhaps Falstaff, Beatrice and Benedick, all of them live apart from the center of society and do not participate in the regular patterns of behavior. Pressures, either personal or social, force them to create a personal style of sharp verbal intensity, a style that Shakespeare never makes the accepted standard of discourse in his plays. Beatrice and Benedick, who conform least to this generalization, modify their style of speech once they have been "converted" to love. *Love's Labor's Lost* explores at length the uses of verbal wit. In keeping with Shakespeare's tendency to broaden our awareness as he moves from comedy to comedy, the characters not only talk wittily but become aware of the way they talk. Yet verbal wit is just one of the problems of communication in this play that raises the full moral issue of adjusting style to substance. As the earlier discussion of rhetoric indicated, Elizabethans did not separate speech from other behavior. The way Richard of Gloucester manipulates language has moral consequences. *Labors* dramatizes the moral dimensions of decorum as it applies to proper and improper speech within, of course, the limits of comedy.

In plotting the story of Navarre and his academy, Shakespeare follows Lyly's way of building scenes, more by theme and variation than by preparing for what happens next, so that the play offers a compendium of the ways characters use verbal wit in adjusting to social circumstances.[18] Already mentioned are passages of courtship. These together with witty exchanges between master and servant, host and guest, pedant and admirer, tend toward mockery. In fact, mockery is the dominant pattern of verbal wit in the play so that the characters could be divided into the mockers and the mocked, a division which may be restated as instructors and pupils. The pupils, who lack a sense of proportion, need to adjust their ideals to their abilities and their style to their subject matter. Mockery of the one entails mockery of the other.

The witty interplay between servant and master which, in *Errors* and *Shrew,* dramatizes the servant holding his own by a swift retort, here works differently because the servants make pertinent criticisms of their masters. Costard resembles Launce in that his criticism of Navarre is more a matter of sheer presence than of what he says, particularly at the outset of the play when he is apprehended with Jaquenetta soon after the academy has renounced the company of women for three years. His words lack the control and sting of a Speed, but they penetrate none the less. When he sums up his behavior in a sentence, "Such is the simplicity of man to hearken after the flesh" (I.i.212), Navarre ignores him, but should have taken his words to heart. Likewise, Goodman Dull's presence during the elaborately ornamented conversation between Holofernes and Sir Nathaniel on the royal hunt, Act IV, scene ii, serves to criticize the pretensions of his betters. Like Costard, Goodman Dull says little, and like Navarre, Holofernes pays no attention to his matter-of-fact viewpoint and his barren style. A third critic, Moth, undercuts his master Armado by double meanings and asides to mock his chivalric pretentions.

> *Armado*
> Fetch hither the swain. He must carry me a letter.
> *Moth* [*aside*]
> A message well sympathized — a horse to be ambassador for an ass.
> *Armado*
> Ha, ha? What sayest thou?
> *Moth*
> Marry, sir, you must send the ass upon the horse, for he is very slow-
> gaited.
>
> (III.i.43–47)

These three critics make their points obliquely and act more to measure their subjects' limitations for the audience's laughter of scorn than to teach their subjects. As such, they function as tentative or preparatory versions of the major critics, the Princess and her ladies, who undertake the central task of instruction through mockery in Act V, scene ii.

At the outset of this scene Shakespeare works with deliberate care to sketch the purpose behind mockery. When Navarre first greets the Princess in Act II, she sets his welcome in perspective by her witty retorts, for he welcomes her, after all, only so far as his park. When in Act V the ladies' banter takes a sharper turn into mockery, Shakespeare inserts a passage to inform the audience that the verbal wit serves here for more than a courtly pastime. The Princess first speaks in terms of sport:

> The effect of my intent is to cross theirs.
> They do it but in mockery merriment,
> And mock for mock is only my intent.
>
> (V.ii.138–40)

That is, she intends to use language like the Dromios or Grumio as a game to score points and hold her own against the men. But Boyet sees that her sport will not be harmless:

> Why, that contempt will kill the speaker's heart,
> And quite divorce his memory from his part.
>
> (V.ii.149–50)

Then the Princess restates her intention:
There's no such sport as sport by sport o'erthrown,
To make theirs ours, and ours none but our own.
So shall we stay, mocking intended game,
And they, well mocked depart away with shame.

(V.ii.153–56)

Mockery is the method and shame the consequence, if not a cure, for those who would pride themselves on their wit.

A former scene, Act IV, scene iii, dramatizes the susceptibility of Navarre's academy for cure because their wit turns into casuistry. Berowne explains away their original oaths by witty renunciation and passes lightly over the act of forswearing. He shapes his speech into a little mock ceremony that may foreshadow Richard II's mock ceremony of unkinging himself. Even if we recognize that Berowne's apology as it stands (IV.iii.285–360) combines a first version (IV.iii.291–312) with a second version (IV.iii.313–60) and settle for the second as the later, what remains is still exuberantly wordy.[19] His overtalk, approved with high spirits by the other lords, sets up the academy for mockery and shame when they carry out their plan of courtship in disguise. Oath-taking happens to be an obvious nexus where words and behavior come together in a clear moral issue. The substance of the lords' oaths fits within the boundaries of behavior suggested by Cicero's and Donatus's definition of comedy, so that shame is sufficient corrective and mockery is appropriate instruction.

Less apparent is the reason why the courtiers woo in disguise. We hear of their plan only through Boyet's report to the Princess rather than directly from them. On the face of it, they stand to gain nothing by disguise. Once they come face to face with the fact of love and decide to engage in courtship, what help can Muscovite costumes give them? Perhaps we do the episode a disservice by looking for motive where the results are apt. Perhaps Shakespeare avoids the weakness in their motive by choosing to disclose it through Boyet's narration rather than expose it through direct discussion. And too, we might well ask why Shakespeare chooses to plot a secondary discovery scene for the lords. During the sonnet-reading sequence they acknowledge the claims of their flesh and decide to abandon their academy. No doubt a lesser playwright would have moved directly to a scene of courtship and acceptance by the ladies. Shakespeare is scrupulous to arrange for the lords to face the consequences of their misdemeanors; their shame brings into focus for them and for the audience the moral dimension of their language. By

their lack of perspective they cheapen the act of oath-taking.[20] Their
decision to woo in disguise as Muscovites, while it has no explicit motivation, is characteristic, for it emphasizes style not well coordinated
with substance. It is not out of line here to recall the old dictum: the
style is the man.

In building toward the mockery, Shakespeare places a scene between
the lords' decision to court the ladies and the execution of their plan.
Intervening is a dialogue of extravagant verbal display by Holofernes,
Sir Nathaniel, and Armado, which serves as an exaggerated analogy to
the indecorum of the lords and intimates how such behavior, by becoming habitual, distorts character. Style is indeed the man. Moth
comments on their discussion in this way:

They have been at a great feast of languages and stolen the scraps.

(V.i.35-36)

The heightened disproportion between what they say and how they say
it sets up our expectation for a corrective, for they obviously need pur-
gation. In tandem with the lords' shaming occurs the Show of the Nine
Worthies. Just as Berowne renounces his ornate style in the process of
rehabilitation, so Armado accepts the consequences of his exposure and
joins Jaquenetta in marriage. Events leave open the question of Holofernes's and Sir Nathaniel's cure because their distortions of style are
deeply embedded as distortions of character. The audience sees that
they are shamed during their show, but the narrative of the play reveals
no more of their careers.

Once the lords realize that they have been mocked by the ladies, they
become self-conscious about language. Shamed, their spokesman
Berowne renounces his ornate style in the process of judging his former
behavior:

Taffeta phrases, silken terms precise,
Three-piled hyperboles, spruce affection,
Figures pedantical — these summer flies
Have blown me full of maggot ostentation.
I do forswear them.

(V.ii.407-11)

Implicit in his experience is a calling into question of all disproportionate style, even verbal wit for the use of shaming. Mockery too has its
shortcomings. Just as the laughter of scorn cannot be a final attitude to
Shakespeare's comedies, for it suppresses the kinship between the scorner
and the scorned, so mockery falls short of fulfilling the purpose of

language to communicate. Events move to bring the witty mockers face to face with their limitations.

Mercade's sudden announcement of the King of France's death serves among other things to call into question the limits of verbal wit and modulates the play into a new key. It softens the Princess and shows her for the first time without the resources of wit that have enabled her to cope with Navarre. As mentioned earlier, she resorts to wit to distract herself from her own feelings, bantering somewhat coldly with the forester after a momentary admiration of Navarre as he spurs his horse uphill (IV.i.1–24). Her retinue, even without the stimulus of the lords, reflects her style. In a peculiar, apparently irrelevant passage at the opening of Act V, scene ii, the Princess and her ladies exercise their wit as sheer pastime. Rosaline mentions that Katharine's sister was killed by Cupid because of love. Katharine replies:

He[Cupid] made her melancholy, sad, and heavy;
And so she died. Had she been light, like you,
Of such a merry, nimble, stirring spirit,
She might ha' been a grandam ere she died;
And so may you, for a light heart lives long.

(V.ii.14–18)

Rosaline bridles at the oblique criticism:

What's your dark meaning, mouse, of this light word?

(V.ii.19)

And their dialogue becomes heated until the Princess intervenes and tactfully redirects the conversation:

Well bandied both; a set of wit well played.
But, Rosaline, you have a favor too:
Who sent it? and what is it?

(V.ii.29–31)

As elsewhere the banter implies more than it states. Although the passage is brief, no more than twenty lines, its position at the opening of the scene where Mercade appears emphasizes it. Death does not lend itself to Rosaline's mode of discourse, and her indiscretion creates a brief moment of uneasiness. Later, Mercade's announcement enforces the matter of decorum by changing the mode of discourse altogether. The pace slows down, the speeches grow longer, and the statements become explicit.

The fact of death clears the air of smart talk and sets everyone's behavior in perspective. The lords' program for an academy, now junked in favor of courtship, appears even more foolish; their intention to waste three years of life, whose span resembles the movement of the seasons, strikes us as unnatural. Paralleling their adjustment is the ladies' acceptance of their courtship, signifying their own willingness to take their place with the ever-so-human lords who woo them. The songs which end the play have stimulated a rich body of critical commentary in recent years because they suggest rather than state meaning. Why do two songs about the seasons conclude a comedy of young courtiers learning about love and courtship? Most critics show how themes relate the songs to the play, either to sum up or contrast, and point the way into a future for the lovers beyond the park.[21] The songs, too, bear directly on this discussion of verbal wit. Significantly, Shakespeare wrote two songs for a "dialogue." It is conceivable that one song, perhaps about the joys and troubles of spring, could have served well enough. Apart from the implications for the cycle of the seasons, the two songs form a debate, each with its pleasures and hardships. Spring's obvious advantage over winter carries the threat of the cuckoo; winter's harshness accommodates the warm pleasures of food and drink about the fire. Together they form a harmony that reflects what they are, harmonic speech. The simple words supplant the jangle of wit and complete the direction in which language has been changing through the play. The songs do not, in my view, act as a contrast to what has preceded. The harmony expressed is one of adjustment between pleasures and troubles. As the courtiers have adjusted their ideals to their human nature, so the ladies make arrangements to deal with the shortcomings of the lords. As the past, so the future. I cannot agree with Bertrand Bronson that the songs constitute an "anti-masque" or with Tillyard that they hold out slim hope for the lords' success.[22]

Shakespeare does not again serve up such a feast of words. In mimetic drama he explores the power of events to modify the power of words. When Lucrece turns to the story of Troy, she indicates that events are as able to convey feelings as rhetorical set-speeches, and consequently words seldom afterwards carry as much of the burden of action as they do in the early chronicles. The introductory public ceremony of challenge and counterchallenge in *Richard II*, for instance, does not state all it means. At approximately the same stage within the development of the comedies, *Labors* dramatizes a narrative that calls into question the proprieties of the characters' style. In Shakespeare's next comedy, *A Midsummer Night's Dream*, the verbal fun arises primarily from confusions and blunders with words. As Bottom says, "and there we may rehearse most obscenely and courageously" (I.ii.96–97). The central predicament of this comedy, the essential blindness of lovers, lunatics, and poets, directs attention to inept rather than to controlled uses of words. Even in the one episode where verbal wit contributes to the fun, the stage audience's response to the playlet, the context shows that wit makes no crucial difference, since both players and audience are of imagination all compact. Yet the realization of this kinship would have little force unless the apparent differences strike us vividly. The ignorance of Peter Quince's crew "which never labored in their minds till now" fulfills this need. Without learning, they confuse genres and speak of "very tragical mirth." Without control of diction, they speak of a "tedious brief scene." Quince mistakes the pointing of the prologue and confuses syntax in a manner that recalls the old play when Matthew Merrygreek misreads Ralph Roister Doister's letter to Dame Custance (III.iv.36–70).[23] On the face of it, laughter at the improprieties of the low comics enforces the sense of social place, a sense that makes all the more amusing the deeper kinship.

The verbal confusions of the playlet add to this irony, for they convey a lunatic truth and reveal the playwright's wit if not the players'.[24] To take "very tragical mirth" as one example, it happens to be an accurate description of the playlet as it is enacted. Peter Quince's jumbled reading of the prologue that states the players' intentions turns out to describe their confusions. For instance:

If we offend, it is with our good will.
    To show our simple skill,
  That is the true beginning of our end. . . .
The actors are at hand: and, by their show,
You shall know all, that you are like to know.

                             (V.i.108ff.)

These distortions, like the passages of conscious wit, act to sharpen our attention to detail and heighten our awareness. So do the absurdities of dramatic conventions. The crude alliterations, the absence of invention, the insistence upon repetition ("Now die, die, die, die, die," V.i.299), and the unerring use of primary devices of the rhetorical lament, all direct our attention to the larger issues of the drama's relation to reality:

  But stay: O spite!
  But mark, poor knight,

What dreadful dole is here?
  Eyes, do you see?
  How can it be?
O dainty duck, O dear!
  Thy mantle good,
  What, stained with blood?
Approach, ye Furies fell!
  O Fates, come, come,
  Cut thread and thrum,
Quail, crush, conclude, and quell!

(V.i.269-80)

The speech reverberates beyond the playlet to the outer play. It echoes Hermia's speeches of fear when she discovers Lysander's disappearance (II.ii.145 ff.) and when she accuses Demetrius of murdering him (III.ii. 65-73). It mocks Shakespeare's own dramatic laments and suggests that from his present vantage point he has seen the full extent of their limitations. In the context of this comedy the mockery of dramatic conventions, like the other verbal inadequacies, attunes the audience to the drama itself and makes them self-conscious as an audience which laughs at the ridiculous behavior while at the same time recognizing the behavior as a mirror of themselves.

The pattern of development that emerges from Shakespeare's use of verbal wit in the early comedies resembles the pattern that appears in the comic characterizations. As he moves from comedy to comedy, he expands the range of our critical awareness of our limitations and adjusts us to this recognition. Our reactions grow correspondingly intense, for the laughter of acceptance depends for its impact upon the extent and nature of the shortcomings to be accepted. Implicit in the energy created by witty dialogue is adaptation to social circumstances, some harsh, like a master's unquestioned control, some delicate, like a tentative loved one's feelings. We delight in a character's energy and the triumph that results from his energetic use of language. Usually his adjustment through wit entails criticism that stimulates our laughter of scorn at whatever he criticizes so that our response approximates the mixture of delight and scorn that Sidney discusses. Just as the later comic characters become critics of themselves and even of drama, so the later comedies expose the limits of verbal wit. Our kinship with the witty character becomes more than a feeling of delight at his triumph and agreement with his scorn; it becomes a mutual recognition of shortcomings inherent in the very tactics of verbal wit which we cannot resist

219

using. Verbal wit, then, fits with the dialectic of criticism and acceptance that Shakespeare's later apprentice comedies embody.

∞

To create laughter, verbal humor depends neither upon surprise nor on unusual use of words. Instead, a discrepancy between what a character says and what circumstances demand causes the laughter. Adriana, as already mentioned, delivers a full-scale deliberative oration in an attempt to win her husband back to the hearthside. The intensities of anaphora, rhetorical question, copious enumeration, all appropriate to her purpose, are ludicrous because the man she addresses is not her husband. Yet verbal humor need not depend upon ignorance of the speaker, for Petruchio, who employs similarly elaborate rhetorical devices in proclaiming chivalric protection for Katharina when he intends to keep her from her wedding feast, is fully aware of his distortions. The more learned the figures, the more forceful the arguments, the louder our laughter. Verbal humor discloses a power of comedy which has not been discussed thus far, a power to make us laugh at what we would otherwise take seriously. Without the respect which Elizabethans gave to rhetoric or the effort they gave to its mastery, it is unlikely that Shakespeare's comedies would have contained such lengthy passages of impeccably tailored language.

Versatility in articulating one's thoughts has always been a staple of comedy, from John Heywood's Merry Report to Shaw's Don Juan, to cite only English secular drama. Yet humanist training in rhetoric seems to have imparted an extra zest to this humor. Ben Jonson, in particular, delights in overtalk. For whole scenes characters spin out webs of words, spiderlike, from almost nothing: Volpone's mountebank scene or Face and Subtle's discussion of alchemical mysteries before Sir Epicure Mammon. Shakespeare capitalizes on this type of humor when he constructs the dialogue of *Shrew*. In an artful passage of *descriptio* Petruchio sums up his impression of Katharina quite contrary to the evidence of their courtship:

For thou art pleasant, gamesome, passing courteous,
But slow in speech, yet sweet as springtime flowers.
Thou canst not frown, thou canst not look askance,
Nor bite the lip, as angry wenches will,
Nor hast thou pleasure to be cross in talk.
But thou with mildness entertain'st thy wooers,
With gentle conference, soft and affable.
Why does the world report that Kate doth limp?

O sland'rous world! Kate like the hazel-twig
Is straight and slender, and as brown in hue
As hazelnuts and sweeter than the kernels.
O let me see thee walk. Thou dost not halt.

(II.i.247-58)

Or again, after the scene with the haberdasher and tailor, Petruchio
thwarts Kate's desires by asserting his own opinion about her gown and
hat, defends her wearing old clothes with the devices of a judicial oration, citing principle, proclaiming values and prudence, all articulated
by an overuse of syntactic figures. His speech, affecting the proverb-
speaker, couches wisdom in terms of animals and sounds remarkably
like Suffolk and Margaret, who argue in a similar way for the emprisonment of Duke Humphrey (*2 Henry VI,* III.i.18-19, 53-56):

Our purses shall be proud, our garments poor,
For 'tis the mind that makes the body rich;
And as the sun breaks through the darkest clouds
So honor peereth in the meanest habit.
What, is the jay more precious than the lark
Because his feathers are more beautiful?
Or is the adder better than the eel
Because his painted skin contents the eye?
O no, good Kate; neither art thou the worse
For this poor furniture and mean array.

(IV.iii.168-77)

We would laugh, of course, even without the copybook methods of
articulating this high-minded talk because of Petruchio's intention, but
his artfulness in guying the pose of the prudent orator adds to our merriment. Tranio exhibits a similar felicity with words, spinning out
declarations of wealth and affection in his contest with Gremio. After
his initial ornate flourishes to the other suitors about his intention to
woo Bianca, Gremio's single-line response makes clear the effect of his
surplus:

What, this gentleman will out-talk us all.

(I.ii.243)

Shakespeare continues to mine this vein of the rhetorically shaped
speeches slightly out of kilter in *Labors* and *Dream.* Berowne's inclination to overtalk, at times consciously excessive, runs throughout the play
and infects even those moments when he intends to be earnest. His re-

nunciation speech, disclaiming three-piled hyperboles for russet yeas, is itself overblown, and to the final statement, "My love to thee is sound, sans crack or flaw," Rosaline answers, "Sans 'sans,' I pray you," thus setting his style in perspective (V.ii.4l6-17). The verbiage in this play should perhaps be set apart as a special case because it relates to the speaker as a symptom of disjointed values, unlike the way it relates to Adriana or Antipholus of Syracuse or Petruchio or the characters in *Dream*. In *Dream* Shakespeare extends verbal humor to include lengthy speeches of lyrical sentiment. Lysander, for instance, awakens to proclaim his adulation to a stunned Helena in a style unusually effusive (II.ii.103-7, 111-22). Although the situation demands his declaration of love, he need not embellish it so thoroughly with the beauties of overtalk. To take a comparable response for contrast, in the next scene, Titania awakes to state her new adoration for Bottom in a series of three brief speeches, beautifully shaped and to the point, as befits a fairy queen. Helena's bewildered response to the sudden love of both Demetrius and Lysander expresses itself in another copiously phrased rhetorical appeal. She shapes her thoughts by introductory address, accusation, argument from facts and values, and summarizes them, all with a formality that would please an orator (*Dream,* III.ii.195-219; again, 222-35 and 237-44). Shakespeare could have fashioned quick-paced dialogue here; in fact, at this moment of highest confusion it would seem that the characters should not keep silent while Helena delivers a twenty-five-line oration. Yet Shakespeare must have been assured that the audience's delight at the inappropriate formality of rhetoric would be warrant enough for Helena's lengthy speech at a moment of sudden reversals in the love of Demetrius, Lysander, and the shock of Hermia.

The ludicrous character is blinded to circumstances that make his language inadequate; the ridiculous character lacks the control to use language adequately, whether or not he is aware of circumstances.[25] Shakespeare does not hesitate to exploit both kinds of verbal humor in his early comedies except in *Two Gentlemen,* where he creates laughter at Launce's distortions of language but takes no occasion to develop passages of verbal humor through rhetoric. Launce struggles to follow the principles of exposition and logical progression in his soliloquies and in the inventory of the milkmaid's qualities. He can "prove" that it is better to have more hair than wit and lives comfortably with contradictions, announcing to the audience:

He lives not now that knows me to be in love, yet I am in love. But a team of horse shall not pluck that from me, nor who 'tis I love.

(III.i.263-66)

Immediately he reveals his love with pedantic care in clarifying his diction:

And yet 'tis a milkmaid. Yet 'tis not a maid, for she hath had gossips.
Yet 'tis a maid, for she is her master's maid, and serves for wages.
(III.i.267–70)

These and similar passages reveal how Shakespeare uses language for
the comic purpose of developing a ridiculous character, but it is difficult to find passages of verbal humor given to the ludicrous characters.[26]
In the four other apprentice comedies the audience's concern for the
characters is either relieved early or is not aroused by serious threats.
Here the audience takes seriously the speeches of sentiment by Valentine
and Julia, who are seriously threatened by Proteus.

This absence of long passages devoted to verbal humor raises a question of the way it depends upon the audience's general attitude. The
power of the comic story to transform what would otherwise be serious
into a matter for laughter is not one that sixteenth-century humanists
discussed, perhaps because it is a property of comedy *qua* comedy
whereas they explicated the power of comedy as instructive. Recently C.
L. Barber, Bertrand Evans, and Elder Olson have drawn our attention
to the power of comedy to release us from everyday involvements.
Comic stories recreate the audience by converting to harmlessness what
appears to be threatening. As Elder Olson puts it, "that emotion [con-
ducive to laughter] is a relaxation, or, as Aristotle would say, a *katastasis*, of concern due to a manifest absurdity of the grounds for concern."[27] Barber sees that a special group of Shakespeare's comedies, not
all of them, approximate the experiment of a holiday, that is, a release
from ordinary responsibilities of life so that one can give rein to his
appetites and reach a clarification about his very human nature. Evans
examines the way that Shakespeare manipulates discrepant awareness
to release the audience's concern for a character's well-being by knowledge that all will eventuate in happiness. While each of these critics, no
doubt, would object to a classification which groups them—they stress
significantly different properties of comedy—all three give prominence
to one characteristic: release, relaxation, recreation. If there is a sixteenth-century counterpart to their general emphasis, it is articulated in
the generalized terms of recreation through mirth. Nicholas Udall referred to recreation in his prologue, already quoted, to *Ralph Roister
Doister*, echoed by the Abbess Emilia in *Errors* (V.i.78–82) and by the
Messenger to Sly (Induction to *Shrew*, ii. 126–33).

From these critics' point of view the plotting of Shakespeare's first five
comedies can be seen to fulfill to varying degrees this potentiality for
pleasing an audience. In *Errors* Egeon's death sentence, Antipholus of
Ephesus's unfaithfulness, Antipholus of Syracuse's incest, and Ephesian

witchcraft turn out to be groundless. Through the power of time—we might say luck—threats are converted to happiness. In *Shrew* and *Labors* threats are overcome by teaching and learning; in *Dream* the nightmares prove to be harmless because of the controls exercised by creatures of imagination (fantastics). Arrangement of information in these four comedies separates the audience from the characters so that it anticipates a happy outcome from the anguish which the characters suffer before their troubles disappear. As Evans observes, it is Shakespeare's characteristic method to contain threats within a framework of warm assurance.[28] Yet he plots *Two Gentlemen* in a different way to realize the potentialities for *katastasis* because the audience remains uncertain about the outcome. Julia and Valentine through constancy and friendship bring about Proteus's conversion, but the audience cannot foresee this. Consequently, the antics of the low comic characters intervene at crucial moments to affect the audience's emotional involvement. The comic manner with which Launce describes his tribulations, tribulations that approximate the troubles of the main characters, deflates our willingness to invest full concern in the analogous troubles of the main characters.

Is the power of comedy to turn the potentially dangerous into laughter to release us from serious concerns a more accurate account of Shakespeare's practices than the stipulations of the sixteenth-century humanists for mirror comedy? I think not, for the key even to release and recreation lies in its usefulness.[29] Udall and the Abbess speak of release as necessary to man's health. C. L. Barber's account of holiday ends in "clarification." Even laughter at the strictest moral principles or at the humanists' own stipulations for comedy can be encompassed within their purposes for comedy as a mirror. The clearest instance of the way drama capitalizes upon release from serious matters can be found in the morality plays where the Vice figure makes fun of the Virtues. An archetypal example appears in one of the earliest, *Mankind* (ca. 1465–70). At the very outset of the play Mercy enters, identifies himself, and exhorts the audience to avoid temptation, repent, and do good works. Then Mischief dances in, followed by New Gyse, Now-a-days, and Nought, who caper, crack jokes, and exchange comments with Mercy. New Gyse asks his name:

Mercy.
Mercy ys my name & my denomynacyon!
I conseyue ye haue but a lytyll fors in my commenycacyon.

New.

Ey, ey, yower body ys full of Englysch Laten!

Now.

I prey yow hertyly, worschypfull clerke —
I haue etun a dysch full of curdes,
Ande I haue schetun yower mowth fulle of turdes;
Now opyn yower sachell with Late [n] wordes,
And sey me this in clerycall maner!

(lines 122–29)[30]

This passage, taken from the beginning of the play, is typical of the irresistible amusement that arises from the Vices' mockery of dignified religious and moral statement. The exuberant merriment of the Vice figures gets much of its force from irresponsibility. A large portion of the appeal of the moralities — some modern readers might say their whole appeal — arises from the release they encourage from the severe restrictions of proper behavior. Mercy makes no attempt to answer New Gyse or Now-a-days on their own terms. He maintains his style as best he can under the circumstances and departs the scene. Like the audience, Mankind is drawn to laughter by these irresistible figures, but his indulgence is temporary. The Vices are contained by the pattern of their names within the framework of the full scope of human life. Man cannot escape responsibility in this play and must face the consequences of his behavior. The Vice figures, of course, need not, since they are temptations by their very nature, not human beings. Thus the morality play recognizes man's anarchic disposition to escape the strenuous demands of Christian precepts and contains it within the larger rhythm of repentance and conversion.

What mockery does in the morality play, discrepant awareness allows in Shakespeare's early comedies, that is, permits the audience to laugh at what it would otherwise take seriously. Shakespeare's subjects, by the nature of his genre, remain limited to everyday concerns, particularly rhetoric, as we have seen, but include romantic tragedy, as the story of Pyramus and Thisbe makes evident. The playlet is in many ways similar to the story of Romeo and Juliet. Although much of our laughter arises from the inadequacies of Peter Quince's players, I would suggest that some of the fun arises from our recognition that the story is the very sort we would otherwise take seriously. As C. L. Barber has shown, many of Shakespeare's comedies after the apprenticeship of *Labors* and *Dream* can be profitably discussed in terms of release to clarification. We can trace the way Shakespeare expands the range of behavior in the holiday world and even see Falstaff encompassed in it. In the earliest comedies a more specific form of clarification, moral judgment about domestic and social behavior, pervades the episodes from beginning to end. Verbal humor in *Errors* and *Shrew* acts together with the harsh treatment of servant by master as counterpoint to the laughter at improprieties and at verbal wit. Laughter at verbal humor resembles the laughter of recognition at harsh social realities because the timbre of both has the force of a breakthrough ("Ha, ha," rather than "He, he"). Yet the dominant laughter of these mirror comedies is directed by improprieties of behavior; it is a laughter of scorn that implies the laugher's dissociation from such behavior. The later apprentice comedies continue to stimulate the audience's awareness of its shortcomings but shift emphasis to a laughter of acceptance, an acknowledgment that most of these shortcomings are part of our human nature. This response, whether or not it is created by a holiday world, resembles the sort of clarification that Barber discusses. In these later plays laughter at verbal humor is not inappropriate, for anarchic laughter at what we would otherwise take seriously reveals our kinship, a recognition of our tendency to chafe under necessary restraints in our temporary mockery of them. But the fact that others laugh when we laugh helps create a sense of community that in effect assures the harmlessness of our impulse. To see the priest join us in laughter at Mercy is not to threaten his position. Like the morality play, the mirror comedies domesticate our tendency toward anarchy by allowing it scope which is restricted, of course, by comparison with the scope of the morality. Given these additions to the power of comedy which the topics of verbal wit and verbal humor have opened, we should return to Shakespeare's early chronicles and tragedies to reconsider the power of rhetorical drama and the ways, if any, that Shakespeare's increasing skill in one genre helped change his practices in the other.

The Powers of Rhetoric
and Mimesis

9

My discussion of Shakespeare's history plays began with patterns of
dialogue in the serious plays and generalized from details to the assumptions that lie behind their creation. My discussion of the apprentice
comedies reversed the procedure by beginning with general principles of
comedy to show how Shakespeare followed them closely at the outset of
his career and modified them when he presented on stage experiences of
romantic love. By way of summary in this chapter I shall try to coordinate the changes Shakespeare made between the earlier and later serious plays with the contemporaneous changes in his comedies. Central to
the chapters on comedy is the way the plays heighten awareness both in
the characters and in the audience. Broadly speaking they begin with
some form of blindness and lead to enlightenment on stage so as to
stimulate perception implicit in the laughter of scorn or the laughter of
acceptance in the audience. The corresponding topic central to the
chapters on the early chronicles and tragedies is power, exerted over the
audience by the uses of rhetoric in stories of the exercise of power.

When sixteenth-century humanists insisted that drama guide men to
virtuous behavior, they were talking about both power and awareness.
Their principle of decorum allowed comedy to come closer to fulfilling
the potentialities of drama *qua* drama than the serious studies about
historical characters. Standards such as "mirror of custom" and "image
of truth" relieved comedies of being insistently didactic. Likewise, a
straightforward presentation of comic events, if they generated laughter, could be sufficiently instructive, for laughter, as the humanists
understood it, entailed judgment so that the playwright felt less need to
accentuate moral principles through illustrative episode and explicit
formulation. Shakespeare's early rhetorical chronicles placed emphasis

upon stimulating our convictions, whereas the earliest comedies, composed with an equal regard for instruction, stressed the audience's awareness of behavior to avoid. In what follows I shall first discuss changes in the audience's responses to the earlier and later apprentice plays, then show how these changes are reflected in characterizations, and finally come full circle to discuss the change reflected in the way characters talk to others and to themselves. These changes will lead us to an estimate of the relative power that the comedies exerted in Shakespeare's early development, for being less explicitly concerned about exerting moral pressure on an audience, the comedies gave him insight into the distinctively dramatic potentialities of his medium.

∞

The rhetorician assumes that in language resides a great potential power to stir men to virtuous behavior. Implicit in this assumption is another about the nature of moral truth: that it can be clearly revealed and that it is generally applicable. Much of the orator's power arises from the fact that he need become entangled neither in demonstrating the truth of moral standards nor in qualifications of them. Instead he can devote his energies to devising a variety of artful restatements to enforce a general truth. Argument and anecdote stimulate listeners to behave according to moral law, not to enlighten them about moral law. Thomas Wilson, for instance, when he illustrates the deliberative oration, takes as his unexceptionable premise, that a young man ought to marry and procreate. When embodied in dramatic episodes, moral truths retain their clarity and apply to all characters equally. In *2 Henry VI* Duke Humphrey concerns himself with the good of the commonwealth while his opponents work for their own interests at the expense of the commonwealth. Behavior squares with moral truth so that the audience can easily categorize the characters. York does not side momentarily with the good Duke, nor does Duke Humphrey momentarily let personal sentiment, such as love for his wife, conflict with his interest in the general welfare. Perhaps the one character who cannot be easily categorized is the King; like Mankind in a morality play, he is influenced by good and bad characters, revealing inadequacy as a leader rather than a wicked nature. Just as behavior and character square with moral truth, so does structure. Similar events accumulate to confirm the audience's understanding; they respond by generalizing from particular episodes to the truth they embody.

Shakespeare's most rhetorically powerful plays, the Henry VI plays, take as their subject power, its uses and misuses. In *1 Henry VI* Bedford states in the opening scene his opposition to the "jars and tears" at home and his approval of war in France. As events unfold, the deeds of Talbot become positive embodiments of his speech, and the quarrels of Winchester, Somerset, York, Vernon, and Basset, become negative embodiments. In Act IV Sir William Lucy's pleas to York and Somerset repeat what Bedford said at the beginning. Citizen and magistrate can leave the playhouse with renewed conviction in the benefits of selfless devotion to the good of the commonwealth. Had Talbot's own countrymen supported him, his valor would have overcome even the spiritual odds of the devil's handmaiden, Joan La Pucelle. In *2 Henry VI* we watch the inevitable disasters attendant upon those who seek to forward their own selfish desires at the expense of the common good. Dramatizing the open struggle between the houses of York and Lancaster, *3 Henry VI* establishes the truth that those who refuse to give the king loyalty bring about disloyalty from their own followers and suffer not only their own destruction but the destruction of those closest to them. York suffers from the death of his son Rutland, a suffering intensified by Margaret's taunts, but later Margaret experiences a similar fate by watching her son stabbed to death. Warwick, who shifts allegiance from York to Lancaster, later is defeated in battle and killed because Clarence shifts allegiance from him to York. Edward IV, who replaces Henry VI as king, suffers but survives the disloyalty of Warwick and Clarence and harbors at the end of the play a traitor in his closest supporter, Richard, who we know will murder his sons and succeed him to the throne.[1] These are only a few of the recurrent patterns that force us to generalize from a proliferation of episodes to the moral law that chaotic behavior bears out.

A similar relationship holds between event and general truth in Shakespeare's two earliest comedies, *Errors* and *Shrew*, even though the given intention of comedy, to hold the mirror of custom and the image of truth up to the audience, emphasizes awareness more than it stimulates them directly to moral behavior. Our laughter of scorn at the crossed purposes of the Antipholi or Katharina's shrewish behavior depends upon the assumption of their proper roles in the order of society. We know from the outset of *Errors* and *Shrew* what ought to be, and subsequent events do not modify our judgments, contrary to the effect of the later comedies, *Two Gentlemen*, *Labors*, and *Dream*. *Errors*, like *1 Henry VI*, supplies us with a multiplicity of events which enforce one another to confirm our general understanding about the proper place of men in the order of things. We watch father, brother, wife, or sister stumble until, enlightened by facts, each assumes his role within the family.

In Shakespeare's later, more mimetic apprentice plays, the general truths of the sort which govern and shine through episodes of the earlier chronicles are modified by particularities of circumstance and character. Structure reveals the difference. Rather than an accumulation of similar events to confirm a general truth, *Richard II* concentrates upon a few events to direct our attention to the details of circumstance and character. We do not leave behind the details in generalizing from episodes to a moral law which they share but take them into account in complicating our understanding of moral law. The absolute application of the theory of divine right is, we come to realize, inadequate to account for Richard's own participation in his unkinging and for Bolingbroke's very practical talent in ruling men. Mimetic drama, far from being without moral purpose, heightens awareness by diminishing the absoluteness of general moral truth. The less certain we are in placing our judgments, the more aware we become of our standards and cautious about simple approval or disapproval of specific behavior.

The later comedies, which modulate the laughter of scorn to the laughter of acceptance, affect the audience's judgment in a similar way. Multiple critics appear in *Two Gentlemen,* perhaps the earliest comedy that takes romantic love for its central experience. Launce's and Speed's point of view qualifies Julia's and Valentine's values and behavior without causing us to agree totally with their judgments. We accept Launce's good sense but take into account the fact that his character with its limitations allows for his common sense. Valentine behaves foolishly from Speed's point of view, but Valentine feels with an intensity that remains outside Speed's ken.

One way to observe the similarity in the way Shakespeare's later comedies and his serious plays relate standards to behavior is to consider those characters who make some claim to authoritative commentary. When the unwinding of the narrative line requires us to modify our judgments by insisting upon the importance of detail, then it follows that choral commentators can have momentary authority and claim our belief for a time, but one may replace another as event supplants event, thereby adding further details for judgment. In *Labors,* for instance, events lead us to see around the edges of even the most convincing critics, such as the Princess of France, while the obviously limited characters in need of mockery and cure, such as Holofernes, can at moments make accurate criticisms of their betters. In *Dream* the most authoritative interpreter, Theseus, gives us the terms for understanding the events in the forest and the playlet, but his major speech cannot be taken at face value. He compares the fantastic behavior of the lunatic, lover, and poet, who see and act under the influence of imagination, and judges these to be out of touch with reality, which can be comprehended only by cool reason. We remember, however, his own youthful exploits under the influence of Titania, when he courted Perigenia, Aegles, Ariadne, and Antiopa (II.i.74–80); nor can we forget that he celebrates marriage to Hippolyta. At the end of the play we should realize that we in the audience have, like Theseus, failed to include ourselves in our judgment, for we too have confused the real with the fanciful in assuming that some of the characters, themselves creations of imagination, are real. Consequently we can laugh at ourselves as we accept the standard of rationality as an ideal.

Likewise, the audience must qualify its attitude toward similar figures of authority in *Romeo and Juliet* and *Richard II,* Friar Laurence and the Bishop of Carlisle. Since *Richard II* has already been discussed in detail, it is necessary only to recall how the theory of divine right and absolute rule whose spokesman is the Bishop of Carlisle resembles Theseus's standard of reason. Both propound ideal standards that measure the inadequacy of behavior which we experience during the dramas; yet the conclusions do not lead us to assume that things could have been different, given the particular characters and the circumstances. Friar Laurence is a man of good sense who meditates, when we first see him, on the interrelation of medicine and poison, birth and death, good and evil in nature and in the soul of men. His resourcefulness and advice through all the troubled events of the young lovers give him a status apart from characters like Mercutio or Tybalt, heedlessly involved in controversy. Yet even at moments when the Friar speaks incontrovertible good sense, such as the scene in his cell when Romeo learns of his banishment and tries to kill himself, Shakespeare does not allow our approval to remain unqualified. The Friar stops Romeo from suicide and defines for him the whole nature of man, a composite of heaven, earth, and birth, that in effect answers Juliet's earlier question, "What's in a name?" by making explicit what events have shown us, that Romeo cannot be now baptized and lose the name of Montague. The Friar then devises a sensible plan for dealing with the problem of banishment, but when he completes his long speech of advice and comfort, the Nurse says:

O Lord, I could have stayed here all the night
To hear good counsel. O, what learning is!

(III.iii.159–60)

231

Our laughter at her response, which we cannot take as fully undercutting the Friar's comment, makes it difficult for us to give the Friar our wholehearted endorsement.

His behavior near the end of the play evokes a more explicit reservation about his wisdom. He enters the tomb after Romeo has slain himself. Fully aware of Juliet's despair, he leaves her alone when an outside noise frightens him away. Circumstances of the story, of course, require Juliet to kill herself, but the Friar's presence when she awakens is necessary to provide her an alternative to death, life among "a sisterhood of holy nuns." Although this is no appealing alternative, it prevents Juliet's suicide from appearing to be automatic. She, like Romeo, makes a deliberate choice in killing herself, a choice which qualifies the absoluteness of the opening statement by the chorus that their lives are star-crossed. Without the Friar's presence, then, the audience would probably interpret Juliet's final act as a passionate reflex. Yet his rapid flight from the watchmen discloses an uncharacteristic weakness. By arranging events in this way, Shakespeare, I think, throws off balance members of the audience who may still cling to the Friar's earlier advice to the lovers as absolute:

Wisely and slow. They stumble that run fast.

(II.iii.94)

These violent delights have violent ends
And in their triumph die, like fire and powder.

(II.vi.9–10)

This interpretation, one encouraged by Arthur Brooke's poem and propounded by subsequent critics of Shakespeare's play (such as John Masefield),[2] Shakespeare articulates within the play to discredit it. The behavior of the Friar at the tomb is too personal for an authoritative choral figure.

Change in the audience's emotional response accompanies, of course, change in the relation of idea to episode. Events of *1 Henry VI,* for instance, arouse the audience's indignation to fever pitch; York's and Somerset's failure to aid Talbot induces a sense of frustration that is intensified by Talbot's son, who argues with his father in vigorous couplets to remain in battle and fight to the death for his and England's honor. The effectiveness of Talbot's death scenes, testified to by Thomas Nashe's contemporary observations, results appropriately from the rhetorical intention. Given the difference which the principle of the mirror makes for comedy, there are close similarities between the way *Errors* and *Shrew* generate the loud laughter of scorn at behavior obviously improper when judged by standards of social types and the way the early chronicles stimulate our approval and disapproval. Petruchio's taming of Katharina makes the clearest comparison with the early rhetorical chronicles. Like a playwright, he arranges events to bring her to accept her proper place in the order of things. So too, the ideal audience of *1 Henry VI*, after watching the English courtiers quarrel and Talbot fight bravely to the death for England's glory, should leave the theater, magistrate and citizen alike, adjusted to their proper roles, each content to accept his given status for the sake of social harmony. Petruchio does not lecture to Katharina, as Luciana does to Adriana. Instead, he appeals viscerally to her will to bring her to acknowledge in action what she already knows, the proper duties of a wife. Comedy, by its very nature, sets the audience one step further back from events on stage than they would appear to the chronicle audience. Shakespeare senses this difference early in his career when he opens *Shrew* with an unnamed lord who orders events to confuse Christopher Sly about his proper place in the order of things. He takes us behind the scenes to tell us that we are watching the playwright-rhetorician arrange his story. Then the professional players enter to perform a play before Sly (and the Lord), thereby revealing how Petruchio arranges events for a real — that is to say, a moral — effect. If we grant that instructive drama, whether comedy or chronicle, gains much of its power from the clarity and generality of its moral truth, it follows that one major way open to the playwright of comedy for exploiting the different potentialities of his genre is to heighten our awareness of the methods for inculcating that truth. It is this step which Shakespeare takes between *Errors* and *Shrew*.

By equating vigor of impact with simple emotional identification, Shakespeare avoids complicating our responses by leading us to sympathize with the characters of whom we disapprove. One major way to control sympathy is through the point of view. We side with Petruchio and watch Katharina's taming from his angle of vision; conversely we are prevented in the earliest chronicles from siding with the wicked intriguer even though the automatic way to plot an intrigue is from the schemer's viewpoint. In *2 Henry VI*, York, Suffolk, and Cade all have secret schemes to forward their selfish ambitions, but when confrontations with their victims occur, their private intentions are known. Duke Humphrey denounces his enemies; Henry VI knows of Suffolk's guilt; and the unnamed captain knows of Suffolk's intimacies with Queen Margaret; Cade's followers know he lies when he claims himself to be a Mortimer. With similar caution, Shakespeare insures the audience against false rhetoric. When Joan persuades Burgundy to change sides or when Jack Cade denounces Lord Say as enemy to the state, we hear in asides their deceptive intentions. At the outset of his career Shakespeare seems to respect the power of oratory so highly that he will not permit dramatic irony to counteract its force.

The rhetorical lament in *3 Henry VI* coincides with the beginning of Shakespeare's willingness to mix sympathy with disapproval. In this play where the civil broils become open clashes, no one can be called completely good. Henry VI intermittently draws us to his side by his sensible comments upon events. Without a clear-cut division between the selfish and unselfish supporters of the commonwealth to bolster, Shakespeare draws us close to many of the characters at moments of intense suffering. The rhetorical lament, through the devices of exclamation, entreaty, command, and hyperbolic wish, works to make us feel as the speaker feels, regardless of his moral character. These highly charged speeches dramatize the suffering of a character who reaps his own whirlwind. York, for instance, suffers from Margaret's taunts, and we sympathize with him, a father whose brow has been wiped with a napkin dipped in his child's blood. Yet our feelings are contained within an attitude of condemnation, for we know that his rebellion unleashed the forces that killed young Rutland. Clifford and Warwick, likewise reprehensible, deliver speeches at the moments of their deaths that make similar claims upon our sympathy. In *2 Henry VI,* a play where the characters do fall into clear moral categories, the wicked deliver no complicating rhetorical laments. Suffolk, Cade, Somerset, and the Duchess of Gloucester, all suffer on stage for their misdeeds; none can be said to speak in a way that would enlist our feelings for their predicaments. The Duchess speaks longer than the others, but she chides her husband rather than laments her downfall. Shakespeare's willingness to complicate our disapproval with sympathy develops in his more mimetic plays, a practice to be explicated in detail as we turn to the problem of characterization.

These later plays, where details of story are crucial to judgment, redirect the custom and purpose of immediate, visceral stimulation to a heightened awareness of our moral categories. Dramatic irony fixes the view of things at a distance from the participants on stage so that the audience becomes detached from any specific character's judgment of events, hesitant to classify absolutely, taking into consideration details of circumstance and idiosyncrasies of character. Shakespeare probably would not have devoted such attention to the specific details of moral experience had he not sensed their great power to teach, but the lesson differs from that of the early chronicles which confirm general moral truths. The later plays dramatize the difficulties of fitting general principles to specific cases. The man who knows only categorically is the man who only thinks he knows. Like happiness which, if to be caught, must be pursued indirectly, the instructive power of drama *qua* drama can be fully realized only by attending first to story in all its specificity.

∞

Characters undergo a change comparable to the audience's. In the earlier rhetorical plays they talk like orators, classify other characters by simple categories, and respond to rhetoric much as the playwright expects the audience to be stimulated by his drama. In the later more mimetic plays, characters gain in awareness of themselves and others, are inclined to express their feelings obliquely, as Lucrece does when she responds to the painting of Troy, and exhibit a mixture of bad and good qualities. Their ability to express modulations of feeling requires us to take into account details of story that inhibit ready, categorical judgments. Along with their capacity to express themselves obliquely, usually through descriptive tableaux, many judge themselves. This extra awareness suggests something apart from the composite qualities of character. Different from "characteristics," it creates the impression of a substance underlying and containing the characteristics so that after we have categorized and judged, something is left over.[3] This something, never fully known, helps make plausible the potentiality for change of character. Characters undergo change at the same time that multiple critics and conflicting points of view occur in drama. If the advantages of a point of view must be balanced by its corresponding limitations, then it follows that something is left over for the audience to judge by itself. Just as there are a few remnants after we have categorized and judged a self-aware character, so there are details left over after we have cut the narrative to our understanding.

The plays where characters of heightened awareness first appear, *Two Gentlemen, Love's Labor's Lost, Richard III*, and *Titus Andronicus*, all dramatize a new relation between understanding and power. For some reason Shakespeare became interested in the experience of irresistible passions. A character can know he does wrong, but this consciousness has no power over the feelings which drive him to wrong behavior. The orator tends to exclude such experience from his assumptions about the relation of knowledge and power: if the rhetorician knows how to manipulate language properly, he can encourage men to virtuous behavior. Concomitantly, if his listener can understand the clear moral truth, stated copiously with *energia* and *enargia,* then he will (be led to) adapt his behavior to his understanding. In response to rhetorical drama, the audience's sympathies correspond for the most part to its judgment, but in response to characters who behave under the influence of irresistible passions, it is inclined to sympathize even though it disapproves of the behavior. Valentine, Julia, or Berowne, who succumb to love and act irrationally against their "better" judgment, raise no moral problem, but Proteus and Titus Andronicus do. Proteus, in two soliloquies, struggles with the principles of moral behavior and yet succumbs to his passion for Silvia; Titus shoots arrows to heaven for justice from the gods, but, knowing that Revenge comes from hell, would drive its chariot to ease his suffering. It would be overstating the case to say that we sympathize with Proteus, but we understand his behavior in a way that we cannot grant, say, to Richard of York, who in *2 Henry VI* speaks an equal number of soliloquies to reveal his secret plans to us. York announces his ambition; he does not, like Proteus struggle with moral alternatives. We sympathize with Titus Andronicus because we sense the irresistible forces that impel him and tacitly acknowledge our own vulnerability to the gnawing desire for revenge. This kind of response approximates the usual description of the audience's reaction to tragedies like *Macbeth* which show the protagonist to be accountable for his actions and yet stimulate our pity.

In the earliest chronicles, characters judge and behave in a manner similar to characters in the earliest comedies. Comic behavior that generates the laughter of scorn resembles political behavior that generates clear-cut approval or disapproval. In *2 Henry VI* Queen Margaret, Suffolk, and Cardinal Beaufort, for instance, plan the murder of Duke Humphrey without hesitation about the morality of their act. When they face punishment or suffer for their deed, they voice no regrets and make no judgment on themselves. Even though the Duchess of Gloucester and Jack Cade are brought low for their foolish ambitions, they exhibit no moment of repentance. Those who enunciate moral principles act morally: Duke Humphrey, Alexander Iden, Exeter, and the Cliffords. Again, Henry VI is an exception in his failure to rule effectively though he knows the right course of action in defending his uncle against his accusers. *Errors* and *Shrew,* while they raise no moral issues of the same scope, do exhibit characters with a similar innocence of introspection. The characters experience no short circuit between the plans and their attempts to execute them. Petruchio undertakes to tame Katharina and carries his intention out; Lucentio desires to win Bianca and fulfills his desire; the unnamed lord undertakes to alter Sly's identity and succeeds. Characters may face reversals, such as Hortensio, Vincentio, or most of the characters in *Errors,* but they scarcely pause to consider whether their actions are proper (as Proteus does) or consider that their behavior might be laughable or foolish (as Julia and Berowne do). Antipholus of Syracuse, the most introspective of the characters in these two comedies, appears to be the exception, but when he stops to wonder about the strangeness of events, he attributes it to the peculiarities of the Ephesians rather than to himself. He posits no conflicting interpretations that would create an impression of awareness as distinct from his motives or feelings.

In the next stage of Shakespeare's development the comedies explore the helplessness of characters in love, and the serious plays explore the paralysis of suffering which those who have sinned undergo. Both kinds of drama insist upon change in the characters and in the audience. Just as the audience comes to realize that the standards of proper rational behavior are ideals after watching the behavior of romantic lovers in *Two Gentlemen,* so they recognize that the "gnawing vulture" of revenge becomes irresistible for Titus Andronicus and his family, placing the act of forgiveness beyond their reach. On the other hand, it never occurs to us that Talbot would lapse from bravery or Duke Humphrey would succumb to his wife's ambitions, or that Suffolk would regret his love for Queen Margaret. By contrast, Proteus undergoes a change of heart, a fact not merely coincident with his soliloquies of introspection. For *Two Gentlemen* to end happily, Proteus must, of course, change his affections. Yet the logic of the story does not necessitate two soliloquies to dramatize his indecisiveness before betraying his friend. It would be too much to claim that his heightened awareness makes possible his change of character, for we see from Katharina's taming or from most of the conversions in the morality plays that external cause is sufficient to make internal change dramatically plausible. When Proteus repents in Act V, the external forces of Valentine's presence, his altruism, and the disclosure of Julia's fidelity, all shock him into change. Yet the two soliloquies of struggle with his better judgment prepare the audience to accept the change. Without his introspection that dramatizes a self apart from his behavior, the audience would classify him simply as villainous. This awareness cuts the circuit of illustration between behavior and character so that we sense something of himself not embodied in his actions. He cannot be summed up by his external behavior as, for instance, Richard of York in *2 Henry VI* can be. If then, a play leads us to understand a character's wrong-headed behavior as more than a matter of sheer perversity, we must take into account details of self-awareness as well as details of circumstances, details which particularize the story and prevent us from ready generalizations.

Titus Andronicus is comparable to *Two Gentlemen* in the way it makes process, both in the audience's judgments and in the characterization, fundamental. Titus's actions direct the audience's judgment against him at the outset and without altering this attitude bring them to pity and even to share his desire for revenge. Titus's first act is to refuse the collective wisdom of Rome in accepting the role of emperor, a rejection whose significance becomes clearer when we recall Gorboduc and King Lear. So too, when he chooses Saturninus to rule in his stead, we notice how his dedication to the principle of primogeniture overrides all indications of Saturninus's unpleasant behavior and Bassianus's moderate behavior. This same dedication to principle over specific realities causes him to sacrifice Tamora's eldest son in a religious ceremony; he remains deaf to her pleas for mercy and sets in motion a sequence of events motivated by the wild justice of revenge which admits no sentiment of forgiveness until all the immediately involved characters are destroyed. Twice in the later part of the play revenge is defined as having a hellish origin and is contrasted with the heavenly justice of Astrea. Yet we have been caught up in the realities of Aaron's and Tamora's brutal acts and recognize how specific deeds can make the principle of forgiveness an unattainable ideal before the hunger for revenge. Wrong Titus certainly is, but he pays so outrageously for his initial mistakes that we are even gratified by his satisfaction in the bloody banquet. Our attitude toward the standard of good behavior resembles our laughter of acceptance in the romantic comedies, for we accept the standards as ideal and recognize that human nature cannot live up to them, at least in certain circumstances.

Titus's heightened awareness of himself helps generate our sympathy. As we have seen elsewhere, he is one of the first of Shakespeare's characters to express his feelings by descriptive tableaux, placing himself in imaginary settings. This awareness creates a sense of inner life apart from his deeds which cannot be summed up by either his initial behavior or his final horrible revenge. Though we hold him fully responsible, we realize that a clear-cut judgment of his deeds is inadequate. Behavior does not illustrate character; hence we cannot label him a villain even though we judge his treatment of Tamora's son and his own Mutius to be villainous.

Heightened awareness, then, makes available to both tragedy and comedy the experience of paralysis before irresistible passions, and this experience in turn helps evoke an audience's complex response. One could object to this account by saying that Shakespeare is experimenting with the form of revenge tragedy which inevitably leads to the audience's complex response. Unquestionably Shakespeare does undertake a play closely resembling Kyd's *The Spanish Tragedy,* but he makes significant changes. Whereas Hieronimo is drawn into a network of revenge that initially has no bearing on his life or his family, Titus initiates the chain of revenge and is fully responsible. And too, we see no abstract figure of Revenge, commenting from the sidelines about the force it exercises upon human affairs, as we do in Kyd's play. Since Hieronimo is both initially innocent and governed by a personified force, our pity and sympathy are much more easily evoked by Kyd's drama than by Shakespeare's. Yet granting the claims of the genre, we still face the question why Shakespeare first chooses to try his hand at it. That he is young and willing to experiment is as good an answer as any, but it is possible to locate his experimentation within the context of his other apprentice plays to see whether or not it had more than random results. When we do, we see that there are significant points of comparison with *Two Gentlemen* and with *Richard III.*

Like Proteus's soliloquies, Richard III's soliloquy before the Battle of Bosworth Field is not demanded by the story itself. Shakespeare adds this moment of debate between Richard's conscience and his "self" to remove the possibility of our simplifying him into a Vice or a puppet. No doubt the Elizabethan playgoer would have sensed something of the abstract figure of the Vice behind Richard's character just as we in the twentieth century, who are readers of Tillyard and Bowers, see Richard's role as God's scourge in the inevitable working out of the providential pattern of justice, necessitated by the Tudor interpretation of the War of the Roses. Margaret's curses, Clarence's and Lord Stanley's dreams, the ghosts appearing to Richmond and Richard, all enforce the impression of a supernatural power at work in human affairs. No such emphasis occurs in the earlier Henry VI plays. In *Richard III* Shakespeare is freed to emphasize repeatedly a providential force and not risk the danger of making his characters puppets, since they have the capacity to judge their past behavior and to choose. In *3 Henry VI,* for instance, neither York nor Warwick nor Clifford, who go to their deaths on stage, experience any moment of regret or self-condemnation for their behavior in the civil struggle. Yet in *Richard III* Hastings, Boling-broke, Lady Anne, Clarence, Rivers, and Gray all face death with an awareness of their misdeeds.

This additional power of consciousness, then, whether it is self-awareness or self-judgment, was a concomitant of Shakespeare's explorations into the complex relationship between external forces and internal choice. Awareness cannot be coordinated with any moral advantage, for if this were the case, then the audience would classify deeds and characters in the same ready way they do in the early rhetorical chronicles. Richard II's introspection leads to his deposition as well as to a kind of personal triumph. By differentiating himself as a man from his role as king, ne allows himself to submit to Bolingbroke and give up the crown, an act which he judges to be mistaken in his final scene when he realizes that this "self" gives no contentment apart from his role. Shakespeare could have dramatized his inadequacy as a ruler by the simple characteristic of weakness. The easiest and most unsatisfactory way would be to show Richard submitting once he recognizes that he has no supporters. Henry VI, another inadequate king, suggests another possibility: he wishes to be a shepherd while sitting on the periphery of a battle that ends the rule of the house of Lancaster. His wish dramatizes inadequacy rather than an awareness of inadequacy. He does not stand back to observe himself and consider the moral consequences of his feelings. To take one of his few other speeches that state his private discontent with his kingship:

Was ever king that joyed an earthly throne
And could command no more content than I?
No sooner was I crept out of my cradle
But I was made a king, at nine months old.
Was never subject longed to be a king
As I do long and wish to be a subject.

(*2 Henry VI,* IV.ix.1–6)

Shakespeare apparently feels this passage in *2 Henry VI* sufficient to reveal the King's awareness of his inadequacy, for this constitutes Henry VI's entire private comment upon his discontent. It is indeed sufficient to fit a clear-cut category: "inadequate king."

Richard II's awareness prevents the audience from making conclusive judgments. His downfall, more than partly his own fault, can hardly be called a defeat in the fullest sense because he comes to see his whole life in perspective, judge himself honestly, and is able not only to converse sympathetically with a groomsman but fight his murderers, an act of opposition he never musters against Bolingbroke. Our general terms for success and failure become as inadequate as do the terms triumph and defeat.

Against this background, the way characters talk in the serious plays can be seen to coordinate with the way they talk in the comedies. Just as characters in the early chronicles reflect Shakespeare's interest in rhetoric, so the later characters in the more mimetic plays approximate with their flexible, expressive verse the range of conversation in the outer world. For those who speak the formal language of rhetoric, their relations to one another tend to be either direct opposition or agreement, just as the characters can be classified directly as enemy or friend, loyal or disloyal, good or bad. Since particularities of story count for more in the later plays, characters not only talk to one another in less formal patterns, but circumstances often count as much as words in our understanding of what a character means.

In the Henry VI plays characters speak the language of power to assert themselves, usually to proclaim their values to an opponent or to persuade a listener. Verbal wit occurs primarily in the quarrel scenes as an instrument of attack. In *Errors* the mistaken identities and crossed purposes force the characters to use language to assert their values, beliefs, or identity. In line with this, the servant makes use of the quick comeback as a safety valve to help him maintain his position in the order of things. In *Shrew* Petruchio's taming, Katharina's responses to his courtship, Grumio's retorts to Petruchio or Curtis, Vincentio's confrontation with the tutor, Tranio's boasts to the other suitors, all employ the language of power to display and assert themselves, for the relationships are all aggressive. One significant difference in the language of the comedies is the freewheeling use of rhetorical devices. In Antipholus's dialogue with Dromio on the proposition that there is a time for all things or in Petruchio's proclamations of his utter devotion to Katharina's welfare, we listen to a mastery of language in excess of any necessity, a display of virtuosity for its own sake that indicates something of the joy in artifice that the genre of comedy released for Shakespeare. While we find similar verbal energy in the chronicles, as in Talbot's debate with his son, the serious intention directs us away from its virtuosity. The consciousness of artifice raises a question about the relative power of the two genres in the development of Shakespeare's apprenticeship to which we must return.

Characters in the more mimetic plays display on the whole less de-

241

cisiveness in their mode of expression because they are less certain about their own natures or have less control over their behavior. The characters who raise no questions about themselves, such as Bottom or Holofernes, become slightly, if not entirely, comic. Hesitations occur at moments of crisis. Titus Andronicus, for instance, reaches a point when horrors so engulf him that language becomes inadequate. For a character to sense the inadequacy of words, the playwright must realize the expressive adequacy of circumstances so that the audience can assess the character's feelings as disproportionate to his speech. The earlier characters are never at a loss for words: York or Henry VI on the molehill in *3 Henry VI*, Suffolk or the Duchess of Gloucester in anger over their banishments in *2 Henry VI*, Antipholus in outrage over being misunderstood. When Lucrece, exhausted from her expostulations, turns to the painting of Troy, Shakespeare in effect was turning to the power of narrative to help relieve language of its expressive duties. Therefore, Richard II need not say all he means, for instance, when he comes down "like glistering Phaeton," so that understatement can be expressive. In the comedies, the characters who talk of love do not say all they mean, intimations oftentimes being more appropriate than direct statement. Julia's disguise may force her into ironic statements, but Silvia's response to Valentine's letter or Navarre's Muscovite mask makes use of the oblique power of language to convey their sentiments. Circumstances operate in combination with Romeo and Juliet's intuitions of disaster and their fascination with death to push the dramatic uses of language beyond conscious ironies to ambiguities. In the earlier comedies and chronicles irony was one of factual information which the characters eventually discover; in the later, ironies reside not only in awareness of facts but also of interpretation. Unless we pay close attention to Puck's final comments, we may not catch Shakespeare's joke of including the audience within the category of lunatics, lovers, and poets.

Likewise, the characters become more attuned to the discrepancy between word and meaning. Richard II can interpret a message falsely in anticipating the worst when Scroop says that Bushy, Bagot, and Green have made their "peace" (III.ii.128–40). Imprecision of words can be expressive: Aaron's "trim" which describes the mutilation of Lavinia (V.i.93–96), or Costard's "guerdon" and "remuneration" (III.i.121–64). Juliet after some sixteen lines of verse knows that Romeo must be her husband, and Mercutio can find the sharpest insult in Tybalt's questions.

Mimetic drama, which stimulates a continuum of shifting responses in the audience and dramatizes changes within characters, also makes room for a range of mental activities that stress spontaneous rather than formally organized language. Characters can visualize scenes apart from immediate events, anticipate, and reflect. Mowbray foresees a life of speechlessness in exile, his tongue imprisoned in his mouth. Juliet's Nurse can interrupt her mistress to recall an irrelevant past or Mercutio can interrupt Romeo to fancify about Queen Mab. In contrast, the syntax of rhetorical speeches tends to be formal; the death scenes of Talbot, Clifford, or Warwick have a staged sense about them. Juliet, on the other hand, before she drinks the potion almost loses control of syntax in her fear. A leap of association in her visualizing the tomb where she will awaken suddenly impels her to drink so that she may save Romeo (IV.iii.24–58). Richard II is able to sense how others see him at the very moment of talking. After a lengthy sentimental speech expressing his grief and despair, he says:

> Well, well, I see
> I talk but idly, and you laugh at me.
>
> (III.iii.170–71)

Concomitant with this flexibility and heightened awareness of self is a consciousness of language that often takes the form of questioning its adequacy to express meaning. Perhaps the first play where characters pay extended attention to the way they talk is *Richard III*. The Duchess of York asks for instance:

> Why should calamity be full of words?
>
> (IV.iv.126)

and Queen Elizabeth answers:

> Windy attorneys to their client's woes,
> Airy succeeders of intestate joys,
> Poor breathing orators of miseries,
> Let them have scope! Though what they will impart
> Help nothing else, yet do they ease the heart.
>
> (IV.iv.127–31)

Consequently the Duchess advises, "Be copious in exclaims" (IV.iv.135) At about the same stage in Shakespeare's development, Lucrece becomes aware that her lament is "in vain" (1016 ff.).

> That she her plaints a little while doth stay,
> Pausing for means to mourn some newer way.
>
> (1364–65)

So too, Proteus advises Sir Thurio about the power of poetry in a successful courtship (*Two Gentlemen*, III.ii.72–86). Berowne renounces his ornate style in an effort to purge himself of affectation (*Labors*, V.ii. 403–16), and Bolingbroke gradually becomes a "silent king" when he acquires Richard II's power (*Richard II*, IV.i.290). Power is no longer coordinated with words as it was when Marlowe wrote *Tamburlaine*, where the hero of the battlefield also triumphs by means of language. Instead the defeated king reveals his anguish and humiliation through lengthy speeches while the new king watches mutely, allowing Northumberland to make the unpleasant commands. Self-consciousness about language is part and parcel of the characters' encroachment upon the perogatives of the playwright, who relinquishes many of the decisions he automatically makes when he composes rhetorical drama.

∞

The ways in which Shakespeare's comic dramaturgy coordinates with his other dramaturgy suggest that, if we consider their relative innovative power, comedy exerts the primary force in his apprenticeship. Part of the cause arises from historical facts and part from the young playwright's stress on artifice. From the outset of his career Shakespeare's comedies lie closer to the distinctive power of drama than his chronicles because the sixteenth-century commentators excluded insistent didacticism from the principles of comedy. They were satisfied to describe a comedy as being an instructive mirror if it resembled Terence's plays. And, too, the conditions for laughter require that an audience be kept at a distance from events on stage. Shakespeare favors artifice as a means to detach his audience. In *Errors*, for instance, he frames the central confusion of the Antipholi within the story narrated by Egeon, who gives us the données that particularize that story. The Induction to *Shrew* encourages us to view the central story of two interwoven courtships as a fiction. Similarly, *Two Gentlemen* depends upon location to place events; it begins not in the Duke's court in Milan but in Verona, and the solution to the problems arising in Milan occurs in a setting still further removed from home, the forest. A strong sense of place helps frame the events to particularize them. In *Labors* the severe rules of Navarre's academy cut off the members from the outside world where normal behavior occurs; the movement of the play is outward into this world. *Dream*, of course, displays the highest artifice of all, approximating, as it does, a masque.[4] It moves first from Athens into the forest, specified by the données of fantasy that are embodied in Oberon and Puck. As a playlet, "Pyramus and Thisbe," the counterpart of an anti-

masque, carries the function of scene about as far as it can go in quali-
fying the kind of behavior that occurs within it.

It is not accidental, I think, that Shakespeare's first play within the
play occurs in comedy rather than in revenge tragedy where, so far as we
know, it occurred for the first time in native drama. As I have observed
in discussing his comic dramaturgy, Shakespeare uses the comic mirror
to heighten the audience's awareness. Through dramatic irony and
verbal wit, he stimulates their laughter at inadequate behavior, but
their awareness, a condition of laughter, includes not only their moral
judgment but also manner of behavior and inevitably manners of
speech as well as drama itself. We can almost mark off the stages of
Shakespeare's increasing control over his dramaturgy by the widening
range of awareness which the comedies stimulate. A comparison between his first use of the playlet in *Shrew* with the later treatment in
Dream shows us how he came to define the distinctiveness of drama in
its own terms. To state the matter by a psychological analogy, self-
awareness is a condition of individuation. Drama becomes fully distinct
when it becomes self-conscious.

Artifice in comedy helps relieve the playwright and the audience from
attitudes of seriousness and sincerity. At least to the twentieth-century
mind playfulness is taken to be a desirable and energizing attitude. One
of the insights which contemporary scholars have given us comes from
the study of the medieval holiday, a time when drama was performed.
Both the holiday and the drama gave release to the rural audience,
whose lives were governed by the cycle of the seasons. By extension,
when drama broke apart from the agrarian economy and became part
of urban life, that is, became professional, it continued to serve men by
releasing them not seasonally but intermittently from their routines and
responsibilities. Even Plautine comedy has recently been interpreted in
this way.[5] Drama is "play" in the sense that the audience can indulge its
fancies without paying the price which such behavior would demand in
everyday life. Tragedy, in this view, allows us to experience disaster
vicariously, so that *Macbeth* can be interpreted, not as a mirror for
magistrates and citizens who would be ambitious, but as a safety valve
for ambitions, allowing the participant to entertain his dangerous desires and thereby set them to rest.

The full power of drama as a distinctive mode arises from its accepting its artifice. The fact that it is artificial is essentially what Aristotle
meant by "mimesis."

In the stricter sense an "imitation" is brought about whenever we succeed, by means of art, in producing an analogue of some natural process or form, endowed with similar powers to affect other things or us, in materials which are not naturally disposed to assume of themselves any such process or form.[6]

Donatus was specifying the particularity of artifice when he differentiated the fiction of comedy from lies.

Counterfeit [*falsum*] is the dissembling of a fact [*factum*], a lie [*vanum*] is what cannot happen, a fiction [*fictum*] is what is not fact but could happen. . . . We are deceived by counterfeits, we are delighted by fictions, we despise lies.[7]

Tragedy, according to the grammarians, must be based on history, whereas the comic story is fiction, a distinction in itself encouraging the playwright, to be playful. That is, he can propose a wildly improbable hypothetical situation and follow it through, just as Shakespeare does when he postulates two sets of identical twins with identical names. As in a game, we accept the rules—or données—at the outset in order to play or follow the various consequences to their conclusion. We make a pact with the dramatist to entertain his hypothesis, and as a result we are entertained.

"Entertain" means literally to hold mutually, a meaning that gets at the effect of drama as distinct from lyric poetry or prose fiction. People gather together in the theater to entertain an hypothesis, and by doing so are shaped by drama into a temporary community which in turn contributes to the drama. Laughter illustrates their mutual dependence. Comedy would lose much of its impact if one person constituted the audience, for laughter grows from laughter, as we know when we watch television comedy alone. Without the canned laughter of an unseen audience we would be hard put to it to sense the fun. Because a twentieth-century audience goes to darkened theaters, sits in rows facing the silver screen or a procenium arched stage, we have lost some sense of the primacy of our responses to drama. Moreover, communities large enough to support live theater usually attract anonymous audiences, whereas the Elizabethans probably enjoyed the familiarity of a restricted and constant theater-going public. We feel vaguely that something is missing when we watch a play, designed for stage performance, enacted on television. Theater in the round, on the other hand, acknowledges the necessary presence of an audience, a fact that the Elizabethan theater took for granted. Leslie Hotson's theory of the Elizabethan and Jacobean stage, however questionable some details of his study may be, made emphatic once and for all the crucial importance of the audience to drama, whether performed at the public theaters or at court.[8]

The structure of the Elizabethan theater militates against total illusion so that members of the audience never fully lose consciousness of their fellows when they watch the stage. The fact that dialogue is primarily in verse indicates one way in which dramaturgy fits with the shape of the theater. Shakespeare's early chronicles with their stylization of dialogue and characterization exploit this double awareness by affecting the audience as an orator his listeners. Mimetic drama also fits the conditions of production, for the audience has no illusions about its reality or its moral authority; it tries to be neither a slice of life nor a sermon. It makes no attempt to duplicate the world, but approximates it as a self-contained, hypothetical, or artificial world. Shakespeare's earliest comedies stress the hypothetical nature of the story; his later push further to encourage a hypothetical attitude toward moral judgments, or as the attitude was described earlier, the comedies stimulated the laughter of acceptance. Gradually his serious dramas stimulated a similar response. The choral openings, for instance, to Acts I and II of *Romeo and Juliet* enclose the story like a frame and prepare the audience to entertain the hypothesis of the stars' power to cross young lovers and end their parents' strife. How moral judgment fits this hypothetical power of mimetic drama can be clarified if we relate it to another twentieth-century predilection, experimentation.

Our modern sense of drama as release from the everyday routine by artifice fits with our unquestioning acceptance of the value of experimentation. It would be a rare critic who could talk about Shakespeare's early plays without using this word approvingly to indicate that the young playwright tried out stories as if they were hypotheses, to see what would happen. The audience responds by submitting themselves to an experiment for several hours. Or as Coleridge stated it, they undergo a willing suspension of disbelief. Disbelief in fact does not entail suspension of judgment. Rather than leave the theater with their general moral truths confirmed, as they would after watching a rhetorical chronicle, they leave, having sensed the difficulty of applying laws and categories absolutely. Shakespeare's mimetic dramas exercise the audience's moral judgment, thereby encouraging it to be flexible. An audience nourished on Shakespeare cannot be easily self-righteous or provincial.

Richard II and *Dream* serve as a convenient terminus for Shakespeare's apprenticeship, but they cannot be taken as models for his later plays. He does not build systematically in one direction onto the mimetic techniques used in these two plays. Between *1 Henry VI* and *Richard II,* for instance, he changes his conception of history so that the clear-cut categories of characterization, such as the selfish and the patriotic, become inadequate. Yet he returns to clear-cut categories, as we see in Iago and Desdemona or Goneril and Cordelia. Maybe a spiral rather than a straight line of ascent would better diagram the uses of dramaturgy throughout his career. Critics have shown Iago to be a sophisticated reworking of the Vice figure; yet he could hardly be mistaken for an earlier characterization.[9] One trait of his villainy appears in his eagerness to categorize others; even when he does not misinterpret their motives, as in the case of Roderigo, his judgment dehumanizes in the way it abstracts from their natures.[10] His habit of mind resembles the method of a melodramatic playwright, a trait that we do not find in earlier villains such as Richard III. How to relate the later to an earlier version of the Vice is a problem which contemporary scholars can most readily handle by isolating the plays from the curve of Shakespeare's development. We lack a scheme for his career such as Dowden proposed, and we shall probably never replace it with a pattern so neat as Shakespeare's early happiness, mythical sorrows, and final golden years.

A scheme would be, of course, no more useful than a first step in criticism, which works by a dialectical interplay between general concepts and particular literary details. That first step, placing the work, influences the terms of analysis and directs our attention to the details we find important. Today we work primarily by genre. We have lost our innocence about the categories "Elizabethan" and "Jacobean," yet they, like "Augustan" and "Victorian," can serve as checks and balances against more extravagant analyses of isolated works now in fashion, such as patterns of light and dark in *Romeo and Juliet* or noise and silence in *1 Henry IV.* I suspect that such essays will be viewed in a generation as we view nineteenth-century essays on Hamlet's personality or the nobility of Shakespeare's women. Certainly no scheme of Shakespeare's development would guarantee a golden age of criticism, nor would a scheme ever escape contemporary assumptions about literature. In helping to place a drama for analysis, it would act to protect the critic from his own extravagant predilections.

When Heming and Condell in 1623 arranged Shakespeare's plays in folio, they grouped them according to genre and placed his comedies first, introducing them with *The Tempest.* This choice suggests that they too were concerned with supplying the reader an appropriate introduction, for *The Tempest,* more than perhaps any other play, is a microcosm of the whole corpus. Prospero has been described, at least when he drowns his book, as a metaphor for Shakespeare's farewell to the stage. While this expresses our sentimental idolization more than it illuminates the play, it does analogize Prospero to a playwright. He arranges events so that the other characters undergo experiences to cleanse and enlighten themselves for their welfare and happiness. The drama, isolated in its own island world that encompasses its own entertainment, a masque, comments obliquely on its own power. Petruchio and the unnamed lord in the outer story of *Shrew* are first tentative versions of Prospero. *Dream* marks the first consolidation of their power. In this comedy the play devours itself, enclosing the devices of drama within its hypothetical comic world, thereby proclaiming its distinctiveness. Here the power of self-dramatization sets the work apart to operate in its own terms. To survey the future of Elizabethan drama from the vantage point of 1595, we can see drama as a discrete art form become increasingly available to playwrights in an expanding theatrical enterprise. If in the general movement of sixteenth-century drama *The Spanish Tragedy* signals the maturity of professional drama in London and marks the period of the University Wits, Shakespeare's apprenticeship marks the second wave of explorers, as he works himself free of explicit didacticism and consolidates drama as an independent mode with its own literary powers. We find no other playwright in the 1590s after the period of the University Wits that terminates in 1592 who could make claims for opening the way to the extraordinary number of careers that suddenly blossom at the turn of the century: Ben Jonson, John Marston, George Chapman, Thomas Dekker, Thomas Heywood, Thomas Middleton, and later Fletcher and Beaumont.

Notes

References to learned journals in these notes follow the standard abbreviations. A list of these can be found in the opening pages of the annual MLA bibliographies.

Introduction

1. "A Dissertation on the Three Parts of King Henry VI," *The Plays and Poems of William Shakspeare,* ed. Edmond Malone (London, 1790), 6, pt. 2, 381–429.

2. For a representative account of Shakespeare as reviser-apprentice, see Brander Matthews, *Shakspere as a Playwright* (New York, 1913), pp. 38, 51, 61, 86–87.

3. See, for example, C. F. Tucker Brooke, *The Tudor Drama* (Boston, 1911), pp. 320–23.

4. Peter Alexander, *Shakespeare's Henry VI and Richard III* (Cambridge, 1929); Madeleine Doran, *Henry VI, Parts II and III: Their Relation to The "Contention" and The "True Tragedy,"* University of Iowa Humanistic Studies, vol. 4, no. 4 (Iowa City, 1928). Those who remained unconvinced are C. A. Greer, "The York and Lancaster Quarto-folio Sequence," *PMLA* 48 (1933): 655–704: "there is a lost text from which the *Contention* and the *True Tragedy,* the *Whole Contention* and the Folio all came separately or independently," p. 655; J. Dover Wilson, editor of the Henry VI plays for The New Shakespeare, Cambridge, 1952; Albert Feuillerat, *The Composition of Shakespeare's Plays* (New Haven, 1953); Charles Tyler Prouty, *"The Contention" and Shakespeare's "2 Henry VI": A Comparative Study* (New Haven, 1954); G. Blakemore Evans, review article on Dover Wilson's editions of the Henry VI plays, *SQ* 4 (1953): 84–92. However, Andrew S. Cairncross has followed Alexander in his editions of the Henry VI plays for The Arden Shakespeare (London, 1957, 1962, 1964), and more recent editors have also followed Alexander's lead: David Bevington, ed., *1 Henry VI,* The Pelican Shakespeare (Baltimore, 1966); Robert K. Turner, Jr., and G. W. Williams, eds., *2 and 3 Henry VI,* The Pelican Shakespeare (Baltimore, 1967); Lawrence V. Ryan, ed., *1 Henry VI,* The Signet Classic Shakespeare (New York and Toronto, 1967); Arthur Freeman, ed., *2 Henry VI,* The Signet Classic Shakespeare (New York and Toronto, 1967); Milton Crane, ed., *3 Henry VI,* The Signet Classic Shakespeare (New York and Toronto, 1968).

5. Alexander located the "upstart Crow" in a tale by Aesop whose primary meaning is deception rather than plagiarism, *Shakespeare's Henry VI and Richard III,* pp. 43–50. Dover Wilson, in support of Malone, traced Greene's "crow" to Horace's Third Epistle, which warns his friend Celsus not to pilfer from other poets, "Malone and the Upstart

Crow," *ShS* 4 (1951): 56–68. Sidney Thomas found two other contemporary references in William Cupper's sermons, 1592, and in Gervase Markham, 1631, to support Horace's crow and bolster Dover Wilson's hypothesis, "The Meaning of Greene's Attack on Shakespeare," *MLN* 66 (1951): 483–84. E. A. J. Honigmann saw Greene's crow as Horatian but related it to a general "war of University Wits and the new professional writers" and stated that Greene accused Shakespeare not of revising their plays but of pilfering *sententiae* and examples, "Shakespeare's 'Lost Source-Plays,'" *MLR* 49 (1954): 293–307. Warren B. Austin, defending Aesop's crow, attacked Dover Wilson's secondary argument for enlisting R. B.'s *Greene's Funerals* to support the attack of plagiarism, "A Supposed Contemporary Allusion to Shakespeare as Plagiarist," *SQ* 6 (1955): 373–80. T. W. Baldwin assessed the various arguments and supported Aesop and Alexander, *On the Literary Genetics of Shakspere's Plays, 1592–1594* (Urbana, Ill., 1959), pp. 1–55. Arthur Freeman added another reference, 1615, to support the Horatian crow, "Notes on the text of *2 Henry VI* and the Upstart Crow," *N & Q* 213 (1968): 128.

6. H. T. Price, "The Authorship of 'Titus Andronicus,'" *JEGP* 42 (1943), 55–81; also H. T. Price on *1 Henry VI* in *Construction in Shakespeare*, University of Michigan Contributions in Modern Philology, no. 17 (Ann Arbor, 1951), pp. 24–37; Leo Kirschbaum, "The Authorship of *1 Henry VI*," *PMLA* 67 (1952): 809–22; Peter Alexander, *TLS*, 8 July 1965, p. 585; and Richard Hosley, "Whenever the 'gap' between *The Shrew* and *A Shrew* seems too large for a 'normal' good and bad text relationship, we can explain the variation by postulating the influence of X [an Ur-*Shrew*]. But the postulate is not strictly necessary. We may suppose *A Shrew* to be simply a bad quarto of *The Shrew* if we concede that it is of rather a different type from the bad quartos of other Shakespearean plays — an 'abnormal' type, that is to say, which involves a good deal more conscious originality on the part of its author or authors than is usually to be observed in bad-quarto texts," "Sources and Analogues of *The Taming of the Shrew*," *HLQ* 27 (1963–64): 293. See also G. I. Duthie, "*The Taming of A Shrew* and *The Taming of the Shrew*," *RES* 19 (1943): 337–56, and J. C. Maxwell, "'The Shrew' and 'A Shrew': The Suitor and the Sisters," *N & Q* 213 (1968): 130–31. John W. Schroeder, however, argues for the priority of *A Shrew* and urges that the question remain open, "*The Taming of A Shrew* and *The Taming of the Shrew*: A Case Reopened," *JEGP* 57 (1958): 424–43.

7. A. W. Pollard, "Introduction," in Alexander, *Shakespeare's Henry VI and Richard III*, pp. 2–3.

8. T. W. Baldwin, *William Shakspere's Small Latine & Lesse Greeke*, 2 vols. (Urbana, Ill., 1944). J. S. Smart much earlier counteracted the picture of a rustic Shakespeare who went to London like Dick Whittington and replaced it with a picture of a learned young man of wide reading, *Shakespeare: Truth and Tradition* (Oxford, 1928, rpt. 1966), pp. 125–62. Subsequent studies have bolstered the impression of Shakespeare's training, such as Sister Mirian Joseph, *Shakespeare's Use of the Arts of Language* (New York, 1947). Even so, one must remain cautious, for there is no external evidence that Shakespeare attended school. We should supplement Baldwin's picture by such accounts of schooling as Craig R. Thompson, *Schools in Tudor England* (Washington, D.C., 1958), and Joan Simon, *Education and Society in Tudor England* (Cambridge, 1966), especially her discussion of London as "the third university," pp. 383–92. Among those who remain cautious about the picture of Shakespeare as scholar are Virgil K. Whitaker, *Shakespeare's Use of Learning: An Inquiry into the Growth of His Mind and Art* (San Marino, Calif., 1953), esp. pp. 3–122, and Matthew W. Black, "The Sources of Shakespeare's 'Richard II,'" *Joseph Quincy Adams Memorial Studies*, ed. J. G. McManaway et al. (Washington, D.C.), pp. 199–216.

9. "We find, not the brilliant apprentice and tinker of others' matter, but an original poet, educated, confident of himself, already dedicated to poetry; a man passing through the states common to any very great artist, akin to Dante and Milton not only through mature achievement but in the manner in which he began his life-work." E. M. W. Tillyard, *Shakespeare's History Plays* (London, 1944), p. 141. "My conclusion is, though I am

frightened at my own temerity in saying so, that for all we know there were no popular plays on English history before the Armada and that Shakespeare may have been the first to write one," F. P. Wilson, *Marlowe and the Early Shakespeare* (Oxford, 1953), p. 108. See also Leo Kirschbaum, "The Authorship of *1 Henry VI*," p. 816.

10. Ernest William Talbert, *Elizabethan Drama and Shakespeare's Early Plays: An Essay in Historical Criticism* (Chapel Hill, N.C., 1963). The concepts of the apprentice's native abilities vary according to one's interpretation of Shakespeare as reviser or innovator. The revisionists assume that he was incapable of writing dull verse; the supporters of innovation stress his ability to construct plays. J. Dover Wilson said, "Shakespeare was a born poet, as Mozart was a born musician," *The Third Part of King Henry VI*, The New Shakespeare (Cambridge, 1952), p. xiv. Feuillerat could well be read as an echo when he stated, "Writers of genius possess from birth qualities which are their own, which can be perfected but not acquired, and every time Shakespeare forgets to imitate and is himself, his liberated originality expresses itself fully, with an innate sense of the richest resources of the English language," *The Composition of Shakespeare's Plays*, p. 66. Both scholars, however, are willing to attribute the plotting of the Henry VI plays to others, such as Robert Greene or George Peele. In the wake of Alexander's book on the text of *2* and *3 Henry VI*, H. T. Price became a major spokesman for Shakespeare's ability to construct; his major statement appears in *Construction in Shakespeare* (1951); in "The Authorship of *Titus Andronicus*" he said, "The plot is superior to anything that Greene, Peele, Marlowe, or Kyd could achieve," p. 72. About the same time, E. M. W. Tillyard was writing, "When we consider how deficient his fellow-dramatists were in the architectonic power, we can only conclude that this was one of the things with which he was conspicuously endowed by nature. Far from being the untidy genius, Shakespeare was in one respect a born classicist," *Shakespeare's History Plays*, p. 161. More recently, Richard Hosley in arguing against *A Shrew* as the source of *The Shrew* says, "In this case, we should be assuming, around 1593, the existence of a dramatist other than Shakespeare who was capable of devising a three-part structure more impressive than the structure of any extant play by Lyly, Peele, Greene, Marlowe, or Kyd. The assumption seems an unlikely one," "Sources and Analogues of *The Taming of the Shrew*," pp. 294-95.

11. *The Idea of the Humanities and Other Essays Critical and Historical* (Chicago, 1967), 2: 90.

12. *Theory of Literature*, 3d ed. (New York, 1956), pp. 27, 142-57. For a survey of literary histories and an evaluation of their methods, see Douglas Bush, "Literary History and Literary Criticism," *Literary History and Literary Criticism*, ed. Leon Edel, Kenneth McKee, and William M. Gibson (New York, 1965), pp. 1-13, and Rosalie L. Colie, "Literature and History," *Relations of Literary Study*, ed. James Thorpe (New York, 1967), pp. 1-26. The problem of relating historical fact to criticism of individual literary work is central to W. K. Wimsatt, Jr.'s "History and Criticism: A Problematic Relationship," *The Verbal Icon* (Lexington, Ky., 1954), pp. 253-65, R. S. Crane, "On Hypotheses in 'Historical Criticism': Apropos of Certain Contemporary Medievalists," *The Idea of the Humanities*, 2: 236-60, and "'The Houyhnhnms, the Yahoos, and the History of Ideas," *Reason and the Imagination: Essays in the History of Ideas, 1600-1800*, ed. Joseph R. Mazzeo (New York, 1962), pp. 231-53, rpt. in *The Idea of the Humanities*, 2: 261-82; Robert Marsh, "Historical Interpretation and the History of Criticism," *Literary Criticism and Historical Understanding*, ed. Phillip Damon, English Institute Essays 1067 (New York, 1967), pp. 1 24. See also the essays in *New Literary History*, vol. 2, no. 1 (Autumn 1970).

13. A. P. Rossiter, among others, has found the analogy to biology useful, not only evolution, but the law of primitive survival and adaptation, in discussing the continuum of early English drama, *English Drama from Early Times to the Elizabethans* (London, 1950, rpt. New York, 1967), pp. 11-12; yet see Wellek's caveat against the use of the metaphor, "The Concept of Evolution in Literary History," *Concepts of Criticism*, ed. Stephen G. Nichols, Jr. (New Haven, Conn., 1963), pp. 37-53.

14. *The Shattered Glass: A Dramatic Pattern in Shakespeare's Early Plays* (Detroit,

1968); *The Early Shakespeare* (San Marino, Calif., 1967). To my mind, the best discussion on the problem of establishing a proper literary continuum is R. S. Crane's "Critical and Historical Principles of Literary History," *The Idea of the Humanities,* 2:45-156, although I cannot pretend to fulfill his requirements for the ideal literary historian who uses Aristotle's four causes to write a "narrative history of forms" (p. 82); see also Crane's "History versus Criticism in the Study of Literature," where he differentiates sharply the task of the literary historian from the task of the literary critic, *The Idea of the Humanities,* 2: 3-24. Recently Geoffrey Hartman has proposed a history "from the point of view of the poets—from within their consciousness of the historical vocation of art"; see especially "Toward Literary History," *Theory in Humanistic Studies, Daedalus,* 1970, pp. 355-83.

15. The first reference to "drama," according to the *OED,* was Barclay's in 1515; the first reference to "play" as a mimetic action or dramatic performance occurs as early as ca. 893 and as a literary composition in the form of dialogue as early as ca. 1440.

16. Among those who have traced the complicated career of "mimesis" are Lane Cooper, *The Poetics of Aristotle: Its Meaning and Influence* (Boston, 1923); Richard McKeon, "Literary Criticism and the Concept of Imitation in Antiquity," *MP* 34 (1936): 1-23, rpt. in *Critics and Criticism Ancient and Modern,* ed. R. S. Crane (Chicago, 1952), pp. 147-75; Marvin T. Herrick, *The Fusion of Horatian and Aristotelian Literary Criticism, 1531-1555,* Illinois Studies in Language and Literature, no. 32 (Urbana, Ill., 1946), Bernard Weinberg, "From Aristotle to Pseudo-Aristotle," *Comparative Literature* 5 (1953): 97-104; see also Weinberg's discussion of Horatian, Aristotelian, and Platonic literary criticism in the sixteenth century, *A History of Literary Criticism in the Italian Renaissance* (Chicago, 1961), vol. 1; and John D. Boyd's similar discussion with emphasis upon eighteenth-century English critics, *The Function of Mimesis and Its Decline* (Cambridge, Mass., 1968).

Concerning Aristotle's meaning of "mimesis," Elder Olson writes, "Art may be said to imitate nature either in the sense that the form of the product derives from natural form (e.g. the human form in the painting resembles the natural human form) or in the sense that the artistic process resembles the natural," "An Outline of Poetic Theory," *Critiques and Essays in Criticism, 1920-1948,* ed. R. W. Stallman (New York, 1949), pp. 264-83, rpt. in *Critics and Criticism,* pp. 546-66; Richard McKeon, "Aristotle is fond of repeating the observation that the objects of art are produced as nature would have produced them, and that in the processes of production and the objects produced, art imitates nature," *Introduction to Aristotle* (New York, 1947), p. 621; see also McKeon, "Rhetoric and Poetic in the Philosophy of Aristotle," *Aristotle's Poetics and English Literature,* ed. Elder Olson (Chicago, 1965), pp. 216-17; Etienne Gilson, *Painting and Reality* (Washington, D.C., 1957, rpt. Cleveland, Ohio, 1959), pp. 137-39; Gerald F. Else, *Aristotle's Poetics: The Argument* (Cambridge, Mass., 1967), p. 322; John D. Boyd endorses Else's comment, *The Function of Mimesis and Its Decline,* pp. 21-24. William K. Wimsatt, Jr., however, says, "but primarily the term *mimesis* in the *Poetics* must be taken as referring not to some kind of aid or parallel to nature but to the making of a likeness or image of nature," *Literary Criticism: A Short History* (New York, 1957), p. 26.

17. I. A. Shapiro, "The Significance of a Date," *ShS* 8 (1955): 100-105.

18. E. K. Chambers, *William Shakespeare: A Study of Facts and Problems* (Oxford, 1930), 1: 270-71. Later discussions of chronology support Chambers's order although the tendency has been to push back the dates of composition; James G. McManaway, "Recent Studies in Shakespeare's Chronology," *ShS* 3 (1950): 22-33. Marco Mincoff reverses the order of *Shrew* and *Errors* and places *Richard III* after *Love's Labor's Lost, Two Gentlemen,* and *Lucrece,* "The Chronology of Shakespeare's Early Works," *SJH* 100-101 (1964-65): 253-65. Peter G. Phialas has more recently assessed the scholarship on the early comedies and confirms Chambers's order, *Shakespeare's Romantic Comedies* (Chapel Hill, N.C., 1966).

19. Kirschbaum, "The Authorship of *1 Henry VI*"; Cairncross, ed., *The First Part of King Henry VI,* The Arden Shakespeare, 3d ed. (London, 1962), pp. xxviii-xxxviii.

20. Honigmann, ed., *King John,* The Arden Shakespeare, 4th ed. (London, 1954), pp. xliii-lviii, 167-76. William H. Matchett, editor of the Signet Classic Shakespeare *King John,* agrees with Honigmann that it is not dependent upon *The Troublesome Reign* and that *The T.R.* is a bad quarto. This leads him to date the Henry VI plays and *Richard III* far earlier than is customary: "Since...I am convinced that it preceded *The Troublesome Reign,* I naturally date Shakespeare's play before 1591, somewhere, probably between 1588 and 1590. I would think that the writing of the three parts of Henry VI, certainly, and of *Richard III,* probably preceded it.... *King John* should be seen as belonging with these early plays, but in its conception, a long step forward from them," *The Life and Death of King John,* The Signet Classic Shakespeare (New York, 1966), p. 148; see also pp. 153-63.

21. Harbage, "*Love's Labor's Lost* and the Early Shakespeare," *PQ* 41 (1962): 18-36.

22. Brooke, "Marlowe as Provocative Agent in Shakespeare's Early Plays, *ShS* 14 (1961): 34-44. See also Irving Ribner, "Marlowe and Shakespeare," *Shakespeare 400,* ed. James G. McManaway (New York, 1964), pp. 41-53. Recently David Riggs placed the Henry VI plays squarely in the tradition of *Tamburlaine,* which he takes to embody a humanistic view of history and heroic ideals, *Shakespeare's Heroical Histories: "Henry VI and Its Literary Tradition* (Cambridge, Mass., 1971).

23. J. C. Maxwell, ed., *Titus Andronicus,* 3d ed., The Arden Shakespeare (London, 1961), pp. xx-xxv. E. M. W. Tillyard also suggests an early date, *Shakespeare's History Plays,* pp. 135-36. R. F. Hill has made the fullest attack upon a late dating, "The Composition of *Titus Andronicus,*" *ShS* 10 (1957): 60-70; an even fuller discussion of dating appears in Hill's *Shakespeare's Use of Formal Rhetoric in His Early Plays up to 1596,* Ph.D. dissertation, St. John's College, Oxford University 1954, microfilm.

24. Hill's stylistic analysis encompasses "excessive alliteration," "general simplicity of metaphor," "tautology," "wordiness," and "epizeuxis." Even the application of such clear-cut categories, if we omit "general simplicity of metaphor" as being too dependent upon personal judgment for statistical reliability, is open to question. To take Hill's conclusions about tautology and wordiness, "In tautology, *Titus* [my italics] topped the list with twelve examples, followed by *2 Henry VI* with eight; no other play yielded more than three. In wordiness, *Titus,* in my judgment, lapsed eighteen times, no other play more than six. When the two faults are taken together, *Titus* wins with thirty examples, the nearest contender for notoriety being *2 Henry VI* with eleven. (It is worth recording that there are twenty-four such lapses in *1 Henry VI),*" "The Composition of *Titus Andronicus,*" p. 67. Hill compiled statistics for all the apprentice plays except *1 Henry VI* whose authorship he felt to be in question; his parenthetical remark signifies, of course, that if Shakespeare collaborated early in his career on it, the strong resemblance of statistics would help fix the dates of both it and *Titus* as early. But let us ask what should be classified as "tautology" (or pleonasm). Hill gives four examples, the clinching one being "That ever ear did hear to such effect." Another is "By working wreakful vengeance on my foes." If we look at *The Rape of Lucrece* (published in 1594 at approximately the time when I would date the play), a work which Hill did not consider in his reckoning, we find such statements as "Her grief is dumb and hath no words" (line 1105) or "Those that much covet are with gain so fond" (134), "Time, cease thy course and last no longer" (1765), "my tongue shall utter all" (1076), "Shame folded up in blind concealing night, / When most unseen" (675-76), "be you mute and dumb" (1123), "Whilst lust and murder wakes to stain and kill" (168), "robbed and ransacked by theft" (line 838), to cite the more flagrant instances. Here we have eight tautologies, equal to the number Hill found in the early *2 Henry VI.* Shakespeare, we know, did not abhor duplication, often piling up similar words for intensification: "But coward-like with trembling terror die" (line 231), "what following sorrow may on this arise" (186), "But will is deaf and hears no heedful friends" (495). When we

consider Hill's category of "wordiness" or redundance, we find such phrases as "mother of dread and fear" (117), "repose and rest" (757), "false thief" (888), "nameless bastardy" (522), "lank and lean" (708), "unseen secrecy" (763), "bold audacity" (1376), "sad dirge" (1612), "quake and tremble" (1393), "immaculate and spotless" (1656), "endless date of never-ending woes" (935), "what following sorrow may on this arise" (186). When we combine these examples, we discover that Shakespeare in 1593–94 wrote twenty-three phrases that can be classified as "tautology or wordiness," comparable in a 1,855-line poem to Hill's count of thirty instances in an approximately 3,000-word play. Epizeuxis, Hill found, appeared excessively in *Titus,* usually broken by a vocative, such as "Help, grandsire, help," p. 68. In *Lucrece* it occurs frequently during the final dramatic disclosure: "No, no, quoth she" (line 1714), "he, he, she says" (1717), "He, he, fair lords, 'tis he"(1721), "Daughter, dear daughter" (1751), "She's mine, O mine she is" (1795), "Woe, woe" (1802); and elsewhere: "Well, well, dear Collatine" (1058), "So, so, quoth he" (330), "his fair fair" (346), "To thee, to thee" (638), "But I alone, alone must sit" (795), "Himself, himself" (998), "Look, look" (1548), "Fool, fool" (1568), "dear, dear" (1602). If we consider slight modifications of the form, we can add: "O eye of eyes" (1088), "he ten times pines that pines" (1115), "grief grieves" (1117), "at each sad strain will strain"(1131), "Poor helpless help" (1056), "lifeless life" (1374), "friend by friend" (1486), "friend to friend" (1487), "thy sorrow to my sorrow" (1676), "harden'd hearts harder" (978), "disdain to himself disdained" (987), "hours of rest with restless trances" (974), "Curse this cursed night" (970), "To wrong the wronger" (943), "his will his willful eye" (417), "modest wantons, wanton modesty" (401). Hill finds no more than two to six examples of epizeuxis, separated by a vocative, in any of Shakespeare's plays beyond *Titus,* where he finds sixteen.

Finally, John Dale Ebbs observed (in 1951) that *Titus* contains an echo from Nashe's *The Unfortunate Traveller,* completed 27 June 1593, entered S.R. on 17 September 1593, and printed in 1594; he remained uncertain about which work was the dependent one, "A Note on Nashe and Shakespeare," *MLN* 66 (1951): 480–81. W. Schrickx proposes that Nashe is the originator, Shakespeare the borrower, "*Titus Andronicus* and Thomas Nashe," *English Studies* 50 (1969): 82–84. Recently Nicholas Brooke argued the close proximity of *Titus* and *Lucrece, Shakespeare's Early Tragedies* (London, 1968), pp. 11, 13.

25. Arthos, "Pericles, Prince of Tyre," *SQ* 4 (1953): 257–70. I regret that his *Shakespeare: The Early Writings* (Totowa, N.J., 1972) appeared too late for me to profit from it.

26. H. B. Charlton proposed an order of composition which began with *Labors,* then a recoil to *Errors, Two Gentlemen,* then another recoil to *Shrew, Shakespearian Comedy* (London, 1938). In *Two Gentlemen,* Act II, scene v, line 1, Speed welcomes Launce to "Padua" rather than Verona; H. F. Brooks suggests that here Shakespeare inadvertently slipped back to *Shrew* where Petruchio travels from Verona to Padua (I.ii.1), cited by Clifford Leech, "Introduction," *The Two Gentlemen of Verona,* The Arden Shakespeare, 2d ed. (London, 1969), p. xxxii.

Chapter 1

1. The best discussion of dramatic dialogue appears in J. L. Styan's *The Elements of Drama* (Cambridge, 1960, rpt. 1963), pp. 11–117. His more specific discussion of Shakespeare's dialogue, "Shakespeare's Aural Craft," I find less helpful mainly because he applies the principles articulated in the earlier book to Shakespeare's entire corpus without much attention to differences between the earlier and later dialogue, *Shakespeare's Stagecraft* (Cambridge, 1967), pp. 141–92. Most of the discussions of Shakespeare's dialogue relate it to the actor's performance rather than to the problem of composition or the principles of

rhetoric. The best of these, in addition to Styan's *Shakespeare's Stagecraft,* is Bernard Beckerman, *Shakespeare at the Globe, 1599-1609* (New York, 1962). Also of interest are Granville-Barker's intermittent comments on dialogue in his *Prefaces to Shakespeare,* 2 vols. (Princeton, 1946); "The Components" in Alfred Harbage, *William Shakespeare: A Reader's Guide* (New York, 1963), pp. 2-91; and "The Text and the Actors," in John Russell Brown, *Shakespeare's Plays in Performance* (London, 1966), pp. 7-112. The influence of Seneca's *controversiae* and *suasoriae* upon the composition of dramatic dialogue other than Shakespeare's has been studied by Eugene Waith, "John Fletcher and the Art of Declamation," *PMLA* 66 (1951): 226-34, and "*Controversia* in the English Drama: Medwall and Massinger," *PMLA* 68 (1953): 286-303. A broader investigation of the influence of education in the sophistic tradition upon dialogue appears in Charles Osborne McDonald, *The Rhetoric of Tragedy: Form in Stuart Drama* (Amherst, Mass., 1966). Two other stylistic analyses of dialogue, tangential though helpful, are Jonas A. Barish, *Ben Jonson and the Language of Prose Comedy* (Cambridge, Mass., 1960), and Howard S. Babb, *Jane Austen's Novels: The Fabric of Dialogue* (Columbus, Ohio, 1962). See also Bertrand L. Joseph, *Elizabethan Acting* (Oxford, 1951) and *Acting Shakespeare* (New York, 1960), esp. pp. 20-109; and Elder Olson, *Tragedy and the Theory of Drama* (Detroit, 1961), pp. 87-125. There are valuable comments on dialogue scattered throughout the criticism of Shakespeare's plays. For instance, E. K. Chambers, in defending Shakespeare's sole authorship of *Richard III* against claims for Marlowe, says, "Nor is Marlowe's the give and take of the dialogue, in which speeches are not merely juxtaposed but articulated, as the ideas of one disputant provoke and determine those of the next. It is a natural and improvised, rather than a prepared dialogue," *William Shakespeare. A Study of Facts and Problems,* 1: 303.

2. According to the "Printer's" foreword, he omitted "some fond and frivolous gestures, digressing and, in my poor opinion, far unmeet for the matter," Irving Ribner, ed., *The Complete Plays of Christopher Marlowe* (New York, 1963), p. 50.

3. W. W. Greg in *Dramatic Documents from the Elizabethan Playhouses* (Oxford, 1931), 2 vols., discusses seven plots (*1 Tamar Cam* is no longer extant). J. Q. Adams describes another in the Folger Library, "The Author-Plot of an Early Seventeenth Century Play," *Library,* 4th ser., 26 (1945): 17-27. Adams surveys the meanings of "plot" as Henslowe uses the word: to apply both to a guide for production and to an author's guide for composition.

4. All quotations from Shakespeare's plays have been taken from Alfred Harbage, et al., eds., *William Shakespeare: The Complete Works,* rev. ed. (Baltimore, 1969).

5. This suggests that the composition of *Errors* precedes the chronicle play. Such an ordering makes more sense than one which assumes that Shakespeare first devised a brief knocking at the gate in *1 Henry VI* and then, when composing *Errors,* searched outside his major source, *The Menaechmi,* for an episode to serve as model for a very similar dialogue.

6. Almost without exception those scholars who find a number of hands in the composition of *1 Henry VI* give the Temple Garden scene to Shakespeare. J. Dover Wilson says, "It would be difficult to find a more characteristic example of Shakespeare's early manner than the Temple Garden scene," *The First Part of King Henry VI,* The New Shakespeare (Cambridge, 1952), p. xlii; see also his discussion, *The Third Part of King Henry VI,* pp. vii-xvi. H. C. Hart delivers the same judgment, *The First Part of King Henry the Sixth,* The Arden Shakespeare, 2d ed. rev. (London, 1930), p. xvi. Allison Gaw says that the scene is "a Shakespearean interpolation," *The Origin and Development of "1 Henry VI,"* University of Southern California Studies, 1st Series, Vol. 1 (1926), p. 107. E. K. Chambers: "Shakespeare's presence is only clear to me in (*e*), the Temple Garden scene, and (*f*), an unrhymed Talbot scene," *William Shakespeare,* 1: 291. Recently even this scene has come into question. G. Blakemore Evans says, "It is unlike Shakespeare to *invent* an important historical moment such as this and the basic idea of the rose-plucking suggests more of the pretty fancifulness of a Greene or Peele than of a Shakespeare," *SQ* 4 (1953):

88. Marco Mincoff says, "actually it has surprisingly little that one could point to as specifically characteristic of Shakespeare's manner," "The Composition of *Henry VI, Part 1*," *SQ* 16 (1965): 283.

7. Elias Schwartz discusses the interplay of the two characters in "On the Quarrel Scene in *Julius Caesar*," *College English* 19 (1957–58): 168–70.

8. *The Institutio Oratoria*, trans. H. E. Butler, Loeb Classical Library (London, 1921), 3:357.

9. Gladys Doidge Willcock and Alice Walker, eds., *The Arte of English Poesie* (Cambridge, 1936), pp. 160, 161, 178.

10. Muir bases his assertion on a passage from *The Winter's Tale, Shakespeare's Sources*, rev. ed. (London, 1961), p. 249; "Shakespeare and Rhetoric," *SJH*, 90 (1954): 49–68. Virgil Whitaker finds evidence of Puttenham in Parts 2 and 3 of *Henry VI* and claims that he along with Lyly and Marlowe were Shakespeare's favorite contemporary authors, *Shakespeare's Use of Learning*, p. 68.

11. *The Arte of English Poesie*, pp. 160–61.

12. Donald Peet, "The Rhetoric of *Tamburlaine*," *ELH* 26 (1959): 137–55. Peet finds the devices of amplification central to Marlowe's purposes and remarks on the absence of repetition, antithesis, and pun.

13. *Elizabethan and Metaphysical Imagery* (Chicago, 1947, rpt. 1961), pp. 89–90. Yet Madeleine Doran has observed, "in effect it was often used synonymously with copiousness. For some of the means of amplification—comparison, example, description, repetition, periphrasis, digression—inevitably led to expansion of the theme," *Endeavors of Art*, p. 49.

14. When the dialogue of *1 Henry VI* is analyzed strictly as verse without regard to the nature of the dramatic experience, several styles may be distinguished. The disintegrators, basing their analyses on parallels and echoes of phrases, imagery, or upon statistics of vocabulary and metrics, find as many as four or five different styles within the play. Dover Wilson based his discriminations upon these standards: the non-Shakespearean style can be discerned in "all lines or passages in halting, forced or prosaic verse," whereas Shakespearean verse "flows freely, with the evident pulse of a powerful mind behind it"; non-Shakespearean images are "hazy, muddled or tawdry," whereas Shakespearean images are "honestly imagined and clearly envisaged, even if at times they are elaborately conceited," *1 Henry VI*, p. xlii; see also Wilson's *2 Henry VI*, p. xx, and *3 Henry VI*, pp. xii–xvi. Allison Gaw, using a similar approach, found evidence for four different hands in *1 Henry VI* in addition to Shakespeare's, *The Origin and Development of "1 Henry VI."* H. C. Hart found Greene's style "toned down" by a "syndicate" of Peele and Shakespeare with perhaps some assistance from Nashe, *The First Part of King Henry the Sixth*, pp. xi–xlviii. E. K. Chambers, who acknowledged Shakespeare to be the sole author of *2* and *3 Henry VI*, declared, "The internal evidence of style I find difficult to handle. I do not think that we have adequate *criteria* for distinguishing with any assurance from the style of his contemporaries that of a young writer still under their influence," *William Shakespeare: A Study of Facts and Problems*, 1: 287. Nevertheless, when he discussed *1 Henry VI* he discovered two main styles that coincide with different subject matter: (*a*) English politics, and (*b*) the matter of fighting in France and Joan of Arc. He found style *b* to be "inferior," with "many flat and some absurd lines, much tautology, and a tendency to drag in learned allusions" (1:290). Recently Marco Mincoff has agreed with Chambers's distinction and suggests that the inferior style belongs to an early version of the play, "If this is Shakespeare at all . . . it is Shakespeare from a period with which we are not familiar," and that the better style belongs to Shakespeare's revision, "somewhere about 1594," "The Composition of *Henry VI, Part I*," *SQ* 16 (1965): 279–87.

15. Antipholus of Syracuse's long speech of praise to Luciana may seem to be an exception. The burden of his speech lies in his willingness to be transformed by her. Yet here too Shakespeare weaves alliteration, rhyme, and antithesis together with the "sensable" fig-

ures, such as paradox, that ornament and depersonalize:

Far more, far more to you do I decline....   (III.ii.44)
Sing, siren, for thyself, and I will dote.
Spread o'er the silver waves thy golden hairs....   (III.iv.47-48)
He gains by death that hath such means to die.
Let Love, being light, be drownèd if she sink!   (III.ii.51-52)

16. Geoffrey Bullough, ed., *Narrative and Dramatic Sources of Shakespeare's Plays*, 3 (London, 1960):73.

17. Sir Arthur Quiller-Couch, for instance, sees the play as an attempt to combine romance and farce, "Introduction," *The Comedy of Errors*, 2d ed., The New Shakespeare (Cambridge, 1962), p. xxiv. Derek Traversi makes an effort to attribute a lyrical quality to the ending by finding in it "intimations of the splendour of reconciliation" that appears so prominently in the late romances, *Shakespeare: The Early Comedies*, Writers and Their Work, no. 129 (London, 1960), p. 14. Yet if the dialogue does not exploit the emotions of reunion, why does Shakespeare arrange events as he does? Francis Fergusson observes shrewdly that an audience cannot be simply released from farce. By analogy to Minsky's burlesque, he sees that "the patrons received the whole treatment, gently eased at last out of their farcical mood into something warmer, damper, and homier," *The Human Image in Dramatic Literature* (Garden City, N.Y., 1957), p. 148.

18. A comparable passage could have been selected from *Errors*: Egeon's speech when he tries to get his son to recognize him. The wrong Antipholus fails to respond, and Egeon delivers a moving speech on the effects of time. Like Mortimer, he makes heavy use of metaphor and simile to present himself through a list of items: "my night of life . . . my wasting lamps . . . my dull deaf ears" (V.i.308-19).

19. See, of course, "The Intentional Fallacy," W. K. Wimsatt, Jr., and Monroe C. Beardsley, *The Verbal Icon*, pp. 3-18; and E. D. Hirsch, Jr., *Validity in Interpretation* (New Haven, Conn., 1967).

20. Ben Jonson delighted in this hyperbole and used it in *Every Man Out of His Humour*, I.i.25-28, in *Volpone*, V.viii.2, and again in *The Devil is An Ass*, II.vii.17; this lineation refers to the Herford and Simpson edition of Jonson's works; see especially *Ben Jonson*, 9 (Oxford, 1950): 425. Alexander H. Sackton comments upon Jonson's use of this hyperbole in *Rhetoric as a Dramatic Language in Ben Jonson* (New York, 1948), p. 157. Shakespeare later used catachresis for ironic and comic purposes. In *Love's Labor's Lost*, for instance, Boyet says:

I only have made a mouth of his eye,
By adding a tongue which I know will not lie.

                                                                                    (II.i.250-51)

and Berowne says:

O, if the street were paved with thine eyes,
Her feet were much too dainty for such tread.

                                                                                    (IV.iii.273-74)

C. L. Barber finds such images in "bad taste," *Shakespeare's Festive Comedy* (Princeton, N.J., 1959, rpt. Cleveland, Ohio, 1963), p. 104

21. Not only speeches, but scenes and whole plays were classified according to the three types of oration. Melanchthon, for instance, classified Terence's *The Andrian* as a deliberative oration; see Marvin T. Herrick, *Comic Theory in the Sixteenth Century*, Illinois Studies in Language and Literature, vol. 34 (Urbana, 1950, rpt. 1964), pp. 12-18. Miss Doran makes clear the shortcomings of such classification, *Endeavors of Art*, p. 34.

22. Miss Doran observes that Elizabethans paid more attention to the demonstrative and ceremonial oration than to the deliberative or judicial and calls attention to the fact that Thomas Wilson in *The Arte of Rhetorique* (1560) devotes much more attention to demonstrative than the other two types, *Endeavors of Art*, pp. 31-32. Milton Boone Kennedy, following Wilson's definition of judicial oration, classifies a number of speeches in

the apprentice plays as judicial because each speech is a "defense of himself," *The Oration in Shakespeare* (Chapel Hill, N.C., 1942), pp. 66–67. He too recognizes the difficulties of clear-cut classification, pp. 64–65. T. W. Baldwin finds, for instance, that Prince Escalus follows "strict judicial rhetoric procedure" in his unraveling of Romeo and Juliet's story, Act V, scene iii, conforming to a "judicial inquiry of the conjectural type," discussed in book 2 of the *Ad Herennium, Small Latine & Lesse Greeke,* 2: 76–81. R. F. Hill's comment on the analyses of structure in orations is salutary: "In fact a survey of the 'orations' in the early plays nowhere reveals careful or complicated structure. Where there is some obvious falling into parts, it is of the simplest kind, and would suggest itself to any writer of commonsense and possessed of an elementary knowledge of composition," *Shakespeare's Use of Formal Rhetoric in His Early Plays up to 1596,* p. 78.

23. *Endeavors of Art,* p. 51.

24. "This gradual progress is not that of a person going up a flight of stairs, say, or climbing a ladder, leaving each stage behind him as he goes: rather it is like the manipulation of a series of optical lenses, which as their operator slowly learns, will under different arrangements reveal ever deeper perspectives. . . . Shakespeare was an economical dramatist, who preferred to creatively redesign extant molds rather than build them anew," Brian Vickers, *The Artistry of Shakespeare's Prose* (London, 1968), p. 52.

Chapter 2

1. "How would it haue ioyed braue *Talbot* (the terror of the French) to thinke that after he had lyne two hundred yeares in his Tombe, hee should triumphe againe on the Stage, and haue his bones newe embalmed with the teares of ten thousand spectators at least (at seuerall times), who, in the Tragedian that represents his person, imagine they behold him fresh bleeding," *Pierce Penilesse his Supplication to the Divell,* ed. R. B. McKerrow and F. P. Wilson, *The Works of Thomas Nashe,* rev. ed. (Oxford, 1958), 1: 212.

2. David Bevington, *From "Mankind" to Marlowe* (Cambridge, Mass., 1962): "In the early sixteenth century, four, five, and six actors are the usual numbers. It is not until the 1560's and 1570's that troupes of seven and eight begin to be indicated; but even at this time, groups of four to six are not unusual," p. 71. My survey appears in an early version of this chapter, "Shakespeare and the Public Confrontation Scene in Early History Plays," *MP* 62 (1964): 1–12.

3. Lineation refers to Irving Ribner's edition, *The Complete Plays of Christopher Marlowe* (New York, 1963).

4. "the open pageant stage which preceded the Elizabethan had its scenic entrances directly opposed at the ends of the oblong, left and right—a transverse axis. And everybody knows that the Restoration stage, which immediately followed the Elizabethan—although alien movable scenery had turned its best open side into a 'back' enclosed by a proscenium arch—on its remaining open half still maintained the transverse axis: entrance doors with window-stages over them, directly opposed at the ends, left and right. . . . The obvious inference is that on the open Elizabethan stage, which chronologically came between the two, the entrances were the same as they were both before and after," *Shakespeare's Wooden O* (New York, 1960), p. 193.

5. "The presence of formal patterns in stage grouping enabled the Globe company to present large-cast plays with a minimum of rehearsal," *Shakespeare at the Globe, 1599–1609* (New York, 1962), p. 173; see also pp. 162–76, 207–13.

6. Line references are to the edition by J. William Hebel and Hoyt H. Hudson, eds., *Poetry of the English Renaissance, 1509–1660* (New York, 1929), p. 173.

7. E. W. Talbert argues that Shakespeare weighted the scales in York's favor in the

Temple Garden scene, *Elizabethan Drama and Shakespeare's Early Plays,* pp. 179-80, 373.

8. From Jonson's prologue to *Every Man in His Humour* (1616 version).

9. Wolfgang Clemen observes that the pun enables a quick interchange of comments, thereby breaking down the older stiff dialogues of sequential monologues typical of Marlowe, *The Development of Shakespeare's Imagery* (London, 1951), p. 32.

10. One of the main interests of E. W. Talbert's analysis of Shakespeare's early history plays is the way he manipulates our sympathies for the Yorkists, then against the Yorkists, for the Lancastrians, then against the Lancastrians, *Elizabethan Drama and Shakespeare's Early Plays.* In an earlier book he showed how the varying interpretations of historians toward Bolingbroke's deposition of Richard II are reflected in *Richard II: The Problem of Order* (Chapel Hill, N.C., 1962). More recently Henry A. Kelly, discussing the various interpretations of divine providence by Renaissance historians, praises Shakespeare for giving each account its fair hearing: "Shakespeare's great contribution was to unsynthesize the syntheses of his contemporaries and to unmoralize their moralizations.... Thus the sentiments of the Lancaster myth are spoken by Lancastrians, and opposing views are voiced by anti-Lancastrians and Yorkists. And the Tudor myth finds its fullest statement in the mouth of Henry Tudor," *Divine Providence in the England of Shakespeare's Histories* (Cambridge, Mass., 1970), pp. 304-5.

11. Irving Ribner discerns such an interpretation underlying the Henry VI plays: 'No matter how superior to the king a claimant to the throne may be, both in legitimacy of birth and in personal attributes, the rule of the *de facto* king must not be challenged, for the worst of all evils is civil war, and even a bad king is preferable to that," *The English History Play in the Age of Shakespeare,* rev. ed. (New York, 1965), p. 109.

12. John Palmer, in my opinion, gives the fullest explication of the opening scene, *Political Characters of Shakespeare* (London, 1945), pp. 122-28.

13. Leonard F. Dean interprets the discrepancies between meaning and ceremony as "theatrical" and symptoms of political malaise, "*Richard II:* The State and the Image of the Theater," *PMLA* 67 (1952): 211-18.

14. The Malone Society reprint of this manuscript play, prepared by Wilhelmina P. Frijlinck, 1929, is entitled *The First Part of the Reign of King Richard the Second* even though Miss Frijlinck says, "but I do not think the relation of Shakespeare's play so close as to make it necessary to assume that it belonged to the same company, or that we are justified in speaking of the play as *The First Part of Richard II,* as Sir Edmund does," p. xxv. She is referring to E. K. Chambers's title of the play, *1 Richard the Second, The Elizabethan Stage* (Oxford, 1923), 4: 42-43. Chambers, following W. Keller's edition in the *Shakespeare Jahrbuch,* vol. 35 (1899), says, "the relation of 1 Rich. II to Shakespeare's play is so close as to make it natural to regard it as having become a Chamberlain's play," p. 43. Samuel Schoenbaum continued to list the play as *1 Richard II,* or *Thomas of Woodstock* in *Annals of English Drama, 975-1700,* 2d ed. (Philadelphia, 1964), p. 56. To my mind, A. P. Rossiter is more convincing. He says, "The play, therefore, is *Woodstock,* and not *1 Richard II,*" in the introduction to his edition, *Woodstock, a Moral History* (London, 1946), p. 26. But in subsequent comments he does not see the distinction so sharply: "That Shakespeare's play has some dependence on *Woodstock* is almost sufficiently demonstrated by its references to Woodstock himself," p. 47. See also his comments in *Angel with Horns,* ed. Graham Storey (London, 1961), pp. 29-30.

15. A survey would probably show that the scenes of brutality were even more popular than the pre-battle confrontations. *Selimus, Part One* (ca. 1587-92), for instance, depicts the brutal triumph of Selimus over Acomat, Acomat over Mahomet, Acomat over Aga, Selimus over Corcut, Selimus over Mustaffa, and Selimus over Acomat's queen.

16. "With more assurance we may say that he [Marlowe] was never so addicted as Shakespeare to what Quintilian (IX.i.17) calls figures of speech," F. P. Wilson, *Marlowe and the Early Shakespeare,* p. 121.

17. A. P. Rossiter has shown how both *Woodstock* and *Edward II* depend upon *2 Henry VI*, "Introduction," *Woodstock, a Moral History,* pp. 63–64, 69–71.

18. "It adds to the horror that in the last two acts Edward is never brought face to face with his two tormentors," F. P. Wilson, *Marlowe and the Early Shakespeare,* p. 98.

19. Richard II's speech of unkinging contains two approximations of the coronation ceremony. In the first, a brief survey, he reverses the ceremonial order of heart, hands, and head:

Now mark me how I will undo myself.
I give this heavy weight from off my head
And this unwieldly sceptre from my hand,
The pride of kingly sway from out my heart.

(IV.i.203-6)

The three general divisions of the coronation service follow this order: (*a*) election of king by the people and oath taken by the king to govern to the best of his power; (*b*) rite of unction, including prayers blessing the king before the unction itself; (*c*) delivery of the royal ornaments: vestments and regalia (crown, scepter, staff, and ring) before enthronement. After enthronement the lords spiritual and temporal come forward to do homage and fealty. See Leopold G. Wickham Legg, ed., *English Coronation Records* (London, 1901), pp. xix–xxxiv; and a discussion of consecration in Percy Ernst Schramm, *A History of the English Coronation,* trans. Leopold G. Wickham Legg (Oxford, 1937), pp. 86–112. Richard II's speech, immediately after the lines just quoted, follows the regular order of the service, beginning with the rite of unction:

With mine own tears I wash away my balm,
With mine own hands I give away my crown,
With mine own tongue deny my sacred state,
With mine own breath release all duty's rites.

(IV.i.207-10)

20. Travis Bogard locates a significant leap in Shakespeare's technique of creating inwardness essential for the tragic character in Richard's comparison of his suffering to Christ's, "Shakespeare's Second Richard," *PMLA* 70 (1955): 192–209. He too senses the discrepancy between what Richard II says and what he feels: "The emotion of the man is obscured by the rhetoric of the king, yet it is alive, coursing below the frigid language, waiting for its moment," p. 207. This essay should be supplemented by R. F. Hill's "Dramatic Techniques and Interpretation in 'Richard II,'" *Early Shakespeare,* Stratford uponAvon Studies, no. 3 (London, 1961), pp. 101–21.

21. One cannot help wondering whether Marlowe was thinking of Rutland's napkin dipped in blood when he devised this gesture. Whereas the bloody handkerchief exercises an overwhelming effect, King Edward's handkerchief is, by contrast, potentially no more than bland. Certainly some more personal token would have intimated a more forceful gesture on the King's part; as it is, the handkerchief bears mute evidence indeed of tears and sighs. Of course, the chronological relationship could be reversed, Shakespeare thereby turning a helpless gesture into a brutal one.

Chapter 3

1. See, among other works, especially Paul J. Aldus, "Analogical Probability in Shakespeare's Plays," *SQ* 6 (1955): 397–414; H. T. Price, "Mirror-Scenes in Shakespeare," *J. Q. Adams Memorial Studies,* ed. James G. McManaway et al. (Washington, D.C., 1948), pp. 101–13; and Thomas B. Stroup, *Microcosmos: The Shape of the Elizabethan Play* (Lexington, Ky., 1965), pp. 88–90.

2. Sigurd Burckhardt takes Joan's comments at face value and finds Shakespeare's implicit criticism of Tudor political drama, "'I am but Shadow of Myself,' Ceremony and

Design in *1 Henry VI*," *MLQ* 28 (1967): 139-58.

3. For instance, in *Like Will to Like* (ca. 1568) Nicolas Newfangle kneels to swear after Lucifer, but turns the oath to nonsense while approximating its sounds and meter, J. S. Farmer, ed., *The Dramatic Writing of Ulpian Fulwell,* Early English Drama Society (London, 1906), p. 11. In *The Marriage of Wit and Wisdom* (1579) Idleness misreads a proclamation given him by Search, J. S. Farmer, ed., *Five Anonymous Plays,* 4th ser., Early English Drama Society (London, 1908), pp. 285-86. Variations on this comic device include the instructions of Moros, who perverts (purposely?) names and blurs lesson with directions, *The Longer Thou Livest, the More Fool Thou Art* (ca. 1559), ed. R. Mark Benbow, Regents Renaissance Drama Series (Lincoln, Neb., 1967), lines 497-505 and 980-85. Matthew Merrygreek, who misreads Ralph Roister Doister's letter to Dame Custance (III.iv) by scrambling the punctuation, can be seen as another variation, which incidentally lies behind Peter Quince's reading of the Prologue to *Pyramus and Thisbe.*

4. Shakespeare's contribution to the revision of *Sir Thomas More,* written perhaps near this time, dramatizes a similar episode where the protagonist exercises rhetorical power over an unruly crowd, a fact that suggests others admired the orations in the Henry VI plays and *Richard III.* R. C. Bald dates the manuscript as we now have it about 1600, "The Booke of *Sir Thomas More* and Its Problems," *ShS* 2 (1949): 53-55; I. A. Shapiro proposes the revisions "about 1593," "The Significance of a Date," *ShS* 8 (1955): 102; Harold Jenkins finds 1590-93 to be likely for the original and 1594-95 for the revisions, "Supplement to the Introduction of Sir Walter Greg's Edition of *Sir Thomas More* (1911)," *Collections,* vol.65 The Malone Society (Oxford, 1961), p. 189. Thomas Clayton sees the problem of dating as still controversial, "The 'Shakespearean' Addition in *The Booke of Sir Thomas Moore*: Some Aids to Scholarly and Critical Shakespearean Studies," *Shakespeare Studies Monograph Series,* vol. 1, ed. J. Leeds Barroll (Dubuque, Iowa, 1969), p. 7.

5. Shakespeare probably chose to omit any confrontation between the Battle of Bosworth Field at least in part out of consideration for Richmond's dignity. Richard III's wit, so sharp elsewhere in the play, would no doubt have left the stately figure of God's minister (and Queen Elizabeth's grandfather) somewhat diminished after the flyting.

6. *A Commentary on Shakespeare's "Richard III,"* trans. Jean Bonheim (London, 1968), pp. 226-27.

7. Ibid., p. 226. Philip Williams finds Richard III's battle oration "essentially a heroic speech," designed to increase our sympathy in him. "In these final scenes he is courageous, competent, and admired by his followers. No disparaging details are introduced," "*Richard the Third*: The Battle Orations," *English Studies in Honor of James Southall Wilson,* ed. Fredson Bowers, University of Virginia Studies, vol. 4 (Charlottesville, Va., 1951), p. 129.

8. W. A. Armstrong clarifies the distinction between a *de facto* tyrant and a *de jure* tyrant and cites Elizabethan sanctions for deposing a *de facto* tyrant, "The Elizabethan Conception of the Tyrant," *RES* 22 (1946): 161-81.

9. *A Commentary on Shakespeare's "Richard III,"* p. 12.

10. *The Arte of Rhetorique,* ed. G. H. Mair (Oxford, 1909), p. 134.

11. Tillyard, *Shakespeare's History Plays,* p. 214. Anne Righter says, "Despite all she knows about Richard, the widowed queen of Edward IV apparently cannot resist, in the wooer's presence, the suit for her daughter's hand," *Shakespeare and the Idea of the Play,* p. 89.

12. Judith M. Karr lists all the similar pleas, "The Pleas in *Titus Andronicus,*" *SQ* 14 (1963): 278-79.

13. Robert L. Montgomery, Jr., denies that the poem is "primarily dramatic" and observes that those critics who would claim this quality for it wish to see the poem as a step in Shakespeare's development. "Shakespeare's Gaudy: The Method of *The Rape of Lucrece,*" *Studies in Honor of DeWitt T. Starnes,* ed. Thomas P. Harrison et al. (Austin, Tex., 1967), p. 35.

14. There is far from unanimous agreement about the success of this episode. Derek Traversi, for instance, says, "The whole of this part of the play suggests that the author's interest in his creation, temporarily exhausted after the presentation of contrasted orders and personalities, was now flagging," *Shakespeare from "Richard II" to "Henry V"* (Stanford, Calif., 1957), p. 46.

15. "This artistry [that is, the shifting Lancastrian and Yorkist interpretations of events] makes *Richard II* a problem drama as purposeful as any of Shakespeare's 'problem comedies'," *Elizabethan Drama and Shakespeare's Early Plays,* p. 321.

Chapter 4

1. J. W. Cunliffe, *The Influence of Seneca on Elizabethan Tragedy* (London, 1893); Wolfgang Clemen, *English Tragedy before Shakespeare,* trans. T. S. Dorsch (London, 1961). Howard Baker's attack on indiscriminate attributions of Senecanism to dramatic conventions of the sixteenth century was healthy, *Induction to Tragedy* (Baton Rouge, La., 1939). R. F. Hill states the precise influence in this way, "The Roman dramatist furnished the idea of a rhetorical tragedy in which verisimilitude of expression was sacrificed to lofty sentiment and polished phrase." "Shakespeare's Early Tragic Mode," *SQ* 9 (1958): 457.

2. Pagination refers to the edition of G. H. Mair (Oxford, 1909). I choose Wilson because he is both traditional and frequently reprinted between 1560 (revised edition) and 1585 (see Russell H. Wagner, "The Text and Editions of Wilson's *Arte of Rhetorique,*" *MLN* 44 [1929]: 421-28). Hardin Craig makes clear that one cannot establish any precise influence between the details of Wilson's text and Shakespeare's plays precisely because he is so traditional, "Shakespeare and Wilson's *Arte of Rhetorique,*" *SP* 28 (1931): 618-30. T. W. Baldwin confirms his judgment, *Small Latine & Lesse Greeke,* 2: 42.

3. Quintilian testifies to his own experience as an orator: "I have frequently been so moved while speaking that I have not merely been wrought upon to tears, but have turned pale and shown all the symptoms of genuine grief" (VI.2.36), *Institutio Oratoria,* trans. H. E. Butler (London, 1921), 2: 439. To emphasize how current this idea was in Shakespeare's lifetime, I cite a similar passage from Thomas Wright, *The Passions of the Mind* (1604), quoted in Bertrand L. Joseph, *Elizabethan Acting* (London, 1951), p. 71:

It cannot be that he which heareth should sorrow, hate, enuie, or fear any thing, that he should be induced to compassion or weeping, except all those motions the oratour would stirre vp in the iudge, be first imprinted and marked in the oratour himselfe…. Furthermore the passion passeth not onely thorow the eyes, but also pierceth the eare, and thereby the heart; for a flexible and pliable voice, accommodated in manner correspondent to the matter whereof a person intreateth, conueyeth the passion most aptly, pathetically, and almost harmonically, and euery accent, exclamation, admiration, increpation, indignation, commiseration, abhomination, exanimation, exultation, fitly (that is distinctly, at time and place, with gesture correspondent, and flexibility of voice proportionat) deliuered, is either a flash of fire to incense a passion, or a bason of water to quench a passion incensed.

4. Even though this speech exhibits a traditional structure, critics have, mainly on the basis of imagery and metrics, praised it as being evidence of Shakespeare's later style, evidence of revision in *2 Henry VI.* E. K. Chambers, *William Shakespeare: A Study of Facts and Problems,* 1: 286; F. P. Wilson finds it "startlingly mature" and may well be "contemporary with *King Lear,*" *Marlowe and the Early Shakespeare,* pp. 117-18; J. P. Brockbank suggests that the speech "was written during or immediately after the composition of *Part 3,* and set back into *Part 2* to offer intimations of the violence to come," and praises it as "simply the most lucid and telling expression of one range of anarchic impulses at large in the tetralogy," "The Frame of Disorder—'Henry VI,'" *Early Shakespeare,* Stratford-upon-Avon Studies, no. 3 (London, 1961), pp. 90-92; still more recently Ken-

neth Muir finds "mature imagery" here and states, "The conclusion is inescapable that Shakespeare made alterations to the play some years after its first performance," "Image and Symbol in Shakespeare's Histories," *Bulletin of the John Rylands Library* 50 (1967-68): 107-8.

5. For instance, Hardin Craig says, "It is as if Shakespeare had learned rather quickly as he went on in his dramatic career the interest that lay in the dramatization of real event and, as he did so, displaced much of his early Senecan rhetoric in favor of a less mannered dramatic style," "Shakespeare and the History Play," *J.Q. Adams Memorial Studies,* p. 57.

6. "Shakespeare's Early Tragic Mode," *SQ* 9 (1958): 455-69; "Richard II," *Early Shakespeare,* pp. 101-21.

7. Albert L. Walker isolates eight devices for constructing "emotional scenes" in Elizabethan drama, "Conventions in Shakespeare's Description of Emotion," *PQ* 17 (1938): 26-66.

8. As the result of two pioneering articles, Clifford Leech, "Document and Ritual," *Durham University Journal* 30 (1937): 283-300, and A. P. Rossiter, "The Structure of *Richard III,*" *Durham University Journal* 21 (1938): 44-75, most critics acknowledge the power of this and similar speeches in *Richard III.* R. F. Hill, for instance, says, "The most successful part of the whole play (*3 H. VI*) is the soliloquy of King Henry at the Battle of Towton and the following episode of the fathers and sons (II.v)," *Shakespeare's Use of Formal Rhetoric in his Early Plays up to 1596,* p. 154. H. M. Richmond, however, says, "The long, flat, fatuous speech of Henry on the battlefield is indefensible in many respects, and the crude parallelisms of this speech are matched by the symmetrically conceived situations . . . that are presented immediately afterwards. . . . Richard is almost justified in getting rid of such a bore," *Shakespeare's Political Plays* (New York, 1967), p. 57.

9. Coleridge's famous defense of Gaunt's quibbles comes to mind here: "The passion that carries off its excess by play on words, as naturally and, therefore, as appropriately to drama, as by gesticulations, looks or tones. This belonging to human nature as *human,* independent of associations and habits from any particular rank of life or mode of employment," *Shakespearean Criticism,* ed. T. M. Raysor, 2d ed., Everyman Library (London, 1960), 1: 135; also 2: 143-45. The key words are "human" and "naturally," for Coleridge relates the passage to character rather than audience. M. M. Mahood also discusses quibbles as operating to release tension, *Shakespeare's Wordplay* (London, 1957), p. 32; see also her discussion of "gaunt," pp. 81-82. Likewise, Derek Traversi differentiates the word-play of Richard II from the stylized speech of Henry VI: "The speaker's feeling, precisely by being aware of its artificiality, becomes more real than that of Henry VI," *Shakespeare from "Richard II" to "Henry V",* p. 38.

10. Again, see Albert L. Walker, "Conventions in Shakespeare's Description of Emotion," *PQ* 17 (1938): 26-66.

11. For the tradition behind Lucrece's declamation see Douglas Bush, *Mythology and the Renaissance Tradition in English Poetry,* rev. ed. (New York, 1963), pp. 150-54. For the function and traditional allegorical interpretations of the fall of Troy, see Horst Oppel, "Das Bild des Brennenden Troja in Shakespeare's 'Rape of Lucrece,'" *SJH* 87-88 (1952): 69-86, and D. C. Allen, "Some Observations on 'The Rape of Lucrece,'" *ShS* 15 (1962): 89-98.

12. M. C. Bradbrook makes a similar point: "This self-dramatisation is necessary for characters who are definitely limited and Humorous, like Marlowe's and Jonson's. They see themselves as a 'picture in the gallery,' and because of this, they can express the total situation as though they were standing outside it," *Themes and Conventions of Elizabethan Tragedy* (Cambridge, 1935 [1960]), p. 133.

13. Max Black, "Metaphor," *Proceedings of the Aristotelian Society* 55 (1954-55): 273-94.

14. A. S. Cairncross adds "prisoner" from F2 to this question: "Is she not prisoner here?" The Arden Shakespeare.

15. Several critics have pointed to the severely formal style in this play that acts as a contrast to moments of "natural" verse between Romeo and Juliet. As Norman Rabkin puts it, "What makes us respond to certain speeches as if they were natural utterances, so that we are scarcely aware of 'style,' when we hear them, is the staginess of others. The inconsistency of style in *Romeo and Juliet* directs our intense response to its most powerful language, and that forces us to attend to its meaning," *Shakespeare and the Common Understanding* (New York, 1967), p. 168. See also Harry Levin, "Form and Formality in *Romeo and Juliet*," *SQ* 11 (1960): 3-11.

16. John Russell Brown postulates a subtext for the actor delivering soliloquies, *Shakespeare's Plays in Performance* (New York, 1967), pp. 50-67.

17. "Lightning before death" is a proverbial expression; see Morris Palmer Tilley, *A Dictionary of the Proverbs in England in the 16th and 17th Centuries* (Ann Arbor, Mich., 1950), p. 381.

18. Denis de Rougemont gave this interpretation its first authoritative statement, *Love in the Western World,* trans. Montgomery Belgion, rev. ed. (Garden City, N.Y., 1956), pp. 193-95. M. M. Mahood brings impressive support to this thesis in the form of iterative images and word-play, *Shakespeare's Wordplay*, pp. 56-72. Not all subsequent critics have fallen into step; John Lawlor, for instance, makes nothing of it, *"Romeo and Juliet,"* *Early Shakespeare,* Stratford-upon-Avon Studies, no. 3, pp. 123-43, nor does Robert O. Evans, *The Osier Cage: Rhetorical Devices in "Romeo and Juliet"* (Lexington, Ky., 1966). Others, however, have affirmed the presence of the love-death motive: for instance, Norman Rabkin, *Shakespeare and the Common Understanding*, pp. 150-51, 180-84; Nicholas Brooke, *Shakespeare's Early Tragedies,* (London, 1968), p. 88.

19. G. B. Harrison, ed., *Shakespeare: The Complete Works* (New York, 1952), p. 507.

20. Bertrand Evans discusses in detail how Shakespeare manipulates the various degrees of the characters' ignorance to carry out the plan of the stars, "The Brevity of Friar Laurence," *PMLA* 65 (1950): 841-65.

Chapter 5

1. That *1 Henry VI* is a didactically clear drama is borne out by the remarkable unanimity among critics who state its general theme, their major disagreement being whether or not England's troubles could be traced to a divine curse placed upon the land for the deposition of Richard II. E. M. W. Tillyard says, "The theme of the play is the testing of England, already guilty and under a sort of curse, by French witchcraft. England is championed by a great and pious soldier, Talbot, and the witchcraft is directed principally at him. If the other chief men of England had all been like him, he could have resisted and saved England. But they are divided against each other, and through this division Talbot dies and the first stage in England's ruin and of the fulfillment of the curse is accomplished." *Shakespeare' History Plays,* p. 163. Lawrence V. Ryan follows this emphasis: "Divine providence allows England to be plagued by infernal as well as political enemies because her people have sinned. How the nation might have remained true to itself is signified by the words and deeds of Talbot. What she is in danger of becoming is signified in the shortcomings of the French.... The dissension that breaks out at home in the opening lines begins immediately to sap the English strength abroad," *Henry VI, Part One,* The Signet Classic Shakespeare (New York, 1967), p. xxxi. Most others narrow the cause to the quarreling nobles. Geoffrey Bullough says, "one basic theme, which can be summed up in the words of Faulconbridge in *King John:* 'Naught can make us rue / If England to itself do rest but true,'" *Narrative and Dramatic Sources of Shakespeare,* 3 (London, 1960): 37. A. S. Cairncross: "If all individual Englishmen had been loyal and

true like them [the Talbots], there would have been no danger of foreign loss and internal disunion," *The First Part of King Henry VI*, The Arden Shakespeare, p. xliv. Leo Kirschbaum: "If all individual Englishmen were as "true" as the Talbots, England would not be in danger of foreign loss and internal disunion," "The Authorship of *1 Henry VI*," *PMLA* 67 (1952):822. H. T. Price places the blame more specifically, "In the end the disunion and treachery resulting from the weakness of the King cause the loss of France," *Construction in Shakespeare*, University of Michigan Contributions in Modern Philology, no. 17 (Ann Arbor, 1951), p. 25. The idea of England being true to itself was prevalent at this time. Of Edmund Campion's trial in 1581 Holinshed says in 1587, "This little Iland, God hauing so bountifullie bestowed his blessings upon it, that except it prooue false within it selfe, no treason whatsoeuer can prevail against it," quoted in Lily B. Campbell, *Shakespeare's "Histories," Mirrors of Elizabethan Policy* (San Marino, Calif., 1947), p. 126, and of course *The Troublesome Reign of King John* (published 1591) ended with the same sentiment.

2. "*The Menaechmi* starts out with the other twin, and with the reassurance of familiar surroundings, into which the disturbing factor will be injected. *The Comedy of Errors* starts with the newcomer, and his impressions of strangeness: the witchery of Ephesus, not the bustle of Epidamnum," "Introduction," *The Comedy of Errors*, The Signet Classic Shakespeare (New York, 1965), p. xxxiii; reprinted in *Refractions* (New York, 1966), p. 145.

3. Tillyard's interpretation of a providential curse upon England, resulting from the deposition of Richard II, has come under increasing attack in recent years. Irving Ribner, for instance, attacked the grand scope of the curse, "It is in part because Shakespeare emphasizes the sins committed during the reign of Henry VI rather than the initial crime against Richard II that I cannot share Tillyard's view that the *Henry VI* plays and *Richard III* form one vast epic unit with the second tetralogy he was to begin some five or six years later to cover the years from Richard II to Henry V," *The English History Play in the Age of Shakespeare*, rev. ed. (New York, 1965), pp. 105–6. More recently, through a deliberate investigation of historiographers' opinions about divine providence in Renaissance England as well as the comments of Shakespeare's characters, Henry A. Kelly agrees with Ribner: "From a providential point of view, what we have in *Richard III* is the Tudor myth more or less as it existed before the time of Polydore Vergil. It includes the recognition of Henry VI as the lawful king, the atrocious cruelty of the York brothers in killing Henry and his son, and the punishment that befell them because of this, especially as manifested in the divinely authorized and supported campaign of Henry Tudor.... There is no indication in this play or in the whole of this tetralogy that Henry VI or his family was divinely punished because of the sins of his grandfather, Henry IV," *Divine Providence in the England of Shakespeare's Histories* (Cambridge, Mass., 1970), p. 295. However, Michael Quinn points to the "scholastic distinction between a general providence and a particular providence" which shows that punishment for local sins does not preclude the operations of a more general providential plan, "Providence in Shakespeare's Yorkist Plays," *SQ* 10 (1959): 45–52. Yet the very concept of providence comes under question, and A. P. Rossiter discerns in *Richard III* ironic details which reveal the limitations of such an interpretation of historical events, "Angel with Horns: The Unity of *Richard III*," *Angel with Horns*, ed. Graham Storey (London, 1961), pp. 1–22. Wilbur Sanders differentiates a meddlesome providence" from a "natural providence" in the play, *The Dramatist and the Received Idea* (Cambridge, 1968), pp. 98–99, also pp. 92–109.

4. "In fact, of those who believed Henry guilty of his [Richard II's] murder, Shakespeare is the first to suggest that Henry was repentant for the deed at the time it was committed. He is also the only one to picture him as projecting his crusade at this time with the motive of making reparation for his part in Richard's death," Kelly, *Divine Providence in the England of Shakespeare's Histories*, p. 213. See also Brents Stirling, "Bolingbroke's 'Decision,'" *SQ* 2 (1951): 27–34.

5. "Richard's fate was settled before the play began,…He has been guilty of an unroyal crime and his just punishment is assured," *The Cease of Majesty: A Study of Shakespeare's History Plays* (London, 1961), pp. 228–29. Irving Ribner agrees with this interpretation, "Bolingbroke is almost a passive instrument of destiny.… His too is a cleansing role; not only does he avenge the death of his uncle," *The English History Play in the Age of Shakespeare,* rev. ed., pp. 162–63. Kelly argues against this hypothesis, *Divine Providence in the England of Shakespeare's Histories,* pp. 204–5.

6. The terms "kingship" and "manhood" are the ones that the play itself gives us in order to understand Richard's acquiescence to deposition. Although "the King's two bodies" are close to "actor" and "poet," they are not equivalent, and to confuse them seems to me to misread the play; Richard is not "acting." See, for instance, George A. Bonnard, "The Actor in Richard II," *SJH* 87–88 (1952): 87–101, or Leonard F. Dean, "*Richard II*: The State and the Image of the Theater," *PMLA* 67 (1952):211–18. The most telling objection to such analyses which import metaphors of poet and actor into plays that do not make them central terms of the dialogue was stated by C. S. Lewis: "We sometimes speak as if the characters in whose mouths Shakespeare put great poetry were poets: in the sense that Shakespeare was depicting men of poetical genius. But surely this is like thinking that Wagner's Wotan is the dramatic portrait of a baritone? In opera song is the medium by which the representation is made and not part of the thing represented. … Similarly in poetical drama poetry is the medium, not part of the delineated characters.… If ever there is occasion to *represent* poetry (as in the play scene from *Hamlet*), it is put into a different metre and strongly stylized so as to prevent confusion," Hamlet: The Prince or the Poem?" reprinted in *Studies in Shakespeare,* British Academy Lectures, selected by Peter Alexander (London, 1964), p. 214.

7. In "The Prophetic Soul: A Note on *Richard II*, V.v.1–66," G. Wilson Knight finds in this soliloquy a compendium of Shakespeare's wisdom, "Thus, Richard, in a poetic mood, becomes a true poet, a miniature of the future Shakespeare," *The Imperial Theme* (London, 1931), p. 362. Others have found it less satisfactory. "The soliloquy, far from showing any penetrating vision in Richard, sums up the evasiveness and moral cowardice which have led to his ruin," Foster Provost, "The Sorrows of Shakespeare's Richard II," *Studies in English Renaissance Literature,* ed. Waldo F. McNeir (Baton Rouge, La., 1962), p. 52. M. M. Reese curiously compares the soliloquy to Lear: "But this perception has brought him [Richard II] only to the threshold of true self-knowledge. If we think of the insight granted to Lear and Timon, we shall realise how little Richard has really achieved.… He could not, as Lear might have done, go back into world and conquer it," *The Cease of Majesty,* p. 244. More in keeping with my reading is H. M. Richmond, "This last scene is marked by an extraordinary fusion of resigned self-knowledge with physical resolution, a fusion that is completely incompatible with the view of Richard as an oversensitive poet, incapable of action," *Shakespeare's Political Plays,* p. 137.

8. Among those who disapprove of York are Alfred Hart, who describes him as "weak and vacillating," *Shakespeare and the Homilies* (Melbourne, Australia, 1934), p. 47, and J. Le Gay Brereton, "He is amiable but weak, and, rather because of his weakness than from any deliberate motive, is ready to accept what is established. Swept out of his depth by the current of circumstance, he feels vainly for a foothold," *Writings on Elizabethan Drama* (Melbourne, Australia, 1948), p. 27; and Leonard F. Dean, "His maxims are turned by circumstances into rootless platitudes. He is so perplexed as he attempts to deal with the unroyal Richard and the usurping Bolingbroke that actors have been misled into playing him as a comic figure. Equally misleading is the attempt to equate him with the undervalued modern parliamentarian," "*Richard II* to *Henry V*: A Closer View," *Studies in Honor of DeWitt R. Starnes,* ed. Thomas P. Harrison et al. (Austin, Tex., 1967), p. 39. On the other hand, Coleridge is kinder to York: "The admirable character of York. Religious loyalty struggling with a deep grief and indignation at the king's vices and follies; and adherence to his word once given, in spite of all, even the most natural, feelings," *Shakespearean Criticism,* ed. T. M. Raysor, 2d ed., 1: 138; but see also 2: 143

and 231-32, passages which are more critical of him. Peter Ure says, "On York's character in general Coleridge's observations . . . are not likely to be bettered." "Introduction," *Richard II*, 4th ed., The Arden Shakespeare (London, 1956), p. lxxii. Homer Nearing, Jr., says, "Shakespeare's purpose in understating any motive on York's part except loyalty to the king was perhaps to hold up to his audience a model of patriotism," "'York in Choller' and Other Unrecorded Allusions to *Richard II*," *N & Q* 191 (1946): 47. Norman Rabkin sees 'the Duke of York, perhaps the first of Shakespeare's 'reflector' characters, who, like Casca and Horatio and Kent and Enobarbus in later plays, epitomizes and directs our shifting sympathies," *Shakespeare and the Common Understanding*, p. 87. Wilbur Sanders notes that "Shakespeare is exceedingly gentle with the old man," but shrewdly observes York's crucial phrasing when he describes his essential position to Bolingbroke, "I do remain as neuter" (II.ii.151), and finds him one more instance in a pessimistic picture about the possibility of "integrity in the political sphere," *The Dramatist and the Received Idea*, pp. 183-85, 193.

9. See A. P. Rossiter, "Ambivalence: The Dialectic of the Histories," *Angel with Horns*, pp. 40-64.

10. R. F. Hill observes the dislocation of tones and appears, for the most part, to disapprove of it: "But the natural comic dialogue thrust crudely into rhetorical tragedy jostles uncomfortably by the side of its predominantly formal diction." The Simpcox and Jack Cade episodes "break the laws of the rhetorical form." "The characters of Aaron and Richard Crookback constantly disturb the overall rhetorical mode. Their vigor and humor are presented with a naturalism which makes the language of the other characters look, indeed, frigid, thin, and artificial." "Shakespeare's Early Tragic Mode," *SQ* 9 (1958): 464. See also Rossiter, "Comic Relief," *Angel with Horns*, pp. 274-92.

11. Peter expresses his fear not only in prose but in asymmetrical syntactic form when parallel construction would have been the readiest way to itemize his various bequests to his friends:

I thank you all. Drink, and pray for me, I pray you; for I think I have taken my last draught in this world. Here, Robin, an if I die, I give thee my apron; and, Will, thou shalt have my hammer; and here, Tom, take all the money that I have. (*2 Henry VI*, II.iii.72-76)

12. After Cade puts on Sir Humphrey Stafford's armor and strikes his staff on London Stone, he reaches his high point in threatening the realm. As he entertains the proposal that he will be the law of England, Shakespeare diminishes him through asides:

Butcher
Only that the laws of England may come out of your mouth.
2 Rebel [aside]
Mass, 'twill be sore law then, for he was thrust in the mouth with a spear, and 'tis not whole yet.
Weaver [aside]
Nay, John, it will be stinking law, for his breath stinks with eating toasted cheese.
Cade
I have thought upon it; it shall be so. Away, burn all the records of the realm! My mouth shall be the parliament of England.
2 Rebel [aside]
Then we are like to have biting statutes, unless his teeth be pulled out.   (IV.vii.5-15)

13. The transition from one style to another in most scenes comes natural and easy "This humanizing and normalizing influence of natural language is most apparent in Richard's own speech, which again and again drops from the rhetorical attitude to an outspoken directness and a stark colloquialism which is unique in the whole range of tragic heroes in the drama before and during Shakespeare's time," "Tradition and Originality in Shakespeare's *Richard III*," *SQ* 5 (1954): 252.

14. Of the York-Aumerle scene, Matthew Black says, "My own feeling about this matter is colored by a belief that the York-Aumerle scenes, in which some of the worst couplets occur, are intended to be funny, and that Shakespeare was impatient with them after the

lyrical flights of the earlier acts," "The Sources of Shakespeare's *Richard II*," *J. Q. Adams Memorial Studies,* p. 210.

Chapter 6

1. Bertrand Evans, *Shakespeare's Comedies* (Oxford, 1960, rpt. 1967), p. 1.

2. Marvin T. Herrick concentrates specifically upon the general tradition of criticism in the sixteenth century as it relates to the genre of comedy, *Comic Theory in the Sixteenth Century,* Illinois Studies in Language and Literature, vol. 34 (Urbana, 1950, rpt. 1964). While he organizes his subject by general topics, it would be a mistake to represent his picture of the tradition as one of general agreement, even with regard to comedy. Yet, as Madeleine Doran has said, "Certain of the critics' general ideas about poetry—*imitation, decorum, verisimilitude,* and the like—are commonplaces met with everywhere," *Endeavors of Art,* p. 10. O. B. Hardison, Jr., sketches three distinct phrases within Italian criticism of this period, "Introduction," *English Literary Criticism: The Renaissance* (New York, 1963), pp. 3–6. Bernard Weinberg's detailed discussion reveals the wide variety of opinion divided along different lines, Horatian, Platonic, and Aristotelian, *A History of Literary Criticism in the Italian Renaissance* (Chicago, 1961), vol. 1. Baxter Hathaway reveals the richness of critical thought by tracing the variety of opinions on one problem in *Marvels and Commonplaces: Renaissance Literary Criticism* (New York, 1968); see also his *The Age of Criticism: The Late Renaissance in Italy* (Ithaca, N.Y., 1962).

3. John Russell Brown, "The Interpretation of Shakespeare's Comedies: 1900–1953," *ShS* 8 (1955): 2.

4. Nevill Coghill, "The Basis of Shakespearian Comedy," *Essays and Studies,* 1950, p. 14. Among those who agree with Coghill are E. M. W. Tillyard, *Shakespeare's Early Comedies* (London, 1965), pp. 13–15, and Arthur Brown, "Shakespeare's Treatment of Comedy," in *Shakespeare's World,* ed. James Sutherland and Joel Hurstfield (New York, 1964), p. 94.

5. Northrop Frye, *A Natural Perspective* (New York, 1965, rpt., n.d.), pp. 44–71. See also his "The Argument of Comedy," *English Institute Essays, 1948* (New York, 1949), pp. 58–73.

6. *Endeavors of Art,* pp. 13 and 228; see also pp. 12–27. J. Dover Wilson also questions the division of comedy into clear-cut "classical" and "romantic" categories: "Modern neo-classical comedy was begotten by classical learning upon the traditions of the late medieval morality play. The doctrine of *instruction*—the typical doctrine of Renaissance dramatic theory—was imposed upon the classical dramatic form, and the result was an almost complete departure from the tone of classical comedy. . . . His [Shakespeare's] comedies belong to the same species (though refined to the point of genius, so that they became in the end something new), as the comedies of sixteenth-century Italy, which were themselves romanticized descendants of Plautus and Terence. Thus, in a way, Shakespearian comedy has a better title to be called classical than has Jonsonian comedy," *Shakespeare's Happy Comedy* (London, 1962), pp. 22–23. F. P. Wilson gives a historical account of the complex interrelations in English comedy between 1540 and 1584, *The English Drama, 1485–1585,* The Oxford History of English Literature (Oxford, 1969), pp. 102–25. See also Marvin T. Herrick's discussion of the Christianized Terence in *Tragicomedy, Its Origin and Development in Italy, France, and England,* Illinois Studies in Language and Literature, vol. 39 (Urbana, 1955, rpt. 1962), pp. 16–62.

7. *Shakespearian Comedy* (London, 1938), p. 23. See also Milton Crane, "I have argued elsewhere for the view that Shakespeare as a comic dramatist was working within the great traditon of classical comedy, reconciling the demands of romance and comedy in a larger harmony. This still seems to me a useful way in which to think about Shakespeare's

treatment of the matter of his comedies, whether in the early classical works, such as *A Midsummer Night's Dream,* the great mature comedies, such as *Twelfth Night,* or the late romantic plays, such as *The Tempest,*" "Shakespeare's Comedies and the Critics," *Shakespeare 400,* ed. James G. McManaway (New York, 1964), p. 71.

8. Translation by John Henry Freese, Loeb Classical Library (London, 1938).

9. See *The Great Critics,* ed. J. H. Smith and E. W. Parks, rev. ed. (New York, 1932), p. 654, for a list of sixteenth-century critics who echoed Donatus's phrase. We hear it, among the English dramatists of the period, from Thomas Heywood in *An Apology for Actors* (1612), reprinted in *English Literary Criticism: The Renaissance,* ed. O. B. Hardison, Jr., p. 225, and, of course, from Cordatus in *Every Man Out of His Humour:*
...let him content himselfe with CICEROS definition (till he haue strength to propose to himselfe a better) who would haue a *Comoedie* to be *Imitatio vitae, Speculum consuetudinis, Imago veritatis;* a thing throughout pleasant, and ridiculous, and accommodated to the correction of manners. (III.vi.204-9)
Ben Jonson, ed. C. H. Herford and Percy Simpson, 3 (Oxford, 1927): 515.

10. Quoted from the edition by Henry Herbert Stephen Croft (London, 1883), 1: 124-25.

11. Quoted from the edition by Edmund Creeth, *Tudor Plays* (Garden City, N.Y., 1966), p. 219. Udall goes on to justify the play by adding that it "against the vayne glorious doth invey."

12. E. K. Chambers lists seventeen reprintings of the play, *The Elizabethan Stage* (Oxford, 1923), 4: 34; see also M. C. Bradbrook, *The Growth and Structure of Elizabethan Comedy* (London, 1955, rpt. Baltimore, 1963), p. 34: "...a debased version of *Mucedorus* was still being played in Shropshire villages in the early nineteenth century."

13. Quoted in Herrick, *Comic Theory in the Sixteenth Century,* p. 65. With regard to Jonson's scorn of romance, it is interesting to compare the hesitant defense from Antonio Minturno's *L'Arte Poetica* (1564) printed by Winsatt and Brooks, *Literary Criticism: A Short History* (New York, 1965), pp. 162-63.

14. Weinberg, in generalizing about vernacular commentaries on *The Poetics* of Aristotle where discussion of "plot" should hardly be equated with argument, says, "It [plot] is thought of largely as a kind of scenario or 'argument' to which episodes are added for purposes of amplification and adornment—episodes which may be considered integral or removable, depending on the decision of individual theorists. In spite of quotations about the 'soul of tragedy,' there is no organic conception of plot as the organizing element of the poem, from which nothing can be removed," *A History of Literary Criticism in the Italian Renaissance,* 1: 562.

15. *The Growth and Structure of Elizabethan Comedy,* p. 94.

16. T. W. Baldwin, *Shakspere's Five-Act Structure* (Urbana, Ill., 1947). See also Herrick, *Comic Theory in the Sixteenth Century,* p. 106-29. Wilfred T. Jewkes in *Act Division in Elizabethan and Jacobean Plays, 1583-1616* (Hamden, Conn., 1958) surveys the act division as it actually occurs in printed drama and observes, "Somewhere about 1607, however, there must have been a gradual change of practice in the public theaters. After that date, the proportion of divided plays rises sharply, until by about 1616, it appears to be universal," pp. 100-101; "But for a period of about sixteen years, from c. 1591 to c. 1607, Dekker, Heywood, Shakespeare, and other playwrights who wrote for the public stage, much more closely connected with the actual operation of the theaters, most of them lacking a university background, seem to have been under no compulsion to divide their plays, probably because the theaters had no practical use for it," p. 103. John Velz criticizes his approach: "Such primary bibliographical inspection as Jewkes makes is unquestionably important, but his cavalier dismissal of Baldwin implies that he is not prepared to admit the validity of literary (as opposed to textual) criticism. Yet he himself can prove little by his own methods," *Shakespeare and the Classical Tradition: A Reference Guide to Published Commentary in English, 1660-1960,* Ph.D. dissertation, University of

Minnesota, 1963 (Ann Arbor, Mich., University Microfilms), p. 155. Henry L. Snuggs in *Shakespeare and Five Acts* (New York, 1960) questions the literary basis for the five-act formula and surveys the bibliographic information; he makes a telling point when he asks, "if the protasis embraces two acts, what is the meaning of the division? If the protasis is a unit, why split it into two parts?" (p. 30); and further he states, "To say that this formula' was learned in grammar school by the Elizabethan dramatists, including Shakespeare, and was a sort of recipe used by them in the making of their plays, would appear to be an extravagant claim," p. 34. Yet like Jewkes he notes the practice of division in the printed plays of Terence as well as plays produced for private theaters, pp. 114-15.

17. *Comic Theory in the Sixteenth Century*, p. 173. Baxter Hathaway makes much the same point with regard to the way critics discussed imagination in heroic poetry: "Presumably, it was unimportant to the sixteenth century critics that by centering the meaning or significance of poetry upon static ideal figures they were forced to separate meaning from action, so that action was useful only because it was pleasing," *The Age of Criticism*, p. 158.

18. See Herrick, *Comic Theory in the Sixteenth Century*, pp. 137-38, and Doran, *Endeavors of Art*, pp. 217-24. Thomas Wilson was but following Cicero and Quintilian in enumerating the places of character. Coordinated with the criticism of dramatic character was rhetorical training in exercises, such as *ethopoeia* and *prosopopoeia* (figures of impersonation), and *descriptio personae, notatio,* and *effictio* (figures of description); see Doran, p. 226-27, and Herrick, pp. 133-36. Trissino in Book VI of his *Poetica* (1563) discusses the traits of character as having a double mode, both universal and particular. In explicating this, Baxter Hathaway says, "It should not be assumed that the Renaissance critic was thinking of a character's universality when he embraced doctrines of decorum. He did not identify universality with typicality of traits according to time, place, or condition. Universality he saved for aspects of man's moral nature," *Age of Criticism*, p. 135.

19. Herrick discusses Badius's comments on characterization, *Comic Theory in the Sixteenth Century*, pp. 137-38; he translates Robortellus's treatise, "On Comedy" (1548), pp. 227-39.

20. Edwin W. Robbins in *Dramatic Characterization in Printed Commentaries on Terence, 1473-1600*, Illinois Studies in Language and Literature, vol. 35 (Urbana, 1951), discusses at length the way Terence individualizes comic characters and the ways sixteenth-century commentators discerned his methods: ". . . the poet's chief method of differentiating between two characters [belonging to the same type] was contrast based upon difference of degree: one old man is more avaricious than the other," p. 112. "The individualization that these Terentian commentators point out is in a sense perhaps still a form of type-portrayal. The individual old man, for instance, may be still considered a subtype; for just as all old men normally fall under a general type, so may they be grouped into sub-categories on the basis of certain qualities not inherent in the type as a whole but also not peculiar to only one human being," p. 95.

21. Quoted by Herrick, *Comic Theory in the Sixteenth Century*, p. 139.

22. Riccobonus, writing near the end of the century, does not differ significantly on matters of characterization from either Robortellus, writing near midcentury, or Badius, writing near the beginning of the century. The quotation appears in Herrick, *Comic Theory*, p. 146. See Weinberg's general commentary which places Riccobonus in his tradition, *A History of Literary Criticism in the Italian Renaissance*, 1: 586, 588, and 608.

23. "*The Taming of the Shrew* has a string-plot as its main action, a plot of incidents simply strung together: a mere series of tricks which Petruchio plays upon Kate, and they might have gone on endlessly, for there is no particular reason why she should reform at one point rather than another," Elder Olson, *The Theory of Comedy* (Bloomington, Ind., 1968), p. 99.

24. Herrick, *Comic Theory in the Sixteenth Century*, pp. 149-50.

25. Translation by H. E. Butler, *The Institutes*, Loeb Classical Library (London,

1921), 2: 421, 423, 427, 429. Quintilian made this distinction in the context of discussing how an orator stimulates emotion in his listeners. Yet it exerted a widespread influence upon literary critics. Dryden observes the distinction in *An Essay on Dramatic Poetry* (1668); Bradbrook speaks of its general importance for sixteenth-century comedy, *Growth and Structure of Elizabethan Comedy*, p. 53; Doran says, "Why should we suppose Elizabethan dramatists not to have known this distinction and not to have shifted, at least partly, the basis of judgment in tragedy from character to passion, from something permanent to something temporary? Shakespeare certainly knew the distinction and counted on his audience's knowing it," *Endeavors of Art*, p. 238; Baxter Hathaway discusses how the distinction was intermixed with Aristotle's comment about the catharsis of pity and fear by Giacopo Mazzoni (1587), *The Age of Criticism*, p. 267.

26. It is interesting that Guarini did not use this line of argument in defending tragicomedy against Denores's attack. See Hathaway, *Age of Criticism*, pp. 268–70; Weinberg, 2: 1074–1105.

27. Translated by E. W. Sutton and H. W. Rackham, Loeb Classical Library (London, 1942).

28. *Poetica*, 127b, printed in *Literary Criticism: Plato to Dryden*, ed. Allan H. Gilbert (1940, rpt. Detroit, 1962), pp. 226–27.

29. Herrick, *Comic Theory in the Sixteenth Century*, pp. 44–45.

30. Quoted from the edition by Forrest G. Robinson (Indianapolis, Ind., 1970), pp. 78–9. Sidney's comment gets its importance more from emphasis than from originality of idea. Trissino, for instance, differentiates laughter from delight, but he does not insist upon the pleasure of delight as being an equally important response to comedy:

Such pleasure [as laughter] does not come from every object that delights and pleases the senses but merely from those objects that have some share of ugliness, for if a man sees a beautiful lady or beautiful jewel or something similar that pleases him, he does not laugh, nor does he laugh on hearing music in praise of him, nor on touching, tasting, and smelling things that to the touch, the taste, and the smell are pleasant and grateful; rather these together with pleasure bring admiration and not laughter.

Allan H. Gilbert, ed., *Literary Criticism: Plato to Dryden*, p. 226.

31. See especially "How to Entertain a Baby" and "Do Babies feel Derisive?" *Enjoyment of Laughter* (New York, 1936), pp. 9–10, 30–33. Edward Hubler makes much the same point in discussing the audience's responses to Falstaff, Bottom, Autolycus, and Pompey of *Measure for Measure*, "The Range of Shakespeare's Comedy," *Shakespeare 400*, ed. James G. McManaway, p. 62.

32. "The Argument of Comedy," *English Institute Essays, 1948*, p. 61.

33. Lyly's terminology in expressing the intention of his comedy is surprisingly apt: "Our intent was at this time to moue inward delight, not outward lightnesse, and to breede (if it might bee) soft smiling, not loude laughing: knowing it to the wise to be as great pleasure to heare counsell mixed with witte, as to the foolish to haue sporte mingled with rudenesse." Prologue to *Sapho and Phao*, ed. R. Warwick Bond, *The Complete Works of John Lyly* (Oxford, 1902), 2: 371. See also Marco Mincoff, "Shakespeare and Lyly," *ShS* 14 (1961): 15–24.

34. Quoted by Herrick, *Comic Theory in the Sixteenth Century*, p. 148.

35. Bradbrook, p. 92. From a different angle Marco Mincoff makes a similar observation: "Counterpoint had, as we saw, long been an element in English comedy. Medwall had opposed the wooing of his heroes with that of the pages, Edwardes had contrasted the true friendship of Damon and Pythias with the selfish alliance of the philosophers; Lyly . . .," "Shakespeare and Lyly," *ShS* 14 (1961): 22.

36. Bradbrook accounts for the taming as a mirror; by his outrageous behavior Petruchio holds up a mirror of Kate's worser self for her to see. "Dramatic Role as Social Image: A Study of *The Taming of The Shrew*," *SJH* 94 (1958): 132–50. Cecil C. Seronsy describes the taming as a kind of "supposes": "Petruchio's is a triumph of the imagina-

tion.... Petruchio has made his supposal, originally fictive but later supported by an insight into the real truth of his wife's nature, a triumphant fact." "'Supposes' as the Unifying Theme in *The Taming of the Shrew*," *SQ* 14 (1963): 24.

37. Charles Brooks psychologizes Katharina and Adriana, finding them to be a composite of "masculine intelligence" at war with "feminine tenderness and sensitivity," "Shakespeare's Romantic Shrews," *SQ* 11 (1960): 356.

38. For instance, "Perhaps the growth of *The Comedy of Errors* out of Plautine material can best be explained as the generous and enthusiastic pouring of the romantic spirit into a mould still influenced by classical restraint," Erma Gill, "The Plot-Structure of 'The Comedy of Errors' in Relation to Its Sources," *University of Texas Studies in English* 10 (1930): 65. A major exception in this approach to source studies is Geoffrey Bullough, who makes little of Gower's *Confessio Amantis, Narrative and Dramatic Sources of Shakespeare,* 1 (London, 1957): 10-11. Louise G. Clubb finds "pathos and tragic import" in the play, but accounts for these by Italian *commedia grave* rather than by some instinctive humanizing spirit in Shakespeare which is unsuited to farce, "Italian Comedy and *The Comedy of Errors*," *Comparative Literature* 19 (1967): 240-51.

39. Peter G. Phialas, *Shakespeare's Romantic Comedies: The Development of Their Form and Meaning* (Chapel Hill, N.C., 1966, rpt. n.d.), p. 16.

40. Harold Brooks, "Themes and Structure in 'The Comedy of Errors,'" *Early Shakespeare,* Stratford-upon-Avon Studies, no. 3 (London, 1961), pp. 67, 69. R. A. Foakes's assumptions can be seen in the following sentences: "The serious force of the presentation of the Antipholus twins is paralleled by a more comic treatment of their servants" (p. xliv); "The growth of this disorder is reflected in two other strands in language and action which reinforce the serious undertones of the comedy," "Introduction," *The Comedy of Errors,* 4th ed., The Arden Shakespeare (London, 1962), p. xlvi.

41. Harry Levin, "Introduction," *The Comedy of Errors,* The Signet Shakespeare (New York, 1965), p. xxix. A more extreme statement appears in Gwyn Williams, "'The Comedy of Errors' Rescued from Tragedy," *Review of English Literature* 5, no. 4 (1964): 69: "The possibilities of the story which interested Shakespeare, his recasting of it and the new elements he introduced, all led headlong toward tragedy, but he may not have felt sufficiently confident at this stage in his career as a dramatist to allow this to happen."

42. G. R. Elliott, "Weirdness in *The Comedy of Errors*," *UTQ* 9 (1939-40): 95-106. Paul A. Jorgensen, "Introduction," *The Comedy of Errors,* The Pelican Shakespeare (Baltimore, 1964), pp. 15-25. Michel Grivelet, in line with them, says, "The subject treated by Shakespeare and by Molière is then a highly serious subject, rooted in the deepest anxieties of the human mind. And yet in spite of its seriousness—or perhaps because of it— it has long proved to be particularly fit for comic treatment," "Shakespeare, Molière, and the Comedy of Ambiguity," *ShS* 22 (1969): 16.

43. As one might expect, the subplot of Bianca and Lucentio has received widely differing judgments about its romantic substance. S. C. Sen Gupta observed that there are no dialogues of love in their story, *Shakespearian Comedy* (Oxford, 1950), p. 117. Peter G. Phialas quotes the five lines of Act IV, scene ii (lines 6-10) and says, "The scene of the lovers, their language and sentiment, and their subsequent romantic elopement—these are surely the most common materials of romantic love," *Shakespeare's Romantic Comedies,* p. 29. E. C. Pettet, on the contrary, says, "in spite of the tone of Lucentio's first words Shakespeare does not afford him a chance to pour out his heart in any scene of genuine courtship. Moreover, our early impression of Lucentio and Bianca is largely effaced by their strange metamorphosis in the last scene of the play," *Shakespeare and the Romance Tradition* (London, 1949), p. 73. E. M. W. Tillyard also observes, "There is less of the element of romance and the feelings this arouses in the *Taming of the Shrew* than in any of Shakespeare's comedies," *Shakespeare's Early Comedies,* p. 108.

44. "Introduction," *The Taming of the Shrew,* The Signet Shakespeare (New York, 1966), p. xxxii. In the appendix he reprints Coghill's and Goddard's accounts of Katha-

rina. See also Heilman, "The *Taming* Untamed, or the Return of the Shrew," *MLQ* 27 (1966): 147-61. Mark Van Doren also classifies the play as farce, *Shakespeare* (New York, 1939, rpt. Garden City, N.Y., 1953), pp. 37-40.

45. M. C. Bradbrook, however, states, "*The Two Gentlemen* is a study of manners rather than sentiments, of behaviour rather than emotion; there is little feeling anywhere," *Shakespeare and Elizabethan Poetry* (London, 1951), p. 147. Oscar J. Campbell, on the other hand, observes,"the nature of the dramatic conventions about love in this play of Shakespeare's—the very essence of romantic comedy—is of exactly the same sort as the similar dialogue of the most highly developed form of *Commedia dell'Arte* that was composed in Shakespeare's time," *The Two Gentlemen of Verona* and Italian Comedy," *Studies in Shakespeare, Milton, and Donne,* University Michigan Publications in Language and Literature, vol. 1 (1925), p. 59. Likewise, M. A. Shaaber finds this play to be unusual in Shakespeare's corpus: "Shakespeare could have made his heroes and heroines analyze the sentiment of love and their own feelings equally well. The proof lies in the fact that, in *The Two Gentlemen of Verona,* he comes so much closer to doing so than in any other play," "The Comic View of Life in Shakespeare's Comedies," *The Drama of the Renaissance: Essays for Leicester Bradner,* ed. Elmer M. Blistein (Providence, R.I., 1970), p. 169.

46. E. W. Talbert's discussion of the comedy emphasizes the "virtue of a true gentility," *Elizabethan Drama and Shakespeare's Early Plays,* pp. 149-56. Karl F. Thompson observes, "'A carter,' says Turberville in his *Tragicall Tales* (1587) 'loves as whotely as a king.' Love is a leveler, perhaps, but Shakespeare never subscribes to this democratization of emotions," *Modesty and Cunning. Shakespeare's Use of Literary Tradition* (Ann Arbor, Mich., 1971), p. 71.

47. Of all the discussions about the conversion of Proteus, I find Karl F. Thompson's in *Modesty and Cunning* to be the most convincing. He sees Valentine's offer of Silvia as a test of the sinner's repentance in the religion of love: "Valentine's offer is, however, so searching a test that it must for a certainty reveal the genuineness of Proteus's repentance," p. 64. Among those who find Proteus's conversion and Valentine's offer unsatisfactory, some explain the "fault" as textual: Edward Dowden, *Shakspere, His Mind and Art,* 1872 (rpt. of 3d edition, New York, 1962), p. 57; also "Q" and Dover Wilson, *The Two Gentlemen of Verona,* The New Cambridge Shakespeare (Cambridge, 1921), pp. xvii-xviii and 102-3; some explain the fault as an unfortunate emphasis on the theme of friendship over love: Phialas, *Shakespeare's Romantic Comedies,* p. 50; and some explain it as part of a general technical ineptitude: Tillyard, *Shakespeare's Early Comedies,* pp. 116-17; Blaze O. Bonazza, *Shakespeare's Early Comedies* (The Hague, 1966), p. 93, 97-98, qualified on p. 82. Others see the unsatisfactory quality of the ending as intentional: Hereward T. Price sees it as criticism of a literary convention which sets friendship between men above the love of man for woman, "Shakespeare as a Critic," *PQ* 20 (1941): 397-98; H. C. Goddard sees it as parody, *The Meaning of Shakespeare* (Chicago, 1951), p. 46. Among those who find the ending satisfactory, some explain the difficulty as a matter of understanding Valentine's offer as "intentionally ambiguous" and not as an unqualified gift, R. Warwick Bond, ed., *The Two Gentlemen of Verona,* The Arden Shakespeare, 2d ed. (London, 1925), p. xxxviii; some see the dramatization of behavior to be consistent with the picture of behavior elsewhere in the play: Alwin Thaler, "Shakspere and the Unhappy Happy Ending," *PMLA* 42 (1927): 744-47; Karl F. Thompson, "Shakespeare's Romantic Comedies," *PMLA* 67 (1952): 1088; William E. Stephenson, "The Adolescent Dream-World of *The Two Gentlemen of Verona,*" *SQ* 17 (1966): 165-68; Clifford Leech, "Introduction," *The Two Gentlemen of Verona,* The Arden Shakespeare, rev. ed. (London, 1969), pp. lxvii-lxix; Larry S. Champion, *The Evolution of Shakespeare's Comedy* (Cambridge, Mass., 1970), pp. 29, 31; some see it as consistent with a general theme such as "blindness and sight": Harold F. Brooks, "Two Clowns in a Comedy ...," *Essays and Studies* (1963), pp. 96, 99. Those who explain the resolution as fitting into a tradition,

either of friendship, magnanimity, or romantic conventions, which a contemporary audience would have accepted without question but which those who would disapprove have lost, are: Ralph M. Sargent, "Sir Thomas Elyot and the Integrity of *The Two Gentlemen of Verona*," *PMLA* 65 (1950): 1177-78; M. C. Bradbrook, *Shakespeare and Elizabethan Poetry*, pp. 150-52; J. F. Danby, "Shakespeare Criticism and *Two Gentlemen of Verona*," *Critical Quarterly* 2 (1960): 319; Stanley Wells, "The Failure of *The Two Gentlemen of Verona*," *SJH* 99 (1963): 172-73; Sargent and Danby emphasize the shock of revelation upon Proteus; so does John Russell Brown, *Shakespeare and His Comedies* (London, 1957), pp. 103-4.

48. Cyrus Hoy finds this movement to be typical of Shakespeare's comedies: "the basic pattern of Shakespearian comedy: a pattern which consists in a movement from the artificial to the natural, always with the objective of finding oneself," "*Love's Labour's Lost* and the Nature of Comedy," *SQ* 13 (1962): 35; in general agreement with him are Northrop Frye, who classifies the play as a "comedy of humour" so that the action is "release from humour," "Shakespeare's Experimental Comedy," *Stratford Papers on Shakespeare, 1961* (1962), p. 7; Granville-Barker, who approximates this conception when he states, "The play is a satire, a comedy of affectations," *Prefaces to Shakespeare* 2 (Princeton, N.J., 1947): 414; Peter G. Phialas, who sees the comic structure to be "the committing by the chief characters of a comic error, which in turn leads to reversal and recognition. The error is of two kinds: one is the rejection of love, the other is the exaggerated idealizing of it," *Shakespeare's Romantic Comedies*, p. 86; and E. M. W. Tillyard, who stresses the more negative part of the movement: "If you detect this initial inability to learn, you will see them, as the play proceeds, plunging from one crude male immaturity to another, until the women ... administer their pungent medicine at the very end of the play. Only then has the educative process been set in motion; and how far it will proceed we are not informed," *Shakespeare's Early Comedies*, pp. 144-45. C. L. Barber fits the action into his formula for holiday, "release to clarification": "the clarification achieved by release is this recognition that love is not wooing games or love talk," *Shakespeare's Festive Comedy* (Princeton, N.J., 1959, rpt. Cleveland, 1963), pp. 11, 93; Gates K. Agnew formulates his statement of the movement in similar fashion: "from the ambivalent sphere of historical experience and psychological realism to the affirmative and symbolic realm of festive comedy," "Berowne and the Progress of Love's Labour's Lost," *Shakespeare Studies* 4 (1968): 41. Even more general is Bobbyann Roesen's (Righter) statement of the movement as "the ultimate victory of reality over artifice and illusion," "Love's Labour's Lost," *SQ* 4 (1953): 416; Philip Edwards agrees with her formulation, *Shakespeare and the Confines of Art* (London, 1968), p. 48.

49. Critics who find love to be the fundamental subject of the comedy show that its primary attribute is "irrationality," and either accept this state of affairs as part of the human condition or show how the play recommends a "rational" love. A second group of critics find imagination to be the fundamental subject, making poetry as well as love central topics, and show how events dramatize a problem about the "reality" of poetry and love. Among those who find love to be central are: H. B. Charlton, "And love refuses to go hand in hand with reason. Its moods and whims are exempt from all constraint but destiny," *Shakespearian Comedy*, p. 112; Thomas Marc Parrott, "The central action is concerned with that phase of human love which the Elizabethans called 'fancy': the irrational emotional impulse that draws man to maid and maid to man," *Shakespearean Comedy* (New York, 1949), p. 133. Some critics push further and find in the play a disapproval of "irrational" love and approval of a love controlled by reason, usually embodied in the person of Theseus: Paul A. Olson, "*A Midsummer Night's Dream* and the Meaning of Court Marriage," *ELH* 24 (1957): 95-119: "Thus Oberon, with his servants, returns the lovers to reason; by allowing them to see for themselves the humor of their situation, he makes it possible for them to extricate themselves permanently from the fond fancy which misdirects the will and leaves one enamoured of an ass," p. 117; Ernest Schanzer, "The Central Theme of *A Midsummer Night's Dream*," *UTQ* 20 (1950-51):

233-38: "But the love which Shakespeare ridicules in *A Midsummer Night's Dream* is engendered in the imagination and blinds both reason and the senses," p. 234; see also G. A. Bonnard, "Shakespeare's Purpose in Midsummer Night's-Dream," *SJH* 92 (1956): 268-79; Peter G. Phialas, *Shakespeare's Romantic Comedies,* pp. 105-6, 115, 130; and Blaze O. Bonazza, *Shakespeare's Early Comedies,* pp. 122-23; E. C. Pettet also asserts that "the love of marriage, which is the consummation of courtship, should be something cooler, more substantial and rational" but says that "we should tolerate" young love which is "transient, irrational, full of frenzy and fantasy," *Shakespeare and the Romance Tradition,* pp. 113-14; likewise, Peter F. Fisher fits with this group of critics, for he analyzes the play into a conflict between "the irrational force of sublunary passion" and the "rationally ordered world of the Athenian court," but he finds no decisive and final triumph of Theseus's world, "The Argument of *A Midsummer Night's Dream,*" *SQ* 8 (1957): 307-10. Among those who assert a contrary evaluation is Frank Kermode: "love considered as a disease of the eye will be enacted in the plot. But so will the contrary interpretation of 'blind love'; that it is a higher power than sight; indeed, above intellect," "The Mature Comedies," *Early Shakespeare,* Stratford-upon-Avon Studies, no. 3, p. 215; see also Thelma N. Greenfield, "*A Midsummer Night's Dream* and *The Praise of Folly,*" *Comparative Literature* 20 (1968): 236-44, and J. Russell Brown; "the play suggests that lovers, like lunatics, poets, and actors, have their own 'truth' which is established as they see the beauty of their beloved, and that they are confident in this truth, for, although it seems the 'silliest stuff' to an outsider, to them it is quite reasonable," *Shakespeare and His Comedies,* p. 90. Among the second group of critics, who see love as one manifestation of the broader faculty of imagination that raises problems about the nature of reality, are C. L. Barber, "The whole night's action is presented as a release of shaping fantasy which brings clarification about the tricks of strong imagination," *Shakespeare's Festive Comedy,* p. 124; R. W. Dent, "Imagination in *A Midsummer Night's Dream,*" *Shakespeare 400,* pp. 115-29; and William J. Martz, *Shakespeare's Universe of Comedy* (New York, 1971), pp. 29-31; David P. Young finds a series of issues raised by the events of the play, such as the relation of nature and art, change and transformation, the opposition of law and love, among which is the relation of reason and imagination; significantly, he entitles the chapter in which he discusses these as "Bottom's Dream," *Something of Great Constancy: The Art of "A Midsummer Night's Dream"* (New Haven, Conn., 1966), pp. 111-66.

50. Rabkin says, "What Shakespeare has done is to present simply, embodied in two characters as two separate principles, the two aspects of love that the neoplatonic Renaissance delighted in seeing paradoxically fused.... For its protagonists not only oppose each other; the poem's theme is the self-contradiction implicit in a central human activity," *Shakespeare and the Common Understanding* (New York, 1967), p. 159; see another version of the essay, "*Venus and Adonis* and the Myth of Love," *Pacific Coast Studies in Shakespeare,* ed. Waldo F. McNeir and Thelma N. Greenfield (Eugene, Ore., 1966), pp. 20-32. J. W. Lever's comments come from "Venus and the Second Chance," *ShS* 15 (1962): 81-88; he also makes a survey of twentieth-century criticism of the poem in the same volume, *ibid.,* pp. 18-30. Like Rabkin, A. C. Hamilton sees the poem as central to Shakespeare's canon: "Venus presides as the goddess of the romantic comedies, and her love for Adonis makes her the archetype of the romantic heroines who yearn to submit to their lovers," but his fine discussion centers upon the relation of the poem to contemporary treatments of the myth, *The Early Shakespeare,* pp. 143-66; reprint from "Venus and Adonis," *SEL* 1 (1961): 1-15.

Chapter 7

1. Text from Joseph Q. Adams, ed., *Chief Pre-Shakespearean Dramas* (Cambridge, Mass., 1924), p. 572.

2. Richard Rainolde, for instance, in *The Foundacion of Rhetorike* (fascimile reprint, Introduction by Francis R. Johnson, New York, 1945) says: "That parte, which is called *Ethopoeia* is that, whiche hath the persone knowne: but only it doeth faigne the manners of the same, and imitate in a Oracion the same," fol. xlixr. See also Madeleine Doran's general discussion of *ethopoeia* and *prosopopoeia, Endeavors of Art,* pp. 218-20, 226-27, and E. W. Talbert on the rhetorical commonplaces for the invention of character, *Elizabethan Drama and Shakespeare's Early Plays,* pp. 375-76.

3. Text from Geoffrey Bullough, ed., *Narrative and Dramatic Sources of Shakespeare,* 2 (London, 1958): 443.

4. Erma M. Gill observes that beatings are threatened several times and found only once in the *Amphitruo,* only threatened in the *Menaechmi,* but occur four times in *Errors,* "The Plot-Structure of 'The Comedy of Errors' in Relation to Its Sources," *University of Texas Studies in English* 10 (1930): 63. C. L. Barber states, "this constant thumping of the Dromios grows tedious and is out of key—the one instance where Roman plot has not been adapted to Elizabethan manners," "Shakespearian Comedy in *The Comedy of Errors,*" *CE* 25 (1963-64): 494. In line with this difference between classical slaves and Renaissance servants, Peter Phialas notes that the servants in *Shrew* do not control or even conceive the intrigue as they do in Plautus, *Shakespeare's Romantic Comedies,* p. 41.

5. John Russell Brown, on the other hand, interprets the final speech by emphasizing its imagery taken from commerce: "Katharina's speech on the duty of wives and the paying of 'tribute' is joyful and elated because, in some mysterious way, she has confidence in Petruchio's love and in his willingness to give away his loan of Nature's bounty," *Shakespeare and His Comedies,* p. 61. Equally prevalent are images of ruler and subject:

What is she but a foul contending rebel
And graceless traitor to her loving lord?
I am ashamed that women are so simple
To offer war where they should kneel for peace,
Or seek for rule, supremacy, and sway,
When they are bound to serve, love, and obey.

(V.ii.164-69)

Her concluding argument is explicit and literal, an argument which sums up her earlier statements:

Why are our bodies soft and weak and smooth,
Unapt to toil and trouble in the world,
But that our soft conditions and our hearts
Should well agree with our external parts? . . .
Our strength [is] weak, our weakness past compare.

(V.ii. 170 ff.)

6. Opinions may differ on Grumio. Is he perverse or dense when he misunderstands Petruchio's command, "Knock me here soundly" (I.ii.8)?

7. John Wain develops this idea with regard to cuckold jokes, "Restoration Comedy and Its Modern Critics," *Preliminary Essays* (London, 1957), pp. 33-34.

8. Among those who have observed these analogies are R. Warwick Bond, ed., *The Two Gentlemen of Verona,* 2d ed., The Arden Shakespeare (London, 1925), pp. xxix-xxx, who finds precedents for the parallels in Lyly's pages; Harold F. Brooks, "Two Clowns in a Comedy . . .," *Essays and Studies* 16 (1963): 91-100; Clifford Leech finds the parallels to be part of a larger structural technique of parody through juxtaposition of scenes, "Introduction," *The Two Gentlemen of Verona,* 3d ed. (London, 1969), pp. lxi-lxvi. Less enthusiastic about their place in the drama are H. B. Charlton, "He [Launce] has no real right within the play, except that gentlemen must have servants, and Elizabethan audiences must have clowns," *Shakespearian Comedy,* p. 41; and Blaze O. Bonazza, "These clowns are not true participants in a dramatic action; they are essentially *bomolochoi* or partakers of the general festivity," *Shakespeare's Early Comedies* (The Hague, 1966), p. 85.

9. Charlton finds Valentine's blindness offensive: "The story renders him a fool," *Shakespearian Comedy,* pp. 35-36; Harold F. Brooks, however, says, "The dullness which prevents his understanding is a perfectly orthodox effect of love-melancholy," "Two Clowns in a Comedy . . .," *Essays and Studies* 16 (1963): 95.

10. John A. Guinn discusses the tradition and possible source of this scene, "The Letter Device in the First Act of *The Two Gentlemen of Verona,*" *University of Texas Studies in English* 20 (1940): 72-81.

11. Most recent critics find some sort of intentional balance created by the presence of Launce and Speed. Charlton understood them to be the "spirit of comedy" that awakens our comic awareness of "incompatibles and the unrealities of romance" and thus that they do not contribute to a harmonious play, *Shakespearian Comedy,* pp. 32-43; however, M. C. Bradbrook says the contrast is appropriate, "like the juxtapositions in Chaucer between the Knight and the Miller," *Shakespeare and Elizabethan Poetry* (London, 1951), p. 153; Derek Traversi sees the servants contributing to "a sane and balanced conception of life," *Shakespeare: The Early Comedies,* p. 26; Peter G. Phialas finds them making possible "an interplay of attitudes toward love," *Shakespeare's Romantic Comedies,* p. 56, 62-63; E. M. W. Tillyard sees in them one more instance of a general principle of Shakespeare's comedies: "In his comedies, Shakespeare (I conjecture more by instinct than deliberation) never allowed any dominant theme or motive to remain pure and uncorrected," *Shakespeare's Early Comedies,* p. 127; Nicholas Brooke finds the same compensating principle in Shakespeare's use of the lower characters in *Romeo and Juliet,* "The Tragic Spectacle in *Titus Andronicus* and *Romeo and Juliet,*" *Shakespeare, the Tragedies: A Collection of Critical Essays,* ed. Clifford Leech (Chicago, 1965), p. 255.

12. Bertrand Evans argues that when Julia comes on the scene in disguise, she becomes the "practiser," and Proteus "the practisee." "The case of Proteus, hero bent on making a villain of himself, is typical: in the comedies, villainy can but peep at what it would, for it is circumscribed and rendered impotent, if not ridiculous, by the bright-eyed heroines who with their superior awareness control everything in this woman's world," *Shakespeare's Comedies,* p. 17. Clifford Leech agrees with him, "Introduction," The Arden edition, p. lxvi. While I grant Julia's superior awareness, I cannot agree that this entails a control assuring to the audience; indeed, the proxy wooing scene with Silvia renders poignant the conflict between what Julia's disguise as Proteus's page leads her to do and what she knows and feels. Likewise, it is hardly Julia who manages events to bring about the happy ending. We may indeed suspect that the predicaments will evolve toward a happy conclusion, but we have little basis for assuming that Julia will control that process.

13. They return to join in the singing of the final songs; this action suggests some sort of reconciliation, but at best it is a suggestion. Modern editors specify the reentrance of Holofernes, Sir Nathaniel, Moth, and Costard, whereas the 1598 Quarto and the first folio state simply "Enter all." See Richard David, ed., *Love's Labour's Lost,* The Arden Shakespeare, 5th ed. (London, 1956), p. 194.

14. R. Warwick Bond finds the Armado-Jaquenetta-Moth trio prefigured in Sir Tophas-Bagoa-Epiton, *The Complete Works of John Lyly,* 3 (Oxford, 1902): 13, and Geoffrey Bullough agrees, *Narrative and Dramatic Sources of Shakespeare,* 1 (London, 1957): 426. Alfred Harbage sees "more than an accidental resemblance" in the two triads, "*Love's Labor's Lost* and the Early Shakespeare," *PQ* 41 (1962): 28. However, Oscar Campbell finds the predecessor to Armado to lie in a different tradition and denies that Lyly served as a single influence, "*Love's Labour's Lost* Restudied," *Studies in Shakespeare, Milton and Donne,* University of Michigan Publications in Language and Literature, vol. 1 (1925), pp. 23-24, 32-33. Richard David agrees with him and denies any "real similarity" between Lyly's earlier characters and Shakespeare's, "Introduction," *Love's Labour's Lost,* The Arden Shakespeare, p. xxxv.

15. Henry David Gray asks, "Did Mercade not appear upon the scene at all?" and proposes that in the original ending, "Jack will never have his Jill," "The Original Version

of 'Love's Labour's Lost,' with a conjecture as to 'Love's Labour's Won,'" *Leland Stanford Junior University Publications* 29 (1918): 13, 40. Richard David asks, "Did Mercade originally bring not the news of her father's death but the missing document required to establish her claim?" "Introduction," *Love's Labour's Lost*, The Arden Shakespeare, pp. xxiii–xxiv. Bobbyann Roesen (Righter) and Gates Agnew, however, see the topic of mortality fundamental to the conception of the play: Roesen, "*Love's Labour's Lost*," *SQ* 4 (1953): 412, 420; Agnew, "Berowne and the Progress of Love's Labour's Lost," *Shakespeare Studies* 4 (1968): 51, 55. On revision, see also Harbage, "*Love's Labor's Lost* and the Early Shakespeare," *PQ* 41 (1962): 18–29, and J. V. Cunningham, "'With That Facility': False Starts and Revisions in *Love's Labour's Lost*," *Essays on Shakespeare*, ed. G. W. Chapman (Princeton, 1965), pp. 91–115.

16. Several recent critics have suggested that events in the forest should be viewed somewhat less than literally. If "allegory" includes the externalization by character and action of internal phenomena, then the following comment by James Calderwood can be taken to confirm my point: "The events and characters of the forest present the drama of the dreaming mind whose imaginative impulses are released from reason (though often rationalized in terms of it) and divorced from daytime fact," *Shakespearean Metadrama* (Minneapolis, Minn., 1971), p. 138. Paul Olson, with a somewhat different meaning of allegory, takes an "iconological" approach to the play; he states that the courtly audience was "consistently interested in that art which builds its meaning from the materials of traditional emblems and allegories," "*A Midsummer Night's Dream* and the Meaning of Court Marriage," *ELH* 24 (1957): 97.

17. Theseus gives the terms for understanding the behavior of the lovers in the forest, but he cannot be taken as a choral figure, speaking for the playwright. That poets, lunatics, and lovers are "of imagination all compact" appears to be correct, but Theseus also says that cool reason can comprehend reality whereas imagination apprehends figments of its own devising. Ideally, this distinction is convincing, but in the world of the play, since all men fall into one of the three categories of lovers, lunatics, or poets, no one can differentiate ultimately between substance and shadow. Some critics, particularly those who read the play as depicting a love "controlled by reason" distinct from love controlled by imagination, take Theseus's speech without irony: H. B. Charlton, *Shakespearian Comedy*, p. 122; S. C. Sen Gupta, *Shakespearian Comedy* (Oxford, 1950), p. 120; Michel Poirier proposes that the speech takes its source from Sidney's *A Defence of Poesie* (1595), "Sidney's Influence upon *A Midsummer Night's Dream*" *SP* 44 (1947): 487–89; Ernest Schanzer, "The Central Theme of *A Midsummer Night's Dream*," *UTQ* 20 (1950–51): 237; Raeburn Miller, "The Persons of Moonshine: *A Midsummer Night's Dream* and the 'Disfigurement' of Realities," *Explorations of Literature*, ed. Rima Drell Reck (Baton Rouge, La., 1966), pp. 30–31; and the judgment is implicit in what Blaze O. Bonazza says about "the eyes of sane judgment as exemplified by Theseus," *Shakespeare's Early Comedies*, p. 122. Paul Olson observes a finer distinction in the speech: "It is only lovers and madmen who are said to exhibit fantasies which descend beyond the comprehension of reason (*MND*, V, 4–6). Implicitly, poets, however much they are possessed by a *furor poesis*, may deal in imaginings apprehensible in more rational terms," "*A Midsummer Night's Dream* and the Meaning of Court Marriage," *ELH* 24 (1957): 97. Among those who find Theseus's speech inadequate are: Howard Nemerov, "The Marriage of Theseus and Hippolyta," *Kenyon Review* 18 (1956): 633–41; Frank Kermode, "The Mature Comedies," *Early Shakespeare*, p. 219; Peter Phialas, *Shakespeare's Romantic Comedies*, p. 131; John A. Allen, "Bottom and Titania," *SQ* 18 (1967): 113; Sidney R. Homan, "The Single World of *A Midsummer Night's Dream*," *Bucknell Review* 17 (1969): 73; Michael Taylor, "The Darker Purpose of *A Midsummer Night's Dream*," *SEL* 9 (1969): 271. Others find Hippolyta's response to Theseus's speech closer to Shakespeare's intention: Bertrand Evans, *Shakespeare's Comedies*, pp. 45–46; Roger Warren, "Three Notes on *A Midsummer Night's Dream*," *N & Q* 214 (1969): 133–34; and James A. S. McPeek, "The Psyche Myth and *A Midsummer Night's Dream*," *SQ* 23 (1972): 79.

18. David P. Young uses the image of the widening circle, *Something of Great Constancy*, pp. 91-92. Bertrand Evans, speaking of discrepant awareness, shows that "the participants' level is not raised to equal ours at the end," *Shakespeare's Comedies*, p. 41, but in fact we must realize that our ability to discriminate reality from shadow is no better than theirs. In addition to Young, those critics who make this point forcefully are James Calderwood, *Shakespearean Metadrama*, pp. 126-46; William Martz, *Shakespeare's Universe of Comedy*, p. 37; Sidney R. Homan, "The Single World of *A Midsummer Night's Dream*," *Bucknell Review* 17 (1969): 72-84; and Michael Taylor, "The Darker Purpose of *A Midsummer Night's Dream*," *SEL* 9 (1969): 271. Peter G. Phialas, too, finds that there is no line of demarcation between the world of dreams and the world of Athens, *Shakespeare's Romantic Comedies*, p. 133. H. B. Charlton speaks just as strongly for the need to discriminate; about Theseus he says, "At once, he sees that mere survival in the world depends upon man's ability to differentiate rapidly and certainly between bears and bushes, and thus perceives that the attribute of supreme value in the world is the 'cool reason,'" *Shakespearian Comedy*, p. 122.

19. M. C. Bradbrook makes this point with regard to Rosalind and Viola in *The Growth and Structure of Elizabethan Comedy*, pp. 97-99.

20. There is no consensus among critics about the relative successes in characterization. G. K. Hunter, for instance, observes that we see Valentine "at merely intellectual focus" whereas in Proteus "we have a psychological dimension as well," *John Lyly, the Humanist as Courtier* (London, 1962), p. 324. Bertrand Evans speaks of Julia as a "flesh-and-blood" heroine, "Introduction," *The Two Gentlemen of Verona*, Signet Edition (New York, 1964), p. xxvi; but Peter G. Phialas feels that Julia "approaches much closer to the sentiments of the conventional lover" and discovers in Silvia the mixture of sentiment and insight that foreshadows the later, greater heroines of Shakespeare's comedies, *Shakespeare's Romantic Comedies*, pp. 59-62.

21. A number of critics have been unsatisfied with characterization in general in *Two Gentlemen* and tend to explain its shortcomings by a discrepancy between "plot" and "character." Madeleine Doran, for instance, says that "story and character rather frown at one another. . . . Too much 'character' in Julia has fouled up the conventional lines of Shakespeare's story," *Endeavors of Art*, p. 325; Larry S. Champion, on the other hand, finds characterization to be determined by the story: "Shakespeare is interested neither in character development nor in credible motivation. Instead he is interested in the comic potential of a situation popular with his audience," *The Evolution of Shakespeare's Comedy* (Cambridge, Mass., 1970) pp. 25-26; J. F. Danby agrees that characters "are pieces moved by the mechanism of the story," "Shakespeare Criticism and *Two Gentlemen of Verona*," *The Critical Quarterly* 2 (1960): 317. E. M. W. Tillyard finds the major flaw in the play to be Shakespeare's "failing to make credible Proteus's treachery" which "comes as a wanton surprise," *Shakespeare's Early Comedies*, pp. 116-17; Derek Travesi feels just the reverse: "Though we shall scarcely find him convincing as a human being, we may feel that the very existence in the play of a character who exposes his inner contradictions represents a meaningful irruption of reality into the closed world of literary convention," *Shakespeare: The Early Comedies*, pp. 24-25.

22. The folio text reads: "It is mine, or *Valentines* praise" while in Folio 2, Malone, Rowe, and Theobald not only try to adjust the meter by adding a word but reverse the order of subject and verb to clarify the statement as a question: "Is it mine,...," see Clifford Leech, ed., *The Two Gentlemen of Verona*, The Arden Shakespeare, p. 43.

23. Tillyard says, "Berowne is a mouth rather than a formed character," *Shakespeare's Early Comedies*, p. 165, but most critics speak more highly of him. Gates K. Agnew, for instance, contrasts him with his fellow courtiers: "They are flat, plodding, stock figures: Berowne is a vivacious, psychologically profound, three-dimensional portrait," "Berowne and the Progress of Love's Labour's Lost," *Shakespeare Studies* 4 (1968): 42.

24. In this regard Gates K. Agnew makes a significant distinction: "self-consciousness

and self-knowledge are not identical and they may be mutually exclusive (especially in the simplified perspective of the drama)," "Berowne and the Progress of Love's Labour's Lost," p. 50.

25. John Palmer, so impressed by Berowne's positive position in the play, makes him the playwright's spokesman: "He speaks for nature, though caught in toils of artifice; and, at the end, delivers the moral of the piece in which he has, in effect, played the part of chorus on his author's behalf," *Comic Characters in Shakespeare* (London, 1946), p. 5.

26. Anne Righter observes a similarity between their characters in her discussion of self-conscious references to the drama, *Shakespeare and the Idea of the Play,* p. 91.

27. This is hardly to be taken as a shortcoming of the play because events do not require complex characterization. Many critics have observed the thinness of characterization; Enid Welsford, for instance, says, "The plot is a pattern, a figure, rather than a series of events occasioned by human character and passion," *The Court Masque* (Cambridge, 1927), p. 331. Some critics find this to be a weakness; R. A. Law says, "The dramatist seems to be more interested in groups than in individuals, with the possible exception of Bottom. The lack of individual characterization in this comedy is its greatest weakness," "The 'Pre-conceived Pattern' of *A Midsummer Night's Dream,*" *University of Texas Studies in English,* vol. 23 (1943), p. 7: see also Larry S. Champion, *The Evolution of Shakespeare's Comedy,* p. 49. Those who do discuss characterization in the play tend to concentrate upon Bottom. Thomas Marc Parrott finds Bottom to be the "supreme character portrayal in the *Dream,*" *Shakespearean Comedy,* p. 130; John Palmer devotes a chapter to him, *Comic Characters of Shakespeare* (London, 1946), pp. 92-109; John A. Allen discusses an apparent contradiction between Bottom's exuberant egotism among his companions and his subdued behavior with Titania, "Bottom and Titania," *SQ* 18 (1967): 107-10; Sen Gupta notes the same problem, *Shakespearean Comedy,* pp. 123-24; Peter F. Fisher finds Bottom to be the "real foundation upon which the whole is based," "The Argument of *A Midsummer Night's Dream,*" *SQ* 8 (1957): 308; and William J. Martz discusses the paradox of Bottom's statureless stature as a comic figure, *Shakespeare's Universe of Comedy,* pp. 21-22, 62-63. Madeleine Doran is exceptional for the extended attention she devotes to the character of Theseus, the tradition that lies behind him, and the way Shakespeare combines both verisimilitude and anachronism in his creation, "*A Midsummer Night's Dream*: A Metamorphosis," *The Rice Institute Pamphlet* 46, no. 4 (1959-60): 113-35.

Chapter 8

1. George Gordon, for instance, says, "I think the best division of the professional comic men in Shakespeare's plays—at any rate, the best technically—would be this: (1) those who play with words; and (2) those who are played with by them," *Shakespearian Comedy and Other Studies* (Oxford, 1944), p. 64. Oscar J. Campbell finds the contrast between slow-witted rustics and quick-witted rogues to be a staple of *Commedia dell'Arte, Studies in Shakespeare, Milton, and Donne,* pp. 60-61; see also Nevill Coghill, "Wags, Clowns and Jesters," *More Talking of Shakespeare,* ed. John Garrett (London, 1959), p. 11.

2. Peter G. Phialas, for instance, disagrees with Francis Fergusson, who finds her speech laughable, Phialas, *Shakespeare's Romantic Comedies,* pp. 11 and 284; Fergusson, "Two Comedies," *The Human Image in Dramatic Literature* (Garden City, N.Y., 1957), pp. 144-57, esp. p. 148.

3. See Marvin T. Herrick's discussion of Madius, *Comic Theory in the Sixteenth Century,* pp. 41-52.

4. Translation by W. Rhys Roberts, *Rhetorica,* III.ii.15-22, from *The Works of Aristotle,* ed. W. D. Ross (Oxford, 1946), vol. 11 (1412a).

5. *Comic Theory in the Sixteenth Century,* pp. 44-45.

6. C. S. Lewis, *Studies in Words,* 2d ed. (Cambridge, 1967), pp. 97-100.

7. William G. Crane, *Wit and Rhetoric in the Renaissance,* Columbia University Studies in English and Comparative Literature, no. 129 (New York, 1937). See also George Williamson, *The Proper Wit of Poetry* (London, 1961): "It was in Jonson's time that 'wit' as distinct from other intellectual virtues began to take on that special sense that Hobbes later defined as 'fancy' or quickness of mind in seeing resemblances between dissimilar things," p. 15.

8. *Shakespeare's Festive Comedy,* pp. 99–100; see also M. M. Mahood, *Shakespeare's Wordplay,* pp. 9–55.

9. See Dodsley's *A Select Collection of Old English Plays,* ed. W. Carew Hazlitt, 4th ed., 6 (London, 1874): 386–404.

10. Lineation refers to the edition by Norman Sanders, *The Scottish History of James the Fourth,* The Revels Plays (London, 1970).

11. Critics who analyze Lyly's style tend to concentrate upon euphuism as it appears in the two early prose tracts. R. Warwick Bond, however, makes general observations on the changes in dialogue from play to play *The Complete Works of John Lyly* (Oxford, 1902), 2: 286–93; Jonas Barish shows that, contrary to G. C. Child's analysis of diminishing euphuism in the plays, the dialogue continues to exhibit the "logicality" that is essential to Lyly's novelistic style even though it sheds some figures of sound, "The Prose Style of John Lyly," *ELH* 23 (1956): 29–34. Peter Sacchio makes an interesting analysis of the dramatic dialogue in *Campaspe* by isolating a basic unit and showing how the units fit together, *The Court Comedies of John Lyly* (Princeton, N.J., 1969), pp. 42–45. Also pertinent to the analysis of repartee are C. L. Barber's comments on the way it develops in *Love's Labor's Lost, Shakespeare's Festive Comedy,* pp. 100–102.

12. All quotations from Lyly's plays come from the edition by R. Warwick Bond, *The Complete Works of John Lyly,* 3 vols. (Oxford, 1902).

13. Hypotheses about the acting of choirboys are, of course, precarious, for we must base them upon our own experience with child actors and by inference from the plays they performed. See, for instance, Jocelyn Powell's different hypothesis about the actors in Lyly's comedies, "John Lyly and the Language of Play," *Elizabethan Theatre,* Stratford-upon-Avon Studies, no. 9 (London, 1966), pp. 164–65. Marston's relatively short scenes, designed to create a single impression, shifting from group to group, strike me as comparable to Lyly's scenes. Anthony J. Caputi, by inference from Marston's plays, finds that the children "emphasized stylization and artificiality," a "burlesque" style appropriate to "caricature," *John Marston, Satirist* (Ithaca, N.Y., 1961), pp. 101, 105, 113. See also H. N. Hillebrand, *The Child Actors,* Illinois Studies in Language and Literature, vol. 11 (Urbana, 1926).

14. From the Prologue to *Endimion,* Bond, 3: 20.

15. Excluded from this is Lyly's one play in verse, written for an adult company, *The Woman in the Moon.* Pandora's relation to her servant Gunophilus helps dramatize the influence of the various planets upon her, a fact signifying Lyly's interest in the dramatic possibilities of servant and master.

16. "What is clear ... is that the Humanist dream forced the learned into dependence on a court which did not really need them.... Yet the dream that the centre of power was the natural home of learning and eloquence was by now so ingrained that it was not to be denied." *John Lyly: The Humanist as Courtier,* pp. 29–30.

17. David Lloyd Stevenson, *The Love-Game Comedy,* Columbia University Studies in English and Comparative Literature, no. 164 (New York, 1946).

18. M. M. Mahood counts "over two-hundred" puns in *Love's Labor's Lost, Shakespeare's Wordplay,* p. 164.

19. J. V. Cunningham relates the revisions to Shakespeare's contemporary reputation: "not a reputation for creation of character or contrivance of plot but precisely for qualities of style, and particularly for pleasant, conceited writing," "'With That Facility': False

Starts and Revisions in *Love's Labour's Lost*," *Essays on Shakespeare,* ed. G. W. Chapman (Princeton, N.J., 1965), p. 92.

20. That Shakespeare was successful in plotting the decision so that his audience would not wonder why the courtiers failed to consider the practicality of their venture can be seen in recent critical essays on the play. When the critics consider motivation at all, they relate it to the character of the lords; usually they concentrate upon the effect of the Muscovite disguise. C. L. Barber finds in their masquing an inadequate festivity: "The game they are playing, without quite knowing it, tries to make love happen by expressing it. to blow up a sort of force-draft passion by capering volubility and wit," *Shakespeare's Festive Comedy,* p. 107. Many critics have followed his lead. Cyrus Hoy, for instance, says, "They have played at being scholars; now, in the concluding act of the comedy, they play at being lovers, and with hardly more success," "*Love's Labour's Lost* and the Nature of Comedy," *SQ* 13 (1962): 35. Restated in terms of language, much the same point appears in James L. Calderwood's *Shakespearean Metadrama* (Minneapolis, Minn., 1971), "love must be truly felt, truly expressed and truly received. This paradigm for the dialogue of love is disregarded in *Love's Labour's Lost,* and love's labor is lost because the scholar-lovers cannot find the verbal *style* in which love can be genuinely expressed and hence genuinely received," p. 68. Among others who see the masquing as one more instance of the youthfulness and inadequacy of the courtiers are Tillyard, *Shakespeare's Early Comedies,* p. 145; Thomas M. Greene, "*Love's Labour's Lost*: The Grace of Society," *SQ* 22 (1971): 317, 321. Richard Cody's diagnosis finds a lack of "self-transcending passion" in the lords: "The inspiration of all their virtuous and amorous posings is not passion but mockery. And when you leave out Bacchus, as Nietzsche says, Apollo leaves you out," *The Landscape of the Mind* (Oxford, 1969), p. 118.

21. Bobbyann Roesen (Righter) sees reflected in the final songs the world of illusion of the play, now fading into the past as the characters face the world "of reality of the greasy kitchen-maid and her pot," "*Love's Labour's Lost,*" *SQ* 4 (1953): 425; also 411, 413, 426. John Russell Brown finds in the songs "the one a reminder of the flesh, the other of death; theirs is the annual reckoning of spring and winter against which all order must be tried," *Shakespeare and His Comedies,* p. 134; Northrop Frye relates the pregnancy of Jacquenetta to the death of the French king and sees implicit in the songs the cycle of the seasons, "Shakespeare's Experimental Comedy," *Stratford Papers on Shakespeare* 2 (1962): 11–12. Peter G. Phialas surveys a number of opinions about the place of the songs in the play and finds Richmond Noble's discussion the most helpful; he adds, "There is spring and winter in love and life, even as there is both beauty and ugliness in both spring and winter.... love and all life partake of the spirit and of the flesh, of the ideal and the real, of mind and body," *Shakespeare's Romantic Comedies,* pp. 99–100. Similar comments can be found in Catherine M. McLay's "The Dialogue of Spring and Winter: A Key to the Unity of *Love's Labour's Lost,*" *SQ* 18 (1967): 121; Joseph Westlund's "Fancy and Achievement in *Love's Labour's Lost,*" *SQ* 18 (1967): 45–46; and Gates K. Agnew, "Berowne and the Progress of Love's Labour's Lost," *Shakespeare Studies* 4 (1968): 65; Ralph Berry, "The Words of Mercury," *ShS* 22 (1969): 76. Thomas M. Greene sees the songs as setting "rhetorical touchstones by which to estimate the foregoing funny abuses of language," "*Love's Labour's Lost*: The Grace of Society," *SQ* 22 (1971): 325.

22. Bertrand H. Bronson, "Daisies Pied and Icicles," *MLN* 63 (1948): 35–38; E. M. W. Tillyard, *Shakespeare's Early Comedies,* pp. 179–81.

23. Lineation refers to the edition by Edmund Creeth, *Tudor Plays,* pp. 269–70.

24. Most critics who pay attention to "Pyramus and Thisbe" call attention to the way it mirrors behavior of the lovers. C. L. Barber, however, observes: "If Shakespeare were chiefly concerned with the nature of love, the clowns would be in love, after their fashion. But instead, they are putting on a play," *Shakespeare's Festive Comedy,* p. 148. Among the critics who comment on the theatrical subjects of parody are J. W. Robinson, who finds the primary focus to be on "those hybrid or transitional plays" that were forerunners to

professional drama, "Palpable Hot Ice: Dramatic Burlesque in *A Midsummer Night's Dream*," *SP* 61 (1964): 202-3; and Larry S. Champion, who sees the object of burlesque to be Shakespeare's "own profession," *The Evolution of Shakespeare's Comedy*, p. 55. Other critics emphasize specifically literary objects of parody: Robert F. Willson sees a parody of Golding's translation of Ovid, "Golding's *Metamorphoses* and Shakespeare's Burlesque Method in *A Midsummer Night's Dream*," *ELN* 7 (1969-70): 18-25. Peter G. Phialas includes a bibliography of those essays which argue for literary objects of parody, *Shakespeare's Romantic Comedy*, p. 292, but claims the parody aims at the romantic and sentimental approach to love typified by earlier versions of the story, p. 109. Still other critics point to both literary and theatrical objects of parody: Kenneth Muir lists six objects of parody, "Shakespeare as Parodist," *N & Q* 199 (1954): 467-68; Geoffrey Bullough finds the playlet mocking "bad literary habits" of contemporary writers as well as amateur entertainments, *Narrative and Dramatic Sources of Shakespeare*, 1 (London, 1957): 374; Madeleine Doran cites parody of language in earlier plays before the development of blank verse, the translations of Seneca's tragedies, and fashionable narrative poems on legendary lovers, "Introduction," *A Midsummer Night's Dream*, The Pelican Shakespeare (Baltimore, 1959), pp. 22-23. Finally, some critics stress the way the playlet comments upon the artistry of the outer play: R. W. Dent says, "It provides a foil to the entire play of which it is a part, not merely to a portion involving the lovers. And not only Bottom's play, but his audience as well, invites comparison with Shakespeare's," "Imagination in *A Midsummer Night's Dream*," *Shakespeare 400*, p. 124; see also Paul N. Siegel, "*A Midsummer Night's Dream* and the Wedding Guests," *SQ* 4 (1953): 142.

25. Elder Olson makes central the distinction between the ridiculous and the ludicrous behavior, *The Theory of Comedy*, pp. 15-16.

26. F. W. Talbert discusses in detail the word-play of Launce and Speed, *Elizabethan Drama and Shakespeare's Early Plays*, pp. 368-69.

27. *The Theory of Comedy*, p. 16.

28. In this connection it is appropriate to mention Evans's careful analysis of discrepant awareness in *Errors*. He points out that Shakespeare withholds the identity of Emilia and intensifies our anxieties unnecessarily, *Shakespeare's Comedies*, pp. 8-9. However, "providing an environment in which comic effects can flourish even in dark moments, this assurance is an indispensable condition and a hall-mark of Shakespearian comedy," p. 40. One might add that, unlike Thaisa and Hermione, whom the audience knows to be essential to a happy ending, Emilia does not hold any key to the difficulties of the twins and Egeon as the audience understands them. When she reveals herself, she adds one more delightful note to the reunion.

29. Jocelyn Powell brings together a number of Elizabethan comments upon "play" and "sport," all of which associate pastime with utility, "John Lyly and the Language of Play," *Elizabethan Theatre*, pp. 148-57.

30. Lineation comes from the edition of John M. Manly, *Specimens of the Pre-Shakesperean Drama* (Boston, 1897, rpt. New York, 1967), 1: 320.

Chapter 9

1. "One objective in aims of its [the family's] importance is the frequent occurrence of eight common nouns of family relationship—brother, daughter, father, husband, mother, sister, son, and wife. They appear 228 times in *3 Henry VI*, nearly three times as often as in each of the other two Henry VI plays," Robert B. Pierce, *Shakespeare's History Plays: The Family and the State* (Columbus, Ohio, 1971), p. 66.

2. John Masefield, *William Shakespeare* (New York and London, 1911), p. 71. Robert O. Evans discusses at length the role of Friar Laurence and of his flight from the tomb; he says, "The friar who throughout the play has shown shortcomings in the reasonable part

of his soul now has his courage flag. He is an old man, and he is only an agent in the play. We should pity him, as the Veronese do, rather than censure him, as do certain of his critics," *The Osier Cage: Rhetorical Devices in "Romeo and Juliet"* (Lexington, Ky., 1966), p. 65.

3. Elias Schwartz has discussed this sense of an irreducible substratum in a fascinating essay, "The Idea of the Person and Shakespearian Tragedy," *SQ* 16 (1965): 39–47.

4. Enid Welsford, *The Court Masque,* pp. 324, 331–32.

5. Erich W. Segal, *Roman Laughter* (Cambridge, Mass., 1968).

6. R. S. Crane, *The Languages of Criticism and the Structure of Poetry,* p. 48.

7. Quoted in Herrick, *Comic Theory in the Sixteenth Century,* p. 65.

8. *Shakespeare's Wooden O* (New York, 1960).

9. See, for instance, Bernard Spivack, *Shakespeare and the Allegory of Evil* (New York, 1958), pp. 3–59.

10. See John Bayley, *The Characters of Love* (London, 1960), pp. 174–201.

Index